NEGOTIATING POWER
IN EZRA-NEHEMIAH

ANCIENT ISRAEL AND ITS LITERATURE

Thomas C. Römer, General Editor

Editorial Board:
Mark G. Brett
Marc Brettler
Corrine L. Carvalho
Cynthia Edenburg
Konrad Schmid
Gale A. Yee

Number 26

NEGOTIATING POWER IN EZRA-NEHEMIAH

Donna Laird

 **PRESS**

Atlanta

Copyright © 2016 by SBL Press

All rights reserved. No part of this work may be reproduced or transmitted in any form or by any means, electronic or mechanical, including photocopying and recording, or by means of any information storage or retrieval system, except as may be expressly permitted by the 1976 Copyright Act or in writing from the publisher. Requests for permission should be addressed in writing to the Rights and Permissions Office, SBL Press, 825 Houston Mill Road, Atlanta, GA 30329 USA.

Library of Congress Cataloging-in-Publication Data

Names: Laird, Donna, author.
Title: Negotiating power in Ezra-Nehemiah / by Donna Laird.
Description: Atlanta : SBL Press, [2016] | Series: Ancient Israel and its literature ; volume 26 | Includes bibliographical references and index.
Identifiers: LCCN 2016021817 (print) | LCCN 2016022680 (ebook) | ISBN 9781628371390 (pbk. : alk. paper) | ISBN 9780884141648 (hardcover : alk. paper) | ISBN 9780884141631 (ebook)
Subjects: LCSH: Bible. Ezra—Criticism, interpretation, etc. | Bible. Nehemiah—Criticism, interpretation, etc.
Classification: LCC BS1355.52 .L35 2016 (print) | LCC BS1355.52 (ebook) | DDC 222/.706—dc23
LC record available at https://lccn.loc.gov/2016021817

Printed on acid-free paper.

Contents

Acknowledgments ix
Abbreviations xi

1. Max Weber, Pierre Bourdieu, and Questions about
   Ezra-Nehemiah 1
   1.1. Research on Ezra-Nehemiah   4
   1.2. Political, Economic, and Social Contexts of the
        Persian Period   15

2. Methodology 37
   2.1. Key Concepts from Weber and Bourdieu   39
   2.2. Critiques and Limitations of Bourdieu's Theory   56

3. Themes and Motifs in Ezra 1–6 59
   3.1. The Temple Building Report   61
   3.2. Legitimating a Temple and Symbolic Capital   74
   3.3. The Exodus Motif   76
   3.4. Prophetic Words and Royal Decrees   80

4. Ezra 2: Defining the Community 89
   4.1. Content of the List in Ezra 2   93
   4.2. List as a Means of Definition   103

5. Ezra 3: Ritual and Identity 111
   5.1. Literary Themes   114
   5.2. Ezra 3 and Nehemiah 8: One Festival, Two Rituals   118
   5.3. Ezra 4:1–5: Drawing Boundaries with a Text   133
   5.4. Ethnicity, Boundaries, and Ritual   138

6. Ezra 4–6: Contesting Legitimacy 147
   6.1. Narrative Structure and Style   148

CONTENTS

6.2. Written Records and Legitimacy	152
6.3. Ezra 4: Conformity, Self-Interest, and Competition	161

7. Ezra 5–6: Support for Temples and Priests 167
7.1. The Jerusalem Temple and Cultural Capital	167
7.2. Weber's Oppositions: Priests, Prophets, and the Laity	169
7.3. God Is Great, Persia Is Good	174
7.4. The Cultural Capital of Writing: Supporting the Scribal Life	180

8. Ezra 1–6: Social Realities and Expectations 189
8.1. Social Trajectory and Expectations	190
8.2. The Author's Capital and the Field of Cultural Production	192
8.3. Minority Ethnic Groups	194

9. The Nehemiah Memoir 197
9.1. Historical Context for the Nehemiah Memoir	199
9.2. The Narrative of Nehemiah's Memoir	202
9.3. Symbolic Capital and Political Strategies	217

10. Nehemiah 5: Economics and the State 229
10.1. Nehemiah's Defense: A Literary Analysis	233
10.2. The Memoir: A Consolidation of Capital	244

11. Penitential Prayers 247
11.1. The Function of Penitential Prayer	250
11.2. Nehemiah 1:5–11: Removing Shame	260
11.3. Nehemiah 9–10: A Response to Corporate Trauma	269

12. Ezra 7–10: (De-)Constructing a Community 285
12.1. The Literary Composition of Ezra 7–10	286
12.2. Ezra 7: The Commission of Ezra, the Priest and Scribe	289
12.3. Ezra 8: The Role of Levites	294
12.4. Contesting Leadership?	298

13. Ezra 9–10: Israel and "Foreign Wives" 303
13.1. Ezra 9: The Confession of the "Holy Seed"	303
13.2. Ezra 10: Resetting Boundaries	312
13.3. The Community: The Holy Seed in Other Words	319
13.4. Leadership and Change	321

13.5. Ezra's Capital, Representation, and Symbolic Power   324
13.6. Mixed Marriages   332
13.7. Conclusions   340

14. Conclusions 345
    14.1. The Date of Writing   346
    14.2. Behind the Text: The Social Context   348
    14.3. In the Text: A Response to the Times   350
    14.4. The Readers: Perspective and Influence   358
    14.5. Reading over the Shoulder   360

Bibliography 365
Ancient Sources Index 387
Modern Authors Index 401

Acknowledgments

No major project, whether it is rebuilding a wall, a temple, or a community, is achieved by one's efforts alone. This book is no exception. I am grateful for the support and guidance of many others. I thank, first and foremost, Danna Nolan Fewell, who sharpened my thinking and provided invaluable guidance for this entire project. I have benefited in countless ways from her insights, her critiques, her wisdom, and her encouragement. Otto Maduro introduced me to the work of Pierre Bourdieu, which opened the biblical text to me in new and, I believe, ethically important ways. He kept me honest with my use of theory and always returned work to me with an encouraging comment even while facing his own serious health issues. Jon Berquist provided much needed guidance on current scholarship on Persian period Yehud as well succinct and helpful advice on writing a more polished work. Thanks are also due Kenneth Ngwa, who graciously read my manuscript, asked thoughtful questions, and provided helpful insights during our discussion. Thanks also to Thomas Römer and the AIL editorial board for their willingness to take on this project and especially for their helpful feedback on the manuscript. Likewise, I appreciate the questions and feedback from scholars at SBL's Ezra-Nehemiah-Chronicles and Social-Scientific sections, where portions of this work have been read and discussed. Thanks are also due the Ramat Raḥel archaeological team led by Oded Lipschits, with whom I spent the 2009 and 2010 seasons. The time with them enriched my understanding of the physical space in which the events of Ezra-Nehemiah took place and provided help in understanding the published results of fieldwork. A special thanks to Ido Koch, who led the team in area D3. I am deeply grateful for the work of the SBL editors who went over this work with a fine-tooth comb and saved me from many errors and made this book a reality. Finally, I would like to thank my spouse, John Laird, for his support. He has sacrificed much for the completion of this project. Yet his encouragement never failed, even when he was compelled to hear me discuss, yet again, my current stage of progress. I could not be more grateful. The final result is better for the aid of all these people. The shortcomings are all my own.

Abbreviations

AB	Anchor Bible
ABS	Archaeology and Biblical Studies
AGJU	Arbeiten zur Geschichte des antiken Judentums und des Urchristentums
AIL	Ancient Israel and Its Literature
ATANT	Abhandlungen zur Theologie des Alten und Neuen Testaments
BibInt	Biblical Interpretation Series
BWANT	Beiträge zur Wissenschaft vom Alten und Neuen Testament
BZ	*Biblische Zeitschrift*
BZAW	Beihefte zur Zeitschrift für die alttestamentliche Wissenschaft
CBQ	*Catholic Biblical Quarterly*
CSCM	*Cultural Studies–Critical Methodologies*
CSR	*Comparative Social Research*
EJL	Early Judaism and Its Literature
ESV	English Standard Version
FAT	Forschungen zum Alten Testament
GPBS	Global Perspectives on Biblical Scholarship
HALOT	*The Hebrew and Aramaic Lexicon of the Old Testament.* Ludwig Koehler, Walter Baumgartner, and Johann J. Stamm. Translated and edited under the supervision of M. E. J. Richardson. 5 vols. Leiden: Brill, 1994–2000.
HBM	Hebrew Bible Monographs
HR	*History of Religions*
HSM	Harvard Semitic Monographs
IBC	Interpretation: A Bible Commentary for Teaching and Preaching
Int	*Interpretation*

JANER	*Journal of Ancient Near Eastern Religions*
JAOS	*Journal of the American Oriental Society*
JBL	*Journal of Biblical Literature*
JBQ	*Jewish Bible Quarterly*
JHebS	*Journal of Hebrew Scriptures*
JJS	*Journal of Jewish Studies*
JNSL	*Journal of Northwest Semitic Languages*
JPSV	Jewish Publication Society Version: *The Holy Scriptures according to the Masoretic Text.* Rev. ed. Philadelphia: Jewish Publication Society, 1955.
JQR	*Jewish Quarterly Review*
JSJ	*Journal for the Study of Judaism in the Persian, Hellenistic, and Roman Periods*
JSJSup	Journal for the Study of Judaism in the Persian, Hellenistic, and Roman Periods Supplement Series
JSNTSup	Journal for the Study of the New Testament Supplement Series
JSOT	*Journal for the Study of the Old Testament*
JSOTSup	Journal for the Study of the Old Testament Supplement Series
JTS	*Journal of Theological Studies*
KJV	King James Version
LHBOTS	Library of Hebrew Bible/Old Testament Studies
LSTS	Library of Second Temple Studies
MTSR	*Method and Theory in the Study of Religion*
NASB	New American Standard Bible
NCBC	New Century Bible Commentary
NIV	New International Version
NJPS	New Jewish Publication Society Version: *Tanakh: A New Translation of the Holy Scriptures according to the Traditional Hebrew Text.* Philadelphia: Jewish Publication Society, 1985.
NRSV	New Revised Standard Version
OTE	*Old Testament Essays*
OTL	Old Testament Library
OTS	Old Testament Studies
PRSt	*Perspectives in Religious Studies*
PTMS	Pittsburgh Theological Monograph Series
SBLDS	Society of Biblical Literature Dissertation Series

SBLMS	Society of Biblical Literature Monograph Series
ScrHier	Scripta Hierosolymitana
SemeiaSt	Semeia Studies
SJOT	*Scandinavian Journal of the Old Testament*
STAR	Studies in Theology and Religion
SymS	Symposium Series
TA	*Tel Aviv*
TBN	Themes in Biblical Narrative
TDOT	*Theological Dictionary of the Old Testament*. Edited by G. Johannes Botterweck, Helmer Ringgren, and Heinz-Josef Fabry. Translated by John T. Willis et al. 15 vols. Grand Rapids: Eerdmans, 1974–2006.
Transeu	*Transeuphratène*
VT Vetus	*Testamentum*
WBC	Word Biblical Commentary
ZAW	*Zeitschrift für die alttestamentliche Wissenschaft*

1
MAX WEBER, PIERRE BOURDIEU, AND QUESTIONS ABOUT EZRA-NEHEMIAH

The social program advocated in Ezra-Nehemiah appears profoundly restrictive to contemporary readers. The rhetoric in these books labels a variety of people as alien and adversaries. It repeatedly urges exclusionary measures against those who do not wish to be excluded and may not perceive themselves as foreign. Nehemiah employs force to gain compliance with his policies that establish and assure social boundaries. Ezra uses a more subtle, but no less coercive, technique of guilt coupled with piety to compel compliance with a covenant that removes wives and their children from the community. Ezra 1–6 capitalizes on political gamesmanship to garner support for the construction of a temple where worship is limited to those who have "separated themselves from the pollutions of the nations of the land" (Ezra 6:21).[1] Although never stated overtly, these persuasive strategies are deployed to convince readers to define and arrange their community in ways most beneficial to the interests of those at the top of the social hierarchy. While such tactics and their underlying motives are no strangers to the human condition, it is disturbing to find them enshrined in what many deem to be sacred text. Their place in the Judeo-Christian canon gives them legitimacy for future communities and invites the perpetuation of these practices.

These policies and the efforts to support and ensure conformity to them interweave two familiar strands of religious practice. First, specific religious beliefs and practices are celebrated and designated as markers of distinction. Often these resonate with habits and views familiar from a person's formative years and family context. These early and durable dispositions generate and organize practices adapted to particular social

---

1. Unless otherwise stated, all translations of biblical texts follow the NRSV.

structures, making inclusion into a particular tradition a smooth fit for some but not for others.[2] Second, criteria are established for membership into the community and participation in leadership and acts of worship. Admittance into this gated community is guarded by written legal documents and by the rulings of elders. Members are granted recognition and status but are required to subscribe to particular beliefs and/or practices that are reinforced through ritual and study. Sacred texts and traditions are employed to support these organizational criteria. Privileges are asserted for some while others are excluded or assigned secondary roles. Rejection of such social constructions is perceived as disobedience to the divine will and endangers a person's standing within the community.

Shared beliefs and habits often form an "unthought" part of the worldview of those immersed in a faith tradition. The strict enforcement of related rules and boundaries can foment dissatisfaction and resistance from those relegated to secondary status, but often these policies remain a largely unchallenged (and unexamined) social milieu. Those who control the community and who most benefit from its organization ensure conformity through the selective interpretation and strategic employment of religious texts. This lends legitimacy to their assertions of privilege and power, strengthening their positions against others' claims.

Ezra-Nehemiah confronts the reader with an extreme form of boundary maintenance. Social boundaries are ritually reinforced and based on rulings established by reference to religious texts. Failure to adhere to established boundaries or practices is countered by threats of divine retribution, and carriers of alternative constructions of the community are delegitimized as untrustworthy adversaries. Ezra 9–10 presents members so unified that they sacrifice their wives and sons in service of their particular definition of the community.

In this investigation, I explore the distinctive character of these strategies. I ask how the ancient social world gave shape to this text and how the text's message and rhetoric attempt to define and control the community addressed. In this study, I identify how competitors and alternative constructions of the community are delegitimized, and the various political, social, economic, or religious constraints that influenced the author.[3]

---

2. Pierre Bourdieu, *The Logic of Practice* (Stanford, CA: Stanford University Press, 1980), 53.

3. For the sake of convenience, I shall generally refer to the "author" and "editor" (singular), though I will not discuss the complex issue of authorship.

Furthermore, an analysis of how these *written* accounts contribute to the author's agenda prompts related questions about the social location of the readership since the audience's social context and position also bear upon authorial strategies. Taken together, these avenues of inquiry may explain how narratives such as these are able to gain traction even among those constrained by these policies.

Historical and archaeological studies provide a framework for understanding the political, geographic, and cultural realities in which these texts arose. A study of this nature would benefit from direct observation of the people involved since the full significance of discourse is understood only in relation to a market.[4] Fortunately the text of Ezra-Nehemiah provides information to bridge this impasse. The writer's symbolic language reflects the world around him, his place in it, and the issues at stake for him. Ezra-Nehemiah is an account of return, reconstruction, restoration, and reform addressed to a reconstituted community that has a temple, a priesthood, the Torah, and a wall. That the history in these books legitimates these religious, social, and physical entities suggests that, although they existed, their importance and roles for the community were contested.

Pierre Bourdieu delineates the relationship between symbolic language and social context. He observes that the most effective religious discourses "derive their efficacy from the hidden correspondence between the structure of the social space within which they are produced ... and the structure of the social classes within which the recipients are situated and in relation to which they interpret the message."[5] Even when the social location and concerns of author and audience are not plainly stated, one can attempt to clarify them by seeking these "hidden correspondences" within the rhetoric of these books.

By identifying and mapping the symbolic language in Ezra-Nehemiah, and examining the logic and social foundations of the author's arguments, I seek in this study to untangle the particular social, economic, and cultural realities of the author and his community. Furthermore, for symbolic language to be effective, the recipients must recognize the author as having authority. The effectiveness of symbolic language to modify the behavior (or beliefs) of others rests on a dynamic, variable (and often unequal)

---

4. Pierre Bourdieu, *Language and Symbolic Power*, ed. John B. Thompson, trans. Gino Raymond and Matthew Adamson (Cambridge: Harvard University Press, 1991), 37.

5. Ibid., 41.

relation between parties.⁶ By employing the theories of Max Weber and Bourdieu in this investigation, I seek to understand these dynamics. The polemics themselves provide material with which we can attempt to construct an ancient social reality and so, with greater clarity, understand what drove the author to advocate so stridently for such a society and why it found acceptance among the people.

1.1. Research on Ezra-Nehemiah

Historical and compositional investigations of Ezra-Nehemiah have postulated a variety of possible historical scenarios and compositional configurations for all or parts of Ezra-Nehemiah. Other studies have used these books as sources to investigate extratextual subjects such as Persian administration and military organization as well as settlement and economic activity in Yehud. The resulting proposals often posit divergent degrees of Persian bureaucratic control, different scenarios for dating construction in Jerusalem, or different arrangements regarding social relations in the region. Since many of these reconstructions are mutually exclusive, these studies cannot be combined to create a coherent chronological or political outline. Nevertheless, these investigations present and evaluate evidence helpful for postulating a social context for the author of these texts and provide a broad framework from which to consider the relationship between social context and argumentation. Furthermore, scholars have identified various themes and lines of reasoning specific to these books that can provide a basis for further study of the social contours of these texts.

The brief survey that follows foregrounds social influences identified by these studies, even though this is often not the primary purpose of many of these works. Other findings related to specific portions of Ezra-Nehemiah are incorporated elsewhere throughout this study, but the following works provide comprehensive treatments of Ezra-Nehemiah, the Persian era context, or share a common thread of sociological analyses in keeping with this investigation. The collective information provided by these investigations provides a helpful introduction to the current study.

---

6. Ibid., 170. So, for example, Bourdieu observes, "The opposition between religion and magic conceals the opposition between differences of religious competence tied to the structure of the distribution of cultural capital" ("Genesis and Structure of the Religious Field," *CSR* 13 [1991]: 12–13).

1. QUESTIONS ABOUT EZRA-NEHEMIAH

1.1.1. The Nature of the Texts

Writing in the early 1900s, Charles Torrey equated the author of Ezra-Nehemiah with the Chronicler and dated the texts to the time of Greek rule.[7] He took a jaundiced view of their historicity and asserted that the books had more to say about the situation at the time of their composition than they had to say about any history they may claim to recount. Torrey believed that the author of Ezra-Nehemiah was engaged in a battle over political and religious legitimacy for the Second Temple, its priesthood, and the returning community; and he argued that the accounts were written to address these issues by establishing ties to the First Temple and priesthood. He stated that the Chronicler wrote "to establish the sole legitimacy of the institutions of Jerusalem in opposition to the Samaritan claims."[8]

Torrey maintained that during this time the priesthood became highly organized and literarily productive partly in response to widely different religious tendencies of the laity, who were affected by changing conditions and an influx of foreign ideas. The priesthood was also compelled to respond to the growing influence of rival sanctuaries with their competing rituals. Competition forced the priests to vie for resources and the loyalty of laity in the region.[9] In these circumstances, the Jerusalem priesthood had to justify the resumption of worship in Jerusalem. Whereas the Samaritans could point to an ongoing religious tradition, the priesthood of Jerusalem had to demonstrate their succession to the preexilic traditions.[10] In Torrey's view, the negative biblical portrait of Samaritans was an effort to undermine the legitimacy of the Samaritan temple, and the Ezra nemoir was an elaborate apology for Jewish institutions that shows "genuine Hebrew men and institutions came from Babylonia."[11] He also maintained that the account was created to "severely score" the sin of intermarriage with foreigners. Ezra's reform became a rebuke to the readership about their alliances.[12]

---

7. Charles C. Torrey, *Ezra Studies* (1910; repr., Eugene OR: Wipf & Stock, 2006), 153.
8. Ibid., 326.
9. Ibid., 291, 311–12.
10. Ibid., 209.
11. Ibid., 212, 238.
12. Ibid., 246–47.

Torrey's analysis was sensitive to the influence of changing and complex social conditions of the Greek period. He recognized that the Chronicler's composition had to defend or account for ongoing Yahwistic religious beliefs given past national losses and new circumstances. His work continues to be relevant today since many of the same issues—the authenticity of documents, dating and authorship, and the circumstances generating the texts' polemics—continue to be debated, often along similar lines of reasoning. Torrey's attribution of polemical argumentation to institutional competition remains a valuable avenue of investigation as scholars try to discern history from the dustup of debate.

More recent studies have also found the historicity of these texts problematic. For example, many agree that Ezra 1–6 is the last major portion of the books to be written and therefore the most distant from the events described.[13] Diana Edelman, for example, identifies several historical errors and claims that these chapters are organized around a standard template for temple building and are derivative of the theme of the foreign nations seeking YHWH found in Haggai and Zechariah.[14] She argues that neither the author nor the editor drew on sources outside those found in the Bible and were "no better informed than we are today about when and why the temple was rebuilt in Jerusalem."[15] In her view, Ezra-Nehemiah is a polemic against those deemed outsiders and an argument for the centrality and legitimacy of the Jerusalem temple.[16] Her observations about literary templates and limited historical evidence are important to understanding these chapters, although the textual claims may be creating outsiders rather than arguing against those already recognized as such.

Others have taken a more moderate stance toward the historicity of these texts. Many scholars credit the Nehemiah memoir as authentic and trust its historical claims. Many also regard the lists, edicts, and letters as authentic documents, and therefore more reliable than the surrounding

---

13. H. G. M. Williamson, "The Composition of Ezra i–vi," *JTS* 34 (1983): 19–30. See also Diana Edelman, *The Origins of the "Second" Temple: Persian Imperial Policy and the Rebuilding of Jerusalem* (London: Equinox, 2005), 158.

14. Edelman, *Origins*, 151, 162. She argues that the author makes historical errors common under the Seleucids: Darius is referred to as "the king of Assyria" in Ezra 6:22 and Artaxerxes is placed between the reigns of Cyrus and Darius in Ezra 4 (170). For similar historical errors, see Dan 6:28 and 9:1.

15. Ibid., 204.

16. Ibid., 193–94.

narratives. In general, the less weight a scholar gives to the text as a historical source, the more he or she is inclined to address the polemical purposes of Ezra-Nehemiah.[17]

Hugh Williamson believes that Ezra 1–6 was composed to justify the temple and cult "after a possible split in its priesthood, the establishment of the Samaritan community, and the first moves to build a temple on Mount Gerizim."[18] In his view, the final redactor is using the history to establish a present identity, one that shows that "no reform movement can be said to have succeeded unless it is followed by 'routinization'—the translation of the values of the reform into a new 'steady state' in the regular life of the community."[19] Joseph Blenkinsopp also identifies legitimacy as a concern in these texts, noting that the author establishes lines of continuity with the past through allusions to the exodus, conquest, and First Temple construction.[20] He also observes that the text highlights the exclusive role of the returnees. They are credited with laying the temple's foundation while delays in the building are attributed to external opposition, a claim that deflects blame away from internal conflict.[21] Likewise, David Clines suggests that the author asserts "the *legitimacy of his own community*, the Judean state of the fourth century BC, as the sole heir of the true theocratic Israel."[22] He notes, for example, that the list in Ezra 2 "shows us a community that is much concerned to draw lines of demarcation both between itself and outsiders and between groups within Israel."[23]

In more recent studies, Juha Pakkala and Jacob Wright posit complex histories of composition for these books. Wright views the books as the

---

17. Mark J. Boda, "Redaction in the Book of Nehemiah: A Fresh Proposal," in *Unity and Disunity in Ezra-Nehemiah: Redaction, Rhetoric and Reader*, ed. Mark J. Boda and Paul L. Redditt, HBM 17 (Sheffield: Sheffield Phoenix, 2008), 33.

18. Williamson, "Composition of Ezra i–vi," 30.

19. H. G. M. Williamson, "The Belief System of the Book of Nehemiah," in *The Crisis of Israelite Religion: Transformation of Religious Tradition in Exilic and Post-exilic Times*, ed. Bob Becking and Marjo C. A. Korpel, OTS 42 (Boston: Brill, 1999), 286.

20. Joseph Blenkinsopp, *Ezra-Nehemiah*, OTL (Philadelphia: Westminster, 1988), 83, 135. For example, 1:4 commands the population to provide material support as did the Egyptians in the exodus; Ezra's journey in Ezra 7 replicates the first exodus; and the use of lists reflects the same style in Joshua regarding the occupation of the land.

21. Ibid., 100.

22. D. J. A. Clines, *Ezra, Nehemiah, Esther*, NCBC (Grand Rapids: Eerdmans, 1984), 25.

23. Ibid., 62.

end result of continuous commentary that transforms Nehemiah's record of Jerusalem's wall construction into an account of Judah's restoration. He suggests that antagonism between Nehemiah and the priesthood generates this composition.[24] Added material focuses on this antagonism and embellishes the report "to criticize enemies and present ideas of what the restoration of Judah entailed."[25] Like Torrey, Wright believes that the writers are creating history rather than recording it and dates the final stage of composition to the Hellenistic age. He concludes that the completed account "is intended to be utilized ideologically and pedagogically—successful relations with one empire illustrate the correct manner of interacting with its successors."[26] This is most certainly true, yet the shifting modes of relating to Persia throughout the text and recourse to Persian rulers for purposes of legitimacy suggest that much of the material was composed earlier and reflects changes in Persian rule.

Focusing on the Ezra memoir, Pakkala argues that a simple account of a return by Ezra to teach Torah has grown into an account that features Levites, exiles, and priests, and whose primary concern is to resolve the intermarriage of community members.[27] The additions are not fostered by a debate such as Wright posits, but from a desire for inclusion. Each editor incorporates references or concepts that align with their own interests.[28] By transforming Ezra into a priest or by incorporating the concerns of the exiles or Levites into the early days of the return, they hope to increase legitimacy for their particular position in the present. Whether literary growth results from conflict or a desire for inclusion, the analyses of both critics indicate various parties, motivated by their own interests, have had a hand in the composition of these books.

In Tamara Eskenazi's narrative analysis, she notes the variety of perspectives conveyed through the content of letters, lists, and edicts as well as

---

24. Jacob L. Wright, *Rebuilding Identity: The Nehemiah Memoir and Its Earliest Readers*, BZAW 348 (Berlin: de Gruyter, 2004), 4, 66. For a critique of his study, see Gary Knoppers, "Revisiting the Composition of Ezra-Nehemiah: In Conversation with Jacob Wright's *Rebuilding Identity: The Nehemiah Memoir and Its Earliest Readers*," *JHebS* 7 (2007): art. 12, 1–36, doi:10.5508/jhs.2007.v7.a12.

25. Wright, *Rebuilding Identity*, 119–20.

26. Ibid., 44.

27. Juha Pakkala, *Ezra the Scribe: The Development of Ezra 7–10 and Nehemiah 8*, BZAW 347 (Berlin: de Gruyter, 2004), 55, 74.

28. Ibid., 28.

shifting first and third person narration.²⁹ She also identifies three major themes: the centrality of community, the written word, and the building of the house of God (which she extends to the city of Jerusalem). The interest in community is accompanied by criteria for membership, but Eskenazi notes that "the exact boundaries of this community of returnees are not yet determined with finality."³⁰ She suggests that Ezra's leadership style provides a critique of Nehemiah's more autocratic methods, and the contrast invites readers to emulate Ezra's power sharing with the community.³¹ The various narrative themes identified by Eskenazi may build on shared values and concerns of the author and the readership, but may also indicate strategies to gain the audience's consent for specific social arrangements linked to these subjects.

1.1.2. The Texts and Contexts

Incorporating earlier lists and records, Ezra-Nehemiah was most likely composed between 445 and 330 BCE. Some editorial activity likely continued into the early Greek era.³² Reconstructions of the political, religious, economic, and social realities of this period are debated, particularly regarding Persian administrative involvement in local governance in Yehud. Joel Weinberg, for example, has posited a community that enjoyed a measure of self-government that was more deeply tied to its temple and the local economy than to Persia.³³ At the other extreme, Kenneth Hoglund contends that Persia exercised tight administrative control over its empire.³⁴ In between these poles are a range of other positions.

---

29. Tamara C. Eskenazi, *In an Age of Prose: A Literary Approach to Ezra-Nehemiah*, SBLMS 36 (Atlanta: Scholars Press, 1988), 131. The emphasis on documents may indicate the importance such materials had for the author at the time of writing. Gordon F. Davies (*Ezra and Nehemiah*, Berit Olam [Collegeville, MN: Liturgical Press, 1999]) provides a rhetorical analysis along similar lines, although his focus is on the theological intent of the text.
30. Eskenazi, *In an Age of Prose*, 49.
31. Ibid., 138, 152.
32. Persian kings and edicts are given important legitimating roles in these texts—their significance goes beyond a model written for later relations with Greece.
33. Joel Weinberg, *The Citizen-Temple Community*, trans. Daniel L. Smith-Christopher, JSOTSup 151 (Sheffield: JSOT Press, 1992).
34. Kenneth G. Hoglund, *Achaemenid Imperial Administration in Syria-Palestine and the Missions of Ezra and Nehemiah*, SBLDS 125 (Atlanta: Scholars Press, 1992).

Peter Bedford posits a reconstruction that began under the reign of Darius rather than Cyrus.[35] He points to the Aramaic documents in Ezra as evidence that the Achaemenid administration issued a decree permitting the construction but notes that there is no evidence to assume it was part of a universal imperial policy. He argues that the project was paid for from local resources, and temple construction was a symbolic act that fostered community integration rather than solidifying division.[36] In contrast, Peter Frei and Lisbeth Fried build theories primarily from evidence external to the biblical account. Frei is especially interested in the relationship between Persia and the promulgation of Torah as law and posits a close, highly structured relationship between the imperial rule and the local authority in Yehud. He contends that laws generated at the local level, such as those contained in the Pentateuch, would have likely received the stamp of imperial authorization, thus raising them to the status of imperial legislation.[37] Fried advocates for a Persian bureaucratic government involved with the appointment of governors and argues against Yehud being a self-governing theocracy with its own assembly.[38]

Hoglund argues that Persia sought to create economic and social relationships that would tie the community more completely into the imperial system.[39] Expanded imperial intervention in the region led to rebuilding

---

35. Peter R. Bedford, *Temple Restoration in Early Achaemenid Judah*, JSJSup 65 (Boston: Brill, 2001), 230. He combines evidence from the prophetic books with the Aramaic account of the Persian governor's investigation of the project in Ezra 5–6 to argue that neither Zerubbabel nor Joshua returned for the purpose of rebuilding. Rather, the local community (as represented by Haggai) viewed their arrival as propitious and commenced the project, prompting the Persian investigation.

36. Ibid., 201, 269.

37. Peter Frei, "Persian Imperial Authorization: A Summary," in *Persia and Torah: The Theory of Imperial Authorization of the Pentateuch*, ed. James W. Watts, SymS 17 (Atlanta: Society of Biblical Literature, 2001), 38–40. He acknowledges that it is unclear whether authorization was obligatory or voluntary for the subordinate bodies (36). Frei's argument has been critiqued for both theory and its application. See esp. Jean Louis Ska, "'Persian Imperial Authorization': Some Question Marks," in Watts, *Persia and Torah*, 161–82.

38. Lisbeth Fried, *The Priest and the Great King: Temple-Palace Relations in the Persian Empire* (Winona Lake, IN: Eisenbrauns, 2004), 233.

39. Hoglund (*Achaemenid Imperial Administration*, 52–96) surveys and argues against three common hypotheses: a local catastrophe such as a failed revolt led by Zerubbabel, Persian efforts to gain local loyalty in response to alleged disturbances at the end of the fifth century, or deliberate political reorganization of the region.

Jerusalem's walls, erecting a citadel associated with the temple, and general complaints about the payment of taxes.[40] Nehemiah's commission to rebuild the city walls reflects Jerusalem's new status as an urban center in the province. Nehemiah's economic reforms were meant to offset the impact of Persia's increased taxation that gave the empire tighter control over the district in the face of Greek pressure. In sum, Hoglund contends that Nehemiah's actions coincided with Persian policies to bring about strategic economic and social changes in Yehud.

Hoglund also asserts that intermarriage was a means of transferring property and social status and therefore smudged the distinction between groups. This blurred distinction threatened communal domain over property. Because intermarriage jeopardized the rights and privileges granted the community by the Persian government, it was perceived as a threat. He concludes that the author of Ezra-Nehemiah submerged political concerns in order to emphasize a theological interpretation of the community's history: imperial collaborators become important reformers.[41] Thus opposition to intermarriage is theologically framed as a motivation for communal self-preservation "in a setting where assimilation and the loss of identity would have been disastrous."[42]

Several studies have further explored the conflict and exclusionary stances within these books in light of theories treating community identity, class, and ethnicity. In 1971, Morton Smith posited competing parties *within* Yehud to explain the polemics of these texts.[43] Smith hypothesized three competing parties: the YHWH alone party of Babylonian returnees led by Nehemiah and Ezra, assimilationists (whom he suggested were Judeans who remained in the land), and the priesthood. He asserted that the groups were divided primarily by religious differences, but he also considered the relevance of economics or social standing. Nehemiah's effort to rebuild the wall, portrayed as an effort to provide security, and his remission of debt would garner an increase in popular support for

---

40. Ibid., 210–12. He believes that Ezra-Nehemiah presents "little direct evidence pertaining to the historical setting of these missions and the motivations that lay behind their actions as reformers" (241).
41. Ibid., 238, 241.
42. Ibid., 247.
43. Morton Smith, *Palestinian Parties and Politics That Shaped the Old Testament* (New York: Columbia University Press, 1971). Smith's analysis relies on comparisons with accounts of Greek tyrants, such as Solon.

him. Meanwhile his religious reforms would strike at the prestige of the priesthood, a possible source of competition.[44] Smith concluded that Nehemiah's memoir was written to defend the Persian appointee's actions and states, "We can infer that the opposition remained strong and that he was never beyond the need of appealing for popular support."[45]

Employing theories on ethnic groups in minority contexts, Daniel Smith posits that the exiles in Babylonia were a conquered minority under domination. They molded their identity from the raw materials of their culture, but it was an identity that had to be *"functional in the new situation."*[46] He believes that "social boundaries erected as a mechanism for survival during the Exile led to conflicts after the return to Palestine."[47] Upon return, the exiles found their land in the hands of new "people of the land" that included Samaritan upper class or former debtors and slaves. Some returnees may have reestablished themselves by intermarriage or independent means, but "the majority of the returned exiles created a separate community with an independent ethos."[48] He states, "Ezra's constant use of exclusive terms regarding these 'sons of the Golah,' the frequent exhortations against intermarriage with the impure of the land,… the priestly reforms of Lev. 25 and Neh. 5, all add up to a self-conscious community that is occupied with self-preservation, both as a pure community in a religious sense and also preservation in a material sense."[49]

Philip R. Davies also describes Ezra's and Nehemiah's concerns for ethnic purity as an issue "inseparable from ethnic integrity … the true Israel is defined simultaneously in both aspects."[50] Davies suggests that the threatened boundary for Yehud was not an issue of "territorial integ-

---

44. Ibid., 98–101. In Neh 13:7–9, Nehemiah counters the high priest by dispossessing Tobiah of temple rooms, and he chases away a son of the high priest over his marriage to the daughter of Sanballat (13:28). He also ensures financial support for the Levites.

45. Ibid., 103.

46. Daniel L. Smith, *The Religion of the Landless: The Social Context of the Babylonian Exile* (Bloomington, IN: Meyer Stone, 1989), 62.

47. Ibid., 197.

48. Ibid., 196.

49. Ibid., 197.

50. Philip R. Davies, "Defending the Boundaries of Israel in the Second Temple Period: 2 Chronicles 20 and the 'Salvation Army,'" in *Priests, Prophets and Scribes: Essays on the Formation and Heritage of Second Temple Judaism in Honour of Joseph Blenkinsopp*, ed. Eugene Ulrich et al., JSOTSup 149 (Sheffield: JSOT Press, 1992), 48.

rity, but one of integrity of the 'congregation of Israel.'"⁵¹ Questions about membership in the community, ownership of the land, and genealogical descent indicate a community anxious over its identity and trying to define it in various ways: "around a cult, an ancestor, an ancient promise, a body of law, a single deity."⁵² These observations highlight how the theology in these texts, and the history they recount, were being put in service of community definition—and it is clearly a contested delineation.

The expulsion of foreign wives recounted in Ezra 9–10 has been of particular interest with regard to ethnicity and social boundaries. David Janzen posits that the expulsion of foreign wives is similar to rituals carried out by other communities with strong external boundaries but weak internal integration.⁵³ He combines work on purity and social boundaries with comparative studies on the phenomenon of witch hunts to explain the events in these chapters. He argues that Yehud was struggling with weak internal integration due to a multitude of causes. This situation combined with the belief that they had been "granted a probationary period by God in which it may either atone for the sins of Israel or face utter destruction."⁵⁴ The confluence of ideology, weak internal integration, and an inability to identify particular causes led to a ritualized purification. The expulsion of the women became the means by which the community, anxious about its social integration, ritually purified itself.⁵⁵

Janzen's work also explores the differences between emic and etic perspectives. With regard to the expulsion of wives, he comments, "From its standpoint it [the community] has purified itself from a dangerous foreign influence that threatened to destroy it; from the standpoint of the anthropologist it has engaged in a ritualized act that has garnered assent from its members to observe social morality, norms and obligations, and to grant legitimacy to social institutions."⁵⁶ By drawing these distinctions, Janzen

---

51. Ibid., 49.
52. Ibid., 54.
53. David Janzen, *Witch-Hunts, Purity and Social Boundaries: The Expulsion of the Foreign Women in Ezra 9–10*, JSOTSup 350 (London: Sheffield Academic, 2002), 22. See also Janzen, "Scholars, Witches, Ideologues, and What the Text Said: Ezra 9–10 and Its Interpretation," in *Approaching Yehud: New Approaches to the Study of the Persian Period*, ed. Jon L. Berquist, SemeiaSt 50 (Atlanta: Society of Biblical Literature, 2007), 49–69.
54. Janzen, *Witch-Hunts*, 162.
55. Ibid., 25.
56. Ibid., 62.

identifies ways in which the religious rhetoric of the text serves a social purpose—one that is often not recognized by either those who wield it or those at whom it is directed.

Katherine Southwood, also informed by social theories regarding ethnicity and forced migration, treats Ezra 9–10. She posits that ethnic difference grew in importance for those in exile, and when immigrants relocated to Yehud these social distinctions continued to operate in this new setting. She comments, "it may be more appropriate to view the extreme ethnic ideology presented through the text as a symptom of a set of circumstances which have resulted in a sense of 'threat' to the community's boundaries and therefore resulted in a drastic effort to establish where such boundaries should lie."[57] She argues, "The complex view of ethnicity presented through the text may ... reflect the ongoing ideology of a returning separatist, literate scribal group, rather than that of the society of the time generally."[58] She further recognizes the value of this written account for those holding this position, "by virtue of being written down and through the prestige of authoritative status as a text which interprets and enforces the 'law,' ... the ethnic boundaries which the text promotes are able to be perpetuated, and strengthened, in later Jewish literature and practice."[59]

1.1.3. Summary

These studies contextualize the polemics of Ezra-Nehemiah, often noting the defensive or legitimating tone of the writing. They clarify the influence of particular institutions of concern in these texts—both local and imperial. They identify competing voices and their possible agendas, and highlight the profound need to define the community using practices or beliefs often reworked during the years of exile. By treating ethnicity, they also demonstrate why the author may have attached such importance to community definition and boundaries. Bourdieu's work on forms of capital, competition within various fields, and symbolic language can be used to reflect further on these same topics and provide added clarity

---

57. Katherine Southwood, *Ethnicity and the Mixed Marriage Crisis in Ezra 9–10: An Anthropological Approach* (Oxford: Oxford University Press, 2012), 132.
58. Ibid., 2.
59. Ibid.

regarding how the various narratives correspond to the social spaces of literary producers and recipients.

1.2. Political, Economic, and Social Contexts of the Persian Period

When the Babylonian army destroyed Jerusalem and its temple in 587 BCE and deported the nation's elite and city residents, it ushered in new economic, social, and political realities. A new Babylonian province and governor replaced the independent Judean state, monarchy, and leadership. The destruction of the temple erased the symbolic center of Judah and the ritual practices associated with it. Those who were exiled and those who remained in Judah lost the political and religious institutions that had shaped their identity.[60]

At least three identifiable Jewish communities arose in the aftermath of these events: one in Egypt, one in Babylon, and one in Palestine. For the exiles, the time following these losses became a time of adjustment to life as a minority within the wealthy and powerful Babylonian empire. New patterns of community life developed, and their faith was reformulated in ways that responded to their new situation. Meanwhile those who remained made adjustments to their new context as well. A new Babylonian-appointed governor was seated at Mizpah. In the absence of the temple, worship was carried out at other sites and perhaps in the ruins of the old temple.[61] When the Achaemenid dynasty arose in 539 BCE, it introduced a new administrative system, one that over time resulted in "a marked enlargement of influence in local Levantine affairs by the imperial administration."[62] The catastrophe and the ensuing changes compelled the production of and shaped the historiography produced during these years as they raised new debates over the identity of Judah, the status of Jerusalem and its temple, and attitudes toward imperial rule.[63] These events and the political, military, ethnic, and social realities of life under Persian rule

---

60. Charles E. Carter, *The Emergence of Yehud in the Persian Period: A Social and Demographic Study*, JSOTSup 294 (Sheffield: Sheffield Academic, 1999), 309.

61. Oded Lipschits, *The Fall and Rise of Jerusalem: Judah under Babylonian Rule* (Winona Lake, IN: Eisenbrauns, 2005), xii. Lipschits suggests that Mizpah, Gibeon, Bethel, and perhaps Shechem were all centers of worship.

62. Hoglund, *Achaemenid Imperial Administration*, 1.

63. Ibid., xiii.

all had a bearing on the rhetorical strategies of the author and the cogency of his arguments.

Over the past century, archaeological studies have produced new evidence regarding Yehud during the time of the Persian Empire (539–333 BCE).[64] The Murashu business archives from Nippur (455–403) and Aramaic texts from Elephantine (ca. 550–400) offer a window into diaspora Jewish communities of the times, providing a comparison for the community in Jerusalem.[65] Excavations and surface surveys of Palestine supply information regarding settlement patterns, population density, and military presence in the region.[66] Coinage and stamp seals testify to administrative activities in the region.[67] Records found at Persepolis and in various

---

64. Ephraim Stern, *The Assyrian, Babylonian, and Persian Periods, 732–332 BCE*, vol. 2 of *Archaeology of the Land of the Bible* (New York: Doubleday, 2001), 360–582; Carter, *Emergence of Yehud*; Lipschits, *Fall and Rise of Jerusalem*. Other useful treatments of this time period are in Oded Lipschits and Manfred Oeming, eds., *Judah and the Judeans in the Persian Period* (Winona Lake, IN: Eisenbrauns, 2006).

65. The Murashu archives consist of some 650 cuneiform tablets from a family business firm in Nippur, about 100 km southeast of Babylon. They provide about 2,200 names of persons. See Elias J. Bickerman, "The Generation of Ezra and Nehemiah," in *Studies in Jewish and Christian History: Part Three*, AGJU 9 (Leiden: Brill, 1986), 299–326; Michael D. Coogan, *West Semitic Personal Names in the Murašû Documents*, HSM 7 (Missoula, MT: Scholars Press, 1976). For details on Elephantine, see Eduard Sachau, *Aramäische Papyrus und Ostraka aus einer jüdischen Militär-Kolonie zu Elephantine* (Leipzig: Hinrichs, 1911); William R. Arnold, "The Passover Papyrus from Elephantine," *JBL* 31 (1912): 1–33; Reinhard G. Kratz, "The Second Temple of Jeb and of Jerusalem," in Lipschits and Oeming, *Persian Period*, 247–64. Emil G. Kraeling provides an interesting history of the discovery and research on the Elephantine papyri in "New Light on the Elephantine Colony," *BA* 15 (1952): 50–67.

66. For details, see Carter, *Emergence of Yehud*; Hoglund, *Achaemenid Imperial Administration*; Yigal Levin, ed., *A Time of Change: Judah and Its Neighbours in the Persian and Early Hellenistic Periods*, LSTS 65 (New York: T&T Clark, 2007).

67. See Carter, *Emergence of Yehud*, 267–79; Oded Lipschits and David Vanderhooft, "Yehud Stamp Impressions in the Fourth Century B.C.E.: A Time of Administrative Consolidation?" in *Judah and the Judeans in the Fourth Century B.C.E.*, ed. Oded Lipschits, Gary N. Knoppers, and Rainer Albertz (Winona Lake, IN: Eisenbrauns, 2007), 75–94; Leo Mildenberg, "Yehud: A Preliminary Study of the Provincial Coinage of Judaea," in *Greek Numismatics and Archaeology: Essays in Honor of Margaret Thompson*, ed. Otto Mørkholm and Nancy M. Waggoner (Wetteren: Cultura, 1979), 183–96; John Wilson Betlyon, "The Provincial Government of Persian Period Judea and the Yehud Coins," *JBL* 105 (1986): 633–42.

temple archives provide a window into Persian administration.[68] Historians have combined this information with ancient Greek histories and the biblical record to propose various possibilities regarding the empire's structure, imperial control, the function of the temple, and the character and governance of the Yehud community.[69]

The Babylonian occupation left little evidence in the material culture. Indeed, the most prominent feature "left by seventy years of Babylonian domination in Palestine was the total destruction and devastation of all the main cities that had flourished during the Assyrian period."[70] Nadav Na'aman observes, "only a network of villages survived in the northern highlands of Judah and Benjamin.... Neither new fortifications, nor new large public buildings have been found in 'exilic' period Judah.... The results of the destructive Babylonian campaigns ... are perceived everywhere in Judah."[71] In particular, the main Babylonian effort was concentrated in the siege of Jerusalem.[72] Settlement continuing in Jerusalem is suggested by Jer 41:5, but "the results of excavations ... do not supply a definitive answer."[73]

While historical considerations have led many scholars to relate the destruction layers at sites in Judah to the Babylonian incursions in the early sixth century, the archaeological data provide no absolute dating or causes of destruction evident in most parts of the country. Nor is there archaeological evidence of extensive deportations from areas of Judah and Benja-

---

68. Pierre Briant, *From Cyrus to Alexander: A History of the Persian Empire*, trans. Peter T. Daniels (Winona Lake, IN: Eisenbrauns, 2002), 8.

69. See, e.g., Briant, *From Cyrus to Alexander*; Muhammed A. Dandamayev and Vladimir G. Lukonin, *The Culture and Social Institutions of Ancient Iran*, trans. Philip L. Kohl and D. J. Dadson (Cambridge: Cambridge University Press, 1989); Lester L. Grabbe, *The Persian and Greek Periods*, vol. 1 of *Judaism from Cyrus to Hadrian*, 2 vols. (Minneapolis: Fortress, 1992); Weinberg, *Citizen-Temple Community*; Fried, *Priest and Great King*; M. Smith, *Palestinian Parties*; Hoglund, *Achaemenid Imperial Administration*; Bedford, *Temple Restoration*.

70. E. Stern, *Assyrian, Babylonian, and Persian Periods*, 308.

71. Nadav Na'aman, *Ancient Israel and Its Neighbors: Interaction and Counteraction*, vol. 1 of *Collected Essays* (Winona Lake, IN: Eisenbrauns, 2005), 411.

72. E. Stern, *Assyrian, Babylonian, and Persian Periods*, 309. He states, "The Babylonian conquest clearly brought total destruction to Jerusalem and the Judaean Hill sites to the south of Jerusalem" (323).

73. Ibid., 324.

min aside from Jerusalem.[74] Taken together, this evidence undermines the biblical suggestion of an empty land (2 Chr 36:21). Oded Lipschits argues that settlement in the Negev may have collapsed gradually after losing the urban center of Jerusalem.[75] Over time seminomadic groups moved into the southern regions, and in the second half of the Persian era they were populated mainly by Edomites and Arabs.[76] Although the southern highlands lost population, the number of northern settlements increased by almost 65 percent. Hans Barstad contends, "This change in the settlement pattern clearly indicates that people from Jerusalem fled to the neighboring areas following the fall of the city in 586 B.C.E."[77] He believes that, although significant, the deportations had less effect on the day-to-day life of those who remained and points to evidence of ongoing agricultural production of wine and oil—both products not grown in Babylonia and therefore desirable commodities that fueled the local economy.[78] Bustenay Oded takes issue with the claim that little changed. He acknowledges continuity but underscores the marked decline in quality and quantity of the population in Judah, arguing for a significant gap in the history of Judah during the exilic period.[79] Lipschits summarizes the situation:

> If we focus the discussion on Judah, the most conspicuous archaeological phenomenon after the destruction of Jerusalem is a sharp decline in urban life, which is in contrast to the continuity of the rural settlements in the highland of Judah, particularly in the area between Hebron and the territory of Benjamin. This settlement pattern continued throughout the Persian Period, when, despite the rebuilding of Jerusalem and the restoration of its status as the capital of the province, urban life remained insubstantial; settlement in Judah continued to be largely rural.[80]

---

74. Lipschits, *Fall and Rise of Jerusalem*, 164.

75. Ibid., 230. This would have been in part because they were dependent on the kingdom of Judah to provide security.

76. E. Stern, *Assyrian, Babylonian, and Persian Periods*, 325. See also his discussion of names on ostraca from this region (443–47).

77. Hans M. Barstad, "After the 'Myth of the Empty Land': Major Challenges in the Study of Neo-Babylonian Judah," in *Judah and the Judeans in the Neo-Babylonian Period*, ed. Oded Lipschits and Joseph Blenkinsopp (Winona Lake, IN: Eisenbrauns, 2003), 9.

78. Ibid., 12–14.

79. Bustenay Oded, "Where Is the 'Myth of the Empty Land' to Be Found? History versus Myth," in Lipschits and Blenkinsopp, *Neo-Babylonian Period*, 71.

80. Lipschits, *Fall and Rise of Jerusalem*, 190.

Four sites in Benjamin—Mizpah, Gibeah, Bethel, and Gibeon—were not destroyed by the Babylonians, and "this small region continued to function and even prosper during the Babylonian period."[81] The pottery at these sites reflects a continuation of vessels attributed to the latest Israelite period, with a gradual increase in Persian styles over time, and is consistent with continuing occupation in Benjamin during the Persian era. Settlement findings substantiate ongoing occupation and support the biblical record of the appointment of a governor at Mizpah, where Gedaliah briefly ruled before his assassination.[82] According to the book of Jeremiah, those who remained in Benjamin apparently accepted Babylonian rule (Jer 40:9–10) while others fled to Egypt (Jer 41–42). During these years the temple site may have continued as a center of pilgrimage; but if so, the visits and any rituals there were unofficial and spontaneous and carried out by small groups or individuals.[83]

During the Persian period, the population of Benjamin gradually declined by about 60 percent. Lipschits assesses the evidence as follows:

> At the end of the sixth century B.C.E. and during the fifth and fourth centuries B.C.E., these four major sites gradually declined in population. This decline may be connected to the transfer of the center of activity to the Jerusalem region after the Return to Zion, which resulted in the decline in status of Mizpah, along with the entire Benjamin region.[84]

Perhaps residents moved to Jerusalem, but the decline may also be explained by a growth of settlements in the northeastern part of the Shephelah. This in turn may have been tied to growing economic activity in the coastal area and the agricultural potential of the region combined

---

81. E. Stern, *Assyrian, Babylonian, and Persian Periods*, 323. Stern suggests six sites, but report of findings from two of them were yet to be published at the time he wrote.

82. Lipschits, *Fall and Rise of Jerusalem*, 98. See Jer 40 for an account of this. Lipschits notes the references to summer fruit harvests and a later grain harvest that he uses to estimate the length of Gedaliah's rule.

83. Ibid., 116.

84. Ibid., 245. Lipschits cites 146 settled sites in Iron Age II and a drop to 59 sites in the Persian period (246). Carter (*Emergence of Yehud*, 235) claims an even steeper decline for Benjamin, from 157 sites in Iron II to a low of 39 settlements in the Persian era. He notes a recovery in the Hellenistic period to 163 inhabited sites.

with proximity to major coastal trade routes.[85] In the late fifth century, Persia built a system of fortresses in the southern part of the Yehud province. Hoglund argues that the widespread military intensification was "to protect primary and subsidiary routes that knit the region together under imperial control."[86] However, it is more likely that the military presence was to stabilize the province's southern border in the face of Egypt's rebellion during the reign of Artaxerxes II (405–359 BCE).[87] This may still have fostered economic development of the region, making it safer, if not a more enticing place to live and work.[88] Ideological conflict between the returned exiles and others may also have been a contributing factor in this migration.[89]

The biblical account claims a numerically significant return to Jerusalem (Neh 7:66 records 42,360 returnees). However, archaeological evidence does not support a growth in settlement consistent with these numbers. Current evidence suggests that the Persian settlement of Jerusalem was small, covering no more than 60 dunams of the city of David, while the western hill remained abandoned until the beginning of the Hellenistic period.[90] Carter estimates that the population of Jerusalem was a maximum of 1,500 people at any given time, with the overall population of Yehud growing to about 20,650 by the end of the fourth century.[91] (Israel Finkelstein argues for significantly smaller estimates, suggesting a city population of 400–500 persons.)[92] Settlements around Jerusalem

---

85. Lipschits, *Fall and Rise of Jerusalem*, 248.

86. Hoglund (*Achaemenid Imperial Administration*, 203) dates their construction to the mid-fifth century. Edelman (*Origins*, 319) associates them with the practice of using fires to send important news to the provincial seat at Jerusalem from the main royal roads to the west and south.

87. Lipschits, *Fall and Rise of Jerusalem*, 183.

88. As Hoglund (*Achaemenid Imperial Administration*, 204) points out, there is some evidence the forts were collection points for tax revenue.

89. Lipschits, *Fall and Rise of Jerusalem*, 248: "At the time of the Return, the ruling authority in Judah was transferred to those who returned from the Babylonian Exile, and they forced their religious, ritual, social, and national views upon the residents of the province. This may have pushed some of the inhabitants of Benjamin to migrate beyond the administrative limits of the province and to settle beyond its borders."

90. Ibid., 212. This contrasts with the pre-Babylonian environs of Jerusalem that reached a size of 900–1,000 dunams (216).

91. Carter, *Emergence of Yehud*, 201, 226.

92. Israel Finkelstein, "Jerusalem in the Persian (and Early Hellenistic) Period

consisted of very small farms, with most located south and west of Ramat Raḥel and Bethlehem. Fourteen farms were counted north and east of Jerusalem compared with sixty in the late Iron Age. Overall settlement around Jerusalem fell from 170 sites prior to the Babylonian invasion to 28 sites.[93]

The settlement pattern represented in the list of returnees in Ezra 2/Neh 7 does not coincide with the archaeological evidence. In the biblical record, approximately 63 percent of the returnees resided in Jerusalem and 24 percent located in Benjamin.[94] In contrast, the archaeological record shows Benjamin had the largest concentration of settlements, with 46 percent; only 10 percent of the population was in Jerusalem.[95] This disparity likely reflects the interest in Jerusalem of the editor of these lists.[96] The biblical lists of settlements may provide an idealized portrait of Yehud, functioning as indicators of "real or fictional ancestral connections, whether or not they were within the borders of the province."[97] Edelman suggests that, by excluding sites in the Negev and placing the returnees primarily in sites within Benjamin and around Jerusalem, the author links the golah (the returned exiles) with Israel.[98]

Over four hundred YHWD (Yehud) seal impressions (stamped on handles or sides of jars) have been found in the region. The jars are not designed for export, and we do not know the exact purpose of the stamps. Perhaps they marked the contents for official consumption or for taxes, or

---

and the Wall of Nehemiah," *JSOT* 32 (2008): 507. He calculates 15,000 for the entire Yehud population.

93. Lipschits, *Fall and Rise of Jerusalem*, 216–17.

94. Ibid., 167. Nine percent are in the northern Shephelah, and none is reported settling in the Judean hills. In the biblical record, the city of residence of approximately 74 percent is unknown.

95. Ibid. The peak settlement pattern of the province of Yehud (probably in the mid-fifth century BCE) provides the following picture: 46 percent of the people live in Benjamin, 10 percent in Jerusalem, 28 percent in the Judean hills, 14 percent in the northern Shephelah, and 1 percent in the eastern strip. These are based on estimates of settled area (in dunams) of: 500 dunams in Benjamin, 110 in Jerusalem and environs, 300 in the Judean hills, 150 in the northern Shephelah, and 10 in the eastern strip.

96. Ibid., 166.

97. Carter, *Emergence of Yehud*, 81, 102.

98. Edelman, *Origins*, 225, 232. She further notes that Neh 11:25–36 has been shaped to reflect the boundaries of the former kingdom of Judah found in the Deuteronomistic History (228).

even that the product originated from official estates.[99] Ninety percent of found seal impressions have only the province name, with about 8 percent also containing the term "governor."[100] Oded Lipschits and David Vanderhooft have identified three chronological stages for the seals.[101] The early seals (sixth-fifth centuries BCE) are the only ones that contain personal names and show a greater variety in form and reflect continuity with late Iron Age seal practices.[102] Middle group stamps (fourth-third centuries BCE) consist of two main types containing only the province name. Titles and personal names are absent. Examples of both the early and middle groups are absent from the western hill of Jerusalem, where only seals from later types were found. Nearly all were found at four major centers: Ramat Raḥel, Jerusalem, Mizpah, and Jericho. Of the forty-two מוצה seals that date to Babylonian rule, 70 percent are located in Mizpah, compared with only 5 percent of the Yehud seals. Meanwhile 80 percent of Persian period Yehud seals have been found at Jerusalem and Ramat Raḥel.[103]

This evidence coincides with some of the shifts in demographics and may indicate that Persia preferred Ramat Raḥel as an administrative center while Jerusalem became the center of the province. Changes in the style, orthography, and location of the finds indicate a change in

---

99. E. Stern (*Archaeology*, 550) lists the following three possibilities; "they represent (a) the seal of the official in charge of tax collection on behalf of the Persian authorities; (b) the seal of the treasurer of the Temple of the autonomous province of Judah; (c) the seal of the high priest, who in this period also functioned as governor." (Stern's work was published prior to the renewed excavations at Ramat Raḥel, the primary source of YHWD stamp seals.)

100. Lipschits, *Fall and Rise of Jerusalem*, 176.

101. Lipschits and Vanderhooft, "Yehud Stamp Impressions," 77. They date the late group to the second century BCE. See also Oded Lipschits and David S. Vanderhooft, *The Yehud Stamp Impressions: A Corpus of Inscribed Impressions from the Persian and Hellenistic Periods in Judah* (Winona Lake, IN: Eisenbrauns, 2011).

102. Lipschits and Vanderhooft, "Yehud Stamp Impressions," 78. Also, Gary N. Knoppers, "Revisiting the Samarian Question in the Persian Period," in Lipschits and Oeming, *Persian Period*, 270.

103. Lipschits, *Fall and Rise of Jerusalem*, 180. Thirty seals from the Babylonian era were found at Mizpah, while only 4 were found in Jerusalem. One was found at Ramat Raḥel and 7 found elsewhere. As of 2005, Jerusalem had 170 Yehud seals, while 194 seals were found at Ramat Raḥel and only 19 at Mizpah. Carter (*Emergence of Yehud*, 267) concurs with this assessment, arguing it supports the hypothesis that Mizpah "declined in importance as Jerusalem rebounded and became the imperial capital of the province."

1. QUESTIONS ABOUT EZRA-NEHEMIAH 23

settlement patterns and an increasing administrative consolidation. The stamping process for Yehud jars grew increasingly consolidated, and the authors conclude that the consolidation "may link to the period when Persia lost control of Egypt [in 404 BCE], increasing the significance of the southern Levantine coast as a border zone. Agricultural resources and perhaps tax revenues for the Persian army would have been more critical and resulted in tighter control in the administration of the distribution system."[104] However, in contrast to the commonly held theory that Yehud was administered by Samaria, the seals (and later the local minting of coins) indicate that Yehud enjoyed a significant level of autonomy from neighboring regions throughout the entire Persian period.[105]

Life in Samaria continued uninterrupted during these centuries. The city grew in size and importance. Imported Attic ware and other finds, including parts to a bronze throne, indicate economic and social elites in the area.[106] Samaria was one of Palestine's largest urban areas, prompting Gary Knoppers to note, "During the Achaemenid era, members of the Judean elite were not dealing with a depopulated outback to the north. Quite the contrary, they were dealing with a province that was larger, better-established, and considerably more populous than was Yehud."[107] The first phase of the Mount Gerizim temple dates to the mid-fifth century, which would parallel the time frame of the construction of the Jerusalem wall. Unlike Samaria, Jerusalem may have remained poor even at the height of the Persian period, and the discrepancy in size and wealth combined with cultural overlap (as evidenced in material culture) would

---

104. Lipschits and Vanderhooft, "Yehud Stamp Impressions," 90.

105. Carter, *Emergence of Yehud*, 279. The theory of Samaritan administration was first posited in 1934 by Albrecht Alt, "Die Rolle Samarias bei der Enstehung des Judentums," reprinted in Alt, *Kleine Schriften zur Geschichte des Volkes Israel*, 3 vols. (Munich: Beck, 1953–1959), 2:316–37. Weinberg (*Citizen-Temple Community*, 135–36) adopts this position, noting primarily that leaders of the early returnees lack governmental titles within the official correspondence in Ezra. For an assessment of Alt's theory, see Hoglund, *Achaemenid Imperial Administration*, 69–71. Carter (*Emergence of Yehud*, 302) critiques Weinberg's position, arguing that the two-governor theory he proposes is impractical from the viewpoint of Persian imperial interests.

106. Oded Lipschits, "Achaemenid Imperial Policy, Settlement Processes in Palestine, and the Status of Jerusalem in the Middle of the Fifth Century B.C.E.," in Lipschits and Oeming, *Persian Period*, 31.

107. Knoppers, "Revisiting the Samarian Question," 273.

have posed challenges for certain members of the Jerusalem elite.[108] This imbalance may have contributed to the policies of the returnees. "The ethnocentrism of [Ezra-Nehemiah] can be regarded as an attempt to resist the dominant culture in which the returnees find themselves."[109]

Although the rebuilding of Jerusalem's wall brought change to the city, it was on a small scale.[110] It replaced Mizpah as the provincial capital and therefore housed a garrison.[111] Jerusalem's new stature may have been initiated by Persia as a reward for loyalty and tied to the revolt of Egypt in the middle of the fifth century (464–454 BCE). However, Lipschits believes that fortifying a garrison in Jerusalem would have held little importance in this conflict and argues for a later time period for increased Persian control.[112] Hoglund associates Nehemiah's wall construction with an imperial citadel in the city (Neh 7:2). He contends that Nehemiah acted in keeping with his position as an imperial appointee, and his mission was *not* to reward the community but "to create a web of economic and social relationships that would tie the community more completely into the imperial system."[113] His mission was associated with tighter control and increased taxes and therefore generated the opposition evident in Nehemiah.[114] However, it is now more certain that garrison construction in the Negev dates to later years. Lipschits links them to Aramaic ostraca that date to the late fifth and early fourth centuries BCE (405–351) and notes that this would coincide with the Levant as a border region with Egypt. Thus the impetus for the reconstruction of Jerusalem was due not to Persian military construction but rather to an internal Judean process.[115]

---

108. Ibid., 279.

109. Tamara C. Eskenazi, "From *Exile and Restoration* to Exile and Reconstruction," in *Exile and Restoration Revisited: Essays on the Babylonian and Persian Periods in Memory of Peter R. Ackroyd*, ed. Gary N. Knoppers and Lester L. Grabbe with Deirdre Fulton, LSTS 73 (London: T&T Clark, 2009), 87.

110. Finkelstein questions whether there was any wall constructed during this time ("Jerusalem," 501–20).

111. Lipschits, "Achaemenid Imperial Policy," 35.

112. Ibid., 38.

113. Hoglund, *Achaemenid Imperial Administration*, 244. Edelman (*Origins*, 349) takes issue with portions of Hoglund's theory but similarly assigns pragmatic concerns of the king for the building of Jerusalem's walls and temple, suggesting an underlying a plan to integrate Yehud into the economic and military imperial system.

114. Hoglund, *Achaemenid Imperial Administration*, 245.

115. Lipschits, "Achaemenid Imperial Policy," 35, 39.

During the Persian era the new territory of Idumea emerged south of Judah. The late-Persian-era boundaries between Yehud and its southern neighbor have been determined by the absence of Yehud seals in Idumea and the presence of figurines found in Idumea but not in Yehud.[116] By the Hellenistic era, Idumea incorporated former regions of the province of Judah: the Negev, the Hebron mountains, and the southern and central Shephelah.[117] However, unlike modern states, borders were porous and should more helpfully be thought of as frontiers where the central political authority "is diffuse or thinly spread."[118] Loyal Judeans likely lived in these frontier areas, marked by their heterogeneity. Epigraphic material from Idumea reflects "a very mixed population within late-Persian-period Idumea."[119] The material reflects Arab, Idumean, West Semitic, Judahite, and Phoenician names, with "only a minority of each group showing ethnic continuity as expressed through their particular ethnic onomasticon."[120]

In summary, Jerusalem began the Persian era desolate, while communities in Benjamin appear to have escaped the destruction by Babylon, and life there continued, although Benjamin shows a loss of population during this era.[121] Seal and textual evidence indicates that Mizpah operated as the local administrative center.[122] In the Persian era, Jerusalem emerged as the

---

116. Amos Kloner and Ian Stern, "Idumea in the Late Persian Period (Fourth Century B.C.E.)," in Lipschits, Knoppers, and Albertz, *Fourth Century B.C.E.*, 140.

117. Lipschits, *Fall and Rise of Jerusalem*, 149.

118. John W. Wright, "Remapping Yehud: The Borders of Yehud and the Genealogies of Chronicles," in Lipschits and Oeming, *Persian Period*, 71.

119. Kloner and Stern, "Idumea," 142.

120. Ibid., 143. Kloner and Stern argue that the coexistence of these various ethnic groups did not result in a competitive atmosphere or ethnocentrism, although each group continued to maintain its own identity. However, this argument is based only on the evidence of name lists, and how people relate may not surface in work detail lists.

121. Joseph Blenkinsopp, "Benjamin Traditions Read in the Early Persian Period," in Lipschits and Oeming, *Persian Period*, 644. Ephraim Stern and Lester Grabbe have argued that there was significant destruction of the Benjamin region ca. 480 BCE: Stern, *Assyrian, Babylonian, and Persian Periods*, 322–23; Grabbe, *Persian and Greek Periods*, 73. However, Blenkinsopp notes that more recent evaluations suggest continuity and that Stern admits that perhaps the towns were only abandoned (Blenkinsopp, "Benjamin Traditions," 645).

122. For a detailed survey of the material culture of Mizpah during the Babylonian era, see Jeffrey R. Zorn, "Tell en-Naṣbeh and the Material Culture of the Sixth Century," in Lipschits and Blenkinsopp, *Neo-Babylonian Period*, 413–47.

provincial capital and grew in numbers—although reaching only 10 percent of its pre-Babylonian population and remaining small and relatively poor throughout this era. The immediate area around the city consisted of a few very small farms. Perhaps both Jerusalem and the northern Shephelah benefited from population movement away from Benjamin. Samaria remained a strong and influential northern neighbor, while regions south of Judah became part of Idumea. There was little change from Persian to early Hellenistic occupation. Evidence shows no distinct increase in the territory of the province or of the city of Jerusalem; Yehud stamp seals remain the same and coins continue in the same denominations.[123]

1.2.1. Imperial Involvement

Following a military conquest, empires need to hold a region by forging a mutual relationship between the crown and the population in the territory. The nature of this relationship between the central Persian government and Yehud is a topic of debate. Arguments about Persia's influence range from benign neglect—except for the matters of taxes, loyalty, and military support—to claims of strong bureaucratic control.

Muhammed Dandamayev surveys the variety that seemed to mark the various regions within the empire and argues for local autonomy in Judah.[124] Following Alt's early thesis, he assumes that the Samaritan governor originally supervised a Judean deputy, but that over time Judah began to enjoy greater independence in domestic affairs. He suggests that the reforms carried out by Nehemiah and Ezra led to a community headed by the high priest that "had its own organs of self-administration, in whose affairs the Persian satrap did not intervene."[125] Frei nuances the argument for local autonomy and suggests that the Persians systematically authorized local customs and religious practices that institutionalized a form of cooperation between the central government and dependent communities.[126] While he argues for local initiative in gaining imperial authorization, he recognizes that "the process also provided the central government a chance to control a self-governing body in a constitutional manner. The

---

123. Oded Lipschits and Oren Tal, "The Settlement Archaeology of the Province of Judah: A Case Study," in Lipschits, Knoppers, and Albertz, *Fourth Century B.C.E.*, 47.
124. Dandamayev and Lukonin, *Culture and Social Institutions*, 104.
125. Ibid.
126. Frei, "Persian Imperial Authorization," 40.

subjects were promised legal protection on the condition that their plans did not contradict imperial interests."[127]

Using archival and inscriptional data, Fried, unconvinced by arguments for local self-governance, points to Persian involvement in the appointments of Ezra and Nehemiah and their ensuing conflicts with local elites. She argues for significant imperial bureaucratic control throughout the empire—including building programs, priestly appointments, the handling of court cases, tax revenues, and the work force.[128]

Hoglund takes imperial involvement further, maintaining that Persia carried out a deliberate policy to integrate the region into the empire in the face the Egyptian revolt of 465–451 BCE. In his view the rebellion was a major crisis in imperial control and, given the Levant's strategic importance as a land bridge to Egypt and access to the Mediterranean, he believes that the empire would naturally be concerned with its security and took "steps to consolidate its hold over territories imperiled by continuing Greek pressure."[129] He posits four policies employed to integrate the region: ruralization, commercialization, militarization, and ethnic collectivization. Ruralization established farming settlements that would have supplied tribute for the crown and required Persian control over land allocation.[130] Commercialization broke traditional economic self-sufficiency and created interdependence. Militarizing the region involved building fortresses that both protected and supervised trade routes in the region.[131] This intensified the imperial presence and created social and economic change as mercenaries of other nationalities came into the region and interacted with the local population.[132] Ethnic collectivization, a policy continued from previous empires, administered ethnic groups as units and pursued policies that kept them dependent on Persia (e.g., prohibiting them from independently securing their own territory).[133]

---

127. Ibid., 38.
128. Fried, *Priest and Great King*, 201, 204.
129. Hoglund, *Achaemenid Imperial Administration*, 163. He partners ancient Greek histories with archaeological evidence taken from excavated sites and ground surveys
130. Kenneth Hoglund, "The Achaemenid Context," in *Second Temple Studies*, ed. Philip R. Davies, JSOTSup 117 (Sheffield: JSOT Press, 1991), 59.
131. Hoglund, *Achaemenid Imperial Administration*, 203. He notes that many of the smaller forts were abandoned within a short period of time.
132. Hoglund, "Achaemenid Context," 64.
133. Ibid., 66. This last point is based primarily on evidence from Ezra-Nehemiah

There is evidence of all four conditions in the Levant, but it is more difficult to prove that they are the result of a deliberate Persian policy of integration. The maintenance of ethnic boundaries may more easily be understood as emerging out of local concerns and conflict rather than due to an external imperial policy. The rural settlements around Jerusalem existed prior to Persian rule, and Jerusalem was renewed as an urban center under Persia. Excavations at Ramat Raḥel provide evidence of imperial interest in, and bureaucratic control over, the collection of agricultural goods from the region, but whether Persia controlled land allocation and determined agricultural production or operated in a more flexible manner with local entities is less obvious. For example, Vadiim Jigoulov argues that Persian monarchs exercised a more flexible policy, which he terms "Managed Autonomy." He suggests that Persian kings demanded "collaboration on imperial economic and military projects and timely payment of tribute" but allowed local autonomy in which local polities had autonomous economies and retained their indigenous cultural distinctiveness.[134]

Although the archaeological evidence demonstrates an increasing, and therefore changing, Persian presence in the Levant over the course of time, giving dates to particular changes proves elusive. Hoglund argues that the construction of the walls of Jerusalem coincided with fortifications built throughout the southern Levant during the time of Artaxerxes I.[135] However; the importance that Hoglund places on the Egyptian rebellion of 460–454 is not shared by Briant, who contends that the rebellion was confined to the Egyptian Delta and lacked full Egyptian support.[136] Hoglund's

---

and the existence of ration lists issued to ethnic groups in small towns. Whether we can extrapolate small town ration lists to a general imperial policy in larger communities remains unclear.

134. Vadiim Jigoulov, "Administration of Achaemenid Phoenicia: A Case for Managed Autonomy," in Knoppers, Grabbe, and Fulton, *Exile and Restoration Revisited*, 145–46. His study is specifically concerned with the Phoenician city-states.

135. Hoglund, *Achaemenid Imperial Administration*, 204. Hoglund and Edelman contend that the garrisons were related to the collection of revenues and the maintenance of the administrative machinery over the territory. For example, Edelman (*Origins*, 9) states, "Zerubbabel, as an agent of Artaxerxes I, rebuilt the temple in Jerusalem probably sometime during the 440s BCE. It was rebuilt as part of a larger Persian policy that established a network of birot, guard stations, inns, and caravanserai along the major road systems of the empire, to facilitate trade, imperial communication, and military mobility."

136. Briant, *From Cyrus to Alexander*, 575.

time frame is further undermined by Lipschits, who dates the southern fortifications to the later period of 405–334. He believes that, although interested in agricultural development earlier in the Persian period, the Achaemenids had no interest in developing urban centers or new social or political structures on the local level. Instead, "they developed an isolated imperial production center, without any cooperation from the local population."[137] This implies that Jerusalem became the capital due to internal Judean processes, and Persian rulers granted permission to build Jerusalem walls when they realized that "Jerusalem had already become the fiscal center of the province (given the usual role of the temple in gathering taxes)."[138]

1.2.2. The Late Persian Era: 404–333 BCE

War with Egypt characterized the late Persian era and provides a backdrop for the completion of Ezra-Nehemiah. The ascension of Artaxerxes II (404–358 BCE) coincided with this military turmoil and brought a stronger Persian presence into the Levant. The Jerusalem temple and Nehemiah's wall had been standing for the author's entire life. In addition to the mainly rural villages of Yehud, the region now also contained centralized administrative centers, and military strongholds.[139] Although constructed at a later date than Hoglund posits, the administrative sites and garrisons were likely a response to the political reality with Egypt.

From 387 to 383, Artaxerxes II "found himself facing multiple rebellions including Egypt, Sidon and Cyprus, which [ancient authors] characterize as not merely simultaneous but coordinated."[140] In 386, Artaxerxes's effort to regain Egypt had failed, and it remained a danger to Persia and "a natural ally to anyone who wanted to take on the Persians."[141] Six years later, Nectanebo I initiated a coalition with allies and fortified the Delta region.[142] In 373 Persia attacked Egypt again but was met with defeat and the army retreated to its Palestinian bases.[143]

---

137. Lipschits, "Achaemenid Imperial Policy," 30.
138. Ibid., 40.
139. Lipschits and Tal, "Settlement Archaeology," 35.
140. Briant, *From Cyrus to Alexander*, 650.
141. Ibid., 651–52.
142. Lipschits and Vanderhooft, "Yehud Stamp Impressions," 87.
143. Briant, *From Cyrus to Alexander*, 655.

Diodorus describes a general revolt by Persian satraps in 361 BCE. But Briant argues, "We are not dealing with a general, coordinated conflagration on the western front in 361 but rather with a series of limited local revolts over the course of a decade."[144] Another Egyptian offensive took place the following year along the coastal plain of Palestine, taking Phoenicia and besieging the cities in Syria. However, Egypt's incursion seems to have dissolved due to its own civil war. Despite these rebellions and satrapal revolts, Briant contends that this is not evidence of a deep and irreversible degradation of the central authority since the monarch shows the capacity to overcome them through military or political offensives.[145]

Artaxerxes III (359–338 BCE) failed twice to regain control of Egypt (359 and 351). In the following years, Sidon and Cyprus revolted. The king finally retook the Phoenician coast by 345 after a bloody suppression of Sidon. It is not known whether Sidon's rebellion extended to Jerusalem. Later writers mention Jews deported to Hyrcania and the destruction of Jericho, but these claims lack external evidence to confirm a revolt in Yehud or Samaria.[146] In 343, Artaxerxes III began a final campaign against Egypt, and this time the pharaoh, Nectanebo, gave ground, withdrawing first to Memphis and finally fleeing to Nubia. Persia regained control of Egypt in 342, fifty years after it had seceded. Diodorus attributes the success of this campaign to a much larger Persian army. If so, this army would have placed demands on the local economy in the Levant. Artaxerxes III remained in power until his death in 338. At that time a son, Arses (Artaxerxes IV), succeeded him.

Prior to the extended revolt by Egypt, Persia may have permitted a larger degree of independence with regard to settlement of the area.[147] Only in the fourth century are municipal jar stamps replaced by uniform Aramaic seal impressions, evidence of increasing imperial control. The growing imperial involvement in the region "most likely included a fixed arrangement of district boundaries, garrisoning of the frontiers, and, most of all, tight Achaemenid control and investment, as is witnessed by the unprecedented construction at many sites in southern Palestine."[148]

---

144. Ibid., 674.
145. Ibid., 665, 675.
146. Ibid., 664, 685.
147. Lipschits and Tal, "Settlement Archaeology," 45.
148. Ibid., 46.

1.2.3. The Jerusalem Temple and the Role of the Exiles

The relationship of the Jerusalem temple to the political and social milieu of Persian Yehud is not entirely clear. Joel Weinberg compared temples operating in Asia Minor with Jerusalem's temple.[149] The temples in his comparative samples were wealthy institutions, had land holdings with a yearly income, and owned slaves. Citizenship was dependent on participation and support of the temple, and could be limited by ethnic membership. Priests often played a major role in the city assembly.[150] However, during these centuries "the Jerusalem temple owned no land and did not have its own economy."[151] In addition, the history of a destroyed and abandoned Jerusalem temple in need of reconstruction compares poorly with the long-standing Babylonian temples cited as parallels.[152] Lacking independent resources, the Jerusalem temple would necessarily be dependent on financial giving by members of the community to maintain its priesthood and rituals. Since the golah community took on this responsibility to the exclusion of the locals, "they were able to claim control of the Jerusalem cult."[153]

The Jerusalem temple also faced competition from the newly constructed temple on Mount Gerizim in Samaria. Evidence from coinage and carbon 14 date its origins to the mid-fifth century BCE.[154] Sanballat was the first governor of the province and, according to Yitzhak Magen, "under-

---

149. Weinberg, *Citizen-Temple Community*.

150. Joseph Blenkinsopp ("Temple and Society in Achaemenid Judah," in Davies, *Second Temple Studies*, 28) provides a survey of the various temple communities used by Weinberg for his comparison. A critique of Weinberg's work appears in Jeremiah Cataldo, "Persian Policy and the Yehud Community," *JSOT* 28 (2003): 131–43.

151. Weinberg, *Citizen-Temple Community*, 103.

152. Bedford, *Temple Restoration*, 226. Bedford (225) critiques Weinberg's analysis and comments, "the putative Judean and Babylonian Bürger-Tempel-Gemeinde as understood by Weinberg are not comparable entities, and his claim that they are examples of the same form of socio-economic organization should be set aside."

153. Blenkinsopp, "Temple and Society," 39–40. Evidence of community control can be seen in Nehemiah's expulsion of Tobiah from the temple precincts (Neh 13:5–9).

154. This counters the claim of Josephus (*Ant.* 11.324) that it dates to the time of Alexander. It was active for 250 years until replaced by a Hellenistic temple in the early second century.

stood the connection between political and religious independence."[155] Consequently he built a temple on a long-established Yahwistic sacred site and managed to engage a high priest from the family of the high priesthood in Jerusalem.[156] By having this priest marry his daughter, Sanballat ensured that his own descendants became high priests.[157] The religion of the early Samaritan community was probably not that different from the Yehudites. The only difference, as evidenced by dedicatory inscriptions, may have been that Samaritans allowed foreigners to make dedications at the cultic site. The building of the temple may have been a first step in a long process of separation.[158] Exacerbating this was the reality that the Persian era population of Judah and Benjamin were largely descendants of those sent into exile under Babylonia. Due to differing contexts, the communities in the two provinces no longer shared the same religious and national worldviews.

Officials in Judah at this time include governors and high priests, as well as prefects, judges, and treasurers. The tax system remained much the same from the Persian to the Hellenistic period. Land taxes were paid in agricultural products, which would require an infrastructure for collection and transport of goods. Taxes were also imposed on craftsmen and trade, including the slave trade, which is attested in the biblical text (Neh 5:2–5; 7:67) and the Samaria papyri.[159] André Lemaire argues that a poll tax in the fourth century prompted the development of coinage in Judah and was collected through the temple, thus making the temple "a kind

---

155. Yitzhak Magen, "The Dating of the First Phase of the Samaritan Temple on Mount Gerizim in Light of the Archaeological Evidence," in Lipschits, Knoppers, and Albertz, *Fourth Century B.C.E.*, 188.

156. Ibid.

157. Bob Becking, "Do the Earliest Samaritan Inscriptions Already Indicate a Parting of the Ways?" in Lipschits, Knoppers, and Albertz, *Fourth Century B.C.E.*, 220. Becking observes that these conclusions interpret "a historical datum from its eventual outcome." Whether Sanballat had these political intentions is not certain.

158. Ibid. During the Persian era, Samaritan religious and provincial political leadership resided in the city of Samaria. When Samaria revolted against Alexander, he responded by destroying the capital and it became a Macedonian city. The priests became the ruling class of a Yahwistic community concentrated around the temple at Gerizim. See Magen, "Dating," 182.

159. André Lemaire, "Administration in Fourth-Century B.C.E. Judah in Light of Epigraphy and Numismatics," in Lipschits, Knoppers, and Albertz, *Fourth Century B.C.E.*, 56, 58.

of public treasury, 'national bank,' and monetary workshop."¹⁶⁰ During these last years of Persian rule, there is evidence of high priests taking on political administrative roles. A silver coin bearing the name "Yohanan the priest" dates to 378–368 BCE (or 340–333 BCE) and may coincide with the priest mentioned in Neh 12:22.¹⁶¹ However, Bedford notes that evidence about the priesthood is slight and comments that it "cannot support the contention that the authority of the priesthood was growing throughout the Achaemenid Persian period at the expense of the Persian-appointed governor."¹⁶²

A variety of causes led to changes in the religious, social, and physical organization in Yehud. The Babylonian destruction and exile were blamed on faulty politics of the past, leading to the disconnection of religious practice from national politics.¹⁶³ Martin Noth maintained that Persian support of religion excluded political independence and compelled changes to religious practice.¹⁶⁴ Religious and/or class conflicts and, in particular, the effect of minority status on ethnic group boundary maintenance also fomented changes in Yehud society.¹⁶⁵

The return of exiles has also been forwarded as essential to understanding these changes. Morton Smith argues that internal conflicts were religious *and* economic—differences that became aggravated with the rebuilding of the temple if membership in the cult was tied to claims to the land.¹⁶⁶ Imposing purity regulations on the priests in Jerusalem by the "Yahweh-alone party" would have produced tension because it reflects an incursion into the priests' field of influence.¹⁶⁷ Ultimately, according to

---

160. Ibid., 60.

161. Ibid., 54. Lemaire suggests that his descendant, Jaddua, may be the priest Josephus states welcomed Alexander (*Ant.* 11.326).

162. Bedford, *Temple Restoration*, 203.

163. Jon L. Berquist, *Judaism in Persia's Shadow: A Social and Historical Approach* (Minneapolis: Fortress, 1995), 4.

164. Ibid., 6.

165. Daniel L. Smith-Christopher, "The Politics of Ezra: Sociological Indicators of Postexilic Judaean Society," in Davies, *Second Temple Studies*, 73–97.

166. M. Smith, *Palestinian Parties*, 99–100, 108. Smith supports this idea with Ezek 11:15, 17, which claim land belongs to YHWH and is not to be sold. Hoglund ("Achaemenid Context," 59) argues that the land was Persia's to dispense with as it pleased and no family or communal land claims were in play.

167. M. Smith, *Palestinian Parties*, 82, 84.

Smith, these two groups of returned exiles forged an alliance in opposition to the surrounding "peoples of the land."[168]

John Kessler proposes a "charter group" model to evaluate the causes and effect of the golah group's return on the political and social dynamics of Yehud. The discourse within Ezra-Nehemiah indicates that the golah recounted history in a way that identified them as the sole heirs of the land in opposition to the local population. Kessler notes that the leadership of the community were golah members appointed by the Persians, giving them key roles in the local institutions. He also identifies a number of advantages of this charter group: literacy, bilingualism, experience with self-administration in a diverse context, and more extensive and direct contact with the imperial administration.[169] In addition, their version of Yahwism was influenced by their experience of exile.

Whether competing parties, charter groups, or ethnic boundary maintenance deployed in a new setting, explanations for the complex of relations during this time are often framed in terms of internal conflict and religious ideals versus external conflict and imperial demands.[170] Each raises interesting possibilities and identifies factors important to a full picture of the two centuries under Persian rule.

1.2.4. Summary

When historical, literary, and archaeological evidence are combined, it is evident that over time Persian control tightened in the region. However, the empire never achieved the status of a nation-state held together by a unified ideology. It began with numerous distinct ethnic groups who practiced distinct religions, spoke different languages, and perceived themselves as Persian through loyalty to the Persian monarch, not due to a shared sense of a nation. The combination of Persian governance, military actions, the "eyes of the king," and record keeping moved the empire toward consolidation.

The final editor or author of Ezra-Nehemiah experienced Persian war with Egypt and Sidon or the conquest of the region in 332 BCE by Alexander. The movements of Egyptian, Persian, or Greek armies through

---

168. Ibid., 86.
169. John Kessler, "Persia's Loyal Yahwists: Power Identity and Ethnicity in Achaemenid Yehud," in Lipschits and Oeming, *Persian Period*, 105.
170. Berquist, *Judaism in Persia's Shadow*, 3–9.

the region, the military conflicts, and the tug by surrounding regions to take sides, as well as local institutional competition, must all have shaped the writer's perceptions.[171] Notably, Ezra-Nehemiah consistently reflects loyalty to the Persians. Their rule is orderly; the kings are inspired by YHWH, but always act at a distance from Jerusalem through intermediaries. Conflict in these books is always local, with each movement of return prompting a distinct source and focus of conflict. Persia's imperial policies create conditions that foster the erection of social boundaries by the ethnic minorities they "collect," such as we see in Ezra-Nehemiah. The shared language, religion, history, and ethnicity of the exiles combine with a concern for identity and anxiety about domination to create an impulse toward communal boundary maintenance. The exclusionary steps taken by the community fostered conflict in Yehud.[172] In Ezra-Nehemiah, the historical and religious traditions of the people are reframed in response to changed circumstances: an impoverished and geographically reduced territory, a well-established diaspora, and a militarily secure Persian Empire.[173] The reshaped traditions are then employed to construct identity.

What might Bourdieu and Weber contribute to analyzing and understanding identity construction in these texts? Weber reminds us that maintaining one's position in the world is never done in a vacuum. It always occurs in competition with others, and is linked to gaining the approval or loyalty of an audience. Bourdieu reminds us of two basic realities regarding identity construction.

> The quest for the "objective" criteria of "regional" or "ethnic" identity should not make one forget that, in social practice, these criteria ... are the object of *mental representations*, that is, of acts of perception and appreciation, of cognition and recognition, in which agents invest their interest and their presuppositions, and of *objectified representations*, in things ... or acts, self-interested strategies of symbolic manipulation

---

171. Alexander Fantalkin and Oren Tal ("The Canonization of the Pentateuch: When and Why?" *ZAW* 124 [2012]: 207) argue that Persia's war with Egypt prompted Egypt's portrayal as a place of slavery and chaos in the Exodus account.

172. Smith-Christopher, "Politics of Ezra," 97.

173. John Kessler, "The Diaspora in Zechariah 1–8 and Ezra-Nehemiah," in *Community Identity in Judean Historiography*, ed. Gary N. Knoppers and Kenneth A. Ristau (Winona Lake, IN: Eisenbrauns, 2009), 144–45.

which aim at determining the (mental) representation that other people may form of these properties and their bearers.[174]

With this in mind, in this investigation I will consider what these texts divulge about those with whom the author competes—and over what. I will examine the mental and objectified representations in these texts and explore the particular ways they are employed to sway the readership.

---

174. Bourdieu, *Language and Symbolic Power*, 220.

2
Methodology

Randal Johnson observes, "The analysis of literary form or language is an essential part of literary study, but has full meaning only when viewed relationally—or, broadly speaking, intertextually—and when reinserted into the objective field of social relations of which it is part and from which it derives."[1] This study is an effort to place the findings of narrative analysis into conversation with the larger field of social relations in postexilic Yehud.[2] The text is in the midst of a conversation—and not just with other texts. The dynamics of the social realities impact what is said and how it is said.[3] Social power and social possibility influence the telling of this history. This means historical reconstructions of life in Persian-period Jerusalem will be relevant to understanding the social context of Ezra-Nehemiah's author. However, since this text grew from a number of sources composed at different times over the course of the two centuries of Persian rule, I will also consider how earlier sources, with perhaps different social constraints and goals, were reshaped to serve different contexts.

In this study I primarily engage the sociological theories of Weber regarding competition among social agents and the theories of Bourdieu regarding social space, symbolic language, and the field of cultural production. Weber's analysis of the competition of religious specialists provides a

---

1. Randal Johnson, introduction to *The Field of Cultural Production: Essays on Art and Literature,*" by Pierre Bourdieu (New York: Columbia University Press, 1993), 14.

2. A synchronic reading focuses on the final form of the text rather than following its development over time.

3. This attention to literary productions embedded in a network of material and ideological practices shares some parallels with New Historicism. However, when exploring these cultural connections, New Historicists avoid employing overarching constructs such as the sociological theories employed in this analysis. See H. Aram Veeser, *The New Historicism* (New York: Routledge, 1989), xi.

framework from which to consider competition among agents for legitimation. Bourdieu's method incorporates three levels of social reality that are relevant to an investigation of the social conditions surrounding the composition of Ezra-Nehemiah: the field of power, the field of cultural production, and habitus.[4] His work also provides ways to investigate forms of capital (economic, social, and cultural) over which agents compete within the relevant economic, social, or cultural fields, and the strategies employed by people as they compete within those fields. He formulates the concepts of *habitus* (a preconscious system of perception) and *doxa* (a shared habitus) that perform structuring roles in how one perceives and constructs the social world. Particularly relevant for analysis of a written text is Bourdieu's description of the nature and role of symbolic language in strategies of legitimation.

Attention to forms of capital as they are contested, rejected, or deployed may allow us to identify, at least partially and hypothetically, the author's loyalties, place in society, economic status, sources of competition, as well as all the resources he draws upon to secure or to improve his position within society. Identifying the author's social context may in turn indicate the general organization of the community at that time. An exploration of the interaction of various fields in the text may also indicate the nature and extent of interaction Persia had with the Jerusalem community and how those conditions were negotiated. Ultimately, it may give us a better understanding of how and why this particular community formed the way that it did.

Evidence of different circumstances reflected in various parts of the text may provide a more nuanced understanding of the book's development and the changing social circumstances of the community. Finally, this study may also allow us to understand more fully the painful texts that advocate the exclusion of others, the divorce of wives, and the expulsion of them with their children and in so doing contribute new insights on the social causes of enforced exclusion within minority communities in general.

---

4. For a helpful introduction to these concepts, see Pierre Bourdieu and Loïc J. D. Wacquant, *An Invitation to Reflexive Sociology* (Chicago: University of Chicago Press, 1992). Particularly useful are the chapters "The Logic of Fields" (94–114) and "Interest, Habitus, Rationality" (115–39).

2. METHODOLOGY

2.1. Key Concepts from Weber and Bourdieu

2.1.1. Competition in Weber

Because the priesthood is of particular interest in Ezra and Nehemiah, Weber's discussion of the competition by religious specialists (nuanced by Bourdieu's attention to the field) provides the first avenue of investigation. Weber evaluated the social dynamics of religious specialists with respect to their interaction with laity. He assumed that all people pursue their own interests and use ideas to further their causes. Competition over the power to modify the worldview of the laity pits different religious specialists—priests who strive for religious order and prophets who seek renewal or change—against each other.[5] Weber states that the power of prophets depends upon their lay followers and that prophecy "by its very nature devalues the magical elements of the priestly enterprise."[6]

> Thus, tensions between the prophets and their lay followers on the one hand, and between the prophets and the representatives of the priestly tradition on the other existed everywhere. To what degree the prophet would succeed in fulfilling his mission, or would become a martyr, depended on the outcome of the struggle for power, which in some instances, e.g., in Israel, was determined by the international situation.[7]

Weber states that depending upon how successful either side is, "the priesthood might compromise with the new policy, surpass its doctrine,

---

5. Weber, *The Sociology of Religion*, trans. Ephraim Fischoff, 4th ed. (Boston: Beacon, 1991), 65–66. Weber states, "Prophets and priests are the twin bearers of the systematization and rationalization of religious ethics. But there is a third significant factor of importance in determining the evolution of religious ethics: the laity, whom prophets and priests seek to influence in an ethical direction" (45). See also Pierre Bourdieu, "Legitimation and Structured Interests in Weber's Sociology of Religion" (trans. Chris Turner), in *Max Weber, Rationality and Modernity*, ed. Scott Lash and Sam Whimster (London: Allen & Unwin, 1987), 126.

6. Weber, *Sociology of Religion*, 66.

7. Ibid. Here Weber also recognizes that forces outside the immediate field of the actors can affect the outcome of the competition. Weber (*Ancient Judaism*, ed. and trans. Hans H. Gerth and Don Martindale [New York: Free Press, 1952], 271) states, "The holders of established power faced these powerful demagogues [prophets] with fear, wrath, or indifference as the situation warranted."

or conquer it, unless [the priesthood] were subjugated itself."[8] His model helps to identify and distinguish how competition may have shaped this text. For example, the prophets Jeremiah, Haggai, and Zechariah are vital for validation of the temple's construction in Ezra, but they are superseded by priests and their messages are carefully shaped to suit the author's concerns. Weber's oppositions provide a framework for examining social causes for these distinctive prophetic presentations.

Weber contends that the authority of the priesthood requires doctrine that meets the needs of the laity and accounts for other forces within the laity, such as prophets, traditionalism, their economic situation, or lay intellectualism. The priesthood takes on the obligation of educating the laity, while competing religious interests lead priests to codify doctrine, produce canonical writings, and assert dogmas (the priestly interpretations of their writings).[9] Weber states that "priests systematized the content of prophecy or of the sacred traditions by supplying them with a casuistical, rationalistic framework of analysis, and by adapting them to the customs of life and thought of their own class and of the laity whom they controlled."[10] This indicates the importance of social context for the ordering and logic expressed in these books. For example, to justify the value of the temple (necessary for priestly legitimacy), the author must rationalize the sovereignty of YHWH in light of the Babylonian destruction and continued Persian influence while also adapting to the changing composition of the laity, now composed of indigenous locals, returnees, and the Diaspora.

Weber tended to work with ideal types with both culture (e.g., laity, classes, pariah groups) and individuals (e.g., prophets, priests, magicians, intellectuals). His analysis employed comparisons based on these rather "unchangeable entities."[11] He argued that prophets possess personal gifts, "charisma," that authenticates their authority and mission, and they therefore do not receive their mission by human agency (a claim Bourdieu argues against). Although he often recognized the social or political events that gave rise to the influence of magicians, prophets, or priests, he contended that their legitimacy arose from other sources.[12] So, for exam-

---

8. Weber, *Sociology of Religion*, 67.
9. Ibid., 65. The scripture tradition then becomes the basis of the religious system.
10. Ibid., 69.
11. Talcott Parsons, "Introduction," in Weber, *Sociology of Religion*, lxxiii.
12. Weber, *Sociology of Religion*, 47, 51. Weber recognizes that prophets often had

ple, prophetic charisma is a personal gift, while priests gain their legitimacy as "functionaries of a regularly organized and permanent enterprise concerned with influencing the gods."[13] However; he was quick to note that distinctions are fluid: "Prophets very often practiced divination as well as magical healing and counseling."[14] The contrast between priests and magicians "is bridged by a sliding scale of transitions."[15] His "types" obscure the social context in which these competing missions might be more or less valued, or deemed legitimate or not. Although Weber never fully articulated the role of laity, his descriptions of the conditions in which religious professionals operate, rituals or practices are embraced, or rationalizations take place, invite attention to the social context of these competitors. Weber's attention to the importance of the material, historical, or class conditions of the social group provided the groundwork for Bourdieu's theory of field. Attention to fields avoids privileging elements over relations.[16]

2.1.2. Fields

Bourdieu builds on Weber's ideal types and develops a more nuanced system or field approach to the sources of legitimation. Bourdieu maintains that "a field is a set of objective power relations that affect all who enter the field."[17] It is "a network, or a configuration of objective relations between positions. These positions are objectively defined ... by their present and potential situation ... in the structure of the distribution of species of power (or capital) whose possession commands access to the specific profits that are at stake in the field, as well as by their objective relation to other positions."[18] Those involved in such arenas agree (implicitly at least) that struggle over control of the field, how the field is defined, and who defines it is important, and that "specific forms of struggle are legitimated

---

to produce evidence of their particular gifts and that the success of prophecy is connected to its lack of remuneration.
    13. Ibid., 28, 47.
    14. Ibid., 47.
    15. Ibid., 28–29. Here he refers to "a pure type" as a clear conceptual distinction that is "fluid in actuality."
    16. Bourdieu, "Legitimation and Structural Interests," 120–21.
    17. Pierre Bourdieu, "The Social Space and the Genesis of Groups," *Theory and Society* 14 (1985): 724.
    18. Bourdieu, *Invitation*, 97.

whereas others are excluded."[19] Bourdieu states, "In highly differentiated societies, the social cosmos is made up of a number of … relatively autonomous social microcosms, i.e., spaces of objective relations that are the site of a logic and a necessity that are *specific* and *irreducible* to those that regulate other fields. For instance, the artistic field, or the religious field, or the economic field all follow specific logics."[20]

Bourdieu often uses the analogy of a game to provide an intuitive grasp of what he understands as a field.[21] By entering the game, players agree that the game is worth playing and oppose each other "to the extent that they concur in their belief (*doxa*) in the game and its stakes."[22] "At each moment, it is the state of the relations of force between players that defines the structure of the field."[23] Agents compete for control of the interests or resources specific to the field in question.[24] These interests are not always either material or conscious, and this is particularly true in the cultural field. Here agents may compete for recognition, consecration, or prestige, each of which confers a form of symbolic authority that may or may not increase one's economic capital.

As a spatial metaphor, "field suggests rank and hierarchy as well as exchange relations between buyers and sellers."[25] People are located within the hierarchy of the field according to the overall volume of the capital they possess.[26] This then affects the possibilities available to and the limits on a person's political effectiveness. Because power relations are reproduced in one's view of the social world, an exploration of how the author of Ezra-Nehemiah portrays his world may offer a more nuanced understanding of both the author's position within various arenas and the implications of his allegiances for his construction of the social world.[27] We can observe

---

19. David Swartz, "Bridging the Study of Culture and Religion: Pierre Bourdieu's Political Economy of Symbolic Power," *Sociology of Religion* 57 (1996): 80.
20. Bourdieu, *Invitation*, 97.
21. Ibid., 98. Bourdieu notes that unlike the field for a game, a field is not a deliberate creation, nor are its regularities (rules) explicit and codified.
22. Ibid.
23. Ibid., 99.
24. Johnson, introduction, 6.
25. Swartz, "Bridging the Study," 79.
26. Bourdieu, "Social Space," 724.
27. Ibid., 729. Bourdieu discusses the reproduction of social location in a person's view of the world.

that in each section of these books characters contend with others, and appeals are made to a variety of parties. Who these various entities are and the nature of their resources provide information about the limits and options available to those composing these texts.

Bourdieu posits a "field of power" (a comprehensive "meta-field") in order to "account for structural effects which are not otherwise easily understood, especially certain properties of the practices and representations of writers or artists, which references to the literary or artistic [or theological] field alone could not completely explain."[28] He employs this concept to describe the dynamics of relations among the various economic, social, political, or cultural fields as they interact in a given society. In particular, in a highly differentiated society, it elucidates the dominated position that fields of cultural production occupy. He therefore defines the field of power somewhat differently from these other fields.

> The field of power (which should not be confused with the political field) is not a field like the others. It is the space of the relations of force between the different kinds of capital or, more precisely, between the agents who possess a sufficient amount of one of the different kinds of capital to be in a position to dominate the corresponding field.[29]

Agents or institutions that hold sufficient capital to dominate their respective fields may then struggle over the "'exchange rate' between different kinds of capital and ... control of the bureaucratic instances which are in a position to modify the exchange rate through administrative measures."[30] Domination in this context is not a direct act of coercion but an indirect effect of "actions engendered within the network of intersecting constraints which each of the dominants endures."[31]

Bourdieu states that individuals may take up a variety of positions with regard to these power relations, depending on the amount and form of capital they possess. The author of Ezra-Nehemiah may thus be competing, with his own forms of cultural capital, against those holding other

---

28. Pierre Bourdieu, *Practical Reason: On the Theory of Action* (Stanford, CA: Stanford University Press, 1998), 33.

29. Ibid., 34.

30. Ibid. Bourdieu suggests that the control of academic titles as an example of controlling the value of those titles and positions.

31. Ibid.

forms of influence (e.g., Persian administrators, landholders, or various clan elders). Notably, both Ezra 1–6 and Nehemiah present the author's capital defeating others, such as the people of the land or Sanballat and Tobiah, who wield their own social, political, or economic power. In the process, the narratives justify for their readership the author's specific forms of capital: Nehemiah's imperial position (a type of political capital) or the scribal skills of the author of Ezra 1–6.

Within the field of power, arenas of contest over particular forms of capital, structured by the positions of the agents within them, operate with their own logic.[32] The level of autonomy of these fields from external determinants can be measured by their ability to refract external demands into their own logic.[33] Within Ezra-Nehemiah, these external influences could include Persian economic demands, expectations of political loyalty, or competing social groups, which are (as much as possible) filtered by the theological logic of the author.

The field of cultural production is situated at the dominant pole in the field of class relations (due to its high degree of symbolic capital) yet occupies a dominated position due to its low degree of economic capital. Bourdieu states, "Whatever its degree of independence, it continues to be affected by the laws of the field which encompasses it, those of economic and political profit."[34] Scribes or priests within the Persian or Greek empires would operate within this cultural field. They possessed a high degree of cultural capital due to their scribal training or priestly ordination. Their skills were embodied and nontransferable except through lengthy periods of training, and they provided necessary resources to their community. This meant they held a high degree of symbolic capital (accumulated prestige, consecration, or honor) due to their knowledge and due

---

32. The differing logic is most obvious if one compares the economic field (where monetary self-interest is paramount) with the fields of art or religion, where there is an interest in "disinterest" in monetary gains. One's symbolic capital increases with a simultaneous disinterest in financial gain: "Art for art's sake."

33. Bourdieu, *Invitation*, 105: "the external determinations that bear on agents situated in a given field … never apply to them directly, but affect them only through the specific mediation of the specific forms and forces of the field, after having undergone a re-structuring that is all the more important the more autonomous the field, that is, the more it is capable of imposing its specific logic, the cumulative product of its particular history." See also Johnson, introduction, 14.

34. Bourdieu, *Field of Cultural Production*, 39.

to others knowing of and valuing the capital of the scribe or priest (in Bourdieu's terms, "recognition").[35]

Bourdieu's work on the relationship of cultural production (e.g., in law, education, art, and religion) to the field of power provides a framework for considering the level of independence of Yehud and its religious specialists with respect to the wider Persian Empire or neighboring provinces. Bourdieu observed that the growing independence of a cultural field from the fields of political, economic, and religious power that often controlled cultural production in the past was discernible through the logic of the cultural field being studied. He states that "the struggle … over the … legitimate mode of cultural production is inseparable from the struggle within the dominant class … to impose … domination."[36] This affects the entire structure of the field and varies over time and place.[37] Contested membership in the Jerusalem community, different ritual descriptions of the Festival of Booths, and different levels of authority for religious specialists testify to competing interests struggling for dominance.

An analysis of the cultural field with regard to the field of power shows a constant struggle between two forms of hierarchy: one that favors those with the most economic or political capital versus a hierarchy that favors a degree of independence from the economy. "The more autonomous the field of cultural production within the field of power (either political or economic) the more it inverts economic principles."[38] In a more nearly autonomous cultural field, an author, free to exclude the pursuit of profit, can narrowly produce work for others within his or her field.[39] "Like prophecy, especially the prophecy of misfortune, which, according to Weber, demonstrates its authenticity by the fact that it brings in no income, a heretical break with the prevailing artistic [religious] traditions proves its claim to authenticity by its disinterestedness."[40]

On the other hand, the need to gain profit, power, or authority might compel an intellectual to be more responsive to external demands of the

---

35. Johnson, introduction, 7.
36. Bourdieu, *Field of Cultural Production*, 41.
37. Ibid., 40.
38. Ibid., 39.
39. Ibid., 41. Bourdieu notes that nineteenth-century poetry was often pursued by those with enough economic capital and skill to allow them to write without regard to sales.
40. Ibid., 40.

dominant. Those literary producers with the least symbolic capital (having the weakest position within the cultural field) are the most vulnerable. They defend their positions in the cultural field by producing "weapons that the dominant agents (within the field of power) turn against the cultural producers most attached to their autonomy."[41] Within a literary field, their arguments, stories, or symbolic reasoning provide weapons that may undermine the prestige of the most independent cultural agents.

Using Bourdieu's theory, we see that local or authorial autonomy may be indicated by a willful neglect of those in the field of power, while careful attention to those with power would suggest less autonomy. Nehemiah, for example, is careful to seek the permission of the Persian monarch, while the exiles in Ezra 4 disdainfully exclude the local population from their construction project. The author's rhetorical strategies would reflect his position with regard to competitors within the field. Does the author seek to overturn or subvert the field's hierarchy, or alternatively does he employ strategies to defend his position in the field? Identifying such strategies allows one to posit subordinate or dominant positions in the field. By pinpointing who or what is targeted or what power relations are protected or subverted, we may be able to reconstruct the religious and cultural fields in which the author competed.

2.1.3. Forms of Capital

Bourdieu's concept of field provides an important corrective to Weber's conception of individual, charismatic, and often isolated cultural producers.[42] It elucidates the ways in which the prophetic independence and charisma are, in fact, products of the larger field and not chiefly a result of individual traits of a person. Lacking the symbolic capital of ordination held by priests, the prophet may accumulate symbolic capital by giving voice to concerns or needs of those in dominated positions within the field of power. Others respond to the prophet's model or teachings because it

---

41. Ibid., 41. Bourdieu adds, "Sampling problems [categorizing people] cannot be resolved by one of those arbitrary decisions of positivist ignorance … these amount to blindly arbitrating on debates which are inscribed in reality itself, such as the question as to whether such and such a group … or such and such an individual claiming the title of writer or artist … belongs to the population of writers or artists or, more precisely, as to who is legitimately entitled to designate legitimate writers or artists."

42. See Weber, *Sociology of Religion*, 46.

2. METHODOLOGY

provides an avenue to contest the power relations in the field and even the structure of the field itself. On the other hand, priests, who benefit from routinization and steady bureaucracy, are inclined to oppose such breaks.

More broadly, Bourdieu defines capital as accumulated labor, "which when appropriated on a private, i.e., exclusive, basis by agents or groups of agents, enables them to appropriate social energy."[43] Capital can exist in different forms: economic, cultural, and social. Economic capital is the most easily recognized and is often institutionalized as property rights. Cultural capital represents an investment of time and talent. It is often embodied and unrecognized as capital but instead viewed as a natural talent or legitimate competence. It can also be found in material objects such as paintings or monuments or it can exist in an institutionalized state. Social capital is "linked to … membership in a group—which provides each of its members with the backing of the collectivity-owned capital, a 'credential' which entitles them to credit."[44] Whether economic, cultural, or social, the amount of capital a person has determines their position in the field, and in each field different kinds of capital may be valued differently.[45] Forms of capital are unequally distributed among social classes, and although they can be exchanged, they are not reducible to one another.

Embodied cultural capital is cultural knowledge or competence. Agents who possess cultural capital are equipped to decipher cultural relations and artifacts. This is acquired by a long process of acquisition through education in the family, group, or social institutions.[46] The acquisition of cultural capital can be institutionalized with academic qualifications or ordination. A certificate of competence "confers on its holder a conventional, constant, legally guaranteed value with respect to culture." The official recognition "makes it possible to compare qualification holders and even to exchange them."[47]

Cultural capital in an objectified state (works of art, including literature or monumental architecture) is given its value through its relationship to capital in its embodied form. While ownership could be transferred,

---

43. Pierre Bourdieu, "The Forms of Capital," in *Handbook of Theory and Research for the Sociology of Education*, ed. John G. Richardson (New York: Greenwood, 1986), 241.
44. Ibid., 248.
45. Bourdieu, "Social Space," 724.
46. Johnson, introduction, 7.
47. Bourdieu, "Forms of Capital," 248.

"the precondition for specific appropriation, namely, the possession of the means of 'consuming' a painting [or using a temple] requires embodied capital."[48] The value of art and the belief that underlies it is "generated in the incessant, innumerable struggles to establish the value of this or that particular work."[49] At the heart of this field (or these struggles) is a disavowal of the commercial benefit of art or of a cultural production. Prestige or authority (symbolic capital) is the only legitimate profit produced in this field and requires a "disinterest" in the commercial economy. Gaining authority or prestige, Bourdieu states, is earning a capital of consecration, which then implies the power to consecrate objects (art, religious times, places, and people), which then gives these objects their value. In turn, the agent who consecrates can appropriate the profits from this act.[50] Thus priests can consecrate a temple due to their embodied capital and in turn appropriate the profits from the now consecrated temple. This suggests that the acts of consecration (for priests, the temple, and even the city walls), the rituals surrounding the reading of Torah, and the covenant agreements are generated by the struggle to establish the value of whatever is the subject of consecration.

"Because the social conditions of its transmission and acquisition are more disguised than those of economic capital, [cultural capital] is predisposed to function as symbolic capital, i.e., to be unrecognized as capital and recognized as legitimate competence."[51] The scarcity of cultural capital, due to the length of time required for its accumulation and its embodied form, also "yields profits of distinction for its holder."[52] Not everyone has the means (economic, cultural, or even time) to secure high levels of cultural capital. This scarcity and the unequal distribution of capital allow the appropriation of profits and underlie the power to organize "the field most favorable to capital and its reproduction."[53] Training, celebrity, or acts of ordination grant certain persons large amounts of cultural capital, such as priests, nobles, or the highly educated. They are "recognized" (given legitimacy) in markets wherever economic capital does not hold full sway, and

---

48. Ibid., 247.
49. Bourdieu, *Field of Cultural Production*, 79.
50. Ibid., 75. Bourdieu cites the example of a recognized name being used as a trademark to add value to an object.
51. Bourdieu, "Forms of Capital," 245.
52. Ibid.
53. Ibid., 246.

they have influence in areas outside their own particular fields because of the recognition they receive for their cultural capital. The particular form of capital available and at stake affects the strategies employed to acquire or increase the capital being sought. Whatever capital is possessed, such as literacy or ordination, is used in efforts to gain something lacking, such as political influence, economic benefit, and/or social connections.

To be effective, the cultural capital one possesses must also be valued by those one wishes to influence. However, every community values particular types of capital over others. Identifying the forms of capital at work in the text and evaluating how they interact (are they legitimated by rhetoric, sought after, dismissed, or exchanged for other capital?) will enable further assessment of the author's social location, concerns, and sources of competition and in addition permit a reconstruction of the social realities of his community.

2.1.4. Habitus, Doxa, and Class Trajectory

The social world inscribes in each person durable and transposable preconscious systems of perception that Bourdieu terms *habitus*.[54] Habitus is produced by the structures of a particular environment, and it creates a "common-sense world" that appears self-evident.[55] Bourdieu makes two important statements about the nature and workings of habitus. He states first that habitus are

---

54. Otto Maduro ("'Habitus' and Action as Strategy: Religious Habitus," lecture, Drew University, Madison, NJ, 4 March 2008) states, "The word *habitus*, rooted in the Latin verb *habere* (to have, to hold, possess), is a noun originally implying habit, condition, bearing, demeanor, disposition, garb, dress, place, nature, character, custom, attitude (both internal and external). Bourdieu understood *habitus* as a conceptual tool (not a 'reality') for researching practice—and first of all as a tool to break with the binary idea of *practice* as either a *mechanical response* to external stimuli or, at the opposite end, as *a free, individually chosen action*."

55. Pierre Bourdieu, *The Logic of Practice* (Stanford, CA: Stanford University Press, 1980), 58. See also Bourdieu, *Outline of a Theory of Practice* (London: Cambridge University Press, 1977), 72; Bourdieu, *Practical Reason*, 8. In this last source he states, "Habitus is a generative and unifying principle which retranslates characteristics of a position into a unitary lifestyle.... Habitus are also classificatory schemes, principles of classification, principles of vision and division, different tastes."

structured structures predisposed to function as structuring structures, that is, as principles which generate and organize practices and representations that can be objectively adapted to their outcomes without presupposing a conscious aiming at ends or an express mastery of the operations necessary in order to attain them.[56]

Various factors (such as one's sex, family, school, social position, and origin) have a determining influence on one's own habitus.[57] For the author of Ezra-Nehemiah, these might include certain practices used to worship YHWH, Persian rule as a condition of existence, or particular familiar boundary maintenance practices.[58] Acquired through training and experience, habitus reflects the social conditions of the individual. It will "generate practices and perceptions, works and appreciations, which concur with the conditions of existence of which the habitus is itself the product."[59] His second observation is that it will continue to operate (often in new ways) even in changed circumstances or different fields.

> The habitus ... produces practices which tend to reproduce the regularities immanent in the objective conditions of the production of their generative principle, while adjusting to the demands inscribed as objective potentialities in the situation, as defined by the cognitive and motivating structures making up the habitus.[60]

In new settings, practices (such as matrimonial exchanges, gift giving, rituals, or eating certain foods) generated by a habitus can make themselves known by being in discord with the new conditions.[61] For example, the religious practices acquired in exile may cause confusion or prompt

---

56. Bourdieu, *Logic of Practice*, 53.
57. Bourdieu, *Language and Symbolic Power*, 82–89. In this section, Bourdieu discusses how linguistic habitus acquired in one setting can either empower or disadvantage a person, but he demonstrates that whenever the social context differs from the origins of one's habitus, adjustments are needed in order to operate in the new setting.
58. Bourdieu, *Outline*, 114.
59. John B. Thompson, "Editor's Introduction," in Bourdieu, *Language and Symbolic Power*, 13.
60. Bourdieu, *Outline*, 78.
61. Bourdieu (*Practical Reason*, 131–32) states that practices are oriented by strategies rather than guided by direct rules. He associates them with agents acting within cultural traditions and oriented toward practical ends although lacking the calculation of intentional actions.

resistance, questioning, or revolt in interactions with a different (or changed) religious field in Yehud.[62] Conflicting practices could extend to issues of preferred language and community and family organization. When imported into a new setting, habitus continue to structure practices while adjusting to the new setting.[63] Thus Torah reading continues—but as a public ritual, led by ordained priests and Levites. Habitus operating in a new context may explain part of the difficulty we see in Neh 13 as Nehemiah tries to instill his religious reforms in a community seemingly indifferent to his concerns.[64]

When a habitus is shared by all or most in a society, Bourdieu refers to this as *doxa*. In a doxic perspective, the order of society seems natural, universal, and self-evident. Bourdieu states,

> when the conditions of existence of which the members of a group are the product are very little differentiated, the dispositions which each of them exercises in his practice are confirmed and hence reinforced both by the practice of the other members of the group ... and also by institutions which constitute collective thought as much as they express it, such as language, myth, and art.[65]

Rites and symbolic exchanges such as feasts and ceremonies reinforce collective belief. This suggests that the many rituals, liturgies, and public acts recorded in this text can be investigated for the role they play in reinforcing a particular condition of existence. The author also draws on doxic beliefs or familiar structures in his argumentation. Narratives are structured by familiar motifs, such as temple building reports, the exodus, or holy war, and then supply "structuring structures" for interpreting the

---

62. Maduro, "'Habitus' and Action as Strategy": "Changes in the religious field or in the larger social space, as well as changes in the location (geographic, social, religious) of religious agents, might prompt the habitus of agents to generate prophetic behavior (individual or collective) and thus to contribute to religious change or broader social transformations."

63. Bourdieu (*Logic of Practice*, 53) acknowledges, "The responses of the *habitus* may be accompanied by a strategic calculation ... performing in a conscious mode the operation that the *habitus* performs quite differently."

64. Bourdieu (ibid., 59) comments that "collective mobilization cannot succeed without a minimum of concordance between the *habitus* of the mobilizing agents (prophet, leader, etc.) and the dispositions of those who recognize themselves in their practices or words."

65. Bourdieu, *Outline*, 167.

community's identity and relations with others. In reality, both the social order and the doxic view of it are constructed, maintained, and promoted by those who are socially dominant. In Bourdieu's words, "Doxa is a particular point of view, the point of view of the dominant, which presents and imposes itself as a universal point of view—the point of view of those who dominate by dominating the state and who have constituted their point of view as universal by constituting the state."[66]

This truth about doxa is only ever fully revealed when there is competition for legitimacy between groups claiming to possess it. The inconsistencies in these texts over ritual practices or the focus of the histories may aid efforts to elucidate competing social arrangements. Often crisis is a necessary condition for doxa to come into question, which suggests that the issues over which the texts lament are related to disparate practices.[67] Attending to doxa draws attention to the unquestioned and unified cultural tradition.[68]

The authors and editors of Ezra-Nehemiah may also be adjusting to changes in class status, whether for good or ill. According to Bourdieu, *class habitus* is "the internalized form of class condition and of the conditionings it entails."[69] Class habitus embodies properties acquired when people share "homogeneous conditions of existence imposing homogeneous conditionings and producing homogeneous systems of dispositions capable of generating similar practices."[70] Because the conditions of acquisition (of a property) persist in the habitus even in new objective class contexts, people "are not completely defined by the properties they possess at a given time" but also by their class trajectory—the "relation between initial capital and present capital (or initial and present position in social space)."[71] He describes this relationship in terms of a space "whose three

---

66. Bourdieu, *Practical Reason*, 57.
67. Bourdieu, *Outline*, 168.
68. Bourdieu (ibid., 169) states, when the definition of the social world is at stake, "the drawing of the line between the field of opinion, of that which is explicitly questioned, and the field of *doxa*, of that which is beyond question and which each agent tacitly accords by the mere fact of acting in accord with social convention, is itself a fundamental objective at stake in that form of class struggle which is the struggle for the imposition of the dominant systems of classification."
69. Pierre Bourdieu, *Distinction: A Social Critique of the Judgement of Taste*, trans. Richard Nice (Cambridge: Harvard University Press, 1984), 101.
70. Ibid.
71. Ibid., 109.

fundamental dimensions are defined by volume of capital, composition of capital, and change in these two properties over time (manifested by past and potential trajectory in social space)."[72] Movement in social space is not random, but trajectories correspond more or less to given volumes of inherited capital. Shifts from one trajectory to another can depend on collective or individual events that are usually considered accidents but, in reality, depend on the person's skill negotiating social connections, or interventions by institutions or others.

Movement in class trajectory elicits particular types of responses depending on the direction of the trajectory, the specific logic of a field (what is at stake and what type of capital is needed to pay for it), as well as the person's type and amount of capital. For example, in contrast to the upwardly mobile, those in decline "endlessly reinvent the discourse of all aristocracies, essentialist faith in the eternity of natures, celebration of tradition and the past, the cult of history and its rituals, because the best they can expect from the future is the return of the old order, from which they expect the restoration of their social being."[73] Analysis of the defensive posture of the text through this lens of class trajectory may allow us to reconstruct not only "what is at stake" but the direction of the trajectory of the author and his community.

2.1.5. Legitimation and Symbolic Language

Bourdieu states that symbolic power is a "misrecognizable, transfigured and legitimated form of the other forms of power."[74] In Ezra-Nehemiah, symbolic acts and language are employed to demonstrate the uniqueness and value of the Jerusalem temple, particular social boundaries of the community, and a particular role for priests within the community of Yehud. In the process, other things and people are delegitimized. A symbolic system (e.g., the ideology of purity) can structure a field because the symbolic system is structured through its logic of division. It "creates difference *ex nihilo*, or else … by exploiting pre-existing difference."[75] It signifies to someone what his identity is and creates the power to dominate. However, the symbolic system is effective at structuring society only when

---

72. Ibid., 114.
73. Ibid., 111.
74. Bourdieu, *Language and Symbolic Power*, 170.
75. Ibid., 120.

those to whom it is directed share "the belief in the legitimacy of the words and of those who utter them." All parties engage in a symbolic struggle "aimed at imposing the definition of the social world that is best suited to their interests. The field of ideological stances thus reproduces in transfigured form the field of social positions."[76]

Ezra-Nehemiah is, in part, an effort to define and control the community's boundaries. The boundaries between ethnicities or geographic regions, claims Bourdieu, are not natural but social, based on characteristics "which are to a great extent the product of an arbitrary imposition … of a previous state of the relations of power in the field of struggle over legitimate delimitation."[77] Defining boundaries is arguably a symbolic, often religious act, one carried out by the person with the highest authority. In Ezra and Nehemiah, the writer appeals to "higher authorities" such as history, royal edicts, Torah, religious purity, and the community in order to create and legitimate the social boundaries that define his vision of the community. Many of these require the cultural capital of literacy to access them, thus placing the author as an arbiter for these sources of legitimacy. A careful analysis of this symbolic work may expose the state of power relations within Yehud at the time of the author, as well as identify aspects of the shared belief system in the community he addresses.

Much of Ezra-Nehemiah reflects efforts to define and control a particular "ethnic" identity. Ethnic groups often appear to be biologically self-perpetuating, but Fredrik Barth states, "ethnic groups are categories of ascription and identification by the actors themselves and thus have the characteristic of organizing interaction between people."[78] In general, efforts to understand this issue have tended to establish an opposition between reality (e.g., language or religious beliefs or genealogy) and representations (perceptions and appreciations). Bourdieu invites us to transcend this dichotomy by including "mental representations" in reality.

---

76. Ibid., 167.
77. Ibid., 222.
78. Fredrik Barth, "Introduction," *Ethnic Groups and Boundaries: The Social Organization of Culture Difference*, ed. Fredrik Barth (Boston: Little, Brown, 1969), 10. Manning Nash (*The Cauldron of Ethnicity in the Modern World*, [Chicago: University of Chicago Press, 1993], 5–6) details common "building blocks" used as identity markers such as language, shared history, and religion. However, not all are always employed nor do all carry the same weight: "Elements are organically interactive and take different shapes according to historical and political circumstances."

These representations include "social demonstrations whose aim it is to manipulate mental images."[79] The account of the marriage covenant and the divorce of foreign wives in Ezra 9–10 and the attention to foreigners in Neh 13 are representations intended to portray a particular understanding of reality. Bourdieu argues that understanding the struggle over classifications represented in the conflict over ethnicity requires treating mental representations as real as other objective categories of reality. He comments,

> Struggles over ethnic or regional identity ... are a particular case of the different struggles over classifications, struggles over the monopoly of the power to make people see and believe, to get them to know and recognize, to impose the legitimate definition of the divisions of the social world and, thereby, to *make and unmake groups*. What is at stake here is the power of imposing a vision of the social world through principles of di-vision which, when they are imposed on a "whole group, establish meaning and a consensus about meaning, and in particular about the identity and unity of the group, which creates the reality of the unity and the identity of the group.[80]

The boundaries between ethnicities or geographic regions, claims Bourdieu, are not "natural" but social, based on characteristics "which are to a great extent the product of an arbitrary imposition ... of a previous state of the relations of power in the field of struggle over legitimate delimitation. The frontier ... produces cultural difference as much as it is produced by it."[81] Bourdieu suggests that the act of defining the boundaries is arguably a religious act, one carried out by the person with the highest authority who "brings into existence what they decree."[82]

In Ezra-Nehemiah, struggles over legitimate definitions of the community play out in these accounts of the construction of the temple, city, and community. In the process, various resources of legitimation are brought to bear. These include recourse to the Persian government, official documents (whether real or contrived), the use of theological language to legitimate social and political actions, and the narrative itself, which asserts the identity of the people constructing the temple and forming the community. Analysis of the capital employed by the author and the logic

---

79. Bourdieu, *Language and Symbolic Power*, 221.
80. Ibid.
81. Ibid., 222.
82. Ibid.

of his arguments can inform us about social location and the community's shared symbolic system. Attention to the role of social or economic capital may allow us to posit other sources of legitimation competing with the strategies present in this text.

2.2. Critiques and Limitations of Bourdieu's Theory

Bourdieu's theory of practice with its concepts of field, habitus, and capital can fruitfully analyze the dynamic structure of the religious field, the influence of habitus on one's actions and perceptions of relations, and the misrecognition of social distinctions as somehow natural and thus acceptable. Yet critics fault Bourdieu's treatment of the religious field for his hierarchical model of religious authority partnered with an economic model of social relations (with its logic of supply and demand). In the religious field, Bourdieu portrays agents acting only in self-interested ways, motivated by the pursuit of capital.[83] Religious capital becomes a resource of power in the competition between orthodoxy and heterodoxy, with the laity reduced to consumers rather than producers of symbolic capital.[84] María Olave states that religious beliefs and activity "are reduced to the possession of assets or the struggle for the accumulation of scarce symbolic goods" and argues that the reduction of religious action to the pursuit of interest makes genuine religious behavior impossible.[85] However, such a critique borders on claiming that people are knowingly pursuing economic self-interest. Bourdieu's theory counters this with his concept of habitus and the nature of cultural capital, which is gained at the expense of economic capital.

Most critiques fault Bourdieu's explicit treatment of the religious field while noting that his theories regarding fields and habitus are more flexible than his specific application to religious institutions.[86] This is in part

---

83. Hugh Urban, "Response: Spiritual Capital, Academic Capital and the Politics of Scholarship: A Response to Bradford Verter," *MTSR* 17 (2005): 171.

84. Terry Rey, *Bourdieu on Religion: Imposing Faith and Legitimacy* (London: Equinox, 2007), 96. See also Michele Dillon, "Pierre Bourdieu, Religion, and Cultural Production," *CSCM* 1 (2001): 425.

85. María Angélica Thumala Olave, "The Aristocracy of the Will: a Critique of Pierre Bourdieu with Illustrations from Chile," *Social Compass* 59 (2012): 62–63.

86. Dillon ("Pierre Bourdieu, Religion," 425) states, "Bourdieu is seen by some sociologists ... as a theorist who opens up the understanding of postmodern culture due to his emphasis on the blurring of boundaries and the indeterminacy of iden-

2. METHODOLOGY

because, as Erwan Dianteill observes, "Bourdieu's sociology of religion is, first and foremost, a sociology of [French] Catholicism. The accent thus falls on the process of monopolization by a single institution: the Catholic Church."[87] The "religious specialists ... struggle against one another to make the laity believe that their products, their religious capital, are legitimate, while the adversary's are illegitimate."[88] This led Bourdieu to develop more fully "religion's function in the establishment and reproduction of social distinctions and domination."[89] He viewed the church as a particularly effective means of conserving "the social order because of its contribution to the legitimation of the power of the dominant and the domestication of the dominated."[90]

Terry Rey believes that Bourdieu overemphasized issues of power, making it easy to overlook other less political forms of religious capital.[91] He further comments, "there is a certain rigidity to Bourdieu's two-dimensional, top-heavy, institutionally focused paradigm [of the religious field], making it less "suitable for incisive or extensive analysis or prediction of anomalies like divergent uses of religion by the powerful or successful rebellious uses of religion by the dominated."[92] Likewise, Hugh Urban believes that "we need to pay more attention to the creative, 'tactical' role of ordinary consumers within the social and religious marketplace; we need to appreciate the ability of the poor and marginalized to subvert, deform, or poach upon an oppressive cultural market where the prices are inflated and the scales are rigged."[93] However, although underdeveloped in

---

tity.... This, however, is not the framework evident in Bourdieu's analysis of religion.... Bourdieu's analysis of Catholicism operates with a mechanistic, pre-Vatican II categorical model in which church officials as producers supply religious meaning to a dispossessed laity."

87. Erwan Dianteill, "Pierre Bourdieu and the Sociology of Religion: A Central and Peripheral Concern," *Theory and Society* 32 (2003): 535.

88. Rey, *Bourdieu on Religion*, 86.

89. Ibid., 79.

90. Ibid. Otto Maduro's study (*Religion and Social Conflicts*, trans. Robert R. Barr [Eugene, OR: Wipf & Stock, 1982]) of postcolonial Latin American religious field identifies the role and methods of religion in the institutionalization of social division. See also Rey's summary of this study in *Bourdieu on Religion*, 108–10.

91. Rey, *Bourdieu on Religion*, 97.

92. Ibid., 103; see also 124.

93. Hugh Urban, "Sacred Capital: Pierre Bourdieu and the Study of Religion," *MTSR* 15 (2003): 356.

Bourdieu's own studies, the general principles of Bourdieu's sociology recognize that religious fields "are structured differently in different times and places."[94] They "differ across time and national context, as they develop historically," which allows for societies where no single group has achieved a monopoly of the goods of salvation.[95] That Bourdieu did not develop this in his own analysis of the religious field in France does not mean his overall theory cannot account for such differences.

Rey suggests that Bourdieu's concept of habitus provides a way to overcome the reductionism related to Bourdieu's "dismissal of both the sacred and the believer's *spiritual* (as opposed to *rational*) engagement thereof, and by their over-emphasis of self interest to the negation of the 'other interest.'"[96] The habitus provides a counter to "rational calculation in explaining religious practice [and] restores the force of the emotional and the somatic."[97]

---

94. Andrew M. McKinnon, Marta Trzebiatowska and Christopher C. Brittain, "Bourdieu, Capital, and Conflict in a Religious Field: The Case of the 'Homosexuality' Conflict in the Anglican Communion," *Journal of Contemporary Religion* 26 (2011): 356.

95. Ibid., 361.

96. Rey, *Bourdieu on Religion*, 137. For such critiques of Bourdieu see Urban, "Sacred Capital," 382; Olave ("Aristocracy of the Will," 52) states, "The religiously inspired ideals of self-control and ethical action cannot be understood fully if they are seen as the result of instrumental behaviour inspired by interests."

97. Rey, *Bourdieu on Religion*, 138.

3
Themes and Motifs in Ezra 1–6

Sometime after the reign of Artaxerxes I (465–424 BCE), and perhaps as late as 335 BCE before Persia fell to Alexander the Great, Ezra 1–6 was added to an earlier work that included the memoir of Nehemiah and the account of Ezra's return in Ezra 7–10.[1] By and large, the events in these chapters are narrated through official Persian decrees and correspondence that not only recount the history of the First Temple but affirm Persian blessing on its restoration.

In this new introduction to Ezra and Nehemiah, exilic descendants journey to the province of Yehud and reconstruct the Jerusalem temple, completing it in the sixth year of Darius (515 BCE). The plot replicates earlier narratives of Ezra and Nehemiah: events begin in exile, the construction is supported by a Persian monarch, and interference at the local level impedes progress. In Ezra 1–4, exiles return to Jerusalem and bring materials for the temple. The temple altar and foundations are laid, but construction is halted by "adversaries" (4:1). In Ezra 5 and 6, prophets prompt renewed building efforts by the community. As the work resumes, the provincial governor conducts an investigation into the legitimacy of the project, but this time construction is unimpeded. Records unearthed

---

1. H. G. M. Williamson, *Ezra, Nehemiah*, WBC 16 (Waco, TX: Word, 1985), xlvii. The motif of writing letters to seek permission or support for temple construction is also characteristic of the Elephantine documents, which date to 410 BCE. Edelman (*Origins*, 158) contends that Ezra 4 is an even later insert, and Jacob Wright (*Rebuilding Identity*, 5) has argued that Ezra 1–6 was composed in response to the negative portrayal of the temple priesthood in the Nehemiah material; Ezra 7–8 was added as a bridge between the two texts, and Ezra 9–10 and Neh 8–10 are later yet. None, however, believes that Ezra 1–6 predates Nehemiah's memoir. See also Jacob L. Wright, "A New Model for the Composition of Ezra-Nehemiah," in Lipschits, Knoppers, and Albertz, *Fourth Century B.C.E.*, 343.

in the royal archives reveal Cyrus's edict and resolve the issue. Darius adds his support to the project and the temple is completed. The dedication of the temple and a celebration of Passover complete this section. Throughout these chapters, the returnees appear committed to the task and unified in their actions.

Scholars debate the historical realities behind this account, especially whether or how much of this actually took place and Persia's role in the reconstruction. They question whether various monarchs issued decrees in its support, supplied funds, or initiated the building. Some argue that it was a local project initiated by the community that remained in Yehud under Babylon, while others believe that the returnees prompt the construction. In addition, the source of opposition has been debated: Did it originate with Samaritans who were descendants of ancient Israel or later immigrants, nonexiled Judeans, Persian appointees, or Levites from local sanctuaries? Space does not allow for a full treatment of these questions, but two assumptions about the historical context do influence this work.

First, evidence suggests that, if Persia did become involved in temple affairs, it was for either economic or military purposes.[2] This would then tie the construction to repopulation and the return of exiles to the region to advance or shore up imperial interests, and it is likely that Egypt's rebellions aided by Greek alliances accelerated this process. Persian organiza-

---

2. Lisbeth Fried, "The House of God Who Dwells in Jerusalem," review of *Temple Restoration in Early Achaemenid Judah*, by Peter Bedford, and *Priester und Leviten im achämenidischen Juda*, by Joachim Schaper, *JAOS* 126 (2006): 98. Fried points out that the Persian monarchy did provide funds for the Egyptian temple at Kharga Oasis in order to populate that area. Archaeological evidence indicates that Jerusalem and its environs were likewise relatively unpopulated at the beginning of the Persian era (although the region of Benjamin was not empty), so it is possible Persia did see an economic benefit from initiating construction of this local temple. This article provides a useful overview of the debate over the status of the temple in Persian era Jerusalem. Fried (*Priest and Great King*) also surveys Persian relations with temples and argues for imperial bureaucratic control over temples. Edelman (*Origins*, 9) dates all the events in these books to the reign of Artaxerxes I but argues for military and economic motivations. She states, "Zerubbabel, as an agent of Artaxerxes I, rebuilt the temple in Jerusalem probably sometime during the 440s BCE. It was rebuilt as part of a larger Persian policy that established a network of birot, guard stations, inns, and caravanserai along the major road systems of the empire, to facilitate trade, imperial communication, and military mobility. The decision by Artaxerxes I to augment the population ... would have been part of a larger plan to supply a labor force and tax base to support a series of new relay stations being built in Yehud."

tion of the province would involve appointment of the local leadership (this is clear in the commissions of Ezra and Nehemiah but never mentioned with regard to the leadership in Ezra 1–6). However, the author's portrayal of Persian support expresses an ideological agenda, and the level of Persian interest and investment in the temple may be less than appears upon a first reading of Ezra 1–6.

Second, although the historical source and reason for local hostilities remains a point of debate among scholars, the author included recurring opposition in the account, and it is likely that a need to address hostilities (possibly of a different sort) in his own time prompted him to do so. How then did this narrative of Persian largesse and local opposition address the author's realities?

Ezra 1–6 is marked by two distinct literary characteristics: a Hebrew text with references to or inclusion of documents containing decrees (1:2–4) or lists of persons (2:1–67) or things (1:9–11), and an entire section in Aramaic (4:8–6:18) that also contains documentary material and decrees. Moreover, the narrative incorporates elements known from ancient Near Eastern temple building reports, alludes to the exodus narrative, and portrays prophets, leaders, and the community in distinctive ways. These features are dispersed throughout the text, and their significance is better understood if approached holistically rather than following a strict narrative sequence. I will examine these literary elements in conversation with Bourdieu's theories in order to consider their social implications.

3.1. The Temple Building Report

Ezra 1–6 is, in part, composed as an ancient Mesopotamian temple building report.[3] Raymond Van Leeuwen identifies an overarching twofold narrative pattern of "building and filling" in building accounts, which he notes has ties to wisdom traditions and commonly describes divine creation.[4] He observes, "National life, cosmic fertility, and well-being are connected

---

3. An earlier version of this study can be found in my article, "The Temple Building Account in Ezra 1–6: Refracting the Social World," *Conversations with the Biblical World: Proceedings of the Eastern Great Lakes Biblical Society and Midwest Region Society of Biblical Literature* 31 (2011): 95–114.

4. Raymond C. Van Leeuwen, "Cosmos, Temple, House: Building and Wisdom in Mesopotamia and Israel," in *Wisdom Literature in Mesopotamia and Israel*, ed. Richard J. Clifford, SymS 36 (Atlanta: Society of Biblical Literature, 2007), 72.

to the god's house, built and provisioned by the king."⁵ So, for example, Esarhaddon boasts that he completed a temple for the welfare and safety of his rule and his country. Providing for the temple and the resident god ensures that the cosmic realm of the nation will also be provisioned.⁶

All ancient Near Eastern temple building accounts celebrate the accomplishment of the builder, and familiar rhetorical tactics legitimate the temple as a deity's place of worship. Divine inspiration has to be confirmed, the details of construction described, the temple successfully dedicated, and blessing given. This model was widespread and employed for centuries.⁷ The tacit and universal assumptions undergirding these accounts are a particular case of Bourdieu's doxa. Beliefs produced by the dominant class are shared by everyone and provide an "unseen and unintended support for the rule of the dominant."⁸ At least two shared presuppositions permeate these accounts: divine desire as a requirement for temple construction, and divine selection and inspiration of the builder. Since the builder is most often the monarch, these accounts would solidify the king's dominant position. An analysis of the doxic assumptions underlying this text may permit us to postulate ways in which these "unrecognized beliefs … motivate the 'ideologue' to action without him or her actually being aware of it."⁹ This might also clarify intentional propaganda "what the biblical author knew and wanted his or her listeners to know as well."¹⁰

---

5. Ibid., 71. Van Leeuwen accepts Hurowitz's more detailed building pattern noted below but draws attention to aspects (such as inspiration of the builder) with links to wisdom traditions (76, 87–88).

6. Ibid., 71.

7. Victor Hurowitz, *I Have Built You an Exalted House: Temple Building in the Bible in the Light of Mesopotamian and Northwest Semitic Writings*, JSOTSup 115 (Sheffield: JSOT Press, 1992), 126. Hurowitz compares over twenty accounts that include Old Babylonian, Assyrian, Neo-Babylonian, and biblical records. He comments that though there are modifications over time regarding certain elements, the overall form remains constant. At the same time, inscriptions from elsewhere differ. In particular, he points to the numerous Egyptian building inscriptions, noting that few resemble those known from Mesopotamia and Israel.

8. Jacques Berlinerblau, "Ideology, Pierre Bourdieu's *Doxa*, and the Hebrew Bible," *Semeia* 87 (1999): 202.

9. Ibid., 203.

10. Ibid., 205.

In his survey of these building accounts, Victor Hurowitz identifies a general tripartite story line: divine decision, implementation, and blessing. He delineates six elements common to the genre.[11] The elements usually occur in the order listed below.

1. The decision to build: This involves divine inspiration of the monarch or divine confirmation of a request by the king to build. Visions or dreams are often involved, and the history of the temple is recounted to explain the circumstances prompting the project.
2. A description of preparations: Materials are gathered, workmen are drafted (often entailing gifts and workforces from foreign nations), and the foundation is laid.
3. A description of the building: This can include furnishings and the building process.
4. Dedication and festivities: This includes the entrance of the god, sacrifices, purifications, music, and feasting, establishment of temple personnel in their posts, and the establishment of justice.
5. Blessing of the king by the god(s) with promises of prosperity.
6. Blessings and curses on future generations: Directed at those who would renew or profane the new temple.

Hurowitz states that the structure of these building stories was not born of necessity (e.g., reflecting the natural course of building); indeed, the stories reflect more idealism than reality.[12] They are also somewhat flexible topoi.

> Not every individual story need contain all the components and all the themes or ideas which seem to typify the pattern. The writer created according to an overall conception or according to a general literary pattern, but he permitted himself to mold the pattern and alter it according

---

11. Hurowitz, *I Have Built*, 97, 126. The template is Mesopotamian with examples extending to the time of Old Babylonia. Egyptian and Northwest Semitic inscriptions (with the exception of the Baal Cycle) do not appear to share this literary style. Hurowitz identifies only two Northwest Semitic narratives that share similarities with the Babylonian template. The Baal Epic shares similarities but also introduces numerous novel details (102).

12. Ibid., 126. For example, all the materials and workers are assembled prior to construction.

to his own views and needs, or in accordance with varying facts and changing realities.[13]

Modifications allowed authors to personalize accounts, while maintenance of the basic structure reaffirmed the underlying message, "the king, by building a temple, had fulfilled in the time-honored manner the traditional role of temple builder and divine servant."[14]

Hurowitz, Edelman, and Fried employ this schema in their analyses of the temple building account in Ezra 1–6. All recognize the addition of later material, but due to differing investigations treat it differently. Fried excludes the Aramaic section of the text, viewing it as an intrusion, while Edelman and Hurowitz include all six chapters.[15] Hurowitz posits a double account. After preparations are completed, the first account ends on an incomplete note due to opposition in chapter 4. The second resumes in 5:1 and reaches completion in 6:22.[16] By positing two accounts, Hurowitz retains the general order of the text and of the identified elements. This corresponds well with the double interruptions to the project that are each resolved through correspondence with the king (4:2–13 and 5:3–10). With some modifications, Hurowitz's framework guides this analysis.

Often tied to a ruler's first year in office, a building project could be initiated by either a god or the builder. Divine desire for the construction

---

13. Ibid., 59. In Neo-Babylonian inscriptions, elements 4 (the dedication) and 6 (the blessings and curses), commonplace in Assyrian inscriptions, are "almost completely absent" (91).

14. Ibid., 90.

15. Edelman, *Origins*, 131–32. Edelman rejects the historical reliability of these chapters, treating them as a single composition, and therefore includes material in the Aramaic correspondence excluded by Fried. (Most notably this includes the history of the temple and a description of the building.) She perceives a more orderly presentation than Fried, although she acknowledges some rearranging of the standard pattern for these accounts. Fried (*Priest and Great King*, 159–77) expands her schema to eight elements and discounts claims that the whole text is a building story given the "hodgepodge" quality of these chapters and an associated disarray of the standard building report elements. She posits an original temple building inscription as a source and therefore seeks to weed out later material to "uncover the building story from the biblical text." She expands her schema to eight elements by breaking the first element into separate parts, eliminates the blessing of the king, and inserts two ceremonies prior to the description of the temple: one for laying the foundation and another for later building stages.

16. Hurowitz, *I Have Built*, 118.

3. THEMES AND MOTIFS IN EZRA 1–6

of a temple was a critical ideological factor—failure to gain divine approval led to disaster.[17] Confirmation was sought and demonstrated in a variety of ways (dreams, omens, extispicy). Ezra 1:1 commences with the divine desire to rebuild the temple. The Lord stirs (העיר) the king's heart, and he immediately dispatches a herald and writes an edict proclaiming his intent to build the temple.

> In the first year of King Cyrus of Persia, in order that the word of the LORD by the mouth of Jeremiah might be accomplished, the LORD stirred up the spirit of King Cyrus of Persia so that he sent a herald throughout all his kingdom, and also in a written edict declared: "Thus says King Cyrus of Persia: The LORD, the God of heaven, has given me all the kingdoms of the earth, and he has charged me to build him a house at Jerusalem in Judah." (Ezra 1:1–2, NRSV)

In Haggai, a famine is judged as an omen to indicate construction should commence (Hag 1:9–11). In contrast, in Ezra, first the prophet Jeremiah (Ezra 1:1) and then Haggai and Zechariah (5:1) are enlisted to confirm the divine will. Hurowitz observes that "the employment of two prophets may be tantamount to sending two messages, one confirming the validity of the other."[18]

The collection of materials and workers present in Ezra 1:4–11 and the entire list of returnees in Ezra 2 are characteristic of Hurowitz's second element. Financial support is "freely offered" by "those around them" (כל־סביבתיהם) in Babylon (1:6), and Cyrus returns vessels from the First Temple (1:7).[19] In 3:7, the returnees hire workmen and purchase wood from Lebanon via the Sidonians and Tyrians. The foreign origin of material and the emphasis on freewill donations are common motifs in building reports and depict a world that "universally recognizes the centrality of the king and the centrality of the building which he is constructing."[20]

---

17. Ibid., 137. "Although the technical methods of expressing divine approval or revealing the divine will differ, it is clear that in the Bible as well as in ancient Mesopotamia divine guidance was desired and considered crucial throughout all stages of the building project and regarding any aspect where human judgment could lead the builder astray" (160).

18. Ibid., 138.

19. The account in 2 Kgs 24:13 states that Nebuchadnezzar cut off all the gold vessels from the temple; many argue that this means there were no vessels to return.

20. Hurowitz, *I Have Built*, 209.

Yet in this account, although Cyrus plays a role, the community is more central than the king as it provides funds and makes arrangements to acquire materials.

The identity of the workers listed in Ezra 2 takes up the lion's share of the second element. In 1:4–5, Cyrus commands "all who remain" (כל־נשאר) wherever he "sojourns" (גר) and whose spirits YHWH has stirred (העיר) to go to Jerusalem to rebuild the temple.[21] The edict encompasses only those living outside Yehud. All the workers and the funds used for the temple come from Mesopotamia (even the restored temple furnishings arrive from there). Additionally, the author pointedly adds that everyone who "went up" were, like Cyrus, inspired (1:5). Eskenazi has argued that the community is a central theme in Ezra-Nehemiah.[22] An inspired community places the people on the same level as the monarch. However, it is the returnees alone who can claim this distinction, as opposed to those who never make this journey.

The decision to build (element 1) often includes a history of the temple to explain why construction is warranted—particularly if it had fallen into ruin and is being rebuilt.[23] In Ezra, Nebuchadnezzar's removal of the temple furnishings (Ezra 1:7) hints at this history. The full account occurs only after materials have been gathered and a foundation is laid. In chapter 4, opponents recite a history of *Jerusalem* as a seat of power and rebellion (4:4–16). Although directed against the city, the complaint placed here implies that any construction will be hurtful to the king and the collection of taxes. Progress halts until the elders provide their own version of the relevant history in 5:11–16. The elders' narrative more directly addresses the *temple's* past and state of disrepair, avoiding the issue of rebellion and placing blame on ancestors who had angered God. Additionally, Cyrus's decree and Sheshbazzar's return of temple vessels now become part of the temple's history. Shifted to this point in the account, the temple's history is used to justify the earlier construction to the current monarch, Darius. It also rebuts the prior accusations—the project is not a threat to the king but, in fact, the exiles are carrying out the orders of a Persian monarch.

---

21. Solomon conscripts labor out of all Israel to construct the First Temple in 1 Kgs 5:13 (27 MT). The Ezra account may assume "Israel" is to be found among the exiles—not among the local population.

22. Eskenazi, *In an Age of Prose*, 42.

23. In 1 Kgs 5:3–5 (17–19 MT), Solomon introduces his building project with a brief history.

In Ezra 3:3, the altar is placed on its support (מכונה). Priests inaugurate sacrifices and festivals, followed by laying the temple foundation (יסד; Ezra 3:6, 10, 11, 12). Accounts of altar construction generally follow the description of the building.[24] But here it precedes the construction of the temple's foundation and becomes part of the preparations for construction. Ezra 3:7 continues preparations for the temple with the collection of materials. Cedar from Sidon and Tyre is purchased with funds collected through local freewill offerings (3:5–7).[25] The temple foundations are laid in 3:10.

Conflict is introduced into the narrative in Ezra 3:3 when the altar is constructed, "because they [the builders] were in dread of the neighboring peoples" (NRSV). Adversaries surrounding the builders impede the project, and, except for the altar and temple foundation, construction is deferred until the next generation. Setbacks to the fulfillment of the divine wish are a common feature in temple reports, and conflict provides this element of uncertainty regarding the temple's completion.[26] It is the most significant plot element in Ezra 1–6, but because it is primarily contained in an Aramaic section of the text (4:8–6:18) and appears intrusive, scholars tend to exclude it from the building report. However, the plot of regional conflict that delays temple construction tracks in parallel with accounts of the First Temple.[27]

In 2 Sam 7, Nathan informs David that the temple will be built by his son once Israel "may live in their own place, and be disturbed no more; and evildoers shall afflict them no more" (7:10). This is confirmed in 1 Kgs 5:3 (17 MT) when Solomon states, "You know that my father David could not build a house for the name of the LORD his God because of the warfare with which his enemies surrounded him, until the LORD put them under the soles of his feet." David prepares for the temple by purchasing the site and constructing the altar in Jerusalem. Just prior to embarking on temple construction, Solomon declares, "But now the LORD my God has given me rest on every side; there is neither adversary nor misfortune" (1 Kgs 5:4

---

24. Fried, *Priest and Great King*, 168.
25. Hurowitz (*I Have Built*, 209) notes that bringing wood from Lebanon by water routes is a common motif in temple building accounts.
26. Ibid., 48.
27. Regarding expansions in reports, Hurowitz (ibid., 96) notes, "the 'historical' temple building stories displayed a tendency to emphasize a certain motif or segment in the story at the price of brevity in describing other segments."

[18 MT]). Overcoming opposition from surrounding peoples becomes a necessary condition for the construction of both temples.[28]

By mimicking the construction of the First Temple, the Ezra account validates the new temple via historical and theological ties. Just as the First Temple had a divinely mandated delay in construction due to conflict, so construction of the Second Temple experiences a delay. Just as David constructed an altar and carried out sacrifices prior to the temple's construction, so the community in Ezra constructs an altar, builds a foundation "on its site," and carries out sacrifices prior to building the temple. The shared plot element of hostile neighbors delaying construction deepens ties to the historic temple, while simultaneously indicating the relations with surrounding peoples as a primary object of concern in Ezra.

Indeed, given the space allotted to countering hostilities, this account is as much about victory over opponents as it is about a restoration of Jerusalem's sacred site. Offers of help from "adversaries" in Ezra 4:1–2 are rebuffed with the claim that "we alone will build to the LORD, the God of Israel, as King Cyrus of Persia has commanded us" (4:3). Normally, temple building reports include foreign workers in a temple's construction.[29] This motif is forgone in Ezra. Notably it is not Persian involvement that is rejected but that of neighboring communities. Bedford has argued that the temple construction was in fact collaborative, and only later conflict arose, leading to the exclusion of local entities.[30] If participation in

---

28. The Chronicler takes the parallels even further when David constructs the altar, accumulates materials for the temple, and organizes the priesthood to await the next generation (1 Chr 22:1–5; 23:6), just as the community does in Ezra 3:7 (although the description in Ezra 3 replicates Solomon's acquisition of materials in 1 Kgs 5:8–11 [22–25 MT]). However, whether the Chronicler is influenced by the scenario in Ezra or vice versa is a matter of debate.

29. For example, 1 Chr 22:2 states that David gathered aliens residing in Israel to construct the temple.

30. Bedford, *Temple Restoration*, 28. "The texts may contain valuable, accurate historical information about this period, but it is often difficult to identify such material in its present literary context. To read these texts is foremost to behold the world as constructed by the authors/editors; to see the issues they considered to be important, and behind those issues the historical conditions that produced them as understood by the authors/editors…. Rather than understand these emphases [social division and centrality of temple] as an accurate, historical representation, they should be read as expressions of their author's/editor's peculiar understanding of Achaemenid Judean society and should be interpreted in light of the time in which the text was written" (31).

construction provided a basis for asserting control over the temple, it may explain why acknowledging collaboration was problematic. This account would then be an effort to overwrite such claims. Describing outsiders as opponents (or opponents as outsiders) permanently repudiates any claims they may make.

Edelman observes that events are communicated through a series of letters and records that highlight the interruption of the building process (Ezra 4:8–6:15).[31] The blow-by-blow description of the challenges to construction contrasts with the brief (and incomplete) note on the temple's appearance in 6:3–4. The exiles and adversaries use identical methods as they battle over the project. The exiles successfully overturn Artaxerxes's imperial decision not by force but through dialogue, effective letter writing campaigns, and archival research. The latter two require specialized training and skills, that is, cultural capital. Embedding the description of the conflict within such literary forms places the community and the ability to navigate records and letter writing in the forefront of the account rather than the building itself.

Cyrus's edict is a specific example of this interest in written documents. It initiates construction and is brought to the reader's attention three times (Ezra 1:1; 4:3; 6:3). However, each subsequent reference underscores the decree's ineffectiveness in contrast to the efforts of the community.[32] The content of Cyrus's order is discovered in a forgotten document and comes to light late in the account (6:3–6). Only at this point in the narrative are temple dimensions given and the information that costs should be paid from the royal treasury. The wider narrative contradicts this scenario as funds are provided through freewill offerings (1:6, 68; 3:5–7) and construction begins without reference to any details from Cyrus regarding the temple's plan. The temple's description occurs late in the narrative and, given its schematic nature, fails to guide the building project. Instead, it indicates only that if the king ordered funds for the project, government authorities never followed through. Instead, it is the exiles alone that have carried on with the project. Upon its *discovery*, its contents still carry force and legitimate the project to Persian investigators. The important role of the *written* text to resolve the stalemate underscores for the reader the value

---

31. Edelman, *Origins*, 162.

32. In Ezra 4:3, Zerubbabel cites Cyrus's order as the basis of refusing help from the adversaries. The immediate result is that the adversaries halt construction until the time of Darius.

of scribal practices. The edict's misplacement highlights the importance of community resources and resolve, without which the temple would never have been built despite imperial authorization. The written validation of the community's labor creates symbolic capital for those whose families contributed to the temple's construction.

After a blessing for the king, an account would normally conclude with blessings for those who repair and maintain the temple and curses directed toward those who might profane it.[33] In this account the order and content are modified. The only curse in the text is pronounced by Darius and occurs prior to the temple's dedication. Those who alter his *edict* are roundly cursed in addition to anyone profaning the temple:

> Furthermore, I decree that if anyone alters this edict, a beam shall be pulled out of the house of the perpetrator, who then shall be impaled on it. The house shall be made a dunghill. May the God who has established his name there overthrow any king or people that shall put forth a hand to alter this, or to destroy this house of God in Jerusalem. I, Darius, make a decree. (Ezra 6:11–12)

The curse's Achaemenid origin, concern for the royal edict, and its narrative location within the Aramaic correspondence prior to the temple's dedication appear to direct the curse toward people external to those who join in the Passover celebration of Ezra 6:19–22. (The distinction is made even more acute by the fact that 6:19 marks the transition from Aramaic to Hebrew.) The absence of a *divine* curse *after* the temple's dedication creates an unmitigated account of success and hope for the future for the celebrating community.

The rebuilt temple is dedicated in Ezra 6:16–18, followed by a celebration of Passover (6:19–22). Both are celebrated with joy (6:16, 22). The dedication and festivities to mark the completion of a temple are the central component in temple building accounts, and Mesopotamian rites always included the entrance of the deity to take up residence in the temple.[34] For example, in the Priestly account the cloud settles on the taber-

---

33. Hurowitz (*I Have Built*, 299) states that in Mesopotamia, gods benefited from the construction of their temples (it provided a place for them to reside.) Therefore monarchs perceived themselves as doing the gods a favor worthy of blessing. He argues that the Deuteronomistic account rejects this view. Divine blessing must come through covenants and "God's own good will."

34. Ibid., 267–68.

nacle as it is filled with divine glory (Exod 40:34–35). The Deuteronomist views the temple as a place where the divine name resides (1 Kgs 8:20–21). Ezra lacks any mention of divine presence. As Hurowitz observes,

> Ezra 6:17–22 reports the dedication of the rebuilt temple, but contains no reference to the crucial event of God's entry into the temple, or to the installation in the temple of any symbol of divine presence. The main events are sacrifices which include twelve purification offerings for the twelve tribes … and initiation of the priests and Levites recalling the initiation of priests marking the Tabernacle dedication (Lev 8; Num 8).[35]

What does the absence of a traditional symbol of divine presence suggest? Perhaps the account reconstructs the evidence of God's arrival to accommodate a new reality. The presence of God seems to be confirmed when they dedicate the priests and Levites "for the service of God at Jerusalem" (6:18), and the joy expressed at the Passover celebration is attributed to YHWH, "for the LORD had made them joyful" (6:22). While only the returnees celebrate the temple dedication, the author records two groups of worshipers for Passover: the returned exiles and "all who had joined them and separated themselves from the pollutions of the nations of the land" (6:21). It may be that the existence of affiliated communities in Babylon and Yehud created a social tension that compelled the author to adjust his account so as not to exclude the Babylonian congregation. The reconstructed temple inaugurates sacrifice and associated rituals, but the Deity is manifested not in glory or image but in worship, sacrifice, and the joy of a purified community. The sacrifices are carried out on behalf of "all Israel" (6:17), thus representing any who did not make the journey. Even though separated from the temple, those in the diaspora could still be assured of the divine presence in their worship if they maintained ethnic purity. While muting the expression of divine presence may accommodate disparate communities, the account maintains the temple's unique role.

The symbolic strategy above that includes those in the diaspora also proscribes others. The criteria for participation in worship address the complicating matter of the exclusion of self-proclaimed Yahwists from worship in Jerusalem. The two rituals of dedication and Passover are each introduced with the delineation of participants. Those participating in the dedication are "the people of Israel, the priests and the Levites, and the

---

35. Ibid., 268.

rest of the returned exiles" (Ezra 6:16). As already mentioned, the celebrants of Passover are the exiles and "all who had joined them and separated themselves from the pollutions of the nations of the land" (6:21). In addition, David Janzen argues that, in Ezra, sacrifice (part of both rituals) "communicates the necessity of Israel's social and geographic separation from outsiders, insofar as only this social group may sacrifice to YHWH in Jerusalem."[36] The surrounding people are portrayed as *not* separate from the nations, *not* exiles, and therefore they are *not* members of the community. The divine presence is now linked to the purity of the worshiping community—purity defined in exclusionary terms.

In a unique move, the divine blessing (element 5), normally directed toward the monarch, is redirected to the community.[37] The community celebrates the Festival of Unleavened Bread, "for the LORD had made them joyful, and had turned the heart of the king of Assyria to them, so that he aided them in the work on the house of God, the God of Israel" (Ezra 6:22b). A king appears at the appropriate point in the text not as the recipient of the blessing but rather as a tool of YHWH to bless the people. (Notably the king is anonymous and incongruously referred to as the king of Assyria.)

The missing blessing for the king (a promise of prosperity, long life, and stable dynasty) may be absent because it causes problems on several levels for the author's agenda. First, it interferes with the temple's connection to Judah's history. As Bedford states, "This temple formerly had been the preeminent national shrine in the kingdom of Judah. Built and maintained by Judean kings, it had been a monarchical institution which served both to legitimate the political order and as an arm of state administration."[38] Blessing a Persian king would cement ties to the Achaemenid crown while severing connections with Judah's monarchy and religious traditions. It would also acknowledge *him* as the primary temple builder and benefactor for YHWH. Although the author acknowledges

---

36. David Janzen, *The Social Meanings of Sacrifice in the Hebrew Bible*, BZAW 344 (Berlin: de Gruyter, 2004), 187. "Sacrifice in Ezra-Nehemiah does what the law in Ezra-Nehemiah does: it communicates the necessity of Israel's separation from the surrounding peoples. Furthermore, we find that the law in Ezra-Nehemiah has almost no other function" (186).

37. Edelman (*Origins*, 133) observes that blessings in Haggai are also democratized (Hag 2:19) or, when directed at Zerubbabel, the Davidic heir, muted (Hag 2:21, 23).

38. Bedford, *Temple Restoration*, 2.

a role for Persian kings, it stands in tension with his presentation of the exilic community. It is the returnees who travel to Jerusalem and provide material, money, and labor needed for building. Pointedly in Ezra 5, the prophetic activity of Haggai and Zechariah is directed not to the Persian monarch but to the Jews in Judah and Jerusalem as Zerubbabel and Joshua, the high priest, lead the reconstruction.[39] The community ordains the priests who all come from the exilic company. It is the community that overcomes the obstacles to construction—a motif associated with the story's protagonist.[40] The Persian king plays only a supporting role. Although the author accepts Persian authority and even presents Persian rule as beneficial, foreign rule remains *foreign*. A blessing bestowed on the Persian king would undermine the carefully constructed argument that the *exiles* are YHWH's representatives.

Indeed, the community even becomes the benefactor for the king! In lieu of bestowing divine blessing on the monarch, the author records Darius's orders that sacrifices and prayers be made "for the life of the king and his children" (6:10). The benefit for the monarch is explicitly mediated through the prayers of the community—making the Persian monarch dependent on this community for divine benefaction. This leads to the logical conclusion that the monarch needs a worshiping community in Jerusalem and that the author regards prayers on behalf of the Persian monarch as an acceptable function of the Jerusalem cult.

The author also avoids positing blessing for a future monarch (element 6) who might restore the temple. Hurowitz notes that this element is commonly dropped in Neo-Babylonian accounts, but in this account it may be modified rather than missing. The narrative moves from the dedication of the temple to a celebration of Passover (Ezra 6:19-22). Passover—celebrating freedom, rescue from oppression, and inaugurating a new future—is now celebrated because of the completed temple. Future hope for this

---

39. Ibid., 184. Bedford argues that Zerubbabel's arrival signaled to the prophets that it was now the proper time to rebuild the temple. In his view, for Haggai and Zechariah, Zerubbabel is monarchical enough, despite his more limited role as governor, to fulfill the royal role in temple building. He also notes that in Second Isaiah, Cyrus's actions become a testimony to YHWH's sovereignty (76). It appears that both images are employed in Ezra 1-6.

40. Hurowitz, *I Have Built*, 49. He states, "the attempt to fulfill the gods' wishes meets with advances and setbacks. The factor which continuously hinders the immediate accomplishment of the plan is the uncertainty which incessantly plagues the leading human character in the story."

community is anchored to the reconstructed temple.[41] Blessings for future monarchs are replaced by a blessing directed toward the community.

3.2. Legitimating a Temple and Symbolic Capital

As a genre, temple building reports legitimate temples and bestow recognition on the builder. They are grounded in the doxic belief that a divine wish communicated to the builder impels temple construction and the deity would bless the faithful servant who successfully accomplishes the task. Because temple building reports had this legitimating purpose, we cannot assume that every polemical statement in this account is born of specific competition over capital. However, Bourdieu posits that wider social relations of power are refracted in the field of cultural production. The less autonomous the cultural field, the more the producers of cultural capital must respond to external economic and political influences. Thus the various distinctive turns identified above can provide evidence of particular concerns generating these literary moves.

The symbolic capital of the Second Temple is enhanced by allusions to the First Temple. This is aided by descriptions of direct connections—temple furnishings are returned and it is rebuilt on the original site. Each gesture underscores a belief that this is *the* legitimate Yahwistic temple. The community's ability to overcome opposition, its celebration of the temple's dedication, and Passover all provide symbolic testimony of divine approval of this construction—God, who controlled the heart of the king, had aided them (Ezra 6:22). The claims bolster both the temple's value (its cultural capital) and the prestige of the community associated with its construction. At the same time, it effectively excludes other worship sites and even other worship practices.

In the narrative, gifts and labor (economic capital) play essential roles. Yet the only resources described in detail come from the exilic community (Ezra 1:6–11; 2:68–69; 5:14–15; 6:5). Cedars from Lebanon are purchased with food, drink, and oil produced by the community, while Cyrus merely provides permission to acquire the wood (3:7). Persian contributions are limited to the return of original temple furnishings. Darius calls for gifts (6:8–9), yet no record is made of their arrival, and adversaries are explicitly

---

41. It also creates a historical tie with the Passover celebrated in Num 9:1–5 after the completion of the tabernacle.

excluded from providing any aid. Through the manipulation of economic capital, the images that provide the community recognition (since they alone are portrayed as contributors to the temple) also exclude others.

Building on doxic beliefs (divine inspiration or blessing for successful temple builders or generosity as a requirement for distinction), this account accumulates prestige and honor for the early community. Those who share the same categories of perception will perceive the qualities as socially pertinent. The text invites those who seek similar recognition to embrace the values of the community portrayed here. They are to give generously to the temple, to accept Persian rule, and to maintain boundaries with the wider population. The persuasiveness of the text lies in the narrative's logic that the earlier community achieved distinction in such actions. The example of the community creates a powerful entreaty to follow suit. Even if one does not initially share similar beliefs, the text appeals to any who recognize and value the capital enlisted in this effort.

Bourdieu states that the fundamental social differences stemming from one's total volume of capital almost always conceals the secondary difference that separates class fractions, for instance, holders of cultural capital and holders of economic capital within the elites.[42] Cultural capital is highly valued in this account, and its narrative intimates competition with those who have greater control over economic resources. Those whose legitimation and power are acquired through cultural capital (e.g., literary production or ordination) are pitted against those whose power rests in economic capital.[43] The author rejects local labor (economic capital), deeming it foreign, and marginalizes Achaemenid political capital. Instead, the successful completion of the temple is accomplished by navigating the arena of royal edicts and letter campaigns through means available only to those invested with cultural capital. Success underscores the value of such capital by demonstrating its strategic importance in constructing the temple. In the process, the author also provides a subversive critique of those holding economic capital and entitlements. The more

---

42. Bourdieu, *Distinction*, 115.

43. Ibid., 176. Regarding the dominant class, Bourdieu comments, "the different fractions of the dominant class are oriented towards cultural practices so different in their style and object and sometimes so antagonistic ... that it is easy to forget that they are variants of the same fundamental relationship to necessity and to those who remain subject to it, and that each pursues the exclusive appropriation of legitimate cultural goods and the associated symbolic profits."

successfully the transmission of other forms of capital are hindered, the more the author's own capital is determinative in the reproduction of the social structure of his community.[44]

The text portrays the community negotiating imperial and external influences in ways that may reflect the author's own negotiations. He holds sufficient capital to influence surrounding fields, but others, with other forms of capital, influence his field as well. Due to Persia's overarching power, the community is not free to ignore or to reject the Persian government's role. Like it or not, they must entreat Persian monarchs for permission to build the temple and to handle opposition, and monarchs must be reciprocated for their efforts. Prayers must be said, credit must be given, orders obeyed. Likely, taxes must be collected. Yet the monarch's role as a builder is limited while the prominence of the worshiping community grows. Both exiles and Cyrus are inspired, but the only clear evidence of resources or labor come from the community, and only they are present for the dedication. In contrast, local competitors holding economic capital are challenged and repudiated. This indicates a more level playing field among these parties. Their close proximity sparks intense hostilities, but the community can rely on God and superior scribal skills to resolve things in their favor.

Finally, composing a temple building report asserts the validity and value of a particular temple. This composition places the Jerusalem temple on a par with all other ancient Near Eastern temples that had their own building accounts. Uniquely, the account celebrates not a monarch but the local community that fulfilled the role of temple builders. Authored well after the temple's actual construction, it hints at competing practices or beliefs that touched on essentials of community identity. For the author, these alternatives threatened the cultural value of the temple itself. The account provides a response that legitimates the temple, a narrowly defined community of builders, and in the process, the author's own cultural capital.

3.3. The Exodus Motif

The journey to Jerusalem in Ezra 1–6 evokes the exodus narrative. Departure from the foreign land of Babylon resembles the departure from Egypt:

---

44. Bourdieu, "Forms of Capital," 254.

In Exodus, the Egyptians encourage the Hebrews to leave, and we are informed that "they had asked the Egyptians for jewelry of silver and gold, and for clothing, and the Lord had given the people favor in the sight of the Egyptians, so that they let them have what they asked" (Exod 12:35–36). Likewise in Ezra, Cyrus commands "the people of their place" to assist the departing people of YHWH with a similar list of materials (Ezra 1:4). As a result, "all their neighbors aided them with silver vessels, with gold, with goods, with animals, and with valuable gifts, besides all that was freely offered" (1:6). Each contingent has two leaders, the journeys fulfill the word of God, and YHWH prompts both monarchs (although Cyrus is an antithesis of Pharaoh, allowing people to depart freely).[45] Both journeys are made with the intent to worship YHWH and construct a temple or tabernacle in order to do so. Upon arrival in the land, both communities face opposition from "adversaries," resulting in discouragement that delays the purposes of the arrivals.

These similarities suggest to Sara Japhet that an ideological motive stands behind the author's presentation. She contends that only in the exodus and in the account of restoration does Israel have a political system of dual leadership, a layman and a priest. Thus the correlation of Moses and Aaron with Zerubbabel and Jeshua may legitimate this type of political situation. In addition, she identifies an analogous first and second generation in both accounts.[46] Williamson pursues a theological purpose for these motifs, suggesting that lines of continuity with the exodus are emphasized to encourage readers' faith "by reminding them of the riches of their heritage and the legitimacy of their present institutions as vehicles through which that heritage could be mediated to them." He suggests that the author is inviting readers to interpret the return "as an act of God's grace that can be compared in its significance with the very birth of the nation of Israel itself."[47]

Both Japhet and Williamson rightly identify the legitimating function of these parallels. However, only certain aspects of the Exodus narrative are in view. Central to the Exodus account is Moses's role as leader and mediator between YHWH and others (despite Aaron's presence). Moreover, the journey out of Egypt and the miracles that overcome Pharaoh's opposi-

---

45. Sara Japhet, "Periodization between History and Ideology II: Chronology and Ideology in Ezra-Nehemiah," in Lipschits and Oeming, *Persian Period*, 502.
46. Ibid., 503–4.
47. Williamson, *Ezra, Nehemiah*, 20.

tion are significant motifs. None of these is developed in Ezra. Indeed, no details of the journey itself are even recorded in Ezra 1–6.[48] The king does not resist the divine will, and the exiles do not fear or hesitate. Instead, YHWH moves hearts, the king commands the return, and the people go. By drawing a sufficient number of parallels with the exodus, the author is able to insinuate sameness despite diverging from other aspects of the exodus. The author draws on those things most helpful for legitimating particular social or institutional arrangements and passes over those that fail to aid his agenda.

The missing miracles and the role of the monarch in Ezra are cases in point. Although miracles are central to the account in Exodus, to draw attention to their absence in Ezra would undermine claims of divine endorsement of the return. Silence on this feature sidesteps questions about the religious validity of the rebuilt temple and priests brought by the returnees. Divine action is not absent from Ezra but is limited to the stirring of hearts (Ezra 1:1, 5) or the narrator's claims (5:5) and is evidenced only in the actions of people. Contrary to expectations grounded in temple building reports or the Exodus narrative, it is not the monarch who is the primary builder of the temple or the chief obstacle to its construction. Rather, local communities either build the temple or thwart construction.[49] The absence of imperial opposition may be due in part to the fact that the author is negotiating the reality that the current emperor is *not* the one who actually deported (enslaved) the people but is rather the one who is *releasing* them.[50] The alacrity with which the exiles embark on the journey coupled with support by an uncoerced king create a positive contrast with the actors in Exodus. Ezra's account translates into a witness to the faithful and noble character of exiles and king.

The selective use of the exodus motif paints a particular portrait of the community. The divine touch on Cyrus hearkens back to God's control over Pharaoh (despite opposing responses by the monarchs) and intimates divine control over foreign monarchs, whether or not they cooperate. Logically, this maintains that Persian rule is not itself a problem. The monarch may be viewed favorably and his administration obeyed unless

---

48. Preparations are made, followed by a list of travelers "who came with Zerubbabel" (Ezra 2:2), and they arrive and make freewill offerings (2:68).

49. Imperial decrees do play a role in halting or supporting construction, but after Cyrus the monarch acts only in response to letters written at the local level.

50. Danna Nolan Fewell, private communication 19 April 2011.

God indicates otherwise. This is an argument for the status quo by someone content with his place in the empire. The symbolic language even insinuates that rebellion against the Persians is rebellion against YHWH, since God has chosen the monarch to accomplish God's purposes.

The community in Ezra responds with alacrity to the call to "go up," which contrasts positively with the hesitancy of the Hebrews in Exodus. Physical manifestations of divine power are not needed to recognize God's will. Both communities transport material goods from the place of exile for the temple. The parallel suggests that providing resources for temple construction is a sign of true Israelites who travel to Canaan. The returnees do not depart to escape bondage but make the journey for altruistic purposes—reestablishing proper worship. The contributions of the returnees become a sign of distinction. Those who worship at the temple will know to whom they are indebted.

Melody Knowles argues that the Ezra descriptions have much in common with religious pilgrimages. The journeys are multiple and voluntary, and those who remain in exile do so without critique.[51] This imagery nuances the Exodus parallels. The motif invites those still in exile to also "go up" to Jerusalem and suggests a reluctance to fault those who remained in Babylon.[52] The repetition invites those still far away to view themselves as members of the community. It reminds those in Yehud to recognize the significant financial contributions of those still in the diaspora who continue to make the pilgrimage to Jerusalem. Close ties between the two communities may be detected in this—perhaps due not only to financial support but also to family relations, as we see the care taken with identification of family lines. The avoidance of negative innuendo for the diaspora indicates the importance of those relations. For both near and far, the text asserts that the reconstructed temple is central to a renewed nation. As Knowles points out, a rebirth reminiscent of the exodus is now defined as a

---

51. Melody D. Knowles, "Pilgrimage Imagery in the Returns in Ezra," *JBL* 123 (2004): 57–59. In Exodus, everyone makes a single trip together. In Ezra, the people do not flee to a new land but return to a land they had previously settled. The city of Jerusalem is the destination in Ezra, while the entire land of Canaan is in view in Exodus. In Exodus, gifts are requested by departing Hebrews and viewed as plunder by the narrator (Exod 3:22; 12:36), but in Ezra, gifts are commanded by Cyrus and givers do not seem to be exploited. Unlike Pharaoh, the monarch is not an opponent in Ezra but a benefactor. Knowles argues that reading the journey in Ezra as a religious pilgrimage rather than escape from bondage has different sociological consequences (64).

52. Ibid., 72.

worshiping community "that places Jerusalem and its temple at the center of its worship life."[53]

Bourdieu states that the construction of a social space rests on how the properties capable of conferring strength or power are distributed within it.[54] The diversity of properties creates an element of uncertainty regarding the formation and cohesiveness of groups. Groups formed in terms of one form of capital might come in tension with groups based on a different form. The uncertainty creates a basis for a plurality of worldviews and also feeds political struggle as agents engage in a symbolic struggle "to produce and impose the legitimate world-view."[55] An account of history is one strategy to impose specific social differences (or mark differences as significant) without directly referencing the present.[56] Ezra 1–6 portrays the exiles gaining dominance over local competitors yet accommodating relations with the Persian monarch and the ongoing diaspora community. Capital held by the author or his community in the present day is linked to the successful construction of the temple by the first returnees. By recounting their success and their gifts for the temple, the narrative overwrites alternative sources of power and social formation. Local competitors are critiqued as opponents to the divine will, and their capital is marginalized. Meanwhile the generosity of those who travel to Jerusalem strengthens ties with the diaspora community. A narrative that includes a monarch stirred by divine touch may reassure Persian loyalists and placate those resistant to Persian rule. These references to the past become tailored to meet needs of the present.[57]

3.4. Prophetic Words and Royal Decrees

Bob Becking contends that Ezra 1 and 2 stress imperial and divine support for a particular Yahwistic group. He comments, "This implies that

---

53. Ibid., 73.
54. Bourdieu, "Social Space," 724.
55. Ibid., 728. Bourdieu states that it is a strategy to produce and impose "the meaning of the objects of the social world by going beyond the directly visible attributes by reference to the future or the past."
56. Ibid., 727.
57. Ibid. Fewell suggests that Exodus may be a contemporary and competing account of release and homecoming that views the monarch and the empire more negatively.

politics and religion were merged in order to attain or defend a position of power both within the community and in connection with the central Persian rule."[58] Evidence bears out this observation, although the two sources of legitimacy do not operate in the same way nor do they address identical goals. In addition, the author of Ezra-Nehemiah portrays prophets and monarchs in ways conducive to supporting his own position within the community.

3.4.1. Jeremiah and Cyrus

Ezra 1:1 states that Cyrus's decree fulfills "the word of the Lord by the mouth of Jeremiah." The statement lacks a clear textual referent, and scholars have most commonly posited Jer 29:10, "For thus says the LORD: Only when Babylon's seventy years are completed will I visit you, and I will fulfill to you my promise and bring you back to this place." However, the immediate literary context of being stirred to action resonates more with Isa 45:13, "I have aroused Cyrus in righteousness, and I will make all his paths straight; he shall build my city and set my exiles free, not for price or reward, says the LORD of hosts."[59] Elias Bickerman suggests that the allusion to Isaiah was intentional because Isaiah anticipates Cyrus as the one who will establish God's kingdom but that Ezra 1:1 refers to Jer 50:18–19, in which Babylon is punished and Israel brought back to pasture.[60] Although Israel's return is a major focus in Ezra 1–6, the punishment of Babylon is not. I suggest that the author's referent is one more consonant with his particular view of restoration.

The reference to Jeremiah is oddly worded in Ezra 1:1: "to complete/fulfill [לכלות] the word of YHWH from the mouth of Jeremiah" (my translation). It does not refer to the words of *Jeremiah* or his vision; rather, it refers to the *Lord's* words in Jeremiah's mouth. This has significant parallels with

---

58. Bob Becking, "'We All Returned As One!': Critical Notes on the Myth of the Mass Return," in Lipschits and Oeming, *Persian Period*, 13.

59. Blenkinsopp, *Ezra-Nehemiah*, 74. Blenkinsopp also posits a relationship with Jer 25:11–14 to the land's Sabbath rest and the destruction of Babylon. These allusions may fit if, like Blenkinsopp, one accepts single authorship of Chronicles and Ezra-Nehemiah. In that case, 2 Chr 36:21–22 fulfills Jeremiah's word twice: once involving the Sabbath rest of the land and Babylon's fall; the second, 36:22, is Cyrus's edict. Even if there is common authorship, however, only 36:22 is included in Ezra, which argues for excluding the first allusion from the author's purposes.

60. Elias J. Bickerman, "The Edict of Cyrus in Ezra 1," *JBL* 65 (1946): 270.

Jeremiah's call: "Then the LORD put out his hand and touched my mouth; and the LORD said to me, 'Now *I have put my words in your mouth.* See, today I appoint you over nations and over kingdoms, to pluck up and to pull down, to destroy and to overthrow, to build and to plant'" (1:9–10). For the author of Ezra 1:1, the completion of the word of the Lord from the mouth of Jeremiah is realized in the concrete acts of building and planting. The theme of building recurs in Jer 24:6, 31:4–5, and 31:28. In every case, building refers to the exiles returning to Israel. Thus the fulfillment of YHWH's word is not seventy years of Sabbath rest, the inspiration of Cyrus, or the end of Babylon, but the rebuilding and the return to life in Judah. Whatever else others may have understood by Jeremiah's words, for this author, the prophetic word is fulfilled if the temple is rebuilt and exiles are planted in the land. This is a different view of the restoration than we find in earlier texts, and it reflects changed social circumstances in the late Persian era.

In Ezra 1:2–4, Cyrus declares that YHWH has charged him to rebuild the house of YHWH in Jerusalem. He therefore commands a return by exiles to Jerusalem to carry out the rebuilding task and calls on "the remainder" (הנשאר; my translation) to provide material support for the task.[61] The decree gains a lot of press in the first six chapters. In 3:7, Zerubbabel and Joshua pay workmen and purchase lumber, "according to the grant that they had from King Cyrus of Persia." In 4:3, leaders of the returnees reject offers of help from "adversaries," insisting the work was theirs alone "as King Cyrus of Persia has commanded us." But the royal edict provides insufficient authority since the work is halted until the reign of Darius (4:5). In 5:13–16, Cyrus's decree to build the temple is again recounted in the letter of Tattenai to Darius. This version does not mention returnees; rather it moves directly to a description of Cyrus's return of temple vessels much like the *narrative* of 1:7–8 (rather than the content of the *edict* in 1:2–4). In 6:3–5, the same decree is different yet—in 1:4–6, the funds for reconstruction come from people who remain in exile, but Ezra 6 states that funds are to come from the imperial treasury. Here again, the return of people goes unmentioned, and the edict describes instead the proportions of the building and the types of materials needed for construction.

Explanations for these differences vary. Some posit two sources: a Hebrew source behind Ezra 1 reflecting the content of an oral proclamation

---

61. הנשאר is given more theological weight in the prayer of Ezra 9:8, 15, where it is frequently translated, "remnant." However, here it may simply mean those left behind. It still implies the idea of being part of the same community.

and an Aramaic administrative memorandum.⁶² Others suggest that the Cyrus edict in Ezra 1 is an authorial invention, while the Aramaic version in Ezra 5 is a possible administrative record.⁶³ Japhet views this difference as an example of Ezra-Nehemiah speaking in "multiple voices, those of its various, unharmonized sources, and that of its author."⁶⁴ The author's perspective, different from his original sources, creates tension between his viewpoint and that of his sources.

Significantly, the command for exiles to return that is so prominent in Ezra 1:1–3 is completely absent in any other reference to Cyrus's edict. Even in 5:14–16, the focus is on temple vessels, and the only returnee mentioned, Sheshbazzar, is charged with the return of temple articles. In contrast, in Ezra 1 a list of materials occurs only in the narrative and is followed by an extensive list of the exiles in chapter 2. The temple vessels, while not unimportant, follow a list of materials donated by neighbors (1:6) or conclude the list of returnees (2:68–69). If Ezra 1 postdates the Aramaic memorandum of Ezra 5, then the author's composition shifts emphasis away from the materials and construction of the temple toward an account centered on the community constructing the temple, a task normally attributed to kings. Eskenazi comments that this "underlines the book's bent toward granting the community real power, power elsewhere assigned to kings."⁶⁵ If so, it may explain the unique reference to Sheshbazzar as "prince" in 1:8.

Narratively, Ezra 1:7–8 brings together three rulers: King Cyrus of Persia, Nebuchadnezzar, and Sheshbazzar, prince (נשיא) of Judah.

> King Cyrus himself brought out the vessels of the house of the LORD that Nebuchadnezzar had carried away from Jerusalem and placed in the house of his gods.⁸ King Cyrus of Persia had them released into the charge of Mithredath the treasurer, who counted them out to Sheshbazzar the prince of Judah. (Ezra 1:7–8)

---

62. Bickerman. "Edict of Cyrus," 252.

63. Blenkinsopp, *Ezra-Nehemiah*, 74; Lester Grabbe, "Ezra," in *Eerdman's Commentary on the Bible*, ed. James D. G. Dunn and John W. Rogerson (Grand Rapids: Eerdmans, 2003), 314, 316.

64. Sara Japhet, "Sheshbazzar and Zerubbabel against the Background of the Historical and Religious Tendencies of Ezra-Nehemiah: Part 1," in *From the Rivers of Babylon to the Highlands of Judah: Collected Studies on the Restoration Period* (Winona Lake, IN: Eisenbrauns, 2006), 83.

65. Eskenazi, *In an Age of Prose*, 53.

These verses are structured in such a way that the actions of Cyrus "bringing forth" (*hiphil* of יצא) utensils of the house of YHWH surround and undo Nebuchadnezzar's action of "bringing forth" (*hiphil* of יצא) those same utensils from Jerusalem. When Cyrus "brings forth" the utensils, his treasurer counts them out to Sheshbazzar. Sheshbazzar is mentioned only with regard to the return of temple furnishings in 1:8 and 11 and again in 5:14–16, although there in the Aramaic section he is called "governor." He appears nowhere else in the biblical text. In all of Ezra-Nehemiah, only here in these verses with two other monarchs present is the title *prince* [נשיא] *of Judah* employed.[66] In usage elsewhere, נשיא is a ruler of a clan (Num 1:44; 1 Chr 2:10), and the term carries an associated genealogical significance. In Ezekiel, נשיא refers to either the king of Israel (e.g., Ezek 46:10–28) or foreign monarchs (Ezek 26:16; 27:21; 30:13; etc.). While there is debate about Sheshbazzar's actual lineage, employing a ruling title at this point places him on similar footing with imperial rulers.[67] Although there is no overt claim to dynastic rule, the present Persian king returns what the Babylonian king removed from the capital of Judah and places it in the hands of a prince of Israel. The transfer is not only of material goods but of responsibility to construct the temple—a task that belongs to kings.

Sheshbazzar's identity as portrayed within this narrative expresses two things at the same time. He carries out a royal decree as a good Persian citizen and acts as a monarch, restoring the symbol of the Judean crown. He immediately disappears from the text; two verses later the list of returnees is headed by Zerubbabel and Jeshua (Ezra 2:2). Later reference to him is only as a distant historical figure (5:14–16). Despite his small role, his

---

66. The term נשיא occurs only four times in Chronicles (1 Chr 2:10; 4:38; 5:6; 7:40) in reference to heads of clans, e.g., "prince of the Reubenites." This usage is also common in Joshua. It occurs only twice in Judges–2 Kings. In 1 Kgs 8:1, נשיא (NRSV "leaders") occurs in combination with "elders" and "heads" of the tribes. In 1 Kgs 11:34, the prophet states that God will make Solomon נשיא (NRSV "ruler") all the days of his life.

67. Debate over Sheshbazzar's linage ranges from identifying him with Shenazzar, son of Jehoiachin, in 1 Chr 3:18, to arguing that there is no royal connection and he is simply a governor. See Ephraim Stern, "The Persian Empire and the Political and Social History of Palestine in the Persian Period," in *Introduction; The Persian Period*, ed. W. D. Davies and Louis Finkelstein (Cambridge: Cambridge University Press, 1984), 70; Peter R. Ackroyd, "The Jewish Community in Palestine in the Persian Period," in Davies and Finkelstein *Introduction; Persian Period*, 138. For a more thorough discussion of his lineage see Japhet, "Sheshbazzar and Zerubbabel," 80.

appearance forms a bridge between the Persian monarch, the historical Judean monarchy, and the ongoing community.

3.4.2. Haggai and Zechariah

In Ezra, the prophets Jeremiah, Haggai, and Zechariah are cited as the motivation for particular actions. Jeremiah's prophecy links the divine will with Cyrus's edict. In Ezra 5:1–2, Haggai and Zechariah prophesy to the Jews and they recommence temple construction. In 6:18, "the book of Moses" provides guidance for the ordination of priests and Levites. No prophetic text is directly quoted. However, the return and the activity of the returnees is clearly presented as directly fulfilling the prophetic message.

Rainer Albertz notes that in Jer 22:24–30 YHWH explicitly rejects the Davidic descendants: "As I live, says the Lord, even if King Coniah son of Jehoiakim of Judah were *the signet ring* on my right hand, even from there I would tear you off." Haggai 2:23, on the other hand, explicitly reverses this oracle, "On that day, says the Lord of hosts, I will take you, O Zerubbabel my servant, son of Shealtiel, says the Lord, and make you *like a signet ring*; for I have chosen you, says the Lord of hosts." He posits that there were two early opposing groups: returnees who were bent on reinstating the Davidic kingship and Palestinian laypeople. The latter were descendants of supporters of "Gedaliah, a non-Davidic governor, and regarded the destruction of the monarchy as the opportunity of realizing in devastated Judah those social reforms of the Deuteronomic legislation" espoused by Jeremiah.[68]

Incorporating references to these two opposing prophetic traditions may suggest that the author of Ezra is pulling on religious texts valued by two historically different and competing groups within his community. He employs them to give legitimacy to his account of events and the particular outcome he supports—an outcome that excludes a Davidic king and supports, as Albertz suggests, "a new kind of political and religious organization, which allowed a safe loyalty to the Persians and corresponded

---

68. Rainer Albertz, "The Thwarted Restoration," in *Yahwism after the Exile: Perspectives on Israelite Religion in the Persian Empire*, ed. Rainer Albertz and Bob Becking, STAR 5 (Assen: Van Gorcum, 2003), 10. See Jer 40. Although forcibly removed later, Jeremiah chooses to remain in Mizpah after the destruction of Jerusalem rather than travel to Babylon.

to the interests of both [reform priests and laymen]."[69] The author avoids directly quoting the prophetic texts; instead, aspects of their messages are incorporated and interpreted in ways that differ from and even contradict the original text.

Haggai's support of the monarchy is eliminated, and Ezra retains only the call to complete the temple. For those who had high political aims, their venerated prophetic tradition is retained but reworked so the temple and the ordination of priests now fulfill the prophetic message. Also absent is Haggai's castigation of community members for investing in their homes to the detriment of temple construction (Hag 1:4). Those living in the land are not faulted for a failure to cough up the necessary funds for construction. In Ezra, the fault lies with opposition from outsiders (Ezra 4:1). Likewise, Jeremiah's critique of the monarchy is absent, perhaps due to support by some returnees. Instead, a rebuilt temple and renewed settlement in the land fulfills this prophet's hope of restoration.[70] Arriving exiles are not a danger to good Persian order, and locals are encouraged to accept them and the changes they bring. Employing these two prophetic traditions symbolically unites the local Palestinians with those who count themselves as descendants of returnees. Only outsiders would go to war with each other, and outsiders are defined in Ezra 1–6 as those who fail to support the temple. These rhetorical moves construct a community united around religious heritage and practice. It is a community that has a number of reasons to be divided. Most of these the author chooses not to identify directly. Rather, he incorporates aspects of each party's particular values or beliefs within his construction while jettisoning the most divisive aspects. This indicates ongoing challenges to the community's cohesion in his own time.

Due to the different histories created by exile, there arose opposing political and cultural practices. Divisive economic realities combine with these to threaten the community's ability to operate as a unit. Albertz suggests that Persia granted the upper class some liberty but demanded loyalty from its appointees in the form of support for its economic and tax policies. The result would have been a growing impoverishment of the poor and a deepening loss of solidarity.[71] For the leadership, choos-

---

69. Ibid.

70. This coincides with Jer 24:5–6, which speaks of the "good figs" returning to the land.

71. Albertz, "Thwarted Restoration," 17.

ing Persian benevolence meant rejecting a resurrection of the Davidic monarchy—a move that may have been perceived as disloyal, especially by those hit hardest by Persian economic policies. In addition, based on religious practices developed in exile, the returnees may have faulted the locals for a perceived lack of religious orthodoxy. Either party could have argued, based on these same texts and realities, for very different social arrangements. The political and economic barriers to building unity compelled the author to rework shared prophetic traditions to build consensus around a reformulated religious ideology.

In these texts, the independence of prophets is brought into line with organized religious practice. The prophets spur the temple's construction and aid the exiles. Once the temple is constructed and priests ordained, the prophetic word is no longer active. For the author's purposes, the continuation of prophetic activity may be problematic. It would suggest that the task is incomplete or inadequate. Their critiques also signal dissension rather than solidarity—solidarity built around temple, priest, and Torah. Because of the social and cultural capital that the prophets hold, they cannot be summarily dismissed. The author therefore incorporates the prophetic voices and aligns them to his purposes. Haggai's criticisms of the community and hope for a king are excised—his message is modified to focus on the construction of the temple. Jeremiah affirms the twin goals of return and rebuilding, while his critique of monarchs is silenced. In addition, Haggai and Zechariah are brought into the narrative in the Aramaic portion (Ezra 5:1), and their presence here ties YHWH's will to Persian royal decrees. This symbolic move works in two directions. YHWH's will aligns with the king's—demonstrating that the desires of this God and this community are no threat to Persian rule—should any Persians happen to read this Aramaic portion. It also communicates that YHWH's will, as given voice by the prophets, is fulfilled by the community carrying out royal decrees to build the temple. It does not matter which king, it only matters which God and which people and which temple.

4
Ezra 2: Defining the Community

Josephus rather famously chose to excise the list in Ezra 2 from his account of the restoration, commenting, "And thus did these men go, a certain and determinate number out of every family, though I do not think it proper to recite particularly the names of those families, that I may not take off the mind of my readers from the connection of the historical facts, and make it hard for them to follow the coherence of my narration" (*Ant.* 11.68 [Whiston]). It is tempting to follow his lead. Yet lists appear repeatedly in Ezra-Nehemiah signaling an importance the compiler places on record keeping and the value placed on lists to communicate the construction of the community. Dalit Rom-Shiloni notes that lists occur in important contexts: the arrival of the repatriates, the reinstitution of temple worship, and the covenant renewal. He argues that their inclusion is a rhetorical strategy that reinforces "a sense of community cohesiveness" that restricts the community to the repatriates alone.[1]

This first roster bridges the preparations for departure in Babylon and the events in Yehud that begin chapter 3. The list becomes the first journey to Jerusalem. It provides information about membership and organization of the returnees and introduces the first indication of problems regarding inclusion (2:62). Its forward placement in the narrative conveys the importance the author places on the arrangement of his society. It is therefore worth exploring what this first list indicates about the social fabric of Yehud.

At first glance, the list in Ezra 2 appears to flow smoothly from the narrative in the first chapter. Ezra 1:5 states, "The heads of the families

---

1. Dalit Rom-Shiloni, *Exclusive Inclusivity: Identity Conflicts between the Exiles and the People Who Remained (6th–5th Centuries BCE)*, LHBOTS 543 (New York: Bloomsbury, 2013), 40.

of Judah and Benjamin, and the priests and the Levites—everyone whose spirit God had stirred—got ready to go up and rebuild the house of the Lord in Jerusalem." Ezra 2 follows this lead by enumerating returnees by family and cultic status beginning with eleven named leaders in Ezra 2:2 (probably originally twelve, as in Neh 7). This is succeeded by tallies for the rest of the community organized by the following categories:

Ezra 2:3–19	Laity identified by family
Ezra 2:20–35	Laity identified by town
Ezra 2:36–58	Priests, Levites, and temple personnel
Ezra 2:59–63	Those unable to prove their family or descent
Ezra 2:64	A final total of people: 42,360
Ezra 2:65–67	Slaves and animals
Ezra 2:68–69	Offerings for the temple building fund

Ezra 2:70 concludes the list with "all Israel in their towns."

The list recurs in Neh 7 (albeit there are small changes in numbers, spellings, and names), and many argue for the priority of Nehemiah.[2] Careful examination shows that the list does not catalog a return under Sheshbazzar, the leader in Ezra 1. Sheshbazzar does not appear in this list, and Ezra 2:2 states rather bluntly, "They came with Zerubbabel and Jeshua," who are said to rebuild the temple during the reign of Darius rather than Cyrus. The number of returnees, nearly fifty thousand if we use the total from Ezra 2:64–65, is quite high for a single caravan or even compared with the number of people taken into exile (ten thousand in 2 Kgs 24:14; eight thousand in 2 Kgs 24:16; and forty-six hundred in Jer 52:28–30). In addition, Jacob Myers notes that the scene has shifted—from the people in Babylon getting ready to go up, to the people of the province in their towns.[3] It is likely an authentic list, but given the change in setting and the list's changing organization—from leaders to family groups to town groups to classes of cultic personnel—it is likely constructed at a later date from several different sources such as tax or census lists.[4]

---

2. Clines, *Ezra, Nehemiah, Esther*, 45. Clines notes that both lists are followed by nearly identical narrative sentences, which suggests borrowing from one to the other; and he believes that the Nehemiah time frame is more authentic.

3. Jacob M. Myers, *Ezra, Nehemiah*, AB 14 (Garden City, NY: Doubleday, 1965), 14.

4. Blenkinsopp, *Ezra-Nehemiah*, 83.

4. EZRA 2: DEFINING THE COMMUNITY

Scholars concerned with the list's original form, date, and priority of placement (Ezra 2 or Neh 7?) have offered various opinions about its role here. Myers reasons that the list is placed here "to magnify the first response of the golah to Cyrus's edict."[5] Clines suggests that the author wanted to provide a list of returnees under Sheshbazzar, and this was "the best list of exiles available."[6] Blenkinsopp argues that its purpose is to establish membership in the cult community. This in turn would have confirmed title to land, which he argues was tied to participation in and support of the cult.[7]

On a literary level, Eskenazi ties the list to a central focus of the book—the people. They are given more attention and detail than the construction or dedication of the temple.[8] Hayyim Angel agrees, noting that "the name lists allow the people to occupy the most important role in E–N."[9] He observes that in Ezra 2, "the sheer magnitude of the list gives the impression that a great many Jews returned to the Promised Land. Similarly, the particular attention ascribed to each group indicates the importance of each individual in the return."[10] However, he also notes that because the community could be counted, it demonstrates the historical limits of the return.[11] Lester Grabbe suggests that the emphasis on large numbers of people and goods, and their return to ancestral towns "would confirm the divine will behind the decree of pagan kings."[12] These observations and interpretations prompt a further question about why the author chose a roster to make such claims.

Mark Throntveit argues that the list of Ezra 2 emphasizes in three ways the community's continuity with the past. (1) Twelve leaders suggest a restoration of the twelve tribes or all of Israel. (2) Descent is calculated by preexilic family or town names, and Throntveit comments, "the individuals so listed ... trace their continuity with the past, particularly the past that constituted preexilic Israel."[13] (3) It recalls the occupation of the land

---

5. Myers, *Ezra, Nehemiah*, 15.
6. Clines, *Ezra, Nehemiah, Esther*, 45.
7. Blenkinsopp, *Ezra-Nehemiah*, 83. Whether he argues that this was its original purpose or its purpose in its present context is unclear.
8. Eskenazi, *In an Age of Prose*, 48.
9. Hayyim Angel, "The Literary Significance of the Name Lists in Ezra-Nehemiah," *JBQ* 35.3 (2007): 150.
10. Ibid., 144.
11. Ibid., 150.
12. Grabbe, *Ezra-Nehemiah*, 16.
13. Mark A. Throntveit, *Ezra-Nehemiah*, IBC (Louisville: John Knox, 1992), 19.

in Josh 14–21 with the expression "all to their own towns" (Ezra 2:1). The phrase creates an inclusio in Ezra 2:1 and 70, and the list of towns in Ezra 2:20–35 is similar to those found in Joshua.[14] In Throntveit's evaluation, continuity with the past performs a theological task: the people are reassured that despite changed circumstances they are not cut off from "the ancient promise of land and posterity made to Abraham."[15] However, as Throntveit acknowledges, the list is demarcated by those who can demonstrate their connections to the past and those who cannot (Ezra 2:59–62).[16] This includes members of the community who made the journey to Yehud and so would seem to undermine the register's ability to reassure these people. Although Throntveit is attuned to the list's purpose in delineating membership, ties to the past may not be the primary connection, since some of the clan names are not Judean, such as Pahath-moab and Bigvai (2:6, 14).

In an analysis of the ideological purpose of the list, Jonathan Dyck proposes that it demonstrates a concern with exilic connections rather than historical ones and contends that the list reproduces ideological tensions relating to group identity and internal hierarchy. It presents the community as a whole—all on the list came up to Jerusalem and Judah "all to their own towns" (Ezra 2:1). Yet it also distinguishes among various families, towns, cultic personnel, and "between those within the community who had the right sort of exilic connection and those who did not."[17] This makes the final product ambivalent. He suggests that these competing presentations of the community reflect two competing cultural biases. The list is primarily the product of an "enclavist" culture of an egalitarian minority community with weak authority structures whose primary concern is boundary maintenance. It has within it evidence of a hierarchist culture, more concerned with articulating the hierarchical structure within a well-defined whole. This latter group tolerates more difference but also fears the

---

14. Ibid. The distribution is also done under two leaders, civil and cultic. "These are the inheritances that the Israelites received in the land of Canaan, which the priest Eleazar, and Joshua son of Nun, and the heads of the families of the tribes of the Israelites distributed to them" (Josh 14:1).

15. Throntveit, *Ezra-Nehemiah*, 20.

16. Ibid., 19.

17. Jonathan E. Dyck, "Ezra 2 in Ideological Critical Perspective," in *Rethinking Contexts, Rereading Texts: Contributions from the Social Sciences to Biblical Interpretation*, ed. M. Daniel Carroll R., JSOTSup 299 (Sheffield: Sheffield Academic, 2000), 130, 145.

4. Ezra 2: Defining the Community

disaffection of the lowest groups, so its discourse highlights the value of various segments of society.[18]

4.1. Content of the List in Ezra 2

The list is introduced as a record of exiles from Babylon who returned to Jerusalem and Judah. "Now these are the children of the province that went up out of the captivity, of those which had been carried away, whom Nebuchadnezzar the king of Babylon had carried away unto Babylon, and came again unto Jerusalem and Judah, every one unto his city" (Ezra 2:1 KJV). In a chiastic arrangement similar to the account of 1:7–8 that described the release of temple vessels, 2:1 describes the release of captives. A double reference to captivity and Babylon is surrounded with movement out of captivity and a return to Judah. The people are united by the experience of exile in Babylon undone by a return to Jerusalem. Grabbe pointedly notes that the list is "an inventory of the population solely in terms of returnees; there is no hint that others were already living in the land or that they might have rights."[19]

The list proper begins with names of men that Blenkinsopp suggests were prominent individuals from different periods.[20] None have the titles that are associated with them elsewhere. It begins with Zerubbabel (governor and Davidic descendant) and Jeshua (elsewhere the high priest), followed by Nehemiah and Seraiah.[21] Seraiah is Ezra's father in Ezra 7:1. The list also includes Bigvai, a governor known from the Elephantine letters, and Rehum, a name that occurs in several contexts: a satrapy official in Ezra 4:8–9, one of the heads of the people in Neh 10:26, and a Levite among those repairing the city walls in Neh 3:17.[22] Five of the names occur in the list of signatories to the covenant in Neh 10.[23] The absence of title,

---

18. Ibid., 141–42.
19. Grabbe, *Ezra-Nehemiah*, 13.
20. Blenkinsopp, *Ezra-Nehemiah*, 85. The names are: Zerubbabel, Jeshua, Nehemiah, Seraiah, Reelaiah, Mordecai, Bilshan, Mispar, Bigvai, Rehum, and Baanah (Ezra 2:2).
21. Sereiah is Azariah in Neh 7. Zerubbabel is governor in Ezra 5:2; elsewhere Zerubbabel is "son of Shealtiel" (Ezra 3:2, 8; 5:2; Neh 12:1; Hag 1:1). In 1 Chr 3:16–17, Shealtiel is a descendant of Jehoiakim, the last Judean king.
22. Rehum is *Nehum* in the parallel text in Neh 7:7.
23. Nehemiah (Neh 10:1), Seraiah (10:2), Bigvai (10:16), Rehum (10:25), and Baanah (10:27).

office, or lineage here, at the beginning, places all these men on equal footing. The lack of titles partners with the introduction's inclusive language to underscore the unity of the returnees. The individuals are subsumed into a single component of the larger community. Eskenazi suggests that this list emphasizes the community by shading out individual claims to leadership.[24] Silence regarding titles may also mask contested power within the local hierarchy.

The laity (rather than the priests) are presented first in 2:2–35 and organized into categories grouped first by descent (2:2–19) and then by place names (2:20–35) primarily in the territory of Benjamin. Clines observes that their inclusion in the list distinguishes them from nonexilic "people of the land," while the organization of the list distinguishes them from priests and temple personnel.[25] The family groups range in size from over two thousand members to as few as ninety-eight. Scholars usually identify the basic social unit, *fathers' houses* (בית־אבות) (Ezra 2:59), with the preexilic *clans* (משפחות) and assume continuity with these earlier kinship groups.[26] However, Weinberg notes that *fathers' houses* and *leaders of the fathers* (ראשי אבות) are distinctive postexilic terms, while the singular *father's house* (בית־אב) is characteristic of preexilic texts. He suggests that the exile and return necessitated "consolidation among the exiles and returnees [that] furthered the formation of a new social construction from the pieces of pre-exilic institutions."[27] In Weinberg's schema, these "collectives" were characterized by large numbers, "a complicated inner structure, an obligatory genealogy and inclusion of the name of the *bêt 'ābôt* in the full name of each of its members and a conscious solidarity based on communal ownership of lands."[28] Dyck also perceives a complicated structure for these groups. He suggests that בית־אבות may be a term used for both the larger clan (משפחות), with kinship established through ties to a no longer living ancestor, and the בית־אב, a smaller "ordinary lineage or residential group" with a living head (grandfather or father) within the larger group.[29] He notes that Ezra 2:16, "Sons of Ater, of Hezekiah, ninety-

---

24. Eskenazi, *In an Age of Prose*, 52.
25. Clines, *Ezra, Nehemiah, Esther*, 47.
26. Dyck, "Ezra 2," 136. "Clan" occurs in these books only in Neh 4:13.
27. Weinberg, *Citizen-Temple Community*, 61.
28. Ibid.
29. Dyck, "Ezra 2," 137.

4. EZRA 2: DEFINING THE COMMUNITY

eight" (my translation), provides an example of a smaller group within a larger one and comments,

> The lack of a category name for these smaller groups and the fact that only one such group is mentioned suggests a weak kinship structure in the postexilic community. I say "weak" because the "strength" of a kinship-based society rests in its being based upon the pre-given family unit. Smaller groups obviously existed at the time but they did not have a well-defined status. This would mean that the בית־אבות is some sort of hybrid quasi-kinship social unit.[30]

Two of the largest groups do not have Israelite names. Ezra 2:6 reads "Of Pahath-moab, namely the descendants of Jeshua and Joab, two thousand eight hundred twelve." Although Jeshua and Joab are Israelite personal names, Pahath-moab is not a family name but means "governor of Moab." Clines suggests that the people may have traced their ancestry to a governor of Moab when it was ruled by Judah.[31] Even if this is so, the use of this title rather than a name creates an alternative to genealogical connections and forms a link with Moab—an ethnic group explicitly excluded later in the book (Ezra 9:1; Neh 13:1, 23). The third largest family group in Ezra 2:14 is that of Bigvai (who also appears among the leaders in the return). Bigvai is Persian, and this suggests a family group organized in an exilic or postexilic setting with little time to grow into such large numbers, suggesting that those attached to this family have had to construct a new family identity. The inclusion of these two family groups problematizes assertions that the list establishes a link to preexilic ancestors or that it is establishing membership based on genealogy. If it is indeed trying to assert genealogical ties, then it may also be trying to include members of these groups under the radar.

The first seventeen family groups (Ezra 2:4–19) are not connected to any particular town. Therefore most assume that they all settled in Jerusalem, especially since Jerusalem is not mentioned among the settled towns. However, this is not asserted in the text.[32] Perhaps this lacuna is to avoid narrative dissonance, as only a few family groups appear to be living in Jerusalem when the city walls are built (Neh 3:23–24). If over

---

30. Ibid., 138.
31. Clines, *Ezra, Nehemiah, Esther*, 48.
32. Jerusalem's mention in 2:70 in the NRSV has been imported from 1 Esd 5:46.

thirteen thousand people are already living there, it would be problematic, as Nehemiah seems to find the city in ruins and has to import people to populate the empty capital.[33] However, resolving narrative dissonance does not seem to be a primary concern of the compiler, but unity is a major theme. Leaving Jerusalem out of the list of settled towns may avoid assertions of privilege founded on claims of priority in the capital city.

To complicate the basis of membership even further, the next grouping (2:20–35) is organized by town rather than family name. Nearly all the towns are known from earlier biblical texts, and most are located within a ten-mile radius of Jerusalem. Citizens of some are labeled using the same terminology as those grouped by descent, "the *sons* of [place name]," but others are "the *men* of [place name]." The two forms occur without a discernible pattern, and Ezra 2 and Neh 7 show no agreement on the usage. The use of descent language in reference to geographic locations indicates a close association of family groups with these geographic locations.

Ten of the twenty-two towns have priestly or cultic connections either historically or associated with the groups settling there. Gibbor in Ezra 2:20 (Gibeon in Neh 7), Kiriatharim, Chephirah, and Beeroth in Ezra 2:25 are four Gibeonite towns identified in Josh 9.[34] Their Hivite citizens lived among the Israelites and worked as temple servants (Josh 9:23). Gibeon is the chief high place during the time of David and Solomon prior to the Jerusalem temple (2 Sam 21:6; 1 Kgs 3:4–5; 1 Chr 16:39). Gibeon's status as a site of worship is complicated by its generally negative character as the site of violence in the books of Samuel and by the Chronicler's identification of it as the home of the rejected king, Saul.[35] The inclusion of these four towns in the list may paper over historical differences by sweeping all citizens under the umbrella of "returnees." At the same time, claims based on exilic lineage now undermine those based on long-term residence.

Anathoth (Ezra 2:23) is the home of the prophet Jeremiah, a priestly city associated with Abiathar in 1 Kgs 2:26, and one of the cities of refuge

---

33. The families listed by descent only (2:4–19) total 13,337.

34. There is some debate about whether Gibbor is identical with Gibeon and whether either is a family name or town name. In 1 Chr 9:35, the father of Gibeon lives in Gibeon.

35. Stanley D. Walters, "Saul of Gibeon," *JSOT* 52 (1991): 70. Scenes of violence at Gibeon frame 2 Samuel (2 Sam 2 and 21). In Chronicles, Saul's lineage is tied to the city of Gibeon rather than Gibeah. In addition, his lineage there lacks a direct link to the tribe of Benjamin.

given to the sons of Aaron in 1 Chr 6:60. Bethel (2:28) is an ancient site of worship for northern Israel (1 Kgs 12:29; Amos 4:4; 7:10) and is associated with Jacob (Gen 28:11–17), early tribal worship in Judges (Judg 20:18, 26), and the prophet Samuel (1 Sam 7:16; 10:3). Nebo of Ezra 2:29 is unknown, but scholars speculate it may be Nob, mentioned in Neh 11:32 and famous for the slaughter of priests there by Doeg the Edomite in 1 Sam 22. Harim (חרם) means "consecrated" or "devoted." Elsewhere (1 Chr 24:8; Ezra 10:21, 31; Neh 10:5, 27; 12:15), it is a priestly family name, and it recurs as such in this list at Ezra 2:39. This suggests that the town of Harim is controlled by this priestly family. Netophah (Ezra 2:22) and Azmaveth (Ezra 2:24) are settled by Levites and temple singers, respectively (1 Chr 9:16; Neh 12:28–29). Thus these towns, separated in the list from priests, Levites, and temple personnel, is in fact filled with allusions to historical priests and shrines and literally populated by Levites and temple employees, and all Israel once again includes the Hivites, descendants of Gibeon, the ancient temple servants. The neatly delineated groups begin to mingle in both ideological and concrete terms.

The last town, Senaah, listed in Ezra 2:35, has the largest numbers associated with it (3,630) and is unknown. Speculations about its referent range from it being a site northeast of Jericho (a rather inhospitable setting), a term meaning "the hated ones/despised ones" and reflecting a lower class of people living in Jerusalem, a family name (Neh 3:3 refers to "the sons of Hassenaah" aiding the wall construction), or people living in Jerusalem who did not belong to one of the identified families.[36] Whatever the reality, this map of the settled towns leaves Jerusalem conspicuously empty and the largest group of returnees lacking a defined home.[37]

It may be that the significance of historical connections of priests to these towns is limited and that this is simply a factual summary of sites occupied upon the return. However, the use of place names indicates that not all those included in the return are known by descent but rather by where they settled and that the citizens living in these sites came to be known as organically linked clans. Dyck believes that during the exile the more traditional name form of father-son used to identify family connections was replaced by surnames to identify one clan from another.[38]

---

36. Clines, *Ezra, Nehemiah, Esther*, 52; and Blenkinsopp, *Ezra-Nehemiah*, 87.

37. The NRSV reference to "priests, Levites, and some of the people *living in Jerusalem*" in Ezra 2:70 is taken from 1 Esd 5:46.

38. Dyck, "Ezra 2," 138–39. He notes that this made fluid genealogical relation-

We may then wonder with him why the terminology of place names is employed for postexilic groups? Why not maintain בית־אבות named after an eponym? As Dyck observes, the list now distinguishes "between exilic and non-exilic groups ... yet cover[s] up this distinction at a higher level in claiming that all these groups came from the exile."[39]

Priests, Levites, and various temple servants round out the list of returnees. Ezra 2:36–39 lists 4,280 priests from four families, beginning with the sons of Jedaiah of the house of Jeshua (the high priest) and followed by the families of Immer, Pashhur, and Harim. Immer is also the name of a Jewish settlement in Babylon (Ezra 2:59). The Pashhur group is the largest (1,247); its eponym is Egyptian and means "son of Horus."[40] Elsewhere Pashhur is counted as a descendant of Immer (Jer 20:1; 1 Chr 9:12); but in the list of priestly courses in 1 Chr 24, Pashhur is absent, leading Blenkinsopp to suggest that these two families separated during the exile.[41] In Ezra 10, all four families have members who married foreign women and sign a pledge to send them away. Most commentators note the large number of priests with respect to the laity—one out of seventeen. Blenkinsopp finds this historically plausible, and Clines notes that it fits with the primary objective of the return.[42]

In contrast, only seventy-four Levites from three eponyms are counted (Ezra 2:40). Ezra will return with only thirty-eight Levites, even though he delays his return as he searches for more (Ezra 8:15–19). Perhaps the division between priests and Levites grew during the exile with the secondary status giving the Levites little incentive to return even with a rebuilt temple and renewed cult.[43] This is supported by the claim in Neh 13:10 that portions had not been given the Levites and they had returned to their fields. The Levitical family names are confusing and probably corrupt. (The same list in 1 Esdras drops Hodaviah and adds two others, while the Levites in

---

ships into more rigid kinship groups and explains the huge numbers associated with some as surnames cannot be divided.

39. Ibid., 140.

40. Blenkinsopp, *Ezra-Nehemiah*, 88. On an unrelated note, it is interesting that Eli's sons in 1 Samuel also have Egyptian names and are shown to be unworthy of their priestly positions.

41. Ibid. In Jer 20, Pashhur son of Immer is the priest who struck the prophet and put him in stocks. In Ezra-Nehemiah they are always two distinct families.

42. Clines, *Ezra, Nehemiah, Esther*, 88.

43. Ibid.

Ezra 3:9 are different yet.)⁴⁴ Temple singers and gatekeepers are distinct from the Levites in this list, yet in other late texts they are included (e.g., 1 Chr 9:33; 15:16). Thus once again we have a grouping that on first appearance seems to be a clearly defined class of returnees, yet close inspection reveals uncertainty about family names, and other texts create ambiguity over what constitutes the Levites.⁴⁵ In addition, this class of temple personnel, second only to the priests, is in short supply, hinting at disagreement over the importance of the project at hand, conflict over the Levitical role among temple personnel, or even a historical abandonment of their position within the temple hierarchy in the absence of the temple.

In this roster, aside from their separate listing, the Levites are given no special attention, and no concern is expressed over their small numbers. In the remainder of Ezra 1–6, they play a role only in the two texts that depict worship and maintenance of the cult: 3:8–12 and 6:16–20. In 3:1–7, only Zerubbabel, the priests, and their families construct the altar, and the conflict in chapters 4 and 5 is handled by the elders. For the author of these six chapters, Levites are important for the work of the temple but play no leadership role in political or communal decisions. This contrasts with their key role in teaching Torah elsewhere in these books.

Musicians (128) and gatekeepers (139) are listed next. Both groups are Levitical temple personnel in Chronicles. They are followed by two classes of temple servants: "the Nethinim" (הנתינים, lit. "the given"; often translated as "temple servants") in Ezra 2:43–54 and "Solomon's servants" (עבדי שלמה) in Ezra 2:55–57. Ezra 8:20 states that the Nethinim were given by David to serve the Levites. However, there is no specific account of this, and the separation here into a separate class of servants is somewhat at odds with the term's usage in Ezra 8:17–20 and Num 8:16–19.⁴⁶ In

---

44. The Levites in Ezra 2:40 are the descendants of Jeshua, Kadmiel, and Hodaviah. In Ezra 3:9, the only Levites mentioned are sons of Henadad.

45. In 1 Chr 15:17–22 and 2 Chr 34:12–13, the Levites carry out the tasks assigned to temple musicians and servants. "The people did the work faithfully. Over them were appointed the Levites Jahath and Obadiah, of the sons of Merari, along with Zechariah and Meshullam, of the sons of the Kohathites, to have oversight. Other Levites, all skillful with instruments of music, were over the burden bearers and directed all who did work in every kind of service; and some of the Levites were scribes, and officials, and gatekeepers" (2 Chr 34:12–13).

46. In the books of Samuel and 1 Kings, the appointment of Levites by David is never mentioned. In 1 Chr 15:2, David appoints Levites to carry the ark, and Levites of a "second order" are appointed to make music and be gatekeepers (15:22–23), but

Ezra 8:17, Iddo, the leader of Casiphia, and his colleagues are "the Nethinims" (KJV). In Numbers, all the Levites are "given" to serve the priests. Scholars note two important characteristics of the Ezra 2 list of Nethinim: there are numerous foreign names that include Arab, Ishmaelite, Egyptian, Edomite, and Aramaic ethnicities. In addition, many other names appear to be nicknames appropriate to slaves: for example, Speedy, White, Crooked, Taciturn, and Faithful. Their total is bundled with that of Solomon's servants. These details indicate a low social status for the Nethinim, although Blenkinsopp argues that they were not slaves as some of them signed the pledge to observe the law in Neh 10:28.[47]

The list of returnees continues in Ezra 2:59–60 with 652 descendants from the families of Delaiah, Tobiah, and Nekoda, originating from five sites in Babylon. These people "could not prove, their families [בית־אבות] or their descent [זרע, lit. 'seed'], whether they belonged to Israel" (2:59). This statement suggests a primary purpose of the list is to define "who and who was not a true member of Israel."[48] Clines points out that no action is reported against the three families and that even the priests unable to find their names in the records (2:61–62) are excluded only from participation in the priesthood until the issue could be resolved. He comments further, "Even under the regime of Ezra only those whose ancestry could be proved to be non-Jewish were expelled (10:16f)."[49] However, the text is careful to differentiate these families from those whose genealogy and thus membership is not contested. Dyck, like most scholars, believes that the families are laity, but their kinship groups are apparently not socially significant, and asks, "why was it so important to have a particular type of kinship connection when, according to the main criterion (being a returnee), one was considered to be an acceptable member of the assembly (as opposed to the slaves and the 'remainees')?"[50] Dyck argues the בית־אבות was not

---

no mention is made of "temple servants." 1 Chr 9:2 lists the first to return to Judah and Jerusalem after the exile and distinguishes "the Nethinim" (JPSV) from priests and Levites. Neh 10:28 and 11:21 also refer to these servants as a distinct class.

47. Blenkinsopp, *Ezra-Nehemiah*, 29, 90.

48. Clines, *Ezra, Nehemiah, Esther*, 57.

49. Ibid., 58. Edelman (*Origins*, 36) concurs with this position: "There would not have been a pressing reason to single out lay families whose historic affiliation with Yehud was not demonstrable, and on the assumption that vv. 61–62 deal with such families, no consequences are given for their lack of clear status."

50. Dyck, "Ezra 2," 140.

only for identity maintenance (who is true Israel) but also a mechanism for social discrimination.

The caveat that these few families on this list could not prove their descent may suggest that they are excluded from the heads of the families who elsewhere are prominent in the leadership of the community.[51] The list indicates a problem only with descent, but evidence elsewhere suggests other causes. *Nekoda* means "sheep raiser" and, as Edelman points out, may be the nickname for a temple servant (Neh 7:50). This indicates that Nekoda's descendants may lack social standing. The other two families in Ezra 2:60 bear names that relate to Nehemiah's traditional enemies. Tobiah appears as an adversary in Neh 2:10–19, 4:7, 6:1–19, and 13:4–8; but the name also appears in Zech 6:10 as a recently arrived exile from whom the prophet was to collect money.[52] Although Delaiah occurs in Chronicles (as a descendant of Zerubbabel or a priest), Delaiah is also known as a son of Sanballat.[53] Edelman argues that Ezra 2:61–62 may "reflect attempts to exclude both of these influential families from claiming priestly prerogatives within Yehud."[54] It is not obvious that priestly roles are in sight since that is treated separately in Ezra 2:61–63. Yet genealogical evidence is not easily contested, and the questionable lineage here justifies limited participation in the community. The list becomes a weapon in the symbolic struggle over the definition of the community. It defines the community by foregrounding and codifying distinctive criteria in response to competing practices. Its rationalization for the community's social organization gains traction because it privileges the political interests of the large number of those granted the greatest participation.[55] Turning to lineage to justify social standing also avoids more easily countered social, economic, or political reasons.

---

51. Ibid., 143–44. Dyck provides evidence for the prominent role of the heads of the families and argues for a growing hierarchical structure represented in the exclusion of these family groups.

52. "Collect silver and gold from the exiles—from Heldai, Tobijah, and Jedaiah—who have arrived from Babylon" (Zech 6:10a).

53. In 1 Chr 3:24, Delaiah is a descendant of Zerubbabel; in 1 Chr 24:18, he is a priest.

54. Edelman (*Origins*, 37) comments that Delaiah "was the name of one of the two sons of Sanballat, governor of Samerina, who was asked c. 410 BCE to become a patron of the temple to Yau in Elephantine and secure permission for its rebuilding after its destruction by the priests of Khnum."

55. Bourdieu, "Legitimation and Structured Interests," 124.

The final grouping is descendants of three priestly families who could not find their names in the records (Ezra 2:61–63). An explanatory note is included that Barzillai had married a daughter of the Gileadite, Barzillai, and taken that name. Several observations can be made here. First, their status as descendants of priests is not revoked, but their ability to perform higher priestly functions is held in limbo. Grabbe contends that their matrilineal descent disqualified those descendants because the priesthood was derived through the male line.[56] Second, the *governor* decides how to handle the issue until "there should be a priest to consult Urim and Thummin" (2:63).[57] The secular (and unnamed) governor makes the decision regarding priestly duties rather than leaders among the priests. Furthermore, his order to await a priest is odd given that the record states they arrived with over four thousand priests. However, in the narrative, the priests who arrive are yet to be purified and ordained by the community prior to being able to carry out official functions such as consulting Urim and Thummin. Later, descendants of Hakkoz appear as "a fully accepted sacerdotal family in other texts (cf. Ezra 8:33; Neh 3:4, 21; 12:3; 1 Macc 8:17)."[58]

The list of those "who went up" concludes with 7,337 male and female slaves, 200 male and female singers, as well as horses, mules, camels, and donkeys (all beasts of burden—no sheep or goats or oxen are included; Ezra 2:65–67). The slaves are not included in the 42,360 total that summarized the community in verse 64. They are possessions and represent sizable wealth—more than one might expect for the descendants of exiles. The focus on wealth continues with a description of a freewill offering for "the house of God, to erect it on its site," given by the heads of families (Ezra 2:68–69). The freewill offering lists gold, silver, and priestly robes—items shared with the same list in Neh 7:70–72. However, here only heads of families make offerings, while in Nehemiah contributions by the governor are singled out, and additional gifts are given by "the rest of the people" (Neh 7:70–72). Just as the list opens with untitled leaders, so the gift giving is done by nameless heads of the families—acting on behalf of the entire community. Sources of political and economic power are submerged in deference to an image of the community unified in its religious

---

56. Grabbe, *Ezra-Nehemiah*, 15.

57. This particular term for governor occurs elsewhere only with regard to Nehemiah in Neh 8:9 and 10:1.

58. Grabbe, *Ezra-Nehemiah*, 15.

4. EZRA 2: DEFINING THE COMMUNITY

commitments—a community whose leadership is linked only to family heads and the priesthood.

4.2. List as a Means of Definition

4.2.1. Membership and Ethnic Definition

This list may have originally served a more mundane task of recording property records or tax rolls, but, as Kenton Sparks observes, its new role is to authenticate the Jewish identity of members. "In these documents the restored community was none other than the ethnic Israelites that returned from Babylon."[59] Building blocks of ethnicity are virtually the same over time. (These include references to the body [genes, flesh, blood, etc.], language, shared history and origins, religion and nationality [associated with a territory].) They are employed "according to historical and political circumstance" in a wide variety of ways.[60] Manning Nash states,

> Which building blocks are invoked to construct a category and what boundary forged to set the category off from others is historically specific, structurally constrained by the economic and political power differentials among the groups, and conditioned by the cultural images of the past and future and the strategies the groups try to enact in view of their divergent agendas.[61]

Ethnic boundaries are constructed from the core elements of kinship, commensality (eating together), and a common cult. Nash goes on to argue that "sometimes the members' basic symbols of ethnicity are not visible, graspable, or available in social interaction, and hence other surface features stand for the index features."[62] To operate as indices of ethnicity, these secondary markers must be related in determinate ways to the basic elements of blood, substance, or cult.

---

59. Kenton L. Sparks, *Ethnicity and Identity in Ancient Israel: Prolegomena to the Study of Ethnic Sentiments and Their Expression in the Hebrew Bible* (Winona Lake, IN: Eisenbrauns, 1998), 296.
60. Nash, *Cauldron of Ethnicity*, 5.
61. Ibid.
62. Ibid., 11.

How, then, does this list constitute ethnic identity? The most significant distinction in this list is the line between returnee and remainee.[63] The people encompassed within "the sons of the golah" include even those identified by local town names or those whose genealogy cannot be determined. The list also points to a doxic belief in kinship as a criterion for determining inclusion. This is discernible when some members are not able to demonstrate a genealogical link to their בית־אבות (lit. "fathers' house"; NRSV "families"), even though the primary distinction, their exilic origin, is well established (2:59). For others, local town names provide the same categorizing function as the בית־אבות. They are genealogically connected to the exiles even when no exilic connection is established except the roster's initial claim: "These were the people of the province who came from those captive exiles" (2:1).[64] Citizens of these towns are incorporated into the founding members of the temple community. Thus "the exiles" (2:1) appears to be a conceptual category rather than one that is easily determined either historically or genealogically.

The kinship language tightly woven into this list of exiles suggests that exilic status is a secondary pointer for group difference. It contributes to indicators of ethnicity but cannot do so alone. Therefore, kinship, the most common and pervasive boundary marker, is brought into service to support this newer category with which it is actually in tension. Bourdieu states that agents not only compete over a given field, but they compete over how the field is defined or constructed. The inconsistency in this text regarding exilic/kinship/class categories may indicate a contested construction of ethnic identity. Ezra 3 follows this chapter with descriptions of the community sharing in worship around an altar rebuilt by the returnees. This would add a second common ethnic boundary, a common cult, to the kinship ties articulated in the list. In addition, the entire account of Ezra 1–6 presents the exilic return as a shared history or origin, another common ethnic marker. Nash comments that shared history "gives the sense of shared struggles, shared fate, common purpose, and [implies] that personal and group fate are one and the same thing with personal fate being itself dependent on group survival."[65] The account stitches together

---

63. Dyck, "Ezra 2," 141.

64. Sparks, *Ethnicity and Identity*, 21. Sparks describes the construction or extension of genealogies for political purposes in Tiv society.

65. Nash, *Cauldron of Ethnicity*, 5.

exilic status with Judean ethnicity as necessary for membership even as it incorporates many for whom such a status is likely fictitious.

Two historical factors may have contributed to the interest in ethnic boundaries: increasing competition for economic resources and exilic experience as a minority group. Ian Stern describes the early conditions in Persian-period Levant as "post-collapse," which he defines as "a situation in which an existing socio-political entity experiences a fast and significant deterioration due to either internal, external or [a] combination of reasons."[66] Under these conditions the territory has lost most of its urban populations, and "this sparsely populated region could create social conditions that would be conducive for co-operation rather than competition over its limited resources, paving the way for low ethnic boundary maintenance."[67] He notes that only in the second half of the fifth century does archaeology indicate a change that would coincide with marked boundaries. This includes the revival of the shekel symbol on weights and the rosette, archaic Hebrew script, and the introduction of Yehud stamps and coins. Combined with evidence from the biblical text (the banishment of foreign wives, the imposition of Sabbath observance, and statements of exclusion), the behavior "reflects high ethnic boundary maintenance" that Stern believes was predicated on political tensions with Samaria.[68] The imposed boundaries would ensure security and justify competition over resources. Opposition to integration was fueled by the ideology of the returnees, whose exilic life as a minority prompted attention to boundary maintenance and who found the low boundary maintenance of the region a threat to their group identity.[69]

---

66. Ian Stern, "The Population of Persian-Period Idumea according to the Ostraca: A Study of Ethnic Boundaries and Ethnogenesis," in *A Time of Change: Judah and Its Neighbours in the Persian and Early Hellenistic Periods*, ed. Yigal Levin, LSTS 65 (New York: T&T Clark, 2007), 214.

67. Ibid., 215.

68. Ibid., 229–32. Based on the total absence of coinage from the opposite province found in the territory of the other, he suggests that by the late Persian period there were virtually no economic ties between them (232).

69. Ibid., 232.

4.2.2. Cultural Capital and Class Standing

Bourdieu's work provides another motive for this exilic focus. He demonstrates a close tie between the acquisition of cultural capital and the social and class standing of one's family.[70] Membership in a family with higher capital allows an earlier age at which members have access to that capital and therefore a longer time frame in which to accumulate it.[71] This gives them an advantage over those who lack that standing in the competition over the accumulation of resources. The exiles may have acquired in their upbringing certain cultural capital that provided this advantage over those raised in the local Judean hills. Bourdieu observes that efforts by disadvantaged groups to close the gap with social groups above them are met "by the efforts of better-placed groups to maintain the scarcity and distinctiveness of their assets."[72] In this case the value of membership in the community is maintained by limiting inclusion to the title of exile. Perhaps this explains why exilic membership is so prized in a text written at least a century after the events it recounts. It betrays a struggle between descendants of exiles who benefit from perpetuating the (previously) established order and those who wish to close the social gap.

The author's overarching context of titleless lay leadership presents a nonhierarchical community of exilic returnees. Groups are differentiated by town or *bet avot*. Dyck argues that the categorization of groups within

---

70. Bourdieu ("Forms of Capital," 243) states, "The notion of cultural capital initially presented itself to me, in the course of research, as a theoretical hypothesis which made it possible to explain the unequal scholastic achievement of children originating from the different social classes by relating academic success, i.e., the specific profits which children from the different classes and class fractions can obtain in the academic market, to the distribution of cultural capital between the classes and class fractions. This starting point implies a break with the presuppositions inherent both in the commonsense view, which sees academic success or failure as an effect of natural aptitudes, and in human capital theories."

71. Ibid., 246. He observed that the ability of an agent to appropriate "the resources objectively available, and hence the profits they produce, is mediated by the relationship of … competition between himself and the other possessors of capital competing for the same goods." The precondition for the fast, easy accumulation of capital "starts at the outset … only for the offspring of families endowed with strong cultural capital." He notes this is a well-hidden form of hereditary capital (as opposed to land, money, or titles).

72. Bourdieu, *Distinction*, 161.

4. EZRA 2: DEFINING THE COMMUNITY

the roster is for social and political purposes.[73] However, the list does not relegate one or the other to a lesser role based on those differences—even those who could not prove their family connections. This coincides with the enclavist ideology identified by Dyck. It is in the area of priestly functions that rank and hierarchy matter. Proven (written) genealogy is enlisted to limit access to sacerdotal roles. Priests who could not find their "writing" (names) in the genealogical records are excluded from the performance of certain duties, and personnel are separated by rank, allocating more or less symbolic capital for discrete positions. Since power relations are reproduced in one's view of the social world, the author may perceive these differences as personally significant. Including such details in this list suggests further benefit if it induces the community to also recognize and value such distinctions.

The list's definition of community boundaries and delineation of the internal structure ought to be understood in its context as part of a religious document. Even without its wider context, the religious interests present in the text are still obvious, as it carefully records thousands of priests and over seven hundred other temple personnel plus towns associated with priests and temple servants and concludes with itemized donations for the temple. When combined with the expressed purpose of returning to Jerusalem to rebuild the temple, these details indicate that the author is intentionally constructing the return as a religious act.

Bourdieu notes that the religious field is not absolutely independent of political influence, and he argues that religious practices contribute to a conservative vision of the world. They render what is relative as absolute and legitimate the arbitrary nature of domination.[74] This literary production legitimates an arbitrary means of determining membership or selecting priests. The accident of birth is treated as determinative for membership. The existence of this list now disqualifies those who may desire membership in Israel on the basis of other criteria. Moreover, the careful attention to genealogical records for priests limits religious specialists, eliminating access to that profession by other means. Both of these categories (membership and priestly office) create opportunities for domination over those lacking these particular qualifications.

---

73. Dyck, "Ezra 2," 138. Dyck compares Scottish clan names in this regard. He suggests that references elsewhere in these books to "the heads of the fathers" (ראשי אבות) exercising leadership also indicates this growing hierarchy.

74. Dianteill, "Pierre Bourdieu," 537.

Such classification struggles always accompany class struggle. If the community, at the time of writing, lacked strong authority structures, then, as Dyck points out, it had "to resort to moral persuasion as its only means of social control."[75] The list itself may be an act of persuasion. It codifies the line between the exiles and the nonexiled and invites the readers to accept the particular differentiation within the community represented in the roster. The list of local towns (nearly all in the area of Benjamin) is now included as territory belonging to the exiles based on a list that is now presented as historically connected to the first arrival of exiles. The incorporation of these Benjaminite towns validates Judean-Jerusalemite hegemony over this territory in the face of local opposition.[76]

Criteria to handle contested membership in Israel or the priesthood are placed in this written record associated with the very first returnees. The use of genealogical records to define the community is not defended, which suggests generalized acceptance of such registers for these purposes. This catalog of members provided a potent weapon in efforts to legitimize specific strategies that limit inclusion and control hierarchy within the community.

4.2.3. Lists of Priestly Robes and Distinction

In Ezra 2:69, priestly garments are recorded among the list of gifts. Priestly robes could be treated as standard gifts to include in an inventory for temple contributions. However, Bourdieu's theory of distinction within the social space suggests that lower-class workers (e.g., fieldworkers) give priority to function over form. Clothes are valued for their functional use, and people make little distinction between top clothes (visible ones) and underclothes. The middle class, however, demonstrate a degree of anxiety about external appearance—at least outside and at work. He comments, "The interest the different classes have in self-presentation, the attention they devote to it, their awareness of the profits it gives and the investment of time, effort, sacrifice and care which they actually put into it are proportionate to the chances of material or symbolic profit they can reasonably expect from it."[77]

---

75. Dyck, "Ezra 2," 141.

76. For a fuller treatment of Benjaminite traditions, see Blenkinsopp, "Benjamin Traditions."

77. Bourdieu, *Distinction*, 202.

The attention to appropriate priestly clothing indicates that it is a valuable marker of social standing. Gifts are given for the temple but also to dress the priests. Temple priests throughout the empire benefit from such ornate dress. Proper tunics provide a substantial increase in symbolic profit for the priest, the temple, and the community that supports them. The clothing also separates the priests from more functionally dressed people and thereby increases their status in relation to ordinary souls. The clothing creates symbolic profit on local and national levels. The right clothing is of concern when physical appearance is valued in the performance of a person's job. Therefore, interest in this detail suggests that the author may possibly be a priest, and his social standing is linked to the symbolic benefit of his attire.

In Nehemiah, both the governor and "some of the people" provide priestly garments (Neh 7:70–72). Yet there the governor's gift of 530 priestly robes overshadows the 67 robes given by others, even though the people's monetary gift is greater. The generous provision by the governor suggests that he too shares an awareness of symbolic profit from properly attired priests. The gift coincides with an increase in symbolic profit for the giver and underscores priestly dependence on the governor's benefaction. In the note in Ezra 2, no specific contributor is mentioned, and thus the recipients of this priestly raiment are free of obligation to an individual. Yet the gift of the robes acts as a sign of distinction for the priests and, by extension, for the community that provided them.

5
Ezra 3: Ritual and Identity

> Because any language that can command attention is an "authorized language," invested with the authority of a group, the things it designates are not simply expressed but also authorized and legitimated.
> —Pierre Bourdieu

Ezra 3 introduces ritual to the ongoing narrative of the exiles' return and reconstruction of the temple. The chapter follows immediately upon the list of first returnees, but the time and characters have all changed. Zerubbabel now leads the community in place of Sheshbazzar, and the section concludes with a reference to the time of Darius. The text bridges a lengthy lacuna in time as the rituals move the narrative through a threshold in time and space.[1] As the chapter commences, the exiles have arrived but taken no corporate action in Judah and nothing yet exists in Jerusalem. At the conclusion, religious life, characterized by particular practices and belonging to a certain people, has been reinstated in Jerusalem

The chapter recounts the sequential construction of the temple's altar and foundation. In 3:1–7, in the seventh month of the first year, the altar is set up "on its foundation," followed by the resumption of sacrifices and the celebration of the Festival of Booths. In 3:8–13, in the second month of the second year, materials are collected, the temple foundation is laid, and a celebration led by priests and Levites marks its completion. Progress remains incomplete as hostilities with neighboring peoples immediately ensue (4:1–5). Ezra 4:5 asserts that the hostilities were ongoing: "they

---

1. The first year of Cyrus was 539 BCE, and the first year of Darius 522 BCE. Ezra 3:1 mentions the seventh month without context other than the first year of Cyrus mentioned in ch. 1. Ezra 3:8 takes place in the second year after their arrival. Other than the events in this chapter, the text is silent on most of the nineteen-year period from Cyrus to Darius.

bribed officials to frustrate their plan throughout the reign of King Cyrus of Persia and until the reign of King Darius of Persia." The text then turns its attention to the escalating conflict, and the narrative shifts into Aramaic in 4:8. Therefore I will treat 3:1 through 4:5 as one unit.

Complicating historical reconstructions is the fact that the duplicated list of returnees in Ezra 2 and Neh 7 is followed by a nearly identical bridge that sets the time frame for two different community religious activities: "When the seventh month came, and the Israelites were in the towns, the people gathered together" (Ezra 3:1; Neh 8:1). The texts differ on the setting: "in Jerusalem" in Ezra and "before the Water Gate" in Nehemiah. Blenkinsopp argues that the list makes more sense in Ezra when connected to the account of donations that end chapter 1.[2] However, Clines and Williamson argue that the list in Ezra is copied from Nehemiah. Clines notes that the reference to the seventh month is associated with a specific year in Nehemiah but stands in isolation in Ezra.[3] Williamson suggests that this textual duplication, combined with the stylized nature of Ezra 3 (particularly its allusions to the construction of the First Temple), means that efforts to identify the seventh month more specifically should not be sought too closely. He points to the importance of the seventh month as the sacred month par excellence, since it includes several of the most important festivals.[4] This provides a theological motivation for this particular time frame for the restoration of worship.

The dating schema and the persons involved in the project also create historical problems (especially when placed in conversation with evidence from Haggai and Zechariah) and are not easily resolved.[5] They are perhaps most obvious in Ezra 3:8: "In the second year after their arrival at the house of God at Jerusalem, in the second month, Zerubbabel son of Shealtiel and Jeshua son of Jozadak made a beginning." In the logic of the narrative, "in the second year" at first appears to be the arrival in

---

2. Blenkinsopp, *Ezra-Nehemiah*, 44.

3. Clines, *Ezra, Nehemiah, Esther*, 45; Williamson, *Ezra, Nehemiah*, 29.

4. Williamson, *Ezra, Nehemiah*, 45. In particular it includes the Day of Atonement as well as the Festival of Booths. For references to the Festival of Booths, see Exod 23:16; 34:22; Lev 23:34–43; Num 29:12–38; Deut 16:13–17; 31:9–13.

5. Ibid., 43. There is no mention of Sheshbazzar in this chapter, although its time referent seems to suggest that the altar construction happened shortly after his arrival in Jerusalem. Instead, Zerubbabel and Jeshua lead the construction, and they continue to lead efforts under Darius. They are the only ones credited with construction in Haggai and Zechariah.

5. EZRA 3: RITUAL AND IDENTITY

Jerusalem under Cyrus, but Sheshbazzar is absent and the work is led instead by Zerubbabel. Williamson surveys two common approaches to handle these historical issues. The first involves attributing the rebuilding to Zerubbabel but positing that he worked under the auspices of Sheshbazzar and so reconciling it with Ezra 5:16, where Sheshbazzar is credited with the foundation: "Then this Sheshbazzar came and laid the foundations of the house of God in Jerusalem; and from that time until now it has been under construction, and it is not yet finished." This explanation rests on the view that there was a twenty-year gap in the project with little evidence of the first effort by the time of Haggai or Zechariah. The second option takes seriously links with Haggai and Zechariah that refer only to Zerubbabel and Jeshua and ascribes all the events to 520 BCE.[6] Both options assume significant historical veracity in the text.[7]

Although Williamson treats details of the account as historical, he suggests that the author has "juxtaposed events from the reigns of both Cyrus and Darius" and offers a theological interpretation of the events based on available sources. He observes: "it is both a mistake of method, and a misunderstanding of the writer's intention, to use this section primarily for the purpose of historical reconstruction."[8] Edelman rejects these early time frames. Working with genealogies and discarding dates from Haggai and Zechariah, she places events much later, under the reign of Artaxerxes I (465–424 BCE).[9] If Williamson or Edelman is correct, mining Ezra for historical details associated with Sheshbazzar or Zerubbabel is a dubious effort. This is especially true since these chapters were composed many decades after the time of Darius. It may be more fruitful to explore what social interests this particular reconstruction of history would address.

---

6. Williamson, *Ezra, Nehemiah*, 43. An example of the first approach can be found in Myers, *Ezra, Nehemiah*, 28. Evidence for Zerubbabel only can be found in Zech 4:9, "Zerubbabel's hands have founded this House and Zerubbabel's hands shall complete it" (NJPS). See also Hag 1:4 and Zech 1:16.

7. Othniel Margalith ("The Political Background of Zerubbabel's Mission and the Samaritan Schism," *VT* 41 [1991]: 320) takes seriously the historical claims in Ezra also and contends that the political situation under Darius explains some of the conflict with adversaries in Ezra 3.

8. Williamson, *Ezra, Nehemiah*, 45.

9. Edelman, *Origins*, 151.

5.1. Literary Themes

5.1.1. Continuity with the Past

Continuity with the past is a recurring theme as each new development is associated with law, tradition, or written texts. In the ancient world, initial temple construction was often tied to an auspicious time. For the author of Ezra, it begins in the seventh month.[10] In addition to importance in the liturgical calendar, the seventh month creates a connection with Solomon's initiation of worship at the First Temple. In 1 Kgs 8, the priests bring the ark into the temple in the seventh month. Moreover, Mark Throntveit notes that the Festival of Booths celebrated during this month commemorates deliverance from Egypt and suggests that the returnees would have recognized parallels to their own experience.[11] However, in Ezra 3, other themes are developed in lieu of this connection with deliverance.

Written texts are also engaged to emphasize continuity. Ezra 3:2 states that the construction of the altar and the offerings were done "as prescribed in the law of Moses the man of God." Blenkinsopp suggests that the "law" refers to Deut 27:6–7, which describes Moses commanding the people to construct an altar immediately upon entering the land.[12] In Ezra 3:4, they keep the Festival of Booths "as prescribed, and offered the daily burnt offerings by number according to the ordinance, as required for each day." Once the temple foundations are laid, the priests lead praise "according to the directions of King David of Israel" (3:10). Williamson states that continuity in this chapter is expressed as "restoration of worship on the site of the first temple, reintroducing the very same forms and expressions that had been previously ordained by Moses and David."[13]

---

10. This reference to the same month is repeated in Neh 7:73, making its origin a matter of debate. In both, it sets a time frame for a significant community religious activity. In Nehemiah the community gathers for the reading of Torah.

11. Throntveit, *Ezra-Nehemiah*, 23.

12. Blenkinsopp, *Ezra-Nehemiah*, 97. "So when you have crossed over the Jordan, you shall set up these stones, about which I am commanding you today, on Mount Ebal, and you shall cover them with plaster. And you shall build an altar there to the Lord your God, an altar of stones on which you have not used an iron tool. You must build the altar of the Lord your God of unhewn stones. Then offer up burnt offerings on it to the Lord your God, make sacrifices of well-being, and eat them there, rejoicing before the Lord your God" (Deut 27:4–7).

13. Williamson, *Ezra, Nehemiah*, 51.

Thematic connections with the past are achieved in this text at the expense of any local worship practice that continued during the exile. Myers, Williamson, and Lipschits, among others, believe it likely that sacrifices of some sort continued during the exilic period.[14] Lipschits suggests that rituals would have been individual and spontaneous rather than conducted in any official manner. Myers believes that any ongoing worship would have required an altar but argues, "the Chronicler … would not have regarded such an altar as legitimate because it was neither in the right place nor constructed by the right people, the golah."[15] Williamson seems to concur when he states, "for the author continuity of religious tradition ran through the community of exile alone … thus making fresh dedication indispensable."[16] These assessments indicate that the author either shares a similar sense of boundaries with his readers or is perhaps concerned to justify those boundaries. Each step toward establishing continuity creates a divide between those who were descendants of exiles and those who were not, making continuity significant not only theologically but relationally.

5.1.2. Unity and Boundaries

Continuity with past worship is related to a second major thematic interest in this chapter—the unity of the community. Although references to Zerubbabel and Jeshua introduce both sections (Ezra 3:2, 8), individuals are marginalized in much of the rest of the text. People do not speak or act independently. Collective terminology introduces the narrative: "Israelites" had settled in their towns, and "the people" gather in Jerusalem (3:1). In 3:3–7, only generic plural subject pronouns are employed when recounting the construction of the altar and resumption of worship. The list of festivals and sacrifices reinstated by the community concludes with "*all* who made a freewill offering," underscoring the participation by the general population. As work commences in the second year (3:8–13), leaders are identified and Levites appointed; but once the celebration ensues, attention returns to the people in general. Companies of Levites and priests play leading roles, but no individuals are named. Eskenazi notes

---

14. Lipschits, *Fall and Rise of Jerusalem*, 116.
15. Myers, *Ezra, Nehemiah*, 27.
16. Williamson, *Ezra, Nehemiah*, 46.

that the people as a whole are highlighted particularly in 3:12–13, where "the people" are mentioned three separate times.[17]

Worship provides the primary means of demonstrating unity. Ezra 3:4–6 highlights the sacrificial calendar, beginning with the all-important symbolic seventh month and continuing with a rehearsal of sacrifices from the daily to the annual festivals. The presentation implies that worship was nonexistent prior to the construction of this altar. Now sacrifices are offered with the regularity of a fully functioning cult. In the second half of the chapter, once the proper personnel are appointed, attention turns to the noise of worship. Here the sound of trumpets, cymbals, and the entire congregation singing, shouting, and weeping rise in a cacophony heard from a great distance. The single coherent voice is the responsive praise by priests and Levites (or by everyone?) of the psalm fragment, praising God for his steadfast love, which is then followed by a shout of praise by the people. Cultic zeal, manifest in an orderly and thorough reinstatement of sacrifices, is celebrated in a wild chorus of noise. The specification of sacrifices and the appointment of priests and Levites conform to prescriptions in the Torah, and descriptions of worship echo those of Chronicles.[18] The combination of history and ritual legitimates worship *in* the text as well as the worship of the community *reading* the text. The worship of the reading audience, most likely enlisted as a basis for the account of worship in Ezra, is portrayed as contiguous with the past, and their ongoing practice is consecrated by the rituals of the first returnees.

This portrayal of the entire community reinstituting past worship practices invites the reader to recognize these practices and this social structure as legitimate.[19] Throntveit suggests that the description proclaims that the solidarity of the community rests on the worship of God.[20] However, it is not just any worship held out as unifying but a very particular worship. This form of worship muscles its way into the reader's view as an image of

---

17. Eskenazi, *In an Age of Prose*, 51 and n. 31.

18. For a helpful comparison of the various descriptions of worship in Ezra-Nehemiah, see Leslie C. Allen, "'For He Is Good...': Worship in Ezra-Nehemiah," in *Worship and the Hebrew Bible: Essays in Honour of John T. Willis*, ed. M. Patrick Graham, Rick R. Marrs, and Steven L. McKenzie, JSOTSup 284 (Sheffield: Sheffield Academic, 1999), 15–34.

19. This description of worship suggests to Williamson (*Ezra, Nehemiah*, 51) that it was an expression of "the heart's affections ... less as a duty than as a delight."

20. Throntveit, *Ezra-Nehemiah*, 22.

the only worship and the only site of worship to be considered legitimate. Now officiates are present who control the sacrifices. No longer are there spontaneous sacrifices or practices carried out in informal ways either at this site or elsewhere. The presence of priests and Levites disenfranchises the laity, and whatever worship was previously engaged in is now, if not taboo, at least inferior to what has taken its place.

The psalm fragment in Ezra 3:11 steers the theme of unity toward community boundaries. Once the temple foundation is laid, the priests and Levites lead musical worship, and all recite the words, "For he is good, for his steadfast love endures forever." Blenkinsopp notes its use elsewhere and deems it a favorite of the Chronicler.[21] In Chronicles, the phrase occurs twice when David brings the ark into Jerusalem (1 Chr 16:31, 34) and three times in the description of the dedication of the First Temple (2 Chr 5:13; 7:3, 6). In 2 Chr 20 the phrase occurs again in verse 22 as Jehoshaphat makes liturgical preparations for war against the Moabites, Ammonites, and Meunites (2 Chr 20:1).[22] There we are reminded that these are people who dwelled in the land, whom God had not allowed Israel to destroy, and so, "they reward us by coming to drive us out of your possession that you have given us to inherit" (20:11). Jehoshaphat prepares the citizens of "Judah and Jerusalem" for war through worship.[23] The army departs for battle against these local people led by a chorus singing this psalm (20:21). The phrase also shows up in several psalms, particularly Pss 118 and 136. In the latter psalm, it is the refrain in all twenty-six verses. The psalm recounts God's creative acts, the exodus, including the destruction of Pharaoh, and the conquest of Sihon, king of the Amorites. (The Amorites are among peoples of the lands to be avoided in Ezra 9:1.)

In Ezra 3:11, the phrase includes an addition, "God's steadfast love [חסד] endures forever *toward Israel.*" It claims חסד explicitly for Israel, the appellation for the exilic community in 2:70 and 3:1 when "all Israel" settled in their towns. The association of the phrase with the institution of worship by David and Solomon and divine protection against surrounding enemies elsewhere makes it particularly suited to this narrative, where worship recommences in the midst of adversaries. Ezra 3:3 introduces "the neighboring peoples" (lit. "the peoples of the lands") as a source of dread, and they appear again as "adversaries" in 4:1. They become active

---

21. Blenkinsopp, *Ezra-Nehemiah*, 101.
22. Some translations replace "Meunites" with "Ammonites."
23. Davies, "Defending the Boundaries," 45.

opponents to the construction effort in 4:4.²⁴ As the community worships, this psalm calls on the God of Israel to keep covenant with Israel alone. Philip Davies believes that the society may be seeking to define itself around the cult. He suggests that the perceived threat is not to the community's territorial integrity (as it was under Jehoshaphat) but to "the integrity of the congregation of Israel." The community draws on a historic pattern of turning inward toward the temple, prompting moves that both consolidate and isolate the community.²⁵

5.2. Ezra 3 and Nehemiah 8: One Festival, Two Rituals

A comparison of Ezra 3 and Neh 8 helps clarify the distinctive rhetorical methods of Ezra 3 and the social structure it represents. These two chapters create distinctly different portraits of worship. Both include the Festival of Booths and are preceded by the same list of returnees. Identical bridges, placing the people in their towns in the seventh month, lead into separate community gatherings. In Ezra, the people gather in Jerusalem (Ezra 3:1), erect an altar, and offer sacrifices on the first day. In Nehemiah, they gather in the square by the Water Gate (Neh 8:1) and read Torah. In Ezra, the Festival of Booths is among the sacrifices resumed upon the completion of the altar. In Nehemiah, it is the concluding festival celebrated in response to Torah reading. The festival is celebrated in very different ways in each account, suggesting divergent authorial perceptions of the festival and purposes for its inclusion in the separate narratives.

In Ezra 3:2–6, the priests and Zerubbabel with his kin construct the altar and "offer burnt offerings on it, as prescribed in the law of Moses the man of God." Calendrical sacrifices are then listed, beginning with daily sacrifices followed directly by the Festival of Booths (normally celebrated beginning on the fifteenth day). The list continues with the New Moon Festival and freewill offerings (3:5) and concludes, "From the first day of the seventh month they began to offer burnt offerings to the Lord" (3:6). The term "burnt offerings" (עלה) occurs five times in these five verses while occurring only four other times in all of Ezra-Nehemiah.²⁶ Easily

---

24. "Then the people of the land discouraged the people of Judah, and made them afraid to build" (Ezra 4:4). Note the singular "the people of the land" rather than the plural form used in 3:3.
25. Davies, "Defending the Boundaries," 49.
26. In Ezra 6:3 and 6:9, royal edicts decree funds to provide for burnt offerings.

overlooked is the lack of specificity about the quantity of the sacrifices.[27] This suggests an authorial interest in the resumption of cultic practices on the altar in Jerusalem, rather than a demonstration of abundance (contra Ezra 6:17).

The Festival of Booths is described in several pentateuchal texts (Exod 23:16; Lev 23:34–36, 39–43; Num 29; Deut 16:13–15). The various pericopes emphasize disparate themes: the celebration of harvest, required sacrifices for the seventh month, the reading of Torah, or historical ties to the wilderness. Among these texts, the festival's ties to harvest are clearly in view in Exod 23:16, Deut 16:13, and Lev 23:39.[28] Neither Ezra 3 nor Neh 8 makes any reference to this connection, although one could argue that the focus on reinstituting calendrical rituals in Ezra leans in that direction. The enumeration of sacrifices in Ezra 3 has the clearest ties to Num 29. There the assemblies of the seventh month are described almost entirely in terms of required sacrifices, and the list of sacrifices for the Festival of Booths is expansive. Numbers 29:13–38 requires seventy bulls plus rams, lambs, grain, and oil for this festival and enumerates the burnt offerings for each day of the festival, beginning with thirteen bulls, two rams, and fourteen male lambs for the first day.[29] Thus the first festival to be celebrated on the new altar in Ezra is the one for which the Torah provides the most extensive list of sacrifices. Other associations for this festival are forgone in deference to the functioning altar.

The emphasis given to sacrifice for this festival is even more apparent when compared with the description of the same festival in Neh 8. Both accounts value the Torah as authoritative, although they employ it differently and appeal to different traditions within it. Ezra 3 celebrates the festival "as prescribed," but in Nehemiah an expansive description of Torah reading leads into the account of the festival's celebration. Twelve verses describe the reading of the law in the square before the Water Gate

---

Ezra 8:35 states that the returnees under Ezra offered burnt offerings and lists the quantity of each type. Neh 10:32–33 states that the people laid an obligation on themselves to provide for the offerings.

27. In contrast, in Ezra 8:35 the animals allotted for offering are listed as a conclusion to a longer list of goods carried by the returnees under Ezra.

28. Num 29 lacks an explicit reference to the harvest, but the festival falls in the logical sequence for a harvest festival after the firstfruits festival in Num 28:26. Deut 31 associates the festival only with the exodus.

29. The total number of animals over the eight-day period is 70 bulls, 14 rams, 98 lambs, 7 goats, plus grain offerings.

on the first and second days of the seventh month. Copious details are provided regarding the setting and time, the reaction of the people, and the list of Levitical interpreters; even Ezra's wooden stand is mentioned.[30] Jacob Wright notes that the reading does not occur on temple grounds, and the Torah is treated as an iconic book with blessings and prostration and liturgical response to its reading.[31] The festival itself, described in Neh 8:16–18, lacks sacrifices and looks nothing like its counterpart in Ezra. What *is* emphasized is the faithful carrying out of the construction of booths by the people and that the Torah was read from the first day to the last (Neh 8:18). The author provides his own appraisal that "from the days of Jeshua son of Nun to that day the people of Israel had not done so. And there was very great rejoicing" (8:16–17). The assessment portrays the community in Nehemiah exceeding all other celebrations of the Festival of Booths.[32] The claim leapfrogs over the intervening time and practices, asserting authenticity and a legitimacy superior to other observances through this tie to ancient practices.

The description of the festival in Nehemiah develops connections with two texts, Deut 31:10–13 and Lev 23:33–43. Deuteronomy requires the reading of Torah every seventh year during the festival.[33]

> Moses commanded them: "Every seventh year, in the scheduled year of remission, during the festival of booths, when all Israel comes to appear before the LORD your God at the place that he will choose, you shall read this law before all Israel in their hearing. Assemble the people—men, women, and children, as well as the aliens residing in your towns—so that they may hear and learn to fear the LORD your God and to observe diligently all the words of this law. (Deut 31:10–12)

---

30. Williamson (*Ezra, Nehemiah*, 288) notes that Solomon also had a specially constructed stand on which he stood to address the people at the inauguration of the First Temple.

31. Jacob L. Wright, "Writing the Restoration: Compositional Agenda and the Role of Ezra in Nehemiah 8," *JHebS* 7 (2007): art. 10, pp. 20, 22, doi:10.5508/jhs.2007.v7.a10.

32. The claim invites a comparison with the Chronicler's assessment of Josiah's Passover: "No passover like it had been kept in Israel since the days of the prophet Samuel" (2 Chr 35:18).

33. Jacob Wright ("Writing the Restoration," 23) notes that Neh 5 calls for the cancellation of all debts and suggests, "it is quite possible that the authors of chap. 8, like many readers since, understood this as 'a year of remittance' and thus portrayed the reading of the Torah as the *haqhēl* in keeping with Deuteronomy."

5. EZRA 3: RITUAL AND IDENTITY

In Nehemiah, men, women, and "those who could understand" are present in the assembly for the reading of the law (Neh 8:3). Moreover, the collection of leaders in the introduction to the Deuteronomic pericope resonates with the gathered leadership in Nehemiah, where "the heads of the fathers of all the people gather with the priests and Levites to study the words of the law with Ezra" (Neh 8:13, my translation). In Deut 31:9, Moses writes the law and gives it to "the priests, the sons of Levi, who carried the ark of the covenant of the Lord, and to all the elders of Israel."

In Neh 8:13–14, the leaders gather to study the law and discover they should live in booths made of branches during the festival. This draws on Lev 23:33–43, which commands the use of leafy branches for rejoicing "as a statute forever," and the people are commanded to live in booths for seven days. Yet Neh 8 conflates these two directives so that the booths are constructed from branches and then equates this with the celebration at the time of Joshua. The combination of booths, branches, and Joshua ties it to the only text that provides a historical motivation for the festival, "so that your generations may know that I made the people of Israel live in booths when I brought them out of the land of Egypt" (Lev 23:43). Notably it is a historical moment associated with leaving a foreign land and living outside Israel, thus creating a connection for those having lived in exile. Unmentioned in Nehemiah are the offerings by fire commanded earlier in Lev 23:36–38.

Both Ezra and Nehemiah claim to carry out their activities in keeping with written texts, but their selective use connotes divergent agendas.[34] Ezra 3 employs texts that coincide with priestly concerns for sacrifice (e.g., Num 29 or Lev 23:34–38, which speak only of sacrifices). In contrast, the texts employed in Nehemiah (Lev 23 and Deut 31) expand the role of laity participation in the celebration with commands to read Torah or construct booths.[35] We see that this coincides with an emphasis on "the people" in

---

34. There is also the possibility that this selectivity indicates separate collections of texts, not fully integrated at the level currently present in the Pentateuch. However, the particular texts they do employ seem to coincide with the interests and perspective of the authors.

35. These texts show evidence of being additions to the main text. Deut 31 is one of several additions to the end of the book as a whole, and the text in Leviticus follows a codicil in Lev 23:37–38. The codicil summarizes the preceding descriptions of festivals, including the Festival of Booths by stating: "These are the appointed festivals of the Lord, which you shall celebrate as times of holy convocation, for presenting to the Lord offerings by fire—burnt offerings and grain offerings, sacrifices and drink

Neh 8.[36] In the absence of the temple to conduct ritual sacrifices, the development of alternative activities makes sense during the Babylonian period. Yet these practices are presented in Neh 8 as if they are newly realized from an older text. In the narrative chronology of Ezra-Nehemiah, the festival in Nehemiah takes place after the construction of the temple, when sacrifice and pilgrimage are now available. Yet the festival most known for its many sacrifices is celebrated without mention of any sacrifices at all. Furthermore, as Jacob Wright notes, Torah is read יוֹם בְּיוֹם ("day by day," Neh 8:18) instead of the sacrifices that were offered יוֹם בְּיוֹם in Ezra 3:4 (NRSV "each day"), and the temple becomes simply another site among several for the construction of booths (Neh 8:16).[37] As Wright points out, the comparison shows us that in Ezra 3, Torah "serves merely to support the building of the Altar and re-inauguration of the sacrificial calendar," while in Neh 8 "it appropriates, or claims a share in, the cultic status of the Altar and sacrifices."[38]

Each text portrays a different structure for society. Throughout Ezra 3 the community is hierarchical, with priests (legitimated through lineage and ordination) controlling the celebrations and rituals. The community gathers in one site and celebrates with one voice. Levites hold secondary roles. They are appointed by others to supervise the temple work crews (3:8-9), and they play the cymbals in worship (3:10). Although important, the scope of their responsibilities is controlled and limited. In Nehemiah, Levites and scribes, legitimated by their ability to read (their cultural capital), lead the community. As the Torah is read to the collected congregation, the Levites give its interpretation (Neh 8:7, 9) and direct the community in their response to the reading (8:11). Only Ezra is given the title "priest," and even he is more often designated "scribe."[39] In response to

---

offerings, each on its proper day—apart from the sabbaths of the LORD, and apart from your gifts, and apart from all your votive offerings, and apart from all your freewill offerings, which you give to the LORD" (Lev 23:37-38).

36. Eskenazi (*In an Age of Prose*, 97-99) details the narrative emphasis on the people as a whole in this chapter. She notes among other things that "the people" are mentioned thirteen times in Neh 8:1-12; *they* call the assembly to have Torah read; and when leaders gather to study the Torah, "they" find it written, rather than Ezra teaching them.

37. Wright, "Writing the Restoration," 22.

38. Ibid., 26.

39. In this chapter, Ezra is titled "scribe" four times (Neh 8:1, 4, 9, 13) and "priest" twice (8:2, 9). In Ezra 7, the joint title, "the priest Ezra, the scribe," is employed three

hearing Torah, people "go out" to eat, drink, and share portions (8:12, my translation). Likewise the Festival of Booths is celebrated in a more diffuse manner. Everyone goes forth to gather branches, and they construct booths at their homes, in courtyards at the temple, and at the gates (8:16). The celebration is enacted without the need of priests, hierarchy, or temple.

The emphasis in Nehemiah on the community gathered for a ritualized reading of Torah and enacting the festival in their own homes contrasts sharply with the stately celebration in Ezra 3 with sacrifices overseen by properly ordained priests. The contrasting customs suggest that the retention of traditions developed in exile and carried back to Jerusalem with the returnees posed problems for priests wishing to reinstate the cult. If *this* festival, distinguished by its many burnt offerings, can be successfully and faithfully celebrated through the reading of Torah and living in booths, what need is there for sacrifice? Thus Ezra 3 provides a potent reminder of a priestly counterperspective on proper worship.[40] Bourdieu's work may allow us to explore evidence of less intentional but equally significant differences in the social structures suggested by these texts and the role that ritual plays in framing these social relations.

5.2.1. Analysis: Habitus, Ritual, and Social Order

Bourdieu states that ritual practices are determined by the material conditions of existence and argues that understanding ritual practice "is not a question of decoding the internal logic of a symbolism but of restoring its practical necessity.... It means ... reconstituting ... the significance and functions that agents in a determinate social formation can (and must) confer on a determinate practice or experience, given the practical taxonomies which organize their perception."[41] For a ritual to be effective, it must share a common sense of the world with the recipients. The practice

---

times (7:11, 12, 21), "scribe" is used once alone (7:6), and when introduced Ezra is given an extensive priestly genealogy (7:1–5).

40. Jacob Wright's ("Writing the Restoration") analysis of these texts demonstrates the differing mind-sets of priests and scribes as they each employ texts to support their differing positions within society.

41. Bourdieu, *Outline*, 114. Bourdieu faults objectivist reduction of ritual because in its effort to bring to light the "so-called objective functions of myths and rites," it "makes it impossible to understand how these functions are fulfilled, because it brackets the agents' own representation of the world and of their practice" (115).

must call on collective dispositions that arise in the context of a shared existence.[42] When a group of agents share the same habitus, practices are "immediately intelligible and foreseeable, and hence taken for granted."[43] In new contexts, groups "persist in their ways, due ... to the fact that they are composed of individuals with durable dispositions that can outlive the economic and social conditions in which they were produced."[44] The rituals in Ezra 3 and Neh 8 all retain aspects of their origins but also show evidence of adjustments to a new setting.

The rituals in Nehemiah are tied to life in exile—living in the wilderness, without territory, state government, or national status. Familiar exilic practices—reading Torah, family-centered celebrations, and leadership exercised by family elders—are reproduced. The practices are transportable and affirm community without regard to possession of the land. In this new situation, the practice of reading Torah, which likely had a more diffuse and egalitarian genesis, is presented in the text as a formal ritual in Jerusalem by a united community.[45] The transfer of cultural capital through communal reading empowers all the members. Yet now a single reader, Ezra, and the interpreters are given greater prestige and authority. The people respond with what originally were family- and community-oriented eating, drinking, and giving of portions that are now an orchestrated ritual.[46] (Giving portions would have fostered solidarity within a community enduring lean economic times.) Furthermore, the gathering

---

42. Bourdieu, *Logic of Practice*, 59. "The corrections and adjustments the agents themselves consciously carry out presuppose mastery of a common code; and undertakings of collective mobilization cannot succeed without a minimum of concordance between the habitus of the mobilizing agents (prophet, leader, etc.) and the dispositions of those who recognize themselves in their practices or words, and, above all, without the inclination towards grouping that springs from the spontaneous orchestration of dispositions."

43. Bourdieu, *Outline*, 80.

44. Bourdieu, *Logic of Practice*, 62.

45. Bourdieu, *Outline*, 78. "The habitus, the durably installed generative principle of regulated improvisations, produces practices which tend to reproduce the regularities immanent in the objective conditions of the production of their generative principle, while adjusting to the demands inscribed as objective potentialities in the situation, as defined by the cognitive and motivating structures making up the habitus."

46. Generally, portions are reserved for priests and Levites (Neh 12:44, 46; 13:10), but Joseph (Gen 43:34) and Elkanah (1 Sam 1:4) provide portions for their families. In 1 Sam 1:4, here, and in Esth 9:19, 22, portions are associated with a festival, and only here and in Esther do community members distribute portions to one another.

to study Torah on the second day includes not only priests and Levites but the "heads of the fathers of all the people" (Neh 8:13, my translation). The response to their findings, once again, has a significant role for all the people as they build booths for a geographically widespread celebration during the seven days of the festival. These details of ritual practice indicate the impact exilic life had on the shape of community life. Community cohesion had been achieved through generally egalitarian relations in the absence of political or ordained religious leadership. Now these same practices, the reading of Torah, the rituals sans sacrifice, become more centralized and confirm the leadership of the educated scribes as evidenced by the people seeking out Ezra to read to them.[47]

In contrast, Ezra 3 requires an established temple hierarchy, enough goods to supply the needs of priest and sacrifices, and rituals that can be practiced only when certain physical conditions are met, such as an altar in Jerusalem. (Links to Solomonic traditions make Jerusalem the only acceptable site.) All of these would require economic conditions that would allow for lavish sacrifices, a priestly class, and perhaps monumental construction.[48] The celebratory rituals here are increasingly centralized, highly orchestrated, and dependent on the leadership of ordained priests. The people take no independent action. Attention focuses on the central altar, sacrifices, the appointment of Levites, priests dressed in robes, and responsive singing. The people's participation is crucial, as it was in Nehemiah; but the community takes orders rather than initiative, and some of them respond in a unison shout of praise while others weep emotionally. Rituals of this magnitude play an important role in maintaining a group's social order as they make a virtue of conformity.[49] The division of labor in Ezra 3 is a "misrecognizable" form of the social order and contributes to its own reproduction by producing practices that make those divisions necessary. As Bourdieu states, "Every established order tends to produce … the naturalization of its own arbitrariness."[50]

The rituals described in these texts contain collective and solemn rites. Bourdieu argues that rites are "much more associated with spatial grouping the more there is collectively at stake: rites thus range in importance from

---

47. Eskenazi (*In an Age of Prose*, 97) notes the centrality of the people in this chapter and their initiative in seeking Ezra.
48. Fewell, private communication, 11 October 2011.
49. Bourdieu, *Outline*, 161.
50. Ibid., 164.

the great solemn rites ... enacted by everyone at the same time, through the rites performed at the same time but by each family separately ... through those which may be practiced at any time."[51] The practices employed in these rituals are orchestrated to adjust to the real divisions of the social order. However, the festival in Nehemiah would have less impact on the social order given its diffuse concluding ritual as multiple booths are constructed throughout the city. In contrast, the collective and highly orchestrated rite that ends Ezra 3 reproduces with more impact the social order from which it is generated. In Ezra 3, the rituals are successfully celebrated only with the aid of priests and Levites, making this arbitrary order appear natural and self-evident and also necessary—without the priesthood, appropriate religious practice cannot take place.

Ritual's important role in articulating a community's social order and self-definition is related in part to its use of the body. Bourdieu states,

> Every social order systematically takes advantage of the disposition of the body and language to function as depositories of deferred thoughts that can be triggered off at a distance in space or time by the simple effect of re-placing the body in an overall posture which *recalls* the associated thoughts and feelings, in one of the inductive states of the body which, as actors know, give rise to states of mind. Thus the attention paid to staging in great collective ceremonies derives not only from the concern to give a solemn representation of the group ... but also ... from the less visible intention of ordering thoughts and suggesting feelings through the rigorous marshalling of practices and the orderly disposition of bodies, in particular the bodily expression of emotion, in laughter or tears.[52]

Both narratives capitalize on ritual practices familiar for two distinct communities. These traditions, for which the participants' doxa (and the reader's habitus) are attuned, affirm particular social orders. In Ezra, the stationing of priests and Levites, the sound of trumpets, cymbals, and singing, form the pinnacle of the community's image of itself. In that snapshot, the priests, whose leadership rests on genealogy and ordination, are presented as the natural leaders. In Nehemiah, the people initiate events as they call Ezra to read to them. He stands above everyone on a specially constructed podium. The people stand as well but only to listen, and they bow before the opened book. In this representation, scribes, whose capital rests on

---

51. Ibid., 163.
52. Bourdieu, *Logic of Practice*, 69.

literacy, prove to be the natural leaders. However, not only is leadership held in different hands, but the order of society is different as well. The initiative and inclusion of the laity present in Nehemiah are replaced in Ezra by a community that affirms the actions of its leadership, who control all aspects of the rituals. The social order of each community is replicated in the bodily practices of the gathered communities. Bourdieu notes that visible manifestations of respect such as bowing or participation in collective ceremonies "always contain political concessions."[53] The portrait of these ceremonies orders the reader's thoughts, suggests feelings, and manages to extort concessions to the hierarchy represented in the text.

5.2.2. Commemorative Rituals and Community Identity

Catherine Bell states, "Many religious traditions define their whole calendar year through a series of rites that express the most basic beliefs of the community."[54] Both texts contain calendrical rituals, providing "socially meaningful definitions to the passage of time."[55] The festival in Neh 8 is a form of calendrical ritual that Bell terms *commemorative*. It reenacts a historical event and "turns the events of a historical narrative into a type of cyclical sacred myth, repeated annually, generating powerful images and activities of corporate identity." The effect is to "remind a community of its identity as represented by and told in a master narrative."[56] Rites of reenactment are distinguished from other rituals "by explicit reference to prototypical persons and events."[57] The life lived becomes a sacred repetition or reanimation of prototypes and is articulated through calendrical repetition, sacred language, and important ritual gestures.[58]

The Festival of Booths in Neh 8 reenacts the wilderness experience following the exodus from Egypt. Replaying this past event affirms the idea that God is with those not in the land. The history and the construction of temporary booths intimate that the situation is temporary and that

---

53. Ibid.
54. Catherine M. Bell, *Ritual: Perspectives and Dimensions* (Oxford: Oxford University Press, 2005), 105.
55. Ibid., 102.
56. Paul Connerton, *How Societies Remember* (Cambridge: Cambridge University Press, 1989), 70.
57. Ibid., 61.
58. Ibid., 65–68.

those exiled were destined to enter and take control of the land as they did in Joshua. In this celebration, no priest is needed to assure purity, no sacrifice or altar necessary to celebrate. Paul Connerton contends, "For the ceremonies to work for their participants … they must be habituated to those performances.… This habituation is to be found … in the bodily substrate of the performance."[59] It is this mix that gives "the cognitive content of what the group remembers in common … persuasive and persistent force."[60] The communal identity underscored in Neh 8 is sensible as a ritual practiced by those in exile. It would make *most* sense to the participants who had become habituated to the practices contained in the ritual through regular practice. Thus reading Torah or sharing portions within the community communicates identity for those sharing those activities in their original habitus. It would be less meaningful (and even alienating) for those who did not share a history of exile.

The Festival of Booths in Ezra 3 is also a calendrical ritual, as its significance in this text is associated with the resumption of repeated sacrifices. However, it is narratively partnered with the dedication of the temple foundation and is not a commemorative ritual such as we find in Neh 8. It does not explicitly reenact any historical event. The account creates allusions to Solomon's dedication of the First Temple but falls short of a historical reenactment. Instead, its textual presentation bears a striking resemblance to political rites that construct and promote the power of political institutions or the interests of particular groups.[61]

Bell states that political rites "define power in a two-dimensional way: first, they use symbols and symbolic action to depict a group of people as a coherent and ordered community based on shared values and goals; second, they demonstrate the legitimacy of these values and goals by establishing their iconicity with the perceived values and order of the cosmos."[62] They make the arbitrary and conventional "into what appears

---

59. Ibid., 71.
60. Ibid., 88.
61. Bell (*Ritual*, 94) outlines a wide variety of strategies for categorizing rituals. For this study, I have chosen to work with the eight categories she put forth in her book. These categories tend to focus on social context, and the categories of calendrical and commemorative rites are shared with Paul Connerton. They are: rites of passage, calendrical and commemorative rites, rites of exchange and communion, rites of affliction, rites of feasting, rites of fasting, and rites of festivals, and political rituals. See also Connerton, *How Societies Remember*, 44–45.
62. Bell, *Ritual*, 129.

to be necessary and natural." Through ritual, "those claiming power demonstrate how their interests are in the natural, real, or fruitful order of things."⁶³ Displays of wealth, resources, or mass approval are employed to legitimate claims to power.

Wealth, resources, and mass approval are prominent in Ezra. Wealth and resources are enumerated in Ezra 2, the acquisition of materials for construction of the temple is detailed in 3:7, and mass approval is implied in the shouted response of the people during the celebration of the temple's completed foundation in 3:11. The rituals describe in detail a society led jointly by secular and priestly leaders with highly differentiated roles for priests, Levites, and laity. The natural and fruitful order of this society is demonstrated by the building accomplishments of the community. While not raised directly in the performance of these rituals, well-defined boundaries for this community are understood as necessary. The exclusion of others deemed adversaries to good social order and success surround these rituals of self-definition.

5.2.3. Reshaping History

The placement of the political ritual in Ezra 3 as the first act of the community upon arrival in Jerusalem suggests that the history has been dramatically altered to serve the author's own community. In his analysis of history writing, David Lowenthal states, "We reshape our heritage to make it attractive in modern terms; we seek to make it part of ourselves, and ourselves part of it; we conform it to our self-images and aspirations. Rendered grand or homely, magnified or tarnished, history is continually altered in our private interests or on behalf of our community or country."⁶⁴ The past in Ezra 3 and Neh 8 is reshaped as more virtuous and successful.⁶⁵ To sustain such a view of the past, "evidence is often ignored or misinterpreted."⁶⁶ Moreover, "Forebears acquire qualities esteemed today ... and their faults are concealed or palliated." Even the past's aesthetic standards are brought into line with current conventions.⁶⁷

---

63. Ibid.
64. David Lowenthal, *The Past Is a Foreign Country* (Cambridge: Cambridge University Press, 1985), 348.
65. Ibid., 340.
66. Ibid., 342.
67. Ibid., 343. Lowenthal details how the expectations of visitors to an Indiana

Both accounts magnify the religious unity of the early returnees. In Nehemiah, the community calls for Torah to be read, obeys the laws they find, and are so committed to Torah that they gather en masse to hear it read each day of the festival. Uncertainties about proper ritual responses are resolved by leaders or by further investigation of sacred texts. In Ezra, the ancestors return for the single purpose of reconstructing the temple, which provides the context for the community's only other activity—sacrificial worship led by ordained priests.[68] There is no disagreement over religious practice, and rebuilding is resisted only by people outside the exilic community. While tears are shed upon completion of the temple foundation, the description of the celebration masks any meagerness in the project. The image dovetails with the conventions of the author's community, connecting his later community to the text and to worship practices their forebears that now, given its literary and chronological placement, predate the celebration in Nehemiah. By antedating these worship practices to the first returnees and constructing allusions to Solomon's inauguration of the First Temple, the author validates his present-day traditions. Rituals now placed among the first returnees become normative, "especially if the precedent is believed ancient and constant."[69] Both texts modify history, shaping it to coincide with current practices, and rely on these historical reconstructions to legitimate the practices of the community. This undermines efforts to reconstruct history from the events in the texts, but it does indicate the nature of the traditions deemed important by the authors and the social practices and structures they valued.

Connerton observes that "we preserve versions of the past by representing it to ourselves in words and images."[70] Both the ritual practices and their written accounts in Ezra 3 and Neh 8 constitute methods of preserving the past. The rituals, because of their embodied character, would have been less open to critique than the inscribed texts that recount them. Inscription "demonstrates, by the fact of being inscribed, a will to be remembered"; yet once inscribed as text, the text can take on a life of its

---

reenactment village of 1836 led the staff to modify the histories of early settlers to permit Christmas talk and activity, which historically was a scarcely recognized holiday (345).

68. The ensuing conflict in Ezra 4–6 continues to be centered on ensuring temple worship.

69. Lowenthal, *Past*, 369.

70. Connerton, *How Societies Remember*, 72.

5. EZRA 3: RITUAL AND IDENTITY

own and the door to scrutiny and critique is opened.[71] Subsequent readers share in the text's meaning.[72]

Each written account claims that revived historical practices are the basis for their rituals, yet each portrays very different worship practices. Perhaps the text of Ezra 3 provides the first critique of the account of the customs in Neh 8: rituals of sacrifice administered by priests replace Torah reading by scribes and booths constructed by the people. Jacob Wright has already argued that Ezra 3 advocates a priestly oriented social structure in direct and deliberate opposition to the scribal centered account in Neh 8.[73] Leadership by trained scribes gives way to leadership determined by lineage. The evidence marshaled here suggests that practices honed in the exile, reflecting a less hierarchical, more family-centered community, are countered in Ezra 3 with priestly leadership and a highly structured community, established around a temple. Important historical references also shift from the untethered wilderness to the temple apparatus of a geographically tied nation-state. Neither account dispenses with the leaders or rituals of the other. Both assume participants are included based on an exilic heritage and (although employing divergent practices) adherence to the singular worship of YHWH.

Through the use of ritual, two separate social orders are presented as normative, divinely instituted, and natural. Both appeal to sacred texts for justification. Yet authorized spokespersons hold their position due to different cultural capital: ordination and genealogy in Ezra, scribal skills in Nehemiah. The legitimate instruments of expression differ in the two texts: reading and study in Nehemiah, and ritual performance in Ezra 3. Access to these sources of capital differentiates between "masqueraders" and the authorized.[74] Each account symbolically reaffirms its own social order. Ezra 3 reinforces a more highly differentiated community granting the priesthood significant control over worship and work. In Nehemiah, the lines of authority are more blurred. The community is directed by Levites and their readings, but family heads share in leadership, and initiative is more equitably shared even with the laity. The rituals in Ezra 3, marked

---

71. Ibid., 102, 96.
72. Ibid., 97. Connerton notes this is especially true of legal and theological texts, although interpreters of religious texts are often bound by confession of a system of religious beliefs.
73. Wright, "Writing the Restoration," 25.
74. Bourdieu, *Language and Symbolic Power*, 109.

by unified, rigidly performed practices, would have a greater impact on the social structure and appear to be an intentional counter not only to the scribal leadership but the less hierarchical society of Neh 8.

How do these two coexisting, competing versions function in the text as we now have it? How would the two practices have been handled in communal practice? Do the two forms coalesce, and these versions represent a compromise?[75] The celebration in Neh 8 not only describes a more egalitarian celebration and one less economically demanding than in Ezra 3, but also draws on texts that counter exclusionary practices. The term "Festival of Booths" occurs only in Leviticus, Deuteronomy, and postexilic texts (Zech 14:16, 18, 19; Ezra 3:4; 2 Chr 8:13).[76] Although only Ezra 3 employs this label (3:4), the title comes from the sources employed by Neh 8 (Neh 8:14 makes reference only to the festival of the seventh month). This suggests that the authors of both Ezra 3 and Neh 8 are familiar with the same passages. Leviticus and Deuteronomy either explicitly include resident aliens in the celebration or require they be treated as full citizens (Deut 16:14; 31:12; Lev 19:33–34).[77] Although the author of Ezra 3 is cognizant of these texts, the inclusion of resident aliens is problematic to the author's interests, so other texts, more focused on temple rituals, come to the fore.

With regard to the physical practice of the Festival of Booths, Milgrom observes,

> The booths of the autumn festival ... strewn on the hillsides that surrounded Jerusalem ... would have been the distinctive visual characteristic of the festival.... It is therefore of ultimate significance that the name "the Festival of Booths" occurs solely in Lev 23:36 and Deut 16:13, 16, the only legal corpora in the Pentateuch that presume *regional preference* over *national centralization*. But when the festivals became national celebrations at the capital, the booths erected by pilgrims probably would match and outnumber the residences in the city.[78]

---

75. Fewell, private communication, 11 October 2011.

76. Jacob Milgrom, *Leviticus: A Book of Ritual and Ethics*, CC (Minneapolis: Fortress, 2004), 282. Milgrom, working with JEPD(H) sources, suggests "the name became preferable at the Jerusalem temple (H) and subsequently became mandatory there (D)."

77. Ibid., 175.

78. Ibid., 287 (italics mine). The Levitical text comes from the Holiness Code (Lev 17–27). Milgrom (175) states that this section of text is characterized by a concern for

The accounts of Ezra 3 and Neh 8 provide two views of the same celebration. One looks toward the temple and the rituals performed there, while the other looks out over the sea of pilgrims and the importance of their presence for the festival. If the name of the festival reflects the many pilgrims in attendance, then the adoption of this name for the festival by late and postexilic texts suggests that the more inclusive stance portrayed in Neh 8 wins out over the highly controlled membership associated with Ezra 3. It acknowledges the arrival of far-flung pilgrims who call themselves "Israel." At the same time, the turn toward the temple celebration in Ezra 3 displaces the leadership of scribes and Levites. By placing the two chapters in conversation, the Festival of Booths incorporates pilgrims with worship now firmly anchored to the temple. Which form of leadership has ascendancy appears linked to geographic proximity to the temple precincts.

5.3. Ezra 4:1–5: Drawing Boundaries with a Text

While historical continuity and unity around worship implicitly draw boundaries, the narrative of the community's temple construction draws explicit lines of demarcation. In Ezra 3, the exiles gather in Jerusalem and set up the altar "because they were in dread of the neighboring peoples" (3:3). In 3:7, the returnees jointly provide funds for the laborers working on the temple foundations and purchase construction materials. Ezra 3:8 more explicitly qualifies who is credited with initiating construction, "In the second year *after their arrival*," and that labor on the temple is carried out by "*all who had come to Jerusalem from the captivity*." "Adversaries of Judah and Benjamin" are explicitly excluded from construction in 4:2–3 when their offers of help are rejected. The rigidly enforced boundaries contribute (in this narrative) to the unity of the community.

Brevard Childs identifies separation as a recurring theme in Ezra. He traces its growing presence in the book through the dissolution of marriages in the final chapter.[79] Although overlooked in Childs's discussion,

---

moral impurity (rather than ritual purity) and an "emphasis on ethical behavior and the granting of civil equality to the resident alien."

79. Brevard S. Childs, *Introduction to the Old Testament as Scripture* (Philadelphia: Fortress, 1979), 634. He suggests that separation is introduced in ch. 2 as a means to protect the purity of the priesthood and that it recurs in 4:1–5 when help on construction is refused, and is developed further in ch. 6 when only those who separate

the narrative construction of worship in Ezra 3 plays an important role in forming a distinct community and identifying criteria on which separation is based. A community unified by worship, joint labor, and exilic status is separated from those whose labor is refused, who do not hold exilic status, and who do not (or no longer) worship in Jerusalem.

The construction of the altar in Ezra 3:3 introduces threatening "others": "They set up the altar on its foundation, *because they were in dread of the neighboring peoples*" ("peoples of the lands," עמי הארצות). Blenkinsopp suggests that the construction of the altar follows David's example in 1 Chr 21:28–22:1 (also in 2 Sam 24:25), where he erects an altar to avert disaster prior to the completion of the temple.[80] Elsewhere both David and Saul (1 Sam 14:34–35) construct altars to avoid retaliation by YHWH; yet in these cases the actions of the *king* create danger and the altar does not protect against an external threat but divine anger.[81] Joshua 8 provides the first biblical account of an altar in Canaan. There it is linked with a ceremonial reading of Torah. That narrative, like Ezra 3, is situated between texts that describe hostilities with surrounding peoples.[82] At this point in Ezra, no clarity is provided about either the exact identity of these adversaries or the nature of the threat. Yet as Ezra links fear with the construction of the altar, it draws on the association of constructing altars to ward off divine wrath or asserting claims to the land in the face of opposition. At the culmination of the foundation account, attention swings explicitly and more fully toward the issue of external threats.

In Ezra 4:1–5, "adversaries" hear of the temple construction, and on the basis of their history and religious beliefs proffer help. "Let us build with you, for we worship [דרש, 'seek'] your God as you do, and we have been sacrificing to him ever since the days of King Esarhaddon of Assyria

---

themselves from the people of the land can keep the Passover (6:21). It becomes dominant in Ezra's prayer of ch. 9 and the abolition of mixed marriages in ch. 10.

80. Blenkinsopp, *Ezra-Nehemiah*, 97. In 1 Chr 21 and 2 Sam 24, David halts a plague after he numbered the people by purchasing a threshing floor and erecting an altar in Jerusalem.

81. In 1 Sam 14, Saul constructs an altar to halt his hungry soldiers from eating meat with its blood after he ordered no rations until a battle was won.

82. The destruction of Ai precedes this chapter, and the following text states, "Now when all the kings who were beyond the Jordan in the hill country and in the lowland all along the coast of the Great Sea toward Lebanon—the Hittites, the Amorites, the Canaanites, the Perizzites, the Hivites, and the Jebusites—heard of this, they gathered together with one accord to fight Joshua and Israel" (Josh 9:1–2).

5. EZRA 3: RITUAL AND IDENTITY 135

who brought us here" (4:2). Upon being rejected, they immediately engage in efforts to discourage the builders and frustrate their efforts by appeals to the Persian rulers. The sudden change in tactics insinuates that the adversaries are not to be trusted with something as crucial to community identity as the temple. Blenkinsopp suggests that the offer would have entailed a share in controlling the temple once completed; and he notes that although their offer is rejected on the basis of not being included in the imperial firman, their identification as foreigners settled by the Assyrian Esarhaddon allows the reader to know that "the real reason was, of course, quite different."[83]

As Blenkinsopp's comment demonstrates, the introduction of the neighboring peoples as something to be feared makes the offer of help by the "adversaries" appear deceptive and a ploy to gain power. Since we have only the author's perspective, the people of the land may have perceived themselves quite differently. They claim solidarity with the exiles on the basis of worship of YHWH —the very thing being celebrated in the text. They indicate they have a long history of sacrificing to and seeking YHWH ever since their ancestors arrived over a century earlier under Esarhaddon (689–661 BCE). They may even have been sacrificing at the site of the Jerusalem temple and perceive themselves as having faithfully maintained worship during that time. If they understood themselves as members of the same community as the exiles, they may have been shocked to discover they are identified as outsiders and interlopers.[84]

In rabbinic literature, "the people of the land" often refers to "ordinary Jews who were not very observant about the finer points of rabbinic law in matters of ritual purity, tithing, and the like. The term is not usually used of non-Jews."[85] Christopher Seitz has argued that in the book of Kings the people of the land are very much members of Judean society but likely refugees displaced to the environs of Jerusalem during the Assyrian incursions

---

83. Blenkinsopp, *Ezra-Nehemiah*, 107.

84. In 1 Esdras, the reference to the people of the land is more ambiguous, as the people of the land are both helpful and a source of hostility: "And some joined them from the other peoples of the land. And they erected the altar in its place, for all the peoples of the land were hostile to them and were stronger than they; and they offered sacrifices at the proper times and burnt offerings to the Lord morning and evening" (1 Esd 5:50). This version suggests more directly a doorway into community membership while still maintaining the boundary and associating outsiders with hostility.

85. Grabbe, *Ezra-Nehemiah*, 18.

in the region.[86] Seitz points to evidence from the book of Jeremiah that suggests that the population outside Jerusalem was composed of Judeans after the destruction of Jerusalem.[87] The prophet was a refugee from Anathoth in Jerusalem (Jer 11:21–23; 32:7–9), and twice it is recorded that Jeremiah remained in Judah at Mizpah under the care of Gedaliah "with his own people" (39:14) or "among the people who were left in the land" (40:6). The king, Zedekiah, expressed concern about falling into the hands of "Judeans who have deserted to the Chaldeans" (38:19). The evidence supports a continuing Yahwistic enclave remaining in the land after the Babylonian conquest.

This understanding of "people of the land" is not shared by Ezra. The term appears to be a label designating foreigners with pagan practices. In Ezra, the people of the land assert that they are foreigners settled by an Assyrian king. Rom-Shiloni notes that this information creates discontinuity with the land and with Israel.[88] This appears to be authorial polemics rather than historical truth.[89] The adversaries in Ezra may not be foreigners, or the confrontation may not be about control over an institution. Instead, it may be a conflict over the basis for inclusion in the community. The claim to worship the same deity is not sufficient for membership in the community.

The term *worship* (NRSV) (דרש) used by the adversaries in Ezra 4:2 recurs in 6:21. In Ezra 6, the community celebrates their first Passover

---

86. Christopher Seitz, *Theology in Conflict: Reactions to the Exile in the Book of Jeremiah*, BZAW 176 (Berlin: de Gruyter, 1989), 64–65: "the use of the term 'people of the land' in the Books of Kings refers to those populations which did in fact come from the 'land' but which had taken up residence in the capital. They were the refugee populations (or their descendants) who, in quite large numbers, had fled from the land to the city for safety, taking up residence both inside the major defensive walls of the capital and also in the immediate environs, both before and after the events of 701 and 721 B.C." (64).

87. Ibid., 69. For a more thorough survey of the evidence from Jeremiah, see Oded Lipschits, "The History of the Benjamin Region under Babylonian Rule," *TA* 26 (1999): 159–65.

88. Rom-Shiloni, *Exclusive Inclusivity*, 42.

89. This is contrary to Williamson (*Ezra, Nehemiah*, 49), who states, "We have no reason to doubt their self-description" (as importees). However, he then qualifies this by noting it may be true of just some of those and that they may have continued sacrifices on visits to Jerusalem. Grabbe notes that this history would still put them in the land for over 150 years (*Ezra-Nehemiah*, 18).

after the completion of the temple. It is celebrated "by all who had joined them and separated themselves from the pollutions of the nations of the land to *worship* the LORD, the God of Israel." דרש is more often translated elsewhere "seek" and is translated as such in these verses by NASB and NIV. Ezra *seeks* (NRSV "study") the law in Ezra 7:10, and the leaders *investigate* (so NASB; NRSV "examine") the issue of mixed marriages in 10:16. In addition, the Chronicler's praise for kings is closely tied to whether the king *seeks* YHWH (1 Chr 28:9; 2 Chr 12:14; 17:3–4). Jacob Wright notes that over time this term shifts in meaning from oracular consultation to textual study.[90] Its usage here may then indicate that these people either study texts to know YHWH or employ prophetic oracles to consult YHWH. Given the word's usage in Ezra 6 and 7 and the book's clear interest in textual authority, it is most likely to be understood as the study of sacred texts. (However, one could argue that the compiler viewed the methods of these adversaries as inappropriate, because they were outside those he deemed legitimate. In a similar way, King Saul's decision to "inquire of" [seek] a medium was condemned even when legitimate means were unavailable to him [1 Sam 28:6–7].)[91]

In Ezra 6:21, all who separate themselves from the pollutions of the nations of the land join the exiles to seek YHWH. The term translated "pollutions," טמאה, covers a lot of ritual, ethical, and theological territory and remains unspecified in the text. The rejection of seekers in Ezra 4:2 suggests that the adversaries' concept of "seeking" fails to incorporate markers valued by the exiles that might have made them acceptable. Yet it appears that Ezra 1–6 provides a door into the community that is not available in the following chapters, unless we assume that the women dismissed in Ezra 10 preferred divorce over taking whatever steps would make them acceptable as members. The silence over criteria used to determine membership invites us to consider how ethnicity is represented in this text, the role ritual plays in maintaining boundaries, and what social realities might be associated with these findings.

---

90. Wright, "Writing the Restoration," 29.
91. 1 Chr 10:13–14 is explicit in its condemnation of Saul, asserting that God put him to death in part because he did not "seek" God but "inquired" of a medium.

5.4. Ethnicity, Boundaries, and Ritual

5.4.1. Ritual: Resisting a Competing Discourse

Ezra 3 introduces a conflict between the exiles and the more ambiguous "peoples of the lands" (3:3) or "people of the land" (4:4). The rival groups are immediately distinguished from one another by their names, which Nash observes is the chief symbolic marker to separate groups from one another. "Names not only mark group boundaries, they also implicate relations of super- and subordination, relative power, status, economic, and moral worth positions of the different entities."[92] Bourdieu concurs, noting that to institute an identity involves "the imposition of a name, i.e. of a social essence," and "to give a social definition, an identity, is also to impose *boundaries*."[93]

In Ezra 3, the designation *Israel* is a term of self-ascription reserved for the exiles (e.g., "But Zerubbabel, Jeshua, and the rest of the heads of families in Israel said to them, 'You shall have no part with us in building a house to our God; but we alone will build to the LORD, the God of Israel'"; Ezra 4:3). Gerhard von Rad observes that, in Ezra and Nehemiah, "Israel" is used in religious contexts while "the Jews" is used in political and organizational contexts.[94] From Ezra 2:59 to 4:5, Israel is mentioned eight times. Half of those are references to the exiles as they worship or defend their right to construct the temple themselves.[95] In Ezra, "the Jews" occurs exclusively in the Aramaic section, which treats the community's external relations. It is employed most often by those outside the community (4:12, 23; 6:7–8) but also by the narrator (4:23, 5:1, 5), and often involves a territorial connection, for example, "the Jews who were in Judah and Jerusalem" (5:1). "Israel" as a designation for the current community recurs in the Aramaic only upon the dedication of the temple (6:16–17) when the narrative focus is turned solely on the community. The usage of "Israel" in contexts of worship probably means it is important to the

---

92. Nash, *Cauldron of Ethnicity*, 9.
93. Bourdieu, *Language and Symbolic Power*, 120.
94. Gerhard von Rad, *Das Geschichtsbild des chronistischen Werkes*, BWANT 4/1 (Stuttgart: Kohlhammer, 1930), 18.
95. Three times it is in reference to the God of Israel, once it refers to David, king of Israel.

author's thinking that the existence of Israel as a distinct community is contingent upon its connection to the constructed temple.

Israel transmits historical and ancestral associations. In contrast, *the people of the land* is a generic, nonspecific identity lacking genealogy or ties to the past, and those so classified are perceived as adversaries. Whatever name they may have employed for themselves is absent from the narrative. Their designation provides a constant reminder of their ties to land outside Judah and excludes them from being exiles, citizens of Jerusalem, and ultimately from Israel. From the author's perspective, their name also excludes them from the imperial decrees, justifying their exclusion from the cult and conferring on them a subordinate status. The persistence of the boundary between the two communities is aided by the use of geographic terminology to designate the separate communities when they interact. Bourdieu states that the most efficacious social distinctions "are those which give the appearance of being based on objective differences."[96] Thus the place of origin, the most obvious difference, becomes the basis for the terminology selected to designate "the people of the land" as opposed to "the Jews in Judah" or "the exiles."

Prior to the conflict that arises in Ezra 3, the exiles are portrayed as an identifiable group with an agreed upon membership. Though the exiles are designated by a variety of terms (people of YHWH, families of Judah and Benjamin, survivors, captive exiles, Israelites), the account proceeds on the understanding that legitimate members of this group can be distinguished from other people groups. The language in Cyrus's edict suggests a level of self-ascription, "Any of those among you who are of his people" (1:3). This in turn points to a collective understanding regarding criteria for group membership. Bourdieu states that practical taxonomies (upon which this belief is constructed) are the product of the social order and reproduce that order "by producing objectively orchestrated practices adjusted to those divisions."[97] He adds, "The instruments of knowledge of the social world are in this case (objectively) political instruments ... producing immediate adherence to the world, seen as self-evident and undisputed."[98] The conditions necessary for membership "go without saying because they

---

96. Bourdieu, *Language and Symbolic Power*, 120.
97. Bourdieu, *Outline*, 163.
98. Ibid., 164.

come without saying," and hence the question of legitimacy arises only after a competing group lays claim to membership.[99]

In Ezra 4:5–6, the people of the land offer their help with temple construction on the basis of shared religious practices. The proposal suggests alternative criteria for determining membership in the community. This poses a direct challenge to the community's doxic understanding of group identity. Bourdieu observes, "The truth of doxa is only ever fully revealed when negatively constituted by the constitution of a field of opinion, the locus of the confrontation of competing discourses—whose political truth may be overtly declared or may remain hidden, even from the eyes of those engaged in it, under the guise of religious or philosophical oppositions."[100]

The challenge brings into the universe of discourse the basis of group membership. However, the confrontation remains focused on religious practice and to whom the imperial decree was addressed. This suggests that the *political* truth, that is, the *arbitrary* nature of the constitution of group membership, remains hidden.[101] The right to exclude others and employ selective criteria to determine membership is unchallenged. This is true in part because the attention placed on religious belief disguises the political power contest underlying the competing discourses. The statement by the adversaries questions the categories relevant for determining inclusion and pushes against the limits of doxa by positing an alternative set of criteria for inclusion. Yet it fails to force change in the dominant system of classification or to question the use of categories in general.

Bourdieu argues that in a contested situation, even as the dominated try to expose the arbitrariness of doxa, "the dominant classes have an interest in defending the integrity of doxa or, short of this, of establishing in its place the necessarily imperfect substitute, *orthodoxy*."[102] Orthodoxy, states Bourdieu, "aims, without ever entirely succeeding, at restoring the primal state of innocence of doxa."[103] In addition, Barth states that even

---

99. Ibid., 168. "The adherence expressed in the doxic relation to the social world is the absolute form of recognition of legitimacy through misrecognition of arbitrariness, since it is unaware of the very question of legitimacy, which arises from competition for legitimacy, and hence from conflict between groups claiming to possess it."

100. Ibid.

101. "Arbitrary" in this sense does not mean capricious or without cause but rather indicates that the criteria employed for determining membership could be otherwise and the group is a social construction.

102. Bourdieu, *Outline*, 169.

103. Ibid. Bourdieu suggests orthodoxy needs competing possibilities for it to

5. EZRA 3: RITUAL AND IDENTITY 141

when confronted by competing discourses, ethnic dichotomies persist if the categories and values employed have a self-fulfilling character. Positive experiential feedback to the categories allows them to be retained. He comments that actors are able to "maintain conventional definitions of the situation in social encounters through selective perception, tact, and sanctions, and because of difficulties in finding other, more adequate codifications of experience. Revision takes place only where the categorization is grossly inadequate—not merely because it is untrue."[104]

In Ezra, there is no revision to the ethnic categories by the exilic group. The religious basis for inclusion suggested by the peoples of the lands is ignored and countered with an imperial decree interpreted as sanctioning only the exiles in the construction. These moves reassert the initial categories of group membership without directly addressing the alternative criteria put forward by the people of the land. However, the boundaries are now no longer self-evident.

When the definition of the social world is at stake, the dividing line between what is discussed and what is doxic and beyond question is at stake as well.[105] The hostilities carried out by "the peoples of the lands" (instilling fear, bribing officials) suggest a political awareness on *their* part as they resist efforts by the community of exiles to proceed with temple construction on their own. The author labels them as outsiders and recounts their hostile response as a sign of their true character and the appropriateness of excluding them from the community. This too is an effort to defend the integrity of doxa. Neither their initial exclusion nor their negative portrait explains the basis for their initial rejection—their behavior is intended to speak for itself, and as a result the boundaries of the community remain intact.

In many ways, this entire chapter of ritual is an effort to restore "the silence of doxa" in the face of a competing discourse.[106] Surrounded by a competing community that seeks admittance, the first action taken by the exiles involves rituals that include the exiles alone. The rituals consecrate the social boundaries of the community "by fostering a misrecognition of the arbitrary nature of the limit and encouraging a recognition of it as

---

exist. He states, "orthodoxy exists only in the objective relationship which opposes it to heterodoxy … made possible by the existence of competing possibles."
104. Barth, "Introduction," 30.
105. Bourdieu, *Outline*, 169.
106. Bourdieu, *Language and Symbolic Power*, 131.

legitimate."[107] Participants in the ritual are specified as "all who had come to Jerusalem from the captivity" (Ezra 3:8). This defines membership, and the rituals sanction this definition with the stamp of divine approval. Reference to Cyrus's decree (4:6) then explicitly sanctions the peoples of the lands as outsiders. Thus, for the reader, YHWH blesses the community as constituted, and the Persian monarch affirms the exclusion of the people of the land. (This same tactic of divine blessing and imperial sanction regarding community boundaries is employed again in 6:6.) Without directly addressing the basis of the community's boundaries or structure, the rituals in Ezra 3 reinforce the clarity and rigidity of the author's categories for inclusion.

The account in Ezra provides one side of a struggle over control of a cultural field. In struggles such as this, cultural producers richest in specific capital and most concerned for autonomy (from economic and political fields) tend to exclude less autonomous producers, whom they see as "enemy agents." Autonomous and less autonomous producers debate not only practices but inclusion in the cultural field, and so Bourdieu argues that to try and determine "whether such and such a group ... belongs to the population of [cultural producers]" or even "who is legitimately entitled to designate legitimate [producers]" amounts to blind arbitration on the part of the researcher since the debate on that "are inscribed in reality itself."[108]

"The strategies which the occupants of the different positions implement in their struggles to defend or improve their positions ... depend ... on the position each agent occupies in the power relations."[109] In this instance, a particular form of worship with specific cultural producers is put forward as legitimate and upheld by appeals to history, ritual, and images of a unified community. This legitimates the temple (a cultural production), the particular structure of the field, and the author's place in it, while delegitimizing his competitors. This strategy bolsters his ability "to say with authority who are authorized to call themselves [worshipers or members]."[110] An unquestioning acceptance of the author's assessment of the "adversaries" as outsiders and enemies is a failure to recognize this description of them as a tactic in the debate.

---

107. Ibid., 118.
108. Bourdieu, *Field of Cultural Production*, 41.
109. Ibid., 30.
110. Ibid., 2.

5.4.2. Appealing to the Reader

The author draws on social mechanisms capable of producing complicity between him and the group as a basis of authority.[111] Familiar rituals and textual authority combine to legitimate social order. Appeals to older traditions are particularly helpful in this endeavor. Bell states, "Appeals to an ancient tradition provide a more faceless, external, and neutral sort of authority."[112] In Ezra 3, ritual practices current at the time of writing are credited to the earlier community. In turn, that community is presented as reinstituting even more ancient rituals. The author enlists a doxic belief in textual authority as he portrays the community in the text employing ancient texts to affirm these particular ritual practices. The homology between the returnees seeking textual guidance for their practices and the readers' current practices establishes the Ezra text as authoritative for the present as well. The use of familiar rituals, textual authority, and ancient traditions exercises "magic" on the readers as they recognize their own social structure and practices as essential to the earlier community.

The author employs these rituals and traditions to legitimate a hierarchical, temple-centered community but also to portray the people of the land as infringing on the community, thus classifying their speech and participation as illegitimate. Evidence from Third Isaiah (e.g., Isa 56:3–8), physical evidence of a sparse population in the early Persian period, and the observations regarding postcollapse economies by Ian Stern indicate that boundaries were probably more open early in the Persian period.[113] However, over time the population and Persian presence grew, making economic resources scarcer and the boundaries of the community increasingly contested and rigid. In defense of community boundaries, the author backdates this conflict and its resolution for the polemical value of situating it among the earliest arrivals. He advocates for an autonomous community and portrays competitors as lacking the proper credentials for inclusion. They lack the symbolic capital held by the exilic leadership, so they compete against them using their access to the wider economic and political powers. This threatens the autonomy of the local cultural field

---

111. Bourdieu, *Language and Symbolic Power*, 109.
112. Bell, *Ritual*, 235.
113. Stern, "Population of Persian-Period Idumea," 214. Isaiah 56:3 (NASB) states in part, "Let not the foreigner who has joined himself to the LORD say, 'The LORD will surely separate me from His people.'"

and those who wield power within it, prompting the redactor to view them as enemies and to label them as distinct from "Israel."

According to Anthony Smith, the impact of imperial cultural classifications and pressures on demotic *ethnie* within their territories contributes to these classification efforts. Intellectuals within the subordinate *ethnie* would respond by formulating "new definitions and goals for their communities, in tune with the ethnic and social realities" of their own people.[114] Integral to this is a selective return to the ethnic past. Using a "historical map," they "transformed the *ethnie* from a passive, subordinate 'object' of history into a mobilized, political aware and active 'subject' of history."[115] This is achieved "by placing the 'masses' at the centre of political concern and by celebrating the role of the 'people' and their collective values, myths and memories."[116] Ezra 3 is a selective history that portrays the community actively engaged in restoring their own place in history in order to mobilize the readers to do the same. Crucial to this goal is representing the community accomplishing the restoration on their own.

Smith states that transforming a community into one with an active stance toward its own history is possible only "when the community controlled its own destiny in its own homeland—a compact, clearly demarcated territory, in which it was united and autonomous."[117] Dyck argues that this situation held for the community of Yehud, and the evidence in Ezra 3 reveals the author mobilizing the people using the tactics described by Smith—placing the people at the center of concern and celebrating their collective myths and values. However, Dyck critiques the emphasis in Ezra that restricts external relations of the community in order to emphasize ethnic depth, noting, "the approach recommended by the writers of Ezra-Nehemiah did not give the community the flexibility to address the need to broaden its territorial basis and to develop social and economic relations with its immediate neighbours."[118] The concern for ethnic survival reduced the scope of economic relationships and made it more difficult for the community to be self-sufficient. Thus, although perhaps persuasive,

---

114. Smith, "Politics of Culture," 720.
115. Ibid.
116. Ibid.
117. Ibid.
118. Jonathan Dyck, "The Ideology of Identity in Chronicles," in *Ethnicity and the Bible*, ed. Mark G. Brett, BibInt 19 (Leiden: Brill, 1996), 102.

the heightened boundaries put forward in this chapter may have come at a high economic cost over the long term.

6
Ezra 4–6: Contesting Legitimacy

The book of Ezra begins with a royal declaration that God has charged the king to construct the Jerusalem temple. Yet Ezra 4 introduces uncertainty regarding the temple's legitimacy, as questions and accusations stall the program. The temple is finally completed at the end of Ezra 6 with the aid of the Persian government. David Beetham notes that stories about origins are consequential because of their relationship to the legitimacy of power in the present.[1] Relations of power, social hierarchies, and political and economic arrangements of the author's own time leave behind telltale footprints in this account of the temple's origins, allowing us, in some measure, to construct his social world.

On the assumption that the text was composed in the last decades of the Persian Empire, the events recounted in Ezra 4–6 occurred a century earlier. Life for the Jerusalem community had changed. Imperial policies had more fully integrated the region into the empire, resulting in increased commercial and social interaction with the wider population.[2] Immigration increased the local population, and the provincial cultural center shifted from Mizpah to Jerusalem. By the early fourth century, conflict with Egypt led to militarization of the region, intensifying imperial presence.[3] At the same time, Melody Knowles comments, "The geographic boundaries of Yahwism extended beyond the borders of Yehud, and thus adherents had to

---

1. David Beetham, *Legitimation of Power* (Atlantic Highlands, NJ: Humanities Press International, 1991), 103.
2. Hoglund, "Achaemenid Context," 59.
3. Fantalkin and Tal, "Canonization of the Pentateuch," 9. Briant concurs (*From Cyrus to Alexander*, 64–66) but bases this primarily on evidence from Ezra-Nehemiah and the existence of ration lists issued to ethnic groups in small towns. Hoglund (*Achaemenid Imperial Administration*, 244) proposes an earlier date for this in the midfifth century.

find other ways to define their relation or non-relation to each other."[4] Thus, as Smith-Christopher notes, exclusionary steps by the Jerusalem community in response to these changes became a source of new conflicts.[5]

By the end of the Persian era, the Jerusalem temple had been standing for a century. Yet it faced competition from worship at Gerizim.[6] Lacking its own property, as Gary Knoppers points out, made it dependent on "the goodwill of patrons for its maintenance."[7] Evidence suggests that the primary patrons were members of the golah community who then, as Blenkinsopp observes, "claimed control of the Jerusalem cult under the supervision and protection of the imperial authorities."[8] Continuing patronage for temple maintenance may have been waning—especially if local political or priestly power was being contested. This narrative is constructed in light of, and perhaps to address, these realities.

6.1. Narrative Structure and Style

Accusations of sedition against the temple builders (Ezra 4:12–16) begin this section. They are confirmed by an archival search of government records. Temple construction resumes only after a second investigation described in Ezra 5–6, and the project is completed in 515 BCE, the sixth year of King Darius (6:14–15). However, this sequence is made problematic by the chronologically dislocated letters to and from Artaxerxes (465–424 BCE) in Ezra 4. These letters deal with construction of Jerusalem's city walls, but narratively are employed to explain the delayed construction of the temple from the time of Cyrus until the reign of Darius. To complicate

---

4. Melody Knowles, *Centrality Practiced: Jerusalem in the Religious Practice of Yehud and the Diaspora during the Persian Period*, ABS 16 (Atlanta: Society of Biblical Literature, 2006), 8.

5. Smith-Christopher, "Politics of Ezra," 97.

6. Stern, *Assyrian, Babylonian, and Persian Periods*, 479; Magen, "Dating," 176. Magen dates the beginning of the Samaritan temple to the mid-fifth century BCE. Edelman (*The Origins of the 'Second' Temple*, 66). suggests that Mizpah also had a temple prior to the rebuilding of Jerusalem.

7. Gary Knoppers, "'The City YHWH Has Chosen': The Chronicler's Promotion of Jerusalem in Light of Recent Archaeology," in *Jerusalem in Bible and Archaeology: The First Temple Period*, ed. Andrew G. Vaughn and Ann E. Killebrew, SymS 18 (Atlanta: Society of Biblical Literature, 2003), 315.

8. Blenkinsopp, "Temple and Society," 39–40. Evidence of community control can be seen in Nehemiah's expulsion of Tobiah from the temple precincts (Neh 13:5–9).

the matter further, Ezra 4:6 refers to an accusation against the Jews sent to Xerxes in his ascension year (486 BCE), but no content is recorded; instead, the complaint to Artaxerxes follows.[9] There has been much discussion regarding the authenticity of the documents and the chronology of the events to which they refer.[10] The most compelling explanation is that 4:6–23 is a digression to justify the exiles' rebuffing proffered help in 4:2–5, and so 4:24 resumes the narrative halted at 4:5.[11] The added material is then thematically related rather than chronologically accurate.[12]

Much, but not all, of this narrative is composed in Aramaic. Aramaic begins in 4:8 at the outset of a letter and continues through narrative and further letters and ends in 6:18, midway through a narrative conclusion that finishes in Hebrew in 6:22. Much of the story is conveyed through letters and imperial edicts. Archival searches produce information that is employed to either halt or support the construction. Each search is suggested by local leadership and decreed by the monarch (4:14–15, 19; 5:17–6:1).[13] It becomes apparent that this pattern reflects authorial purpose in the use of whatever older documents are employed. The author has literary and,

---

9. The authors of this complaint are also problematic: Ezra 4:7 refers to Bishlam, Mithredath, and Tabeel, while 4:8 cites Rehum and Shimshai as the authors.

10. Grabbe (*Ezra-Nehemiah*, 21) contends that the author is ignorant of the sequence of Persian rulers and states, "When the *contents* of the chapter are compared with *external history* … the message becomes nonsense." Jacob Wright argues on the basis of inconsistencies between Nehemiah's approach to Artaxerxes (Neh 2) and the king's edict in Ezra 4 that the correspondence in this chapter is not authentic but composed ad hoc for the book. He suggests that the final proviso, "the city should not be built until a command be given from me" (Ezra 4:21), makes sense only in the narrative of the book that anticipates future permission to build (*Rebuilding Identity*, 35, 38).

11. Williamson, *Ezra, Nehemiah*, xlvii, 57. Williamson suggests that the work stoppage in Ezra 4 may historically have been related to Ezra's mission.

12. Baruch Halpern, "A Historiographic Commentary on Ezra 1–6: A Chronological Narrative and Dual Chronology in Israelite Historiography," in *The Hebrew Bible and Its Interpreters*, ed. William H. Propp, Baruch Halpern, and David Noel Freedman (Winona Lake, IN: Eisenbrauns, 1990), 105, 111.

13. Wright, *Rebuilding Identity*, 39–40. Wright identifies textual searching as a recurring theme within the book as a whole and suggests that it reflects a reverence for written texts. He lists the search for the priests' registration (2:59), Ezra's search for missing Levites, the inquiry into those who had married foreign wives, the gathering to study Torah in Neh 9, as well as the Persian rulers seeking to find records (Ezra 4:15, 19; 5:17–6:1).

even more importantly, ideological motives for this tangled text. Although issues regarding dates and authenticity remain unresolved, the rhetorical strategies and purposes of this account can still be investigated.[14]

Hans Mallau identifies a considerable number of parallels between Ezra 4:1–24 and 5:1–6:22 and demonstrates that these parallel panels should be treated as a unit.[15] Each account follows the same general outline: both describe the same building effort under Zerubbabel and Jeshua (4:1–2; 5:2), a confrontation with outsiders that prompts spokesmen to justify their activity as obedience to Cyrus's command (4:3; 5:13), and a royal edict that resolves the conflict over construction. Further structural correspondence include the outsiders' effect on the progress of the work (4:4; 5:5), the emperor seeking background information from archives prior to rendering a decision (4:15; 5:17), and a description of the outcome for the project (4:24; 6:14–15). Mallau deems it unlikely that two documents regarding two separate events would have the many close parallels he identifies, and so he suggests that a skillful redactor has composed two separate accounts of the same event.[16]

Stefan Matzal has identified further points of correspondence and organizes the narratives into four general sections (see the table below): an initial encounter (4:1–5 and 5:1–5), a request (4:6–16 and 5:6–17), a royal decree (4:17–22 and 6:1–12), and a concluding enactment of the decree (4:23–24 and 6:13–15). He also notes that the Hebrew introduction (4:1–7) and conclusion (6:19–22) share terminology and create a framework for the three chapters.[17] Mallau suggests that the contrasting accounts demonstrate that important goals are achieved through persuasion and political skills rather than curt and tactless confrontations.[18]

---

14. H. G. M. Williamson, "The Aramaic Documents in Ezra Revisited," *JTS* 59 (2008): 41–62. Williamson provides a helpful summary and analysis of the issues regarding the Aramaic text.

15. Hans H. Mallau, "The Redaction of Ezra 4–6: A Plea for a Theology of Scribes," *PRSt* 15.4 (1988): 70–75.

16. Ibid., 71–72, 78.

17. Stefan Matzal, "Short Notes on the Structure of Ezra 4–6," *VT* 50 (2000): 566–68. He cites the double repetition of "YHWH, the God of Israel," occurring in the introduction and conclusion as well as references to Israel and the root דרש, "to seek." This structure results in Ezra 4:1–5 becoming a literary hinge. It frames the previous chapter as it parallels the mention of the people of the land in 3:3 and introduces the following section.

18. Mallau, "Redaction of Ezra 4–6," 78.

6. EZRA 4–6: CONTESTING LEGITIMACY

Narrative Structure of Ezra 4:1–6:22

Panel 1: Ezra 4		Panel 2: Ezra 5–6
4:1–5	Initial encounter with outsiders	5:1–5
4:3	Actions are obedience to Cyrus's command	5:13
4:4	Effect of outsiders on progress of work	5:5
4:6–16	A request	5:6–17
4:15	Search for background information in archives	5:17
4:17–22	A royal decree	6:1–12
4:23–24	Enactment of the decree	6:13–15
	Conclusion	6:19–22

Although the introduction in Ezra 4:1–5 shares terminology with the conclusion in Ezra 6:19–22, this pericope shares a similar plot structure with the beginning of panel 2 in Ezra 5:1–5. In each, as construction commences, the work comes to the attention of outsiders whose inquiry threatens the project. However, the parallel plots involve opposing royal decisions that reverse outcomes. In Ezra 4:4–5, the adversaries use intimidation and bribery to successfully frustrate the construction, and Artaxerxes suspends building "until I make a decree" (4:21). In 5:3–4, Tattenai and his associates make inquiries, but the text states, "the eye of their God was upon the elders of the Jews, and they did not stop them" (5:5). Darius then decrees that the building should continue and adds an oath condemning anyone who would "put forth a hand to alter this" (6:8–12).[19] The turnaround may be signaled by the modified introduction in 5:1, where Haggai and Zechariah spur construction just as Jeremiah anticipates the return of exiles in 1:1. Prophetic proclamations lead to successful outcomes and legitimate the events that follow, including any political skill and persuasion employed by the community. As events replay within the same narrative structure, variations signal the author's perspective regarding interactions with surrounding peoples and the imperial government.

---

19. Ibid., 72.

Both accounts describe a confrontation between exiles and others that creates a problem to be overcome. In chapter 4, "adversaries" make what appears to be a conciliatory offer of help, only to be unequivocally rejected. In response, they garner a royal decree that thwarts the project. Ezra 4:6–23 explains the hostile actions of the adversaries in their own words, which also serve to distinguish between their community and the exiles. In the second account, Tattenai, representing the imperial government, requires an explanation, "Who gave you a decree to build this house and to finish this structure?" (5:3). The response by the elders is informative and nonconfrontational, and the project continues unimpeded. As Baruch Halpern notes, Tattenai's inquiry in Ezra 5 "reflects official interest, not a history of opposition"; but the more pointed inquiry receives a more conciliatory response.[20]

The account attributes the delayed construction to hostile actions by neighbors. Williamson notes that the theme of continuity, so positive with regard to the exiles, finds new meaning when applied to others. They are continuously opposed to reconstruction and dangerous to the community.[21] However, an alternative explanation for the delay already exists in Haggai—community indifference (Hag 1:2–4).[22] Yet in Ezra the exiles eagerly pursue construction until compelled to stop. Given Haggai's earlier explanation, it seems that charging nonmembers for the setback is not meant merely to explain a delay in the temple's construction. Rather, it roots sectarian division in the author's time to antagonism directed at the earliest repatriates. The enmity is never resolved, but it is effectively overwritten by successful diplomacy with the empire.

6.2. Written Records and Legitimacy

6.2.1. Changing Languages, Changing Views: The Role of Aramaic

The role of language creates a conundrum in Ezra-Nehemiah. The Torah requires translation in Neh 8:8 (assumedly from Hebrew into the vernacular), yet Nehemiah contends with the people over marrying foreign

---

20. Halpern, "Historiographic Commentary," 112. Halpern notes that although divine anger led to the temple's destruction, the problem to be resolved is gaining not divine forgiveness but imperial permission.
21. Williamson, *Ezra, Nehemiah*, 66.
22. Blenkinsopp, *Ezra-Nehemiah*, 105.

women in part because the children "could not speak the language of Judah" (13:24). For a text that presents foreign language as problematic, it is indeed odd that the book itself is written in two languages: Aramaic and Biblical Hebrew. Aramaic, introduced in the beginning of a report by the people of the land to the imperial government, sits in the midst of Biblical Hebrew. Yet Aramaic is the language that describes the construction of the temple, the heart of the new Judean community. Below I consider the narrative role of Aramaic. Its implications for legitimacy and cultural capital I will take up in the following chapter.

Ernst Knauf suggests a complex linguistic context early in the Persian era, with Mishnaic Hebrew used locally, Aramaic employed in government and diplomacy (and most familiar to returning exiles), and Biblical Hebrew used for literary composition. He posits that local scribes may have been trilingual—fluent in Aramaic, speaking locally in Mishnaic Hebrew, and mastering Biblical Hebrew.[23] Joachim Schaper contends that the local Hebrew and Aramaic coincide with a social division. A vernacular Hebrew would have been retained by the lower-class, nonexiled inhabitants of Judah.[24] In Ezra, the people of the land converse with the exiles in Hebrew and communicate with the court in Aramaic, which perhaps reflects changed linguistic habits in the late Persian era.[25] By the Hellenistic period, evidence reveals that Aramaic was employed locally for letters and court cases as well as marriage and divorce contracts (even during the

---

23. Ernst Axel Knauf, "Bethel: The Israelite Impact on Judean Language and Literature," in Lipschits and Oeming, *Persian Period*, 309. This raises the question about who would be able to understand these texts if only priests were trained in Biblical Hebrew.

24. Joachim Schaper, "Hebrew and Its Study in the Persian Period," in *Hebrew Study from Ezra to Ben-Yehuda*, ed. William Horbury (Edinburgh: T&T Clark, 1999), 16–17.

25. Ingo Kottsieper, "'And They Did Not Care to Speak Yehudit': On Linguistic Change in Judah during the Late Persian Era," in Lipschits, Knoppers, and Albertz, *Fourth Century B.C.E.*, 103, 109. Kottsieper posits an evolution from a bilingual society that spoke both Aramaic and Hebrew prior to the fifth century to one where Aramaic superseded Hebrew as a spoken language. He suggests that local opposition to Aramaic had religious motivations because it separated "the uneducated people from the Hebrew Torah, which had just been propagated as the unifying document for the Jewish people" (110).

Hasmonean revolts), while Hebrew continued in use in temple business and in religious circles.²⁶

In this narrative, Aramaic is not confined to the body of documents. Nearly one third of the Aramaic is narrative that introduces, links, and ends the Aramaic documents.²⁷ Many suggest that the author is employing authentic documents, and the Aramaic narrative is explained through proximity or thematic connections.²⁸ These explanations are unconvincing, especially when considering the point at which the Aramaic ends. Furthermore, B. T. Arnold rightly points out that reference to Haggai and Zechariah appears in the Aramaic section (5:1–2), which suggests access to these prophetic *Hebrew* texts, thus making the selection of Aramaic for these verses even more curious.²⁹

Arnold investigates the role of Aramaic through the lens of literary artistry using the work of Boris Uspensky.³⁰ Uspensky notes, "The rendition of speech in one language or another has purely functional aims, directly related to the problem of the authorial point of view."³¹ Arnold suggests that changing languages introduces differences in "point of view" to express differing ideological perspectives. He posits that the Aramaic allows the author to present an outsider's perspective of the events described by "faithful transmission of the character's native language" and identifies a number of terms distinctive to the Aramaic section that reflect this different viewpoint.³² In particular, he cites, "the Jews who were in Judah and Jerusalem" (Ezra 5:1) as opposed to "exiles" in 2:1 or "children of Israel" in 3:1. In addition, God is אלה (4:24; 5:1, 2, 5, etc.), not YHWH, and the temple is "the house of God that is in Jerusalem."³³ Joshua Berman

---

26. Ibid., 111–15.

27. Joshua Berman, "The Narratological Purpose of Aramaic Prose in Ezra 4:8–6:18," *AS* 5 (2007): 166.

28. See Daniel C. Snell, "Why Is There Aramaic in the Bible?" *JSOT* 18 (1980): 32–51; Williamson, "Aramaic Documents," 50.

29. B. T. Arnold, "The Use of Aramaic in the Hebrew Bible: Another Look at Bilingualism in Ezra and Daniel," *JNSL* 22.2 (1996): 5.

30. Ibid., 1–16.

31. Boris Uspenski, *The Poetics of Composition: The Structure of the Artistic Text and Typology of Compositional Form*, trans. Valentina Zavarin and Susan Wittig (Berkeley: University of California Press, 1973), 46. Uspenski treats the use of French and Russian in *War and Peace* by Leo Tolstoy.

32. Arnold, "Use of Aramaic," 4.

33. Ibid., 6.

supplements Arnold's list, noting the reference to the book of Moses (6:18) also reflects an external viewpoint since it fails to refer to its divine source in contrast with other references in the Hebrew portions of Ezra.[34]

Berman posits an unnamed Samarian scribe, associated with Tattenai's investigation in chapter 5, as a literary explanation for the external voice. He suggests that it operates in the same way the words of outsiders are often used in other biblical passages, for example, Rahab, the outsider, who proclaims YHWH's power over the Canaanites (Josh 2:9–13), or the Midianite soldiers overheard by Gideon as they express fear prior to battle (Judg 7:13–14). The words of the outsider confirm what the reader may not have taken to heart, "the foes of his time are not as formidable as he may have thought them, and … the God of Israel works in ways he may not have appreciated without this external testimony."[35] As in these other texts, Ezra 4–6 addresses internal doubts or fears by overturning the adversaries' strategies or plans. However, in Joshua and Judges the identity of the speakers is clear, as is their stance with regard to the Israelites. In Ezra, an outsider's perspective is less obvious, and Arnold and Berman must develop arguments that rely on the use of Aramaic, terminology, and subtle or contested readings, plus positing an unidentified character to defend this external viewpoint for the entire Aramaic section.[36] Arnold further suggests that the point of view shifts gradually from an external to an internal perspective.[37] Berman adds that the scribe's perspective slowly shifts from belligerence in Rehum's rescript to a cautious and impartial tone, so that by the end of the account the Samarian narrator is "nearly converted to a fully Judean orientation."[38] This final move becomes a vindication of identity that delivers a message for the readership, who, Berman states, "struggle with the maintenance of a strong Jewish identity in Achaemenid Judah."[39]

---

34. Ezra 3:2 cites "the law of Moses the man of God," and 7:6–26 refers to the divine source all seven times the law is mentioned.

35. Berman, "Narratological Purpose," 190.

36. For example, Berman (ibid., 168) bases the Samarian scribal identity on the first person plural pronoun in 5:4: "*We* asked them, 'What are the names of the men who are engaged in the building?'" He discounts a scribal dittography from 5:10, where the same question is repeated.

37. Arnold, "Use of Aramaic," 6.

38. Berman "Narratological Purpose," 191.

39. Ibid., 190.

Although their argument is difficult to justify for the entire Aramaic section, the claim of Arnold and Berman that the terminology and language reflect an external perspective is worth considering. However, I would argue that rather than a single (albeit changing) view of the community from outside, Ezra 4–6 reflects negotiations *with* outsiders from two different perspectives. Ezra 4 presents communication with the monarch by those external to Yehud. But Ezra 5–6 represents an insider's presentation of how to interact or present oneself *to* those outside the community—in particular the imperial and provincial authorities. The Aramaic acts as an interface and signals the boundary between the Jerusalem community and the rest of the world.

6.2.2. Ezra 4: Writing Wrongs

The hostile actions that begin Ezra 4 turn quickly into a letter writing campaign aimed at halting construction. In 4:7–23, outsiders talk with outsiders and give their perspective on the Yehud community. The foreign identity of the two sets of letter writers—first, Bishlam, Mithredath, and Tabeel, then Rehum the commissioner and Shimshai the scribe (4:7–8)—are underscored by associating them with a long list of nationalities in 4:9–10: "the Persians, the people of Erech, the Babylonians, the people of Susa, that is, the Elamites, and the rest of the nations whom the great and noble Osnappar deported and settled in the cities of Samaria and in the rest of the province Beyond the River." They admit they are foreigners settled by Assyrian and Babylonian kings (Esarhaddon and Osnappar; 4:2, 10).[40] The complainants' foreignness is unambiguous, but their specific nationalities are vague. Gordon Davies observes that they are introduced "in a detailed mixture of name, rank, nationality, and history" (4:7–9).[41] Without a clear identity, they "are too blurred to gain prestige in [the reader's] sight despite their successful association with the ruler."[42] Davies notes that even the name of the king is obscured, and so his authority is undermined. (Who settled these people? Which Persian monarch is addressed: Xerxes, Artaxerxes, or Darius?) Moreover, the imperial decrees by Cyrus, Artaxerxes,

---

40. Although it is commonly assumed that Ashurbanipal is intended by the reference to Osnappar, the mangled name makes even this identification tenuous.
41. Davies, *Ezra and Nehemiah*, 23.
42. Ibid., 20.

and Darius are successively reversed, and the contradictory rulings further undermine royal authority.

The unfavorable account of the history of Jerusalem, and the purpose for construction, is composed without the input of the Judean community. The city is described as rebellious and wicked (4:12), a threat to the royal revenue (4:13), hurtful to kings, and historically seditious (4:15). It is a hostile and damning account of Jerusalem's history and warns that any reconstruction will revive these ancient dangers and leave the king with "no possession in the province" (4:16). The letter mentions the completion of the city walls three times (4:12, 13, 16), always partnered with either rebellion or a loss of tax monies, and encourages the monarch to search the royal annals for confirmation (4:15). The king demands an inquiry (4:19), the accusations are confirmed, and the monarch halts the work "until I make a decree" (4:21). The correspondents also underscore their close relationship to and concern for the monarch: "we share the salt of the palace and it is not fitting for us to witness the king's dishonor" (4:14).

Davies contends that even as the claims of loyalty "win the king's ear," they diminish the stature of the adversaries in the reader's eyes.[43] In contrast, the reputation and identity of the Judahites is enhanced, as the letters describe the might and influence of the ancient kings of Jerusalem. Even though these letters detail a setback, their rhetoric gives the Judahites "greater status in our [the readers'] eyes … and anticipates the repatriates' eventual resurgence."[44]

Ezra 3 describes a unified, carefully defined, and ritually sanctified community. Ezra 4 then draws a portrait of those outside the community. Their identities and geographical associations are obscure and their behavior treacherous as they unite in countering the exiles' restoration efforts. The distinctions between the communities are lent moral authority by integrating them into a controversy over the temple's legitimacy. The struggle to build the temple is now coupled with a struggle to define

---

43. Ibid., 21.
44. Ibid., 23. Davies also notes that vocabulary combines with conflict to signal the estrangement of the two camps: *people of the land* vs. *the people of Judah* (Ezra 4:4), counselors frustrate counsel (יוֹעֲצִים לְהָפֵר עֲצָתָם; 4:5), the heads of the *fathers'* houses (4:2–3) are stymied by records of the king's *fathers* (4:15), the peoples of the lands are denied a share in building the *temple* of YHWH (4:1) but share the salt of the king's *temple* (palace) (4:14).

the community and its boundaries.[45] This written account then acts as a source of authority in future debates over the nature of the community.

6.2.3. Ezra 5–6: Rewriting Wrongs

In chapters 5–6, the scenario of construction, inquiry, and edict is replayed, and this time the elders have input into the letter that goes to the king (5:11–16). Their considerate reply indicates "awareness that the audience now includes the king of Persia and not only their local adversaries."[46] Tattenai asks questions, and the letter provides a different version of history and their project. In response, Darius, the monarch in these chapters, completely repeals the previous results. Not only does the project continue unimpeded, but Darius supplies materials and issues an edict in support of the temple's future care.

The reader is reminded in 5:2 that Zerubbabel and Shealtiel lead the community. However, despite twice stating that Tattenai asks for the names of the people (5:4, 10), they are never listed. Instead, the narrator states that the eye of God was upon the elders of the Jews (5:5) or that the elders identify themselves as servants of the God of heaven (5:11). Unlike those who drafted the letter in Ezra 4, this identity marks the elders with distinction. They state they are rebuilding a temple built by a great king of Israel but destroyed by Nebuchadnezzar (5:11–12). Much the same as the adversaries in Ezra 4, the elders refer to a historic king of Jerusalem. Berman argues that a reference to past "great kings" would not be a wise tactic when addressing the Persian monarch, since he is unlikely to welcome any suggestion of loyalty to a different crown.[47] Perhaps the reference reflects a bit of clever manipulation, just as the reference to ancient kings of Judah in chapter 4 was cleverly manipulated. In 4:20, the king of Jerusalem is specifically associated with collecting "tribute, custom, and toll," while the city is tied to sedition and rebellion that would endanger the current monarch's tribute, custom, and toll (4:12–13, 15, 16, 19).[48] In

---

45. Bourdieu, *Language and Symbolic Power*, 128.
46. Berman, "Narratological Purpose," 180.
47. Ibid., 181.
48. Ezra 4:20 contains wording that could be understood as referring to *foreign* kings who ruled over Jerusalem rather than Judean kings since it includes a reference to the province by name. A more literal translation would read, "mighty kings have ruled over Jerusalem, governing all the provinces beyond the River" (NASB), rather

Ezra 5, the "great king of Israel" is cited *only* as one who builds temples (5:11), and the elders acknowledge the legitimacy of the Babylonian king's destruction of the Jerusalem temple (5:12). Thus one could infer that Persian decisions regarding the temple are also regarded as legitimate—and their narrative testifies that *great* kings *build temples*! Expressing fondness for past kings who built temples might suggest to any current king that building a temple would likewise lead to esteem for him. The response also asserts that these people have learned their lesson. Angering God resulted in destruction by imperial forces, and this community wants no more of that! Indeed, they assert that their actions are an effort to obey a Persian monarch's decree (5:13–16). Their loyalty is offered in exchange for royal investment in the local cultural capital of the temple.

6.2.4. Contrasting Outcomes: Everyone Needs a Good Scribe

The two competing letter campaigns of Ezra 4 and Ezra 5–6 diverge over the histories recounted, imperial responses, and the outcome for the Yehud community. Ineffective resistance to confrontation recorded in chapter 4 is replaced with effective explanation and dialogue in chapter 5. The reader can then conclude that one does not need to respond to confrontation with overt resistance. Rather, carefully worded responses designed to navigate around conflict and work the system accomplish the task at hand. These chapters also further distinguish between the community of Israel and the people of the land and address the issue of the political legitimacy of the temple.

Berman contends that the twofold explanations of the temple's destruction (God allowed it/kings enacted it) promotes a theology of dual causality as actions of foreign kings are attributed to God. He notes in Ezra 4 that the Jews claim only Cyrus's edict—not God's will—as the basis for their construction (4:3) and suggests the failure of this first building episode is due to a failure to attribute efforts to divine impetus, which then sets up the alternative presented in Ezra 5–6.[49] In Ezra 5, Haggai and Zechariah

---

than the more common, "Jerusalem has had mighty kings" (NRSV). In the NASB, the king may be expressing concern about losing control over a city that had been compliant under previous monarchs of his own empire. The less literal translation suits the context better with all the warnings about the seditious city and provides a better counterpoint with the reference to the great king of Jerusalem in 5:20.

49. Berman, "Narratological Purpose," 182.

motivate the builders (5:1–2; 6:14), and the elders identify themselves as servants of God carrying out Cyrus's order (5:13)—thus pairing the two sources of legitimation. Furthermore, the content of the newly discovered edict now demonstrates a keen interest by Cyrus in the dimensions of the temple—however incomplete they may be (6:3–5). Berman states that by joining both sources of legitimation the author "wishes to cast the Jews' behavior in this episode as a paradigm for future generations to emulate."[50] Noting a series of contrasting uses of identical terms by Artaxerxes in Ezra 4 and Darius in Ezra 5, he suggests that the two accounts "are an index of change … from … capitulation and surrender to … covenantal commitment to build the temple."[51]

Is Ezra 4 a warning against capitulation and Ezra 5–6 a model of perseverance under pressure? These may be valid theological readings. However, divine instigation of royal builders who overcome adversity was standard literary fare in temple building accounts. Furthermore, the lack of reference to the divine will in connection to Cyrus's edict in Ezra 4 may be because the divine impetus occurs in 1:1 when the decree is first introduced. Additionally the project's failure *and* success are achieved by obedience to the Persian monarch—not by resisting Persian rule. It is only *local* resistance that is portrayed as problematic, and it is the monarch's permission, not God's, that the exiles need to continue their project. What has changed most significantly from chapter 4 is not persistence but the inclusion of the *Judean* explanation of the building program *in writing* in the letter to Darius. The dual causality of divine will and royal decrees is mediated through the texts that carry the messages between the community and the king. Carefully worded documents accomplish the will of God and king.

The threat of adversaries to again thwart the construction as they did in Ezra 4 is hinted at in 5:3. Tattenai and his associates "descend upon" the builders, but this time the issues are resolved in favor of the building project. The evidence underscores the value of negotiating with the authorities and accepting their right to license such projects. Such a stance achieves the sought-after goal of excluding the people of the land as declared in

---

50. Ibid., 183.
51. Ibid., 185. Berman notes that Artaxerxes orders construction to "cease" (בטל; 4:21), while Darius orders that it not "cease" (6:11). Likewise negligence is a concern (4:22; 6:9), with Artaxerxes concerned with the profit and Darius with the temple. Similarly, injury is of concern in 4:22 and 6:12.

4:3, while also achieving the successful completion of the temple. Effective tactics now involve careful negotiation by wise leaders and skillful scribes who know how to turn a phrase instead of aggressively stonewalling.

6.3. Ezra 4: Conformity, Self-Interest, and Competition

In Ezra 4, the community's boundaries grow as a matter of concern. The people of the land are constructed as unworthy of inclusion as their character is impugned by the content of their letter, ostensibly in their own words, to halt the temple construction. The text also defends the authority of the Jerusalem power structure by demonstrating that its leadership, contrary to those outside the community, is devoted to promoting the public interest as they labor to construct the temple.[52] The details of this argument reflect a concern for legitimacy and political power.

Beetham states that every power seeks to establish and cultivate a belief in its legitimacy.[53] He argues that this is done chiefly by the powerful respecting the limits set to their power. The monarchs in Ezra 4–6 abide by previous edicts and historical evidence found in archives, accepting limits on their right to enact their rulings. The adversaries, on the contrary, are portrayed as overstepping boundaries as they override Cyrus's edict to impede the construction of a temple that is not their own. Beetham identifies four typical means of power whereby one social group is able to dominate another: possession of material resources, physical force, control of socially necessary activities (skills), and positional power (command defined by rules).[54] The two social groups lack positional power over each other. So they compete over or employ the remaining sources of power, even as they each appeal to the monarch who holds positional control over both groups.

The letters in Ezra 4 and 5 do not question the legitimacy of the king's laws, his power, or its acquisition. Instead, the monarch's claim to legitimate power operates on a doxic level in the narrative. Both the exiles and the people of the land accede to Persian rule. In this case, the acceptance of Persian legitimacy rests not on the regime's conformity to local religious or ethnic values but on the king's ability to satisfy, and/or mediate between, the interests of either party. The letter by Rehum and Shimshai appears as

---

52. Beetham, *Legitimation of Power*, 237.
53. Ibid., 34.
54. Ibid., 47–49.

a transparent effort to win the king's good graces. Richard Jenkins associates this desire for approval with conformity and contends that it has a great impact on public behavior.[55] The adversaries warn the king that the rebuilding threatens his coffers and regional control. Their letter contrasts their loyalty with the intentions of the builders. They describe themselves to the king as "your servants" (4:11) who "share the salt of the palace and it is not fitting for us to witness the king's dishonor" (4:14). They contrast this with the potential nonconforming behavior of the builders: "this is a rebellious city, hurtful to kings and provinces, and that sedition was stirred up in it from long ago" (4:15), "if this city is rebuilt and its walls finished, you will then have no possession in the province Beyond the River" (4:16). The either/or rhetoric is a means of manipulating the king's perception of the exiles, while simultaneously identifying themselves with the king's interests. The concern for the affairs of the king indicates compliance with his rule, acknowledging his legitimacy. The exilic community also defers to the Persian monarch, as evidenced in Ezra 5–6. They conscientiously obey royal edicts but never claim to be dependent upon the monarch nor do they malign their adversaries. The letter's more muted form is in part due to the author's concern to gain the approval of the readers/hearers of Ezra. As each community vies against the other, their letters provide evidence of their own compliance.

The temple construction is a catalyst for hostilities due to its role as a visible and public symbol of the community. Jenkins comments,

> Typically organizations have a substantial and visible presence in the human world: in buildings, artifacts and public symbols, organization of time, uniforms, etc. An individual's organizational identification may be framed at least as much by that organization's public image as by her presentation of self.... The public presence of organizations is an important dimension of their impact on non-members.[56]

The temple is a visible reminder of a community of which people *are* or are *not* a part. Jenkins comments further,

> Identification and allocation are, in fact, mutually entailed in each other. Identity is consequential in terms of allocation: how you are identified

---

55. Richard Jenkins, *Social Identity* (New York: Routledge, 2008), 149.
56. Ibid., 186.

may influence what, and how much, you get. Allocation is part of the process of identification: being deprived of or given access to particular resources is likely to color the individual sense of what it means to be an X or a Y. A shared experience of being treated in particular ways may even generate a sense of collectivity where none existed before.[57]

The temple is a visible manifestation of the allocation of resources and a constant reminder to the exiles of their distinction and to the people of the land of their exclusion from membership.

The accusers raise the possibility of the exiles engaging in treason, rebellion, and withholding taxes as possible motives and actions accompanying the construction of the temple (or the city walls). Such strategies may have been considerations among the exiles. (We certainly have some evidence of messianic hopes and economic hardship in the writings of Haggai, Zechariah, and Neh 5.) However, in this text these maneuvers are placed as accusations in the mouth of the adversaries so that they can be dismissed as contrary to the community's purposes. Here rebellion does *not* serve the community. Instead, the community survives through compliance, moderated by those who have mastered the techniques that allow them to "'get [their] motion carried,' not to mention the mastery of the procedures and tactics which ... directly control the very production of the group."[58]

The letters (4:11–16 and 5:7–17) stereotype the two communities (for bad or good). As the separate contentions are presented in their own words, the letters give the author's caricature of his opponents, or portrayal of his own community, greater legitimacy. Jenkins states that stereotyping and attribution are important dimensions of classification and identification. He notes that stereotyping is "a collective process, involving the creation and maintenance of group values and ideologies, and the positive valorization of the in-group," and it demarcates boundaries "with a particular, albeit illusory clarity."[59] However, he adds,

> At the margins of the group, where the frameworks of predictability are less firm and intrusive, there is likely to be ambiguity about membership criteria and appropriate behavior. Group boundaries may thus

---

57. Ibid., 198.
58. Bourdieu, *Language and Symbolic Power*, 182.
59. Jenkins, *Social Identity*, 152.

be generated by uncertainty, emerging as an ordering response to the relative unpredictability of encounters. Strong pressures encouraging conforming behavior—with penalties attaching to deviance—may oppress most those whose membership or identity is insecure. Powerful signals about conformity and deviance, dramatizing group membership and boundaries, are easily expressed as stereotypes of insiders and outsiders.[60]

Bourdieu adds, "Struggles over ethnic or regional identity … are a particular case of the different struggles over classifications … to impose the legitimate definition of the divisions of the social world and, thereby, to make and unmake groups."[61] When these classifications are imposed on a whole group, they establish a consensus about, and thus create the reality of, the identity and unity of the group.[62] Bourdieu further states that this political action can "transform the social world in accordance with their interests—by producing, reproducing or destroying the representations that make groups visible for themselves and for others."[63] The account in Ezra 4 produces a negative representation of the people of the land by ascribing to them actions and words that malign the character of the exiles and are detrimental to their rebuilding efforts. The author then employs this depiction to classify membership among the people of the land as repugnant for any who value the good of the Judean community.

The scribal professional who composed these chapters competed with other professionals (such as Rehum or Shimshai) even as they all competed over legitimate ideas about the social world that would resonate with the people and therefore grant them the power to mobilize them. Bourdieu terms this a "Double Game" and comments,

> So as to ensure [an] enduring mobilization comes about, political parties must on the one hand develop and impose a representation of the social world capable of obtaining the support of the greatest possible number of citizens, and on the other hand win positions … capable of ensuring that they can wield power over those who grant that power to them.[64]

---

60. Ibid., 154.
61. Bourdieu, *Language and Symbolic Power*, 221.
62. Ibid.
63. Ibid., 127.
64. Ibid., 181.

6. EZRA 4–6: CONTESTING LEGITIMACY

Therefore, "professionals [are] required who can manipulate ideas and groups at the same time: Producing ideas capable of producing groups by manipulating ideas in such a way as to ensure that they gain the support of a group."[65] Bourdieu identifies a homology between the structure of the political field and the structure of the world represented, commenting,

> Homology means that, in adopting stances that are most in conformity with the interests of those whom they represent, the professionals are still pursuing—without necessarily admitting it to themselves—the satisfaction of their own interests, as these are assigned to them by the structure of positions and oppositions constitutive of the internal space of the political field.[66]

The interests of the author of this text are hidden in part because, as Bourdieu states, the cultural producer's ideologies tend to be presented "as universal interests, shared by the group as a whole."[67] The author defines the social world to suit the interests of his community, while at the same time defining it in such a way that his mastery of the scribal skills needed to achieve this goal grants him a position of power, and so suits his interests as well. Bourdieu observes that "the production of ideas about the social world is always in fact subordinated to the logic of the conquest of power, which is the logic of the mobilization of the greatest number."[68]

This text portrays a society organized for a specific purpose, and Beetham observes that society organized for the pursuit of a collective purpose requires belief in the validity of that purpose for its legitimacy.[69] Thus legitimacy rests on a shared belief in that purpose and ongoing evidence that those wielding power do so in keeping with that goal. He observes that a central belief system defines goals, provides stimulus, and is a source of authority for rulers, but becomes "both its strength and weakness." Although shared belief accomplishes all three criteria, it is required to do too much, making it vulnerable to forces of erosion (e.g., class division, ethnic divides, or external forces).[70] The system becomes

---

65. Ibid., 182.
66. Ibid., 183.
67. Ibid., 167.
68. Ibid., 181.
69. Beetham, *Legitimation of Power*, 185. He discusses this in terms of Soviet Communism.
70. Ibid., 239.

vulnerable to collapse when credibility of its belief system is eroded or if the bureaucratic framework designed to support the society's goal begins to contradict the goal. External competition can fuel the collapse of such a system, as alternatives arise and people claim a right to decide their interests themselves. Thus the author's belief about society is defended as the text portrays that all are committed to the collective purpose and, despite adversity and alternatives, successfully achieve their shared goal.

The legitimacy of Judah's leadership rests not on social utility but on the extent to which the people's beliefs converge with the purposes for which the leadership exercises authority. The more the use of power conforms to the people's values or satisfies their normative expectations, the more likely it is given consent as legitimate.[71] Failure to meet expectations by those exercising power can result in erosion of the support of those subordinate to them. Here the successful construction of the temple in Ezra 5–6 operates as a symbol of the exercise of local power for the good of the community. At the same time, the legitimacy of the people of the land is undermined by their interference in the project. Their use of power is shown to be counter to the common interests of the community. When combined with their obsequious attitude toward the monarch, they appear willing to exchange the good of others for their own privilege before the king. In contrast, the concern for the sanctification of tradition confers authority upon the "elders" and those whose role is to study and perpetuate the cultural legacy.[72] The author achieves this dichotomy by enlisting stereotypes to classify, demarcate, and delegitimize his competitors. Their use dramatizes the importance of community membership and the maintenance of boundaries. The author employs this account of the earliest returnees to call on the reader to embrace membership in an ethnically bounded community centered on the temple, led by those most skilled to navigate the political landscape.

---

71. Ibid., 11.
72. Ibid., 74.

7
Ezra 5–6: Support for Temples and Priests

In Ezra 5 and 6, the stymied rebuilding efforts are renewed. Although Tattenai questions the legitimacy of the project, work continues unhindered until the task is complete. In these chapters, Persian rule is orderly, carried out by documents kept in long-standing archives. The distant kings are inspired by YHWH, initiate the rebuilding effort, and provide resources for the project but always operate through intermediaries. The Yehud community works in concert to build the temple despite the inquiry regarding imperial permission to build it. The text concludes with the dedication of the temple and a community-wide celebration of Passover. As a whole, this creates an idealized portrait of the community united around the temple, perhaps in contrast to the author's own divided community. Purity language and institution rites are particularly prominent, as symbolic acts and language legitimize a particular role for the Jerusalem temple, particular social boundaries of the community, and a particular function for priests within the community of Yehud.

7.1. The Jerusalem Temple and Cultural Capital

The struggle over the temple represents a fight over cultural capital in an objectified state (rather than embodied). Bourdieu comments that this form of capital "can be appropriated both materially—which presupposes economic capital—and symbolically—which presupposes cultural capital."[1] The temple, like a piece of fine art, can be the possession of the community and priests. However, economic or social benefit comes only by appropriating the services of those who use the temple, which makes the temple's symbolic value important to priests whose livelihood depends

---

1. Bourdieu, "Forms of Capital," 247.

on the temple economy. (This requires access to embodied cultural capital—people who know how to appreciate the temple and find it of value.)

Although the temple already existed, the author composes a text that asserts its importance, making its construction *the* stake in the narrative. Prophets encourage the community to build it (5:1–2; 6:14), and despite an official inquiry, construction continues "because the eye of their God was on the elders of the Judahites" (5:5, my translation). Silent on the accusation of sedition directed against them in Ezra 4, the Judahites provide a historical account that centers on rebuilding the house that their king had previously built and completed. They acknowledge that Nebuchadnezzar had destroyed "this house." Yet Tattenai's query, "Who gave you a decree to build this house?" (5:4, 9), is answered with, "Cyrus, the king of Babylon, Cyrus the king gave a command to build this house," and to return the temple vessels (5:13–14). Prophets, YHWH, the Judeans, and even Persian monarchs all agree the Jerusalem temple should be built. The terminology itself directs the reader's attention again and again to the temple. In 5:12–17, terms referring to the temple (*house of God, this house, temple in Jerusalem*) occur eight times. In addition, the writer is specific about the location "in Jerusalem" (three times) or "this place/this house" (two times). The marshaling of support suggests that the temple's cultural value is in jeopardy. Although never mentioned, another sanctuary in another place may be competing with this one. Or there may be those who simply question rebuilding a sanctuary that all agree was destroyed by the will of its own god. Tattenai may be giving voice to another issue as well: will this new temple affect Persia's rule? For the governor or others, the social and economic capital of Persia's good graces would be worth more than any cultural capital of this temple. What they do not question is whether YHWH should be worshiped but rather in what form, and where, and perhaps by whom.

The solicitous and respectful stance toward the Persian representatives and imperial rule may largely be a manifestation of the author's habitus. Acquired through experience, "the objective order and the subjective principles of organization of the natural and social world appear as self-evident."[2] When shared by society, Bourdieu terms this correspondence *doxa*. In reality, doxa represents the view of the dominant in society, their

---

2. Bourdieu, *Outline*, 164. He "distinguishes [doxa] from orthodox or heterodox belief [as those which imply] awareness and recognition of the possibility of different or antagonistic beliefs."

ruling positions appearing universal and self-evident. One of the conditions of existence for our author is the status of Yehud as a secondary state in the empire. The author's composition presents foreign rule as a foregone conclusion and rebellion nearly unthinkable—working with the imperial authorities is the only option he entertains. Despite the author's subject position, he shares the view of the dominant, that Persian hegemony is unassailable. Persia's power cannot be denied, and the temple, in his mind, depends on Persia's largesse and grace.

When a doxic view of the world becomes contested, efforts to defend the integrity of doxa often result in the imperfect substitute, orthodoxy.[3] Orthodox discourse is a conscious rationalization that imposes a censorship, "the official way of speaking and thinking the world"; it is distinguished not by its content but by its ability to manage those within the community who deviate from it.[4] The author's position in the religious field depends on the temple retaining an active stake in the field of cultural capital. A failure in this regard is his loss. Its abandonment threatens his own identity and, he believes, the identity of his community. These twin assumptions—Persian rule and the temple's centrality—lead him to marshal whatever shared cultural capital he has with the readers to espouse social arrangements that coincide with his social existence.

7.2. Weber's Oppositions: Priests, Prophets, and the Laity

Competition over the power to modify the worldview of the laity pits different religious specialists, prophets and priests, against each other.[5] Priests are specialists in "the continuous operation of a cultic enterprise" who strive for orderly obedience of the laity.[6] On the other hand, the prophet breaks with routine and contests the accepted order; the prophetic word is exceptional and discontinuous. "Thus the prophet stands

---

3. Jacques Berlinerblau, "Toward a Sociology of Heresy, Orthodoxy, and *Doxa*," *HR* 40 (2001): 347. Bourdieu (*Outline*, 169) states, "when social classifications become the object and instrument of class struggle ... the arbitrary principles of the prevailing classification can appear as such and it therefore becomes necessary to undertake the work of conscious systematization and express rationalization which marks the passage from doxa to orthodoxy."
4. Berlinerblau, "Toward a Sociology," 350.
5. Bourdieu, "Legitimation and Structured Interests," 126.
6. Weber, *Sociology of Religion*, 30.

opposed to an administrative apparatus."[7] Ezra 5 and 6 reflect a priestly attempt to control the practice and worldview of the laity. Ezra 5, however, begins with prophets: "Now the prophets, Haggai and Zechariah son of Iddo, prophesied to the Jews who were in Judah and Jerusalem, in the name of the God of Israel who was over them" (5:1). Two wordless prophets prompt the twin leadership of Zerubbabel and Jeshua to restart the building of the house of God (5:1–2). Once the legitimacy of the temple is resolved, the author concludes, "So the elders of the Jews built and prospered, through the prophesying of the prophet Haggai and Zechariah son of Iddo. They finished their building by command of the God of Israel and by decree of Cyrus, Darius, and King Artaxerxes of Persia" (6:14). A celebration ensues: "The people of Israel, the priests and the Levites, and the rest of the returned exiles, celebrated the dedication of this house of God with joy" (6:16). The consecration of priests and Levites follows, and all is done "as it is written in the book of Moses" (6:18); the celebration of Passover completes the narrative. The prophetic message that calls the community to renewed action culminates in the ordination of priests and the return of ritual.[8]

The opposition that Weber's theory leads us to expect is not immediately obvious. The community lives out the message of Haggai and Zechariah in worship at the temple led by consecrated priests—a community analogous to the author's own.[9] However, although the prophets support the temple, the author does not retain them as participants in the concluding celebration of Passover. Once the prophetic appeal is fulfilled in the completed temple, they are removed from the stage, replaced by the priests. The author may not criticize the prophets, but replacing them with priests signals the passing of prophetic agents. This marks as unnecessary any who may continue the prophetic tradition in the ongoing religious life of the community. The traditional source of critique of the priesthood is presented as the impetus to its revival, and rebuilding the temple is now the desire of prophets, God, and king. The growing power of the priests is a sign of success, and the account becomes an argument for the status of priests in the author's own time. This reasoning marks the author of these

---

7. Bourdieu, "Legitimation and Structured Interests," 127.

8. In the chapter's conclusion, in the space of five verses (6:16–20), priests and Levites are mentioned three times. Purity, separation, and pollution are also in focus.

9. On the survival of a prophetic message through routinization, see Weber, *Sociology of Religion*, 62.

7. EZRA 5–6: SUPPORT FOR TEMPLES AND PRIESTS

chapters as a member of the priestly class, in that he defines and defends priests as the apex in the local religious and social hierarchy.

The description of Passover (Ezra 6:19–22) also advances priestly interests as details of priestly organization and purification alternate with notices that the community celebrated Passover, signaling the priests as necessary for this formative ritual.

> Then *they set the priests in their divisions and the Levites in their courses* for the service of God at Jerusalem, as it is written in the book of Moses. *On the fourteenth day of the first month the returned exiles kept the passover.* For *both the priests and the Levites had purified themselves*; all of them were clean. *So they killed the passover lamb* for all the returned exiles, for their fellow priests, and for themselves. (6:18–20)

To be considered legitimate agents of the temple, the priests need to be viewed by supplicants as recognized authorities.[10] To that end, *they* organize the priests and Levites, after which the clerics purify themselves for service. Significantly the symbolic language is "aimed at underlining the fact that [the priest] is not acting in his own name and under his own authority."[11] Rather, it is the community that institutes and legitimates the priesthood. Even as the text asserts the community's role in setting apart the priests, it also underscores the division between priests and laity and extends the distance between them. The act of purification becomes a symbol of the authority of the priestly office. As a consequence, the pronouncements of priests are given greater authority by the laity. Priestly discourse is now recognized as containing "the accumulated symbolic capital of the group that has delegated him and of which he is the authorized representative."[12]

When laity and priests are distinct classes, the priests must recognize the needs of the laity they have created in order to maintain their priestly positions. An indifferent laity can make the priesthood obsolete.[13] Bourdieu observes that what laity need or are interested in "is determined by the agents' conditions of existence."[14] Advantaged and disadvantaged

---

10. Bourdieu, *Language and Symbolic Power*, 73.
11. Ibid., 75.
12. Ibid., 111.
13. Weber, *Sociology of Religion*, 65, 71.
14. Bourdieu, "Legitimation and Structured Interests," 122.

groups often have opposing needs. The privileged desire to have their position affirmed based on their good conduct. For the underprivileged, need rests on a promise of redemption from suffering—a focus on what they are to become.[15] If the priests fail to address these needs, doubts grow about the effectiveness of religious practice and skepticism about the function of priests, or even, as Weber mentions, indifference. In Weber's mind, concern about laity indifference leads the priesthood to push "distinctive criteria and differential doctrines."[16]

The inclusion of a celebration of Passover may demonstrate how the author tackles the competing needs of the disadvantaged and the fortunate. This dichotomy forces priestly discourse toward rationalization in order to meet the needs of all concerned with a single message. In this case, through the polysemy of meaning, Passover speaks to both groups.[17] Its history ties the current religious practice to YHWH's saving act in Exodus and to previous accounts of religious renewal under the devout kings Hezekiah and Josiah.[18] For the disprivileged, the tie to Exodus speaks of YHWH's rescue from domination, while the affiliation with religious renewal affirms the righteous character (and place) of the privileged. For either group to experience the Passover requires the mediation of the priests. The celebration in Ezra 6 is liturgical and centralized, similar to descriptions by the Chronicler, rather than the more family-oriented celebration in Exod 12. As in 2 Chr 30 and 35, priests and Levites control the celebration in Jerusalem, with purity and pollution constituting a major theme. The essential role of purified priests and Levites in the celebration of Passover legitimates their control over this religious practice and guarantees that they receive a substantial share of the sacrifices involved (2 Chr 35:14).[19] So our author employs a shared historic faith to meet the needs of the laity and in the process legitimates priestly authority. The combination of the promise of divine care for the people with commendation for religious fidelity also validates a distinctive and elite status for the community as divinely chosen, rescued,

---

15. Ibid., 125.
16. Weber, *Sociology of Religion*, 70.
17. Bourdieu, *Language and Symbolic Power*, 40.
18. 2 Chr 30 and 35 record the earlier Passovers. Both involve the sanctification of priests and the community. 2 Chr 30:27 concludes Hezekiah's Passover by noting the effective prayer of the priests, "Then the priests and the Levites stood up and blessed the people, and their voice was heard; their prayer came to his holy dwelling in heaven."
19. Danna Nolan Fewell, private communication, 20 April 2012.

and assured of land with its produce. This identity calls for separation from adjacent communities or competing practices. The purification carried out by the priests and the community's separation from "the pollutions of the nations" (Ezra 6:21) provide ritual definition and assurance of this distinctive identity.

The symbolic action of purification and the literary ties connecting priests with Passover add to priestly legitimacy and authority. Prophets, the king, and the community lend their support to priestly power as well—all groups that may have cause to contest such an arrangement since enhanced priestly authority requires a reciprocating diminishment of their own influence. These sources of support may indicate bases of opposition in the writer's world. Levites likely contested the priests' arrogating control over the temple and its income solely to themselves. Imperial or local financial support of the temple may have been waning. (The monarch orders financial costs to be paid, "from the royal revenue, the tribute of the province Beyond the River" [Ezra 6:8]. This is not a royal gift but a further demand placed on the local tax base, placing pressure on citizens to increase production if they are to meet the added obligation.) Prophetic voices may be questioning priestly rulings or teachings or offering their own new teachings (such as those filled with messianic hope) that might threaten the state of affairs beneficial for priests. Laity may be indifferent or resistant to religious requirements and the associated economic demands—for example, traveling to Jerusalem to celebrate Passover. (This may be especially so since they would retain a larger share of the Passover offering if they stayed at home!) Or perhaps tying worship (and priests) entirely to the Jerusalem temple is contested. Thus our author argues that, from the beginning, all these factions were in agreement regarding the importance of the temple, the place of priests in the local hierarchy, and the priestly institution's benefit to the laity. Loss of the temple's cultural capital would directly affect the recognition that priests receive from the group.[20] For the author, world order and his place in it stands or falls on the community's recognition of the Jerusalem temple. To that end, he employs all the symbolic power of this history of the early community acting in concord to complete and celebrate the temple.

---

20. Bourdieu, *Language and Symbolic Power*, 73. He comments, "The symbolic efficacy of religious language is threatened when the set of mechanisms capable of ensuring the reproduction of the relationship of recognition, which is the basis of its authority, ceases to function."

7.3. God Is Great, Persia Is Good

7.3.1. Hiding Political Interests

The wider political realities of Yehud also impinged on theological constructions. Weber comments that generally, "as soon as a religion has progressed to anything like a status of equality with the sphere of political associations," tensions erupt.[21] This would have been augmented by the ancient Near East conviction that a deity "existed merely for the protection of the political interests of his followers' associations."[22] Weber states, "even for the ancient religion of Yahweh, political victory and especially vengeance against the enemy constituted the real reward granted by god."[23]

As the Jerusalem community grew in size and local influence, their loyalty to the empire (or lack thereof) would grow in importance as well. To navigate this difficulty, the author of Ezra 5–6 does not give up the idea of the divine granting of victory over enemies. However, enemies are narrowly defined—unlike the reasoning of Deutero-Isaiah, it is not the empire but local others who are to be overcome. The battle is waged with letters rather than physical combat, and victory is portrayed in construction rather than on the battlefield. Thus YHWH's power and reward for the community is maintained, as is the community's loyalty to the crown. This last is demonstrated not by the community declaring loyalty to the Persian monarch or rejecting Israel's history of independent kings (Ezra 5:11). Rather, the Persian monarchs are positively disposed toward *them*. Darius pays for the temple from the royal coffers and commands Tattenai and the officials to stand aside so work can commence (6:7). Then the monarch acknowledges the temple's beneficial role as a place of prayers for the king (6:10). Indeed, it is not one king but three kings who, along with the God of Israel, decree that the temple be built. "They finished their building by command of the God of Israel and by decree of Cyrus, Darius, and King Artaxerxes of Persia" (6:14b).[24]

---

21. Weber, *Sociology of Religion*, 223.
22. Ibid. In Deutero-Isaiah, the sovereignty of YHWH is elucidated to convince hearers that exiles will return to Jerusalem and Babylon will fall.
23. Ibid., 224.
24. Temple building initiated by kings and desired by the god is a staple in ancient Near Eastern temple building accounts. The account in Ezra follows this tradition and thus incorporates another type of shared cultural capital—any temple worth its salt

Theologically the author portrays YHWH as still powerful, still worthy of worship, despite political and military failures. Depicting a strong deity masks efforts to protect political interests. An insubstantial YHWH would lead to abandonment of the cult and would weaken the priests' position within Yehud. Yet local power also depends in large part on Persia, whose good graces the writer depicts through royal decrees and the obvious munificence of the monarch for YHWH's temple. If the priest or community wishes to assert YHWH's unmitigated power, they have little choice but to see the empire's rule as the will of YHWH. This would also allow them to make theological sense of the benefits of good standing in the empire. Political reality combines with the author's doxic beliefs in Persian domination and an almighty deity. His defense of YHWH must account for the limits of being a tributary province. Efforts to create a cohesive response to these diverse and competing concerns results in still further ordering of religious beliefs.

The importance of the priesthood is also supported by moving the *God of heaven* (a politically strategic title as opposed to YHWH) to the house in Jerusalem, where the priests carry out their duties.[25] In Ezra 5:1–13, God is primarily cited for his care for the temple builders.[26] Through the rest of the section the focus shifts to "the house of God *in Jerusalem*" (5:14–17; 6:5, 9, 12). Moving the God "of heaven" (5:11, 12) to "the house of God in Jerusalem" collects divine providence to a particular location and project. The destruction of the First Temple is attributed not to divine weakness but to God's anger toward the ancestors (5:12). This logic allows the writer to maintain YHWH's power and the value of the temple (and thus the priests' power and value) while at the same time maintaining the goodwill and confidence of the present community.

While this logic, designed to avert defection to stronger gods, is a common tactic of religious thinking in general, it is significant that it occurs here in this text. It represents a need to persuade others at the time of the author's composition. The temple exists, but the questions remain.

---

would need this type of royal/divine initiative. For discussion of building accounts, see Edelman, *Origins*, 132; or Fried, *Priest and Great King*, 161.

25. In Ezra, "the God of heaven" is used by the monarchs Cyrus and Darius (1:1; 6:9, 10) and by the Judeans when speaking with Tattenai (5:11, 12).

26. Ezra 5:5: "But the eye of their God was upon the elders of the Jews." See also 5:1, 8, and 11. Later references become focused on God's location at Jerusalem and the "house of God" there.

Persian rule impinges on an assertion of God's power, as does the reality of the First Temple's destruction. This nuanced history provides a defense that counters such uncertainty within the author's community. At the same time, it champions the institution necessary for the priest's place in the social and religious hierarchy.

James Trotter argues that the temple was not the result of religious fervor and unified community desire and effort. He notes that Haggai explains the delay in construction with reference to economic hardship. Haggai never mentions external interference with the building, never mentions a difference between the golah community and those living in the land, and never mentions an earlier or interrupted start (Hag 1:5–11).[27] Following Jon Berquist, he suggests that Persian economic and political interests finally gave impetus to the temple building—perhaps a reward for cooperation during the army's travels through the Levant during the war with Egypt and a way of consolidating power in the region.[28] (Berquist notes that military campaigns would have demanded substantial agricultural support from the local communities. This might coincide with the economic hardship addressed in Haggai.)[29] Trotter contends that the author of Ezra 1–6 has retrojected opposition "to explain the fact that his own expectations regarding the immediate rebuilding of the temple were not fulfilled."[30] I agree that the author has placed external opposition into the text, but not because of disappointment over rebuilding—after all, the writer is living well after the temple has been completed, so any delay would have been ancient history. Rather, he writes to address his reality. The centrality of the Jerusalem temple and cult seem to be at stake due to questions regarding YHWH's commitment to the temple and whether worship there is efficacious—doubts fomented by economic hardship and lack of political autonomy.

---

27. James M. Trotter, "Was the Second Temple a Primarily Persian Project?" *SJOT* 15 (2001): 284. See Hag 1:9: "You have looked for much, and, lo, it came to little; and when you brought it home, I blew it away. Why? says the Lord of hosts. Because my house lies in ruins, while all of you hurry off to your own houses."

28. Ibid., 290. Berquist (*Judaism in Persia's Shadow*, 62) claims that the temple was constructed by Persia in a reaction to uncertainty surrounding Darius's ascension. He still places construction during his reign but views Persian support as recompense for military supplies, following the conflict with Egypt.

29. Berquist, *Judaism in Persia's Shadow*, 65.

30. Trotter, "Primarily Persian Project," 286.

7. EZRA 5–6: SUPPORT FOR TEMPLES AND PRIESTS 177

Purity language sets apart the priests and redefines the Judean community. The Passover is eaten "by the people of Israel who had returned from exile, and also by all who had joined them and separated themselves from the pollutions of the nations of the land to worship the LORD, the God of Israel" (Ezra 6:21). Those barred from the community are classified as aliens, and the rationale for exclusion is articulated in the language of ritual impurity.[31] It reflects the authorial belief that ethnic purity is inseparable from ethnic integrity. In the past, Israel could be defined by possession of the land or by its own political identity. Now, with identity defined in ethnic terms, the issue is not "territorial integrity, but one of the integrity of the 'congregation of Israel.'… Thus the first reaction to the threat is an inward turn, towards the Temple, towards YHWH."[32] This reaction leads ultimately to separation of the populace at large "into those who participate in such sacred occasions and those who do not."[33] Separation from competing doctrines, now defined as alien, maintains the community's superiority in propaganda.[34] The purity language justifies the existence of the laity as occupants of a particular position in the social structure. The language grounds the dignity of the community in a conviction of their own excellence.[35]

Interestingly, Ezra 1–6 lacks the strong tactics of expulsion found elsewhere in Ezra-Nehemiah. While the nations are impure, boundaries are enforced through mutually exclusive rhetoric. In addition, there is some vacillation over inclusion, as 4:3 excludes the people of the land from participation in the temple construction, while 6:21 allows "all who had joined them and separated themselves from the pollutions of the nations

---

31. Saul Olyan, "Purity Ideology in Ezra-Nehemiah as a Tool to Reconstitute the Community," *JSJ* 35 (2004): 11. Olyan discusses ritual impurity with regard to Neh 13:4–9. The term טמאה ("pollutions" or "impurity"), for which they are rejected, is used of bodily discharges in Leviticus and occurs elsewhere in Ezra only in 9:11; there the land is unclean because of the *impurity* of the people of the land: "The land that you are about to possess is a land unclean through the uncleanness of the peoples of the land, through their abhorrent practices with which they, in their *impurity*, have filled it from one end to the other" (NJPS).

32. Davies, "Defending the Boundaries," 48. Although Davies's discussion focuses on 2 Chr 20, his conclusions depend on the social setting of Yehud and converge with the temple and worship focus in Ezra 6.

33. Berquist, *Judaism in Persia's Shadow*, 149.

34. Weber, *Sociology of Religion*, 70.

35. Bourdieu, "Legitimation and Structured Interests," 125.

of the land to worship the LORD." Yet incorporating these people is not a merger but an act of assimilation. The previous group to which these people belonged is not recognized, and the exclusive nature of the exilic community remains intact.[36]

The inclusion of others at this point in the narrative is linked to two significant and related events: the temple is finished, and the priests who will officiate are already ordained. The work and the ongoing leadership of the temple are now firmly within the hands of the exilic descendants. At this point, those who wish to join them may provide additional financial support, while the requirement that they "separate" from the surrounding nations reduces any threat to control over the institution. Furthermore, their participation (and any benefit they perceive from worship in Jerusalem) now makes them indebted to those who govern the temple. "After all, it is the priesthood and its elaborate sacrificial system that will keep the people 'pure.'"[37]

7.3.2. Whose Temple Is This?

The economic security of the Jerusalem temple and its priests depends on investment by the wider community. Therefore the author must demonstrate that the temple is worth its economic and social investment. He addresses in religious (or symbolic) terms two logical challenges that arise due to the intersection of the political and economic fields with the temple's religious function.

First, he addresses the relationship of YHWH to the rebuilt temple. The account begins by linking the "God of *Israel*" (5:1) to "the house of God *in Jerusalem*" (5:2). Ezra 5:5 states that the God of Israel is over the Jews in Judah and Jerusalem. The temple builders are self-proclaimed "servants of the God of heaven" (5:11).[38] The elders, Tattenai (5:8), Cyrus (5:15), and Darius (6:7) all agree that the temple in Jerusalem is the house of God. By 6:12, Darius asserts that God "has established his name there," and the narrator states that the building was finished "by command of the God of Israel" (6:14). This literary move collects divine approval for this

---

36. Rom-Shiloni, *Exclusive Inclusivity*, 46–47.
37. Fewell, private communication, 20 April 2012.
38. Ezra 5:5: "But the eye of their God was upon the elders of the Jews." See also 5:1, 8, and 11. Later references become focused on God's location at Jerusalem and the "house of God" there.

particular location and project. Those disinclined to continue support for this temple are now confronted by the possibility of failing to support God, who is both the "God of Israel" and the "God of heaven"—the latter label invites Persian inclusion.

To justify YHWH's approval of the rebuilding effort, the destruction of the previous temple must be explained. A loss of this magnitude would suggest either a failure on the part of the Deity or of those who represented the Deity. The interpretation of the failure must be done "in such a manner that the responsibility falls, not upon the god or themselves, but upon the behavior of the god's worshippers."[39] In Ezra 4, the adversaries attribute the destruction to Jerusalem's rebellion against the empire (4:15). In 5:12, blame is deflected to the ancestors who rebelled *against their own God*, and it is God who then allowed the destruction. This logic allows the writer to maintain YHWH's power and the value of the temple (and thus the priests' power and value) while at the same time maintaining the goodwill of the present community and of Persian rulers since the fault lies in *religious* failures of *past* generations.

How the Yahwistic temple can be authentic when constructed under the auspices of the Persian crown also requires explanation. Imperial involvement *in* the temple likely indicates imperial benefit *from* the temple. The local taxpayers might wonder, "Whose interests are being served?" In response, YHWH's commitment to the temple is shown operating through the edicts, records, and funds of Persian monarchs. Though kings may think they are operating independently, the narrative shows YHWH orchestrating the events; and at the end of the day, as Eskenazi observes, in 6:14 the decrees of the monarchs are in agreement with the decree of God.[40] Opposition to the temple now becomes opposition to the community, God, and king, and comes only from outsiders—and this implies therefore that divine and imperial sanctions should be directed at those who oppose the temple.

Persian rule and the temple's past destruction impinge on a simplistic assertion of YHWH's power and the temple's efficacy. The author confronts

---

39. Weber, *Sociology of Religion*, 33.
40. Eskenazi, *In an Age of Prose*, 60. She states, "Here the edict of God and the edict of the three kings combine to explain the success of the Judeans.... The singular, 'king of Persia,' applies to all three kings as a single unit, as if they spoke with one voice. Likewise the *decree* of the three kings is spoken of in the singular as if it were a single decree.... Divine command and royal decree ... are .... one" (59–60).

these issues by deflecting blame and so averts defection by worshipers. The evidence is embedded in a seemingly objective historical report that obscures the underlying purpose of the account. Economic hardship, alternative sites for worship, and waning commitment by the wider community are pasted over with a show of community solidarity. The need to raise this defense suggests substantial disagreement over or appealing alternatives to the Jerusalem temple.

7.4. The Cultural Capital of Writing: Supporting the Scribal Life

There is an ongoing debate regarding the authenticity of the Aramaic documents in Ezra-Nehemiah. Early scholarship, with the important exception of Torrey, treated the royal edicts, lists of exiles, and letters in Ezra-Nehemiah as authentic documents that the author felt compelled to include. While some continue to treat them as authentic (Briant, Blenkinsopp, Williamson, Steiner, Steinmann), recent work by Dirk Schwiderski and others has weakened that claim based on linguistics, theology within the documents, archaeology, and evidence from known edicts of the Persian kings.[41] Whether the documents are authentic or not, evidence indicates that editing has shaped these texts so they may not reflect what was originally stated.[42]

However, Grabbe argues that, of all the documents, the most likely to be authentic is the Aramaic letter from Tattenai found in Ezra 5:7–17. We know Tattenai was a real Persian official, the letter contains only early grammatical forms, and the role of Sheshbazzar differs from the description of him in Ezra 1–3. Some scribal insertions (e.g., regarding the role of elders) may still be present.[43] Edelman disagrees, asserting there was

---

41. See, e.g., Dirk Schwiderski, *Handbuch des nordwestsemitischen Briefformulars: Ein Beitrag zur Echtheitsfrage der aramäischen Briefe des Esrabuches*, BZAW 295 (Berlin: de Gruyter, 2013), 343–53. Although often discounting details of ancient historical authors, Briant (*From Cyrus to Alexander*, 488) treats Darius's edict in Ezra 6:6–12 as historical. See Grabbe (*Ezra-Nehemiah*, 125–30) or Edeleman (*Origins*, 180–206) for detailed arguments against their authenticity.

42. Grabbe, *Ezra-Nehemiah*, 130. Grabbe demonstrates this editing with an example from Josephus, who quotes a decree from Claudius claiming that Jews have equal rights with the Greeks (*Ant.* 19.281). An authentic decree found in Egypt shows this not to be the case.

43. Grabbe, *Ezra-Nehemiah*, 131.

no decree from Cyrus or a return of temple vessels with Sheshbazzar, and she argues that "the contents of the letter betray its inauthentic nature." Its purpose, she claims, "is to bolster the credibility of [the author's] account of a two-stage construction of the temple."[44] Whether these documents are authentic or not, edited or not, tied to the appropriate historical setting or not, most scholars agree that the inclusion of edicts and letters in this narrative is tied to authorial purpose. These forms of communication, even if modified, serve a persuasive purpose in the present context.

Eskenazi has already noted that "Ezra-Nehemiah emphasizes the primacy of the written text over the oral as a source of authority."[45] Yet the context in which these writings first appeared would have generated a different perception and use of written texts than is found in today's modern print culture. Literacy was rare and confined to specialists. Embedded in an oral environment, writing was "often understood as sacred or numinous."[46] In general, written texts played a subsidiary role to the process of oral learning and oral performance.[47] Written literary texts would have had a very small reading audience.[48] They were not easily accessible, public, or generally used for archival consultation. Instead, they provided proof of a society's legacy, "proof of their status and history in a more wholesale and symbolic fashion."[49]

Halpern compares Ezra 1–6 with Nabonidus's Sippar cylinder and concludes that our author was a scribe with a Babylonian education.[50] In these chapters, written *legal* texts are primary, suggesting an author with a governmental role. This author's particular use of documents, royal edicts,

---

44. Edelman, *Origins*, 188.
45. Eskenazi, *In an Age of Prose*, 2.
46. Richard Horsley, *Scribes, Visionaries, and the Politics of Second Temple Judea* (Louisville: Westminster John Knox, 2007), 8. Susan Niditch (*Oral World and Written Words: Ancient Israelite Literature* [Louisville: Westminster John Knox, 1996], 44) concurs, commenting, "People at home in oral cultures sometimes treat writing with a respect accorded the numinous. Writing comes to be regarded as capable of transformation and magic, the letters and words shimmering with the very power of the gods."
47. Horsley, *Scribes, Visionaries*, 104.
48. Niditch, *Oral World*, 41.
49. Ibid., 42.
50. Halpern, "Historiographic Commentary," 129. Halpern argues that evidence of shared concerns and techniques of Ezra 1–6 with Nabonidus's Sippar cylinder indicate that "this historian was … an assiduous scribe, versed in the models of an establishment Babylonian education."

references to archives, and facility with Aramaic suggest an underlying assertion that textuality was an authoritative social practice.[51] His account valorizes scribal practices and echoes how he negotiates with the local and imperial authorities.

In Ezra 5 and 6, the temple project begins with the oral encouragement of Haggai and Zechariah, but a written edict of the king assures its completion. In addition, as Richard Steiner demonstrates, the narrative unfolds primarily through the reading of documents contained inside other documents (5:7–6:12).[52] Even the narrative outside the documents, Andrew Steinmann suggests, is taken from the letters themselves.[53] Governor Tattenai's oral query, "Who gave you a decree to build this house and to finish this structure?" (5:3), seeks recorded confirmation for the project, and the investigation is conducted via written correspondence. In 5:5–7, the triple repetition that a letter is sent to Darius highlights dependence on writing.[54] The Jehudite response to Tattenai is revealed only in his written letter to Darius, where he quotes their *written* response (5:11).[55] Darius, upon receiving the letter (in which he is told to perform a search through the royal archives for a written edict) is guided by the discovered written scroll (6:1–2). Although within the monarch's power to modify or cancel the order, he not only confirms it but adds his own written decree of sup-

---

51. Donald C. Polaski, "What Mean These Stones? Inscriptions, Textuality and Power in Persia and Yehud," in *Approaching Yehud: New Approaches to the Study of the Persian Period*, ed. Jon L. Berquist, SemeiaSt 50 (Atlanta: Society of Biblical Literature, 2007), 48.

52. Richard C. Steiner, "Bishlam's Archival Search Report in Nehemiah's Archive: Multiple Introductions and Reverse Chronological Order as Clues to the Origin of the Aramaic Letters in Ezra 4–6," *JBL* 125 (2006): 659. Steiner suggests that chs. 4–6 are records kept by Nehemiah that summarize an archival search prior to rebuilding the Jerusalem walls. Williamson concurs, arguing that disjoined verses and complicated introductions are better explained by someone copying an existing document than creating a false one ("Aramaic Documents in Ezra Revisited," 52).

53. Andrew E. Steinmann, "Letters of Kings about Votive Offerings, the God of Israel and the Aramaic Document in Ezra 4:8–6:18," *JHebS* 8 (2008): art. 23, p. 3, doi:10.5508/jhs.v.8.a23.

54. While Steiner ("Bishlam's Archival Search Report") demonstrates that this is due to the copyist's copy of headings on documents, the narrative effect is to highlight the dependence on writing and documents.

55. The Aramaic for "the answer" in 5:11 is פתגמא. Its use elsewhere indicates a written reply (4:17; 6:11).

port.⁵⁶ He provides for the temple construction financially and threatens anyone (or any king) who interferes with its completion (6:11–12). All the actors in this episode rely on writing to guide them, and when they find something in writing it is upheld. Upon completion of the temple, priests and Levites are appointed and the temple is dedicated, "as it is written in the book of Moses" (6:18).

Mallau also observes the importance given documents in this text and suggests that this may reflect a scribal theology.⁵⁷ The important role documents play in achieving desired results buttresses the author's scribal capital. Facility with legal documents (a form of cultural capital) benefits the author's social position among those in his audience who already value reading or writing. The temple's completion and imperial provision for the project due to written decrees confirms the importance of scribes within the political sphere. Conversely, for those who may *not* recognize the value of his particular form of capital, everyone in the narrative expresses both need and respect for written correspondence. The correspondence itself is portrayed as powerful and effective for good even to the level of the monarchy—*especially* at the level of the monarchy. Material goods flow to Yehud when the king reads records! In the end, even the divine will is communicated through writing, as priests are appointed according to the book of Moses.⁵⁸ Documents become necessary for official decisions and are critical to the movement of the plot itself. Multiple people, at all levels of government, accede to their contents. The nature of the author's material and the content of his narrative demonstrate that without scribes

---

56. Even when Artaxerxes halted the building project, he does so in response to a written document (Ezra 4:19).

57. Mallau ("Redaction of Ezra 4–6," 79) observes, "The redactor presents himself as a learned man. He is acquainted with a fair number of documents. He knows the authors. He is able to quote the texts if it suits his purpose. He knows where documents are archived. He is aware of the fact that literary documents play a decisive role in political decisions. He has learned that those who know how to present the right documents have a tremendous influence upon the decisions of the mighty. He even knows about dangerous documents."

58. Davies (*Ezra and Nehemiah*, 34) comments, "Rhetorically … [the book of Moses] is literally incomparable and unalterable because it is never quoted. It is the only document here that is without contradiction or adaptation. It is not even open to archival verification or strategic rewording." Davies and many other scholars note that the royal decree attributed to Cyrus is not identical with the decree as it appears in Ezra 1, thus reflecting a tendency to adapt written documents for new contexts.

who can read, write, and maintain government archives, his community's religious centerpiece, the temple, would never have come to fruition, and YHWH's will would have been hindered and unknown. The importance of writing for this outcome heightens the value of the scribe's cultural capital (his scribal training and occupation). The procurement of economic capital for the temple increases its cultural capital, which then produces economic capital for those most closely affiliated with the temple's workings.

The connection of biblical scribes to either the temple or government institutions is currently under debate.[59] The textual evidence points to someone familiar with the composition, uses, and handling of governmental records, namely, a governmental scribe. The narrative demonstrates a concern for textuality as a practice—to be able to compose documents is an essential skill in this narrative.[60] This is a separate issue from the veracity of the texts in the story, but the complete fabrication of such documents might bring into question the basis for the scribe's legitimacy. That he employs his capital in support and defense of the temple suggests dual commitments for this particular scribe. Further evidence of the scribe's governmental role is the author's use of Aramaic. Ezra 4:8 through 6:18 is Aramaic, the lingua franca and governmental language of the Persian Empire.[61] Not confined to particular documents, the Aramaic covers the portion of text when the building project is being contested or justified before Persian officials. Once the completed temple is dedicated, the account reverts to Hebrew.

Bourdieu's discussion of official language offers an approach from which to consider the presence and purpose of this Aramaic text. Official language, he argues, "is bound up with the state in its genesis and its social uses." It becomes viewed "as the only legitimate language" especially in formal or official situations, and it is "produced by authors who have the authority to write."[62] Its formal usage and codification establishes norms regulating linguistic practice.[63] Reflecting on France's own linguistic history, he comments,

---

59. For a summary of the issues, see John Van Seters, "The Role of the Scribe in the Making of the Hebrew Bible," *JANER* 8 (2008): 99–129.

60. Polaski, "What Mean These Stones," 48.

61. Ezra 7:12–26 is also in Aramaic, but since it is outside the scope of this chapter, I will not treat it in this discussion, although the same logic holds true for its use.

62. Bourdieu, *Language and Symbolic Power*, 45.

63. Ibid.

The imposition of French as the official language did not result in the total abolition of the written use of dialects.... A situation of bilingualism tended to arise. Whereas the lower classes, particularly the peasantry, were limited to the local dialect, the aristocracy, particularly the literate ... had access much more frequently to the use of the official language, written or spoken, while at the same time possessing the dialect,... a situation in which they were destined to fulfil the function of intermediaries.[64]

He further argues that the imposition of the legitimate language in opposition to the dialects was not solely for the technical need for communication or from a desire to crush local characteristics but was rather "gaining recognition for a new language of authority, its terms of address and reference ... and the representation of the social world which it conveys."[65]

Bourdieu's discussion treated a form of French initially imposed by those in power, but he contends that this could not compel its generalized use. Rather, its growing circulation accompanied a growing unification of the production and circulation of economic and cultural goods.[66] Likewise the spread of Aramaic reflected a growing economic and cultural unification of the empire. Unlike French, there was no government effort by the Persians to impose the language, but rather it was an earlier language shared throughout the wider empire, making it useful for general and official communication. As Aramaic grew increasingly widespread, it led to the progressive obsolescence of Hebrew.[67] Even Jewish communities within the empire communicated with one another in Aramaic (e.g., the Elephantine letters) and employed Aramaic in their legal contracts. While not imposed from the top down, it would still carry the distinctiveness of symbolic domination associated with the language of the imperial government. Aramaic's currency as the language of business and government meant facility with Aramaic, particularly *written* Aramaic, would have been a form of cultural capital that created prestige for anyone capable of using it.

The Aramaic section of Ezra may be exploiting this symbolic power. Within this section of Ezra, the legality of the building program is twice

---

64. Ibid., 47.
65. Ibid., 48.
66. Ibid., 51.
67. Ibid., 50.

brought to the attention of the Persian monarch, first by outside neighbors and then by Persian officials (Ezra 4:8; 5:6). In the second episode, local Persian representatives ascertain the legitimacy of the building project and resolve the issue positively—all in the formal, legitimate language of the empire. It is carried out in measures coinciding with Persian governmental requirements. Legal legitimacy for the temple is asserted by legal documents in the authorized language. By the same means, the official status of Aramaic is recognized and the political institution and class to which it is attached. This enhances the standing of those capable of handling legal documents in that language, such as our author, but also acknowledges the political sovereignty of Persia.

Once the legitimacy of the temple is established, it is dedicated, and priests are selected, the Aramaic section of the text ends and the account reverts to Hebrew. The use of two languages in this text is associated with dominant and subordinate standings within the empire.[68] Aramaic, the language of imperial power, is necessary for negotiations with the empire and enhances the standing of those capable of using it. Those empowered by literacy and facility with Aramaic would be more integrated into the dominant class, while concomitantly those who spoke exclusively in Hebrew and were illiterate would be entrenched in social impotence.[69] Due to its role as a tool of Persian hegemony, Aramaic would be an intrusion into the community. The resumption of Hebrew in this text for the description of local religious practice may reflect solidarity with the dominated community, but retains the dichotomy between the language of power and the local dialect.[70] James Scott observes that its use also provides a "barrier and veil that the dominant find difficult or impossible

---

68. Ibid., 53. Bourdieu makes this point with regard to speaking the same language with different dialects, grammar, etc.; but the relationship between Hebrew and Aramaic may reflect similar valuation when Hebrew has a subordinate social place within the empire.

69. Terry Rey, "Marketing the Goods of Salvation: Bourdieu on Religion," *Religion* 34 (2004): 339. Rey describes the roles of language and religion in the subordination of classes in Haiti. He notes that those who speak Creole and are excluded by illiteracy from the use of French ultimately view the social order as legitimate because it establishes distinctions tied to a competence they lack.

70. In Bourdieu's schema (*Language and Symbolic Power*, 68) condescension is a denial of "difference" that in reality reinforces social difference. "Such a strategy is possible whenever the objective disparity between the persons present … is sufficiently known and recognized by everyone."

to penetrate."[71] Hebrew carves out some autonomy for the Yehud community. The Aramaic sections of Ezra were the most accessible to people outside Yehud. It is in these sections that the argument is made for the legitimacy of the temple of YHWH within the Persian Empire. Local and more exclusionary policies of Yehud are expressed in Hebrew. In Hebrew, God is *YHWH*, the God of *Israel*. In Hebrew, the community separates itself from the polluted nations of the land (Ezra 6:21); and Passover, the celebration of freedom from imperial oppression, is described. Hebrew provides a safer context in which to voice these views concerning those outside the community.

Royal edicts, a form of legal discourse, play an important role in the author's account of the creation of the temple and community. In Ezra 5:3, Tattenai's request for the source of the builders' decree to build assumes that royal edicts provide legitimacy.[72] A string of royal decrees constructs the legitimate temple. In 5:13, the Judeans claim that Cyrus issued a decree; and once it is found, Darius issues his own decree (6:8) in support of the temple. The completion of the project is summarized by the statement, "They finished their building by *decree* of the God of Israel and by *decree* of Cyrus, Darius, and King Artaxerxes of Persia" (6:14b). Halpern comments that "the king's word, then, is so charged as to be virtually indistinguishable from its accomplishment." He sees in this an "exaggerated deference to authority" and an effort to demonstrate "the loyalty of the returnees."[73]

Bourdieu would agree with Halpern's depiction but adds, "Legal discourse is … the divine word, which creates what it states, in contrast to all derived, observational statements, which simply record a pre-existent given."[74] He contends that three criteria are necessary for legal discourse to be effective. It must be "uttered by the person legitimately licensed to do so, in a legitimate situation [and] enunciated according to the legitimate forms."[75]

---

71. James C. Scott, *Domination and the Arts of Resistance: Hidden Transcripts* (New Haven: Yale University Press, 1990), 32.
72. The Aramaic term for "decree," טעם, is also rendered "order" (e.g., 5:9, 6:1, 3) or "command" (6:14) and occurs frequently in these chapters.
73. Halpern, "Historiographic Commentary," 123.
74. Bourdieu, *Language and Symbolic Power*, 42.
75. Ibid., 113.

In these chapters, official language combines with official discourse contained in official correspondence between Tattenai and the king.[76] Legality and legitimacy are heightened for the project in a way unavailable in a narrative alone. The edict creates the temple that a narrative could only describe, and only the edict of the king can accomplish that. An impasse over the temple between two equal parties cannot be resolved through decrees rooted in their own authority. Instead, both parties, dependent on the Persian king, await a royal verdict. This standoff may mirror similar conflicts in the author's own time. Local disagreements are resolved by imperial intervention, often at the request of the competing parties, and facilitated by the work of government scribes.

The narrator also uses these edicts to create a particular and limited view of the community. In Ezra 5:12, the builders are identified as descendants of those carried into exile.[77] This correspondingly excludes from the community all who do not share that particular history. Consistent with that, Darius's edict in 6:6–7 orders Tattenai to "*keep away*; let the work on this house of God *alone*; let the *governor of the Jews* and the *elders of the Jews* rebuild this house of God on its site." Royal edicts establish the temple as a center for the community and give the exiles its exclusive oversight. Meanwhile the history, couched within Darius's uncontested legal decree, defines in ethnic terms the community's perimeter.

---

76. In Ezra 5–6 only in these legal documents are we told of Cyrus's decree or the history of the first temple.

77. Ezra 5:12: "But because *our ancestors* had angered the God of heaven, he gave them into the hand of King Nebuchadnezzar of Babylon, the Chaldean, who destroyed this house and *carried away the people to Babylonia*."

8
Ezra 1–6: Social Realities and Expectations

David Beetham observes, "Stories about origins are important; and therefore who tells them, or who controls their telling, is of great consequence. Historical accounts are significant and contentious precisely because of their relationship to the legitimacy of power in the present, and because of their contribution to disputes about it."[1] This account of the temple's origins is tied to strategies that produce and maintain legitimacy of institutions and social arrangements important to the author. As a dominant member of society, he possesses the means to influence the beliefs of others, and the most important beliefs are those that justify his own power.[2]

The author adopts a cautious acceptance of the political power of others. Persian monarchs support the temple, yet the traditional role of the monarch is limited. Individual exilic leaders are named but narratively subsumed under the umbrella of elders, and their actions are incorporated into those of the efforts of the wider community. However, support for the current temple hierarchy is sustained by ties to idealized religious practices of preexilic monarchs, and by portraying the return and construction as the fulfillment of prophetic calls and imperial decrees. The controlled presentation of the monarch and historical traditions, the unified presentation of the community, and the limited role of named leaders coalesce to legitimate the temple and the cultural producers instrumental to its construction—in terms appealing to the local community.

---

1. Beetham, *Legitimation of Power*, 103.
2. Ibid., 104.

8.1. Social Trajectory and Expectations

Sara Japhet observes that early aspirations toward political independence found in the prophetic books of Haggai and Zechariah are absent from Ezra 1–6. Instead, we have "a complete acceptance of the political present and a complete absence of any perspective of change.... The existing political reality, as it stands, is understood and described as divine benevolence and as God's special blessing upon His people."[3] At first blush the author's lack of aspiration in Ezra 1–6 appears to conflict with his purpose in writing a history that establishes the legitimacy of the temple and celebrates and defines the uniqueness of the community. However, the connection between ethnic minorities and social trajectories may help to explain such an account.

Bourdieu associates social trajectories of individuals or classes with social aging. He describes this process in terms of the adjustment of aspirations to objective chances of success.[4] He also states that "practices cannot be completely accounted for solely in terms of the properties defining the position occupied in social space at a given time."[5] Rather, one must consider the correlation between a practice or belief and the person's or community's social trajectory from their point of origin to the present (the relation between initial capital and present capital). Social rise or decline (class trajectory) affects dispositions and opinions. He observes that conflicting stances in religion or politics within the same class can be explained by "the different relations to the social world which [agents] owe to divergent individual trajectories, having, for example, succeeded or failed in the reconversion strategies necessary to escape the collective decline of their class."[6]

The author of Ezra 1–6 accepts the limitations imposed by Persian rule—even when it overrides the hopes expressed in his own religious

---

3. Japhet, "Sheshbazzar and Zerubbabel," 59.
4. Bourdieu, *Distinction*, 110–11. "Social ageing is nothing other than the slow renunciation or disinvestment (socially assisted and encouraged) which leads agents to adjust their aspirations to their objective chances, to espouse their condition, become what they are and make do with what they have ... and accepting bereavement of all the 'lateral possibles' they have abandoned along the way."
5. Ibid., 111. In other words, one cannot assume that all members of a class have always been in that class.
6. Ibid.

8. EZRA 1–6: SOCIAL REALITIES AND EXPECTATIONS

texts (Haggai and Zechariah), or reflects a decline from the earlier history of David and Solomon with which he works, or threatens to halt the community's efforts to rebuild. This indicates a downward social trajectory that is "making do" with the restrictions imposed by Persia. There is no hope for a restored monarchy or independence as promoted in the prophetic texts. Although the people's history and the initial return may have raised higher expectations, the author's outlook is adjusted to match a more limited reality. His political and religious opinions are not simply the product of his current position, but the product of a collective (downward) transformation.

A downward trajectory may explain the author's impulse to idealize a past community, to compose an account that celebrates the resumption of the "good old days" with its traditions and underscores the present community's genealogical continuity with the past. Bourdieu comments:

> In contrast to upwardly mobile individuals or groups … who have their future … before them, individuals or groups in decline endlessly reinvent the discourse of all aristocracies, essentialist faith in the eternity of natures, celebration of tradition and the past, the cult of history and its rituals, because the best they can expect from the future is the return of the old order, from which they expect the restoration of their social being.[7]

With little influence over Persia, the author draws heavily on the past and the reinvigoration of rituals associated with the Judean monarchy but conformed to the reality of Persian rule. The restoration of the temple holds within it a hoped-for return of the old religious order, and an accompanying restoration of the author's place in society. Ties to the past and resumption of historic traditions form the basis of confidence for the future.

Although Persia's rule limits the author's hopes, he may have still resisted a downward trajectory by shifting attention to the local community. He employs their history not just to rehash what was lost but to reassert ethnic identity and to define and promote a community within which he has a dominant position. Anthony Smith states that intellectuals within subordinate *ethnie* would respond to imperial cultural classifications and pressures by formulating "new definitions and goals for their communities, in tune with the ethnic and social realities" of their own

---

7. Bourdieu, *Distinction*, 111.

people.⁸ Integral to this is a selective return to the ethnic past. Using a "historical map," the *ethnie* are transformed "from a passive, subordinate 'object' of history into a mobilized, political aware and active 'subject' of history. This was to be achieved by placing the 'masses' at the center of political concern and by celebrating the role of the 'people' and their collective values, myths and memories."⁹ Ezra 1–6 is exactly such an account. It is a selective history that portrays the community actively engaged in restoring their own place in the world.

Smith states that this transformation was possible only "when the community controlled its own destiny in its own homeland—a compact, clearly demarcated territory, in which it was united and autonomous."¹⁰ Dyck contends that this situation held for the community of Yehud, and the evidence in these chapters reveals the author mobilizing the people, not to overthrow imperial rule, but to control the boundaries of their own *ethnie*. However, Dyck argues that this mobilization limited economic interaction, noting, "The approach recommended by the writers of Ezra-Nehemiah did not give the community the flexibility to address the need to broaden its territorial basis and to develop social and economic relations with its immediate neighbours."¹¹ The effort to resolve the political limitations due to Persian rule by reinforcing ethnic identity and boundaries exacerbated economic isolation. Although perhaps beneficial for the author, the heightened boundaries that provided an autonomous cultural field had an economic cost.

8.2. The Author's Capital and the Field of Cultural Production

Ezra 1–6 represents a struggle over the value of the Jerusalem temple. Its value rests on the doxic belief, inherent in this particular field, of the value of temples in general. Previous struggles over the value of numerous other temples structure this particular field. Temples, like works of art (or cultural icons), exist as symbolic objects "only if they are known and recognized as works of art and received by spectators capable of knowing and recognizing them as such."¹² This recognition is not intrinsic to the art or

---

8. Smith, "Politics of Culture," 720.
9. Ibid.
10. Ibid.
11. Dyck, "Ideology of Identity," 102.
12. Bourdieu, *Field of Cultural Production*, 37.

temple but is produced by a belief in the value of the work. Strategies to halt the temple's construction and thus subvert its value succeed only by overturning "the hierarchy of the field without disturbing the principles on which the field is based."[13] (The goal is not to make all temples worthless, but to gain ascendancy for a competing position, and the competition heightens the value given temples in general.) This narrative counters such strategies by demonstrating the value of the Jerusalem temple. While the biblical text itself may be a piece of literary art (having its own symbolic value), it also produces symbolic value for the temple.

This text has all the earmarks of a composition by a Jerusalem scribe. Independent prophetic voices quietly give way to scribal compositions of formal letters and royal edicts, the realm of literate agents, much like the author. The account contends that the temple is *the* legitimate Yahwistic site for worship. It portrays the local community working in concert to reinstitute worship at this location and scribal practices as essential for the success of the project. The social organization promoted is one beneficial for a local governmental scribe who also held a position within the temple.

Such a defense composed in the late Persian era suggests that the temple is faced with declining support. If so, those dependent on the temple for their livelihood also face economic hardship. The author's arguments contend with those who question the temple's efficacy or unique standing, or who envision other less exclusionary social boundaries, and who may be unconvinced that government employees are working in the best interests of their communities. He meets these challenges by producing evidence of divine approval of work on behalf of the community. It all comes from his own scribal and priestly context: documents, imperial and religious, reveal the divine will, and religious rituals consecrate the temple community.

The author's account reflects the influence of the larger field of power. Bourdieu posits that a field has its own laws in which "external determinants can have an effect only through transformations in the structure of the field itself. In other words, the field's structure *refracts* ... external determinants in terms of its own logic.... The degree of autonomy of a particular field is measured precisely by its ability to refract external demands into its own logic."[14] In this instance, the narrative symbolically discounts

---

13. Ibid.
14. Johnson, introduction, 14.

claims by local adversaries but respects the local imperial representatives, accepts imperial interference, and imperial edicts are authoritative and lend legitimacy to local claims. In this manner, the author suggests that his community can tolerate the pervasive influence of Persia—its kings, its edicts, its representatives, its language—by using those very things to create a space in Yehud for the local community. The temple creates a focal point for this subordinate community, while language, exilic status, and shared history mark the boundaries. Given these social arrangements, the author's pen, his own particular capital, performs a key function—mediating the distance between king and people.[15] In his effort to mediate Persian rule, however, he also reinscribes the political and social hierarchies of his world.

Other forms of capital are also refracted in this narrative, modified to lend support to the author's claims or position.[16] Competitors are undermined as the power of literary production shifts from adversaries to the people of Judah. The king's political power and economic resources are conveyed through letters and edicts and are valuable only when employed for the construction and maintenance of the temple. The author transfigures the power of the dominant class into symbolic support for the temple to enhance the autonomy of the author's own community and his position within the field of cultural production.

8.3. Minority Ethnic Groups

Minority ethnic groups arise due to external historical events when a preestablished cultural contrast is brought into conjunction with a preestablished social system.[17] In the public sphere, interaction takes place within the statuses and discourse of the dominant population.[18] This may explain, in part, why competition with neighbors is recounted in the Aramaic portion of the text. In this most publically accessible portion of the text, the legitimation of the temple is presented in terms respected by the Persian envoy, and the citizens of Jerusalem are presented as knowledgeable and compliant citizens of the empire.

---

15. Bourdieu, *Language and Symbolic Power*, 167.
16. Bourdieu and Wacquant, *Invitation*, 105.
17. Barth, *Ethnic Groups and Boundaries*, 30.
18. Harald Eidheim, "When Ethnic Identity Is a Social Stigma," in *Ethnic Groups and Boundaries*, ed. Fredrik Barth (Boston: Little, Brown, 1969), 48.

When ethnic identity is a stigma, members seek to qualify themselves as full participants in the larger society by developing techniques to avoid or tolerate sanctions from the wider population.[19] Discourse with outsiders may involve showing off knowledge and competence in areas prized by the wider population, while themes that point to ethnic differentiation are avoided. In Ezra's narrative, the returnees demonstrate a comfortable "Persian" identity toward locals as they claim to carry out an imperial edict. At the same time, they cover up their own non-Persian traits that true Persians would take as signs of local Judean identity.[20] Even recounting these events represents efforts to secure standing with regard to the wider Persian culture. Competence in Aramaic and bureaucratic expertise permeate these texts that employ edicts and letters in keeping with governmental form. The community is obedient to imperial decrees, and the Babylonian origin of the exiles is stressed. YHWH is the "God of heaven," a trait repeatedly attributed to the Persian deity, Ahura Mazda, yet new in its attribution to YHWH.[21] Although the temple is constructed for the local deity, it is a site of prayer for the Persian monarch. The temple in every way is described on equal terms to any other Persian temple. Reserved for the closed stage of the local community, the distinctive Judean festival of Passover is described only in the Hebrew portion of the text, out of the purview of anyone who speaks only Aramaic.

Although these Judeans operate successfully in the public arena, the narrative does not hide their ethnic identity. For Jewish readers, this proves they can successfully compete in the wider culture without abandoning their local and historical identity. Persian formalities can gain administrative backing for local initiatives by presenting one's case in terms respected by royal administrators. The demonstration of knowledge and competence portrays schooling in "Persian" culture and administration beneficial to gaining goods, services, and legitimacy for the community of Yehud.

---

19. Ibid., 40.

20. Ibid., 45. In Eidheim's study of coastal Lapps, he comments, "Lapps act out a 'Norwegian' identity toward Nomad Lapps but relations with those they classify as Norwegians show quite another aspect of their situation … in order to achieve the material and social goods they appreciate, and to share the opportunities available in the society, people have to get rid of, or cover up, those social characteristics which Norwegians take as signs of Lappishness."

21. The term "God of heaven" occurs only in Gen 24:3, 7, and 2 Chr 36:23, but appears in Ezra 1–7 nine times and Neh 1–2 four times. Elsewhere it occurs in Daniel, Tobit, Judith, and 3 Maccabees.

9
The Nehemiah Memoir

The book of Nehemiah traces the reconstruction of Jerusalem's walls (Neh 1–6) as two external antagonists hamper the ongoing project. Nehemiah 5 digresses to internal economic problems that threaten the cohesion of the community. Once the wall is completed, Neh 8–10 shifts to the community as they learn the law, celebrate the Festival of Booths, and commit to maintaining the law. Following this, the narrative returns to the "holy city." It is populated, and the purified priests and people (12:30) together dedicate the wall. The book does not end on a note of grand celebration; instead, the final chapter takes up reforms that respond to failures to maintain commitments made as part of the covenant renewal in Neh 10.

The first-person narrative in Neh 1:1–7:5 and portions of Neh 12–13 are commonly identified as the Nehemiah memoir. It is possible that Nehemiah, son of Hacaliah, authored some portion of these chapters. The memoir is often given credence as authentic and as authored in the time and place it describes.[1] The account of the wall's construction (Neh 1–4, 6) likely comprises the earliest portion of the entire Ezra-Nehemiah corpus.[2] Nehemiah 5 and 13 expand the earlier material and redirect attention from the wall building to address concerns over the character of the community.

---

1. Wright, *Rebuilding Identity*, 91.
2. Not all scholars are in agreement on this. Peter Ackroyd ("Jewish Community in Palestine," 132) views the Nehemiah material as a final addition to Ezra added in the Greek period. Margaret Cohen ("Leave Nehemiah Alone: Nehemiah's 'Tales' and Fifth-Century BCE Historiography," in *Unity and Disunity in Ezra-Nehemiah: Redaction, Rhetoric and Reader*, ed. Mark J. Boda and Paul L. Redditt, HBM 17 [Sheffield: Sheffield Phoenix, 2008], 73) dissects Nehemiah into storytelling and document "tales." On this basis she argues that the lists (Neh 3 and 7) are part of Nehemiah's original historiography, but the material regarding Sanballat (Neh 4 and 6) is a later addition.

Nehemiah may have composed these additions at a subsequent time in his rule or they may come from a later and different hand.[3] Nehemiah 5 departs from the concern for external combatants to address internal economic problems. This makes it suited to a different method of analysis from the rest of the memoir, and I will treat it separately despite its literary connections to Neh 13 (particularly the "Remember" formulas). The measures taken in Neh 13 (separation from foreigners, Sabbath observance, and support for the temple) coincide with commitments in the covenant in Neh 10, yet other evidence suggests that chapter 10 postdates the composition of these chapters.[4] The list of wall builders in chapter 3 and the list of returnees in 7:6–73 (nearly identical to Ezra 2) derive from independent sources. Nehemiah 3 is generally assigned an early date for its inclusion, although the prominence of the priests among the builders appears out of place with the rest of the memoir. The time and occasion for the addition of the list of returnees (Neh 7) is debated.[5]

Nehemiah 8:1–12:26 consists of late additions to Nehemiah, although there is lack of unanimity regarding their origins.[6] It is likely that a portion of the Ezra narrative has been moved to Neh 8, given the prominence of Ezra in that chapter, and 9:1–12:26 is the work of the final compiler, with the lists of 11:21–36 and 12:1–26 possibly added later yet.[7] These later additions are distinguished by a change in focus: they stress the participation

---

3. Williamson (*Ezra, Nehemiah*, xxvi–xxvii) points to Nehemiah's absence and return (13:6) as support for a two-stage composition by Nehemiah. (He places Neh 5:14–19; 13:4–14, 15–22, 23–31 in the second phase.) Jacob Wright (*Rebuilding Identity*, 191–97), on the other hand, contends that the material in 13:4–9 originally followed 6:17–19 and refers to the situation prior to the wall building. He argues that 13:6 is an addition to the text that would indicate an earlier date for the narrative than what Williamson posits.

4. Williamson, *Ezra, Nehemiah*, xxvi, 330–31. Williamson argues Neh that 10 was part of an originally independent document inserted by the composer of Neh 8–9 who also added the list of signatories.

5. Jacob Wright (*Rebuilding Identity*, 340) contends that Neh 7 was added at the last stage of composition of the books. Blenkinsopp (*Ezra-Nehemiah*, 44) argues that the list of Neh 7 was copied from Ezra 2, against Williamson (*Ezra, Nehemiah*, 29), who maintains that the list of Neh 7 preceded its placement in Ezra 2.

6. For a survey of issues see Boda, "Redaction," 25–54.

7. In 1 Esdras, Neh 8 follows the solution to the marriage crisis of Ezra 10. Based on chronology and the logic of a law reading followed by its implementation, Blenkinsopp places Neh 8 after Ezra 8 (*Ezra-Nehemiah*, 45).

of all the people and appear less enamored with Nehemiah.[8] The narrative moves from wall building to a concern for the law and proper maintenance of the cult.[9] These thematic differences hint at distinctive agendas and perhaps changing time periods.

9.1. Historical Context for the Nehemiah Memoir

Because this material predates much of the rest of the book, I will initially analyze the rhetorical strategies in the autobiography as a unit and evaluate them with regard to social conditions during Nehemiah's tenure as governor. Nehemiah held the position of governor of Yehud under Artaxerxes I (Neh 5:14; 12:26). This monarch ruled from 465 to 424 BCE, and Nehemiah's tenure as governor is frequently dated from 445 to 433.[10] In his survey of Achaemenid administrators, M. A. Dandamayev states that, under Cyrus, the governor of Across-the-River handled both civil and military functions. By the time of Darius, "the governor's functions were mainly limited to civil ones."[11] The term for "governor," פחה, is used for provincial governors as well as a variety of administrators such as city governors and minor civil servants. This makes Nehemiah's exact jurisdiction less clear. Yet Dandamayev comments,

> The governors of all levels were at the head of the administration of their own regions and had at their disposal various officials, as well as scribes, messengers, and sometimes even merchants. They were obliged to keep order and carry out justice, as well as supervising the economics of their districts and their local civil servants, and overseeing the receipt of state taxes and tolls and the fulfillment of duties.[12]

There is evidence that governors of Uruk influenced the management of the Eanna Temple, chaired the local assembly, exercised judicial authority, and acted as witnesses for documents.[13] Aside from Nehemiah, only

---

8. Williamson, *Ezra, Nehemiah*, xxxiii.
9. Boda, "Redaction," 54.
10. Blenkinsopp, *Ezra-Nehemiah*, 140. Neh 2:1 states that Nehemiah made his request to go to Jerusalem in Artaxerxes's twentieth year.
11. M. A. Dandamayev, "Neo-Babylonian and Achaemenid State Administration in Mesopotamia," in Lipschits and Oeming, *Persian Period*, 394.
12. Ibid.
13. Ibid., 395.

Tattenai is called "governor" in Ezra-Nehemiah (Ezra 5:3). Pointedly, although Sanballat operates like a governor in Nehemiah, he is nowhere given the title. Evidence suggests that he may have been the first governor of the northern territory of Samaria.[14]

A protracted war with Egypt was a primary concern of the "Great King" from 460 to 454 BCE. The rebellion was led by a Libyan, Inarus, who enlisted Athenian forces with promises of shared rule. Eventually the Persian navy, led by Megabyzus, defeated the Egyptians.[15] Egypt's proximity to the Levant has led scholars to connect Nehemiah's arrival with this conflict. However, as noted in the introduction, there is debate as to the strength of this rebellion and how wide ranging its influence was.[16] In addition, the fortification of Jerusalem was unlikely to have had much significance for troop movement or military operations along the coastal plain.

Hoglund contends that the Persians engaged in a deliberate strategy of consolidation and militarization during this period and that garrisoning the region was "directly related to the collection of revenues and the maintenance of the administrative machinery over the territory."[17] However, Lipschits argues that the construction of garrisons occurred later. Persian-era Yehud stamped jar handles from Mizpah, Jerusalem, and Ramat Raḥel still show significant diversity in design during this era. Only at the beginning of the fourth century BCE does there appear a consolidation of form indicating increasing imperial regulation over the region.[18] However,

---

14. Magen, "Dating," 187–88. Sanballat's presence and importance at this time is consistent with later references in the Elephantine papyri to Sanballat's son in 407 BCE. See also Hannan Eshel, "The Governors of Samaria in the Fifth and Fourth Centuries B.C.E.," in Lipschits, Knoppers, and Albertz, *Fourth Century B.C.E.*, 223–34.

15. Briant, *From Cyrus to Alexander*, 573–75. Briant relies mostly on Diodorus and Thucydides for his reconstruction. See Briant or Hoglund (*Achaemenid Imperial Administration*, 137–64) for more detailed descriptions of this event.

16. Briant (*From Cyrus to Alexander*, 575) argues that the rebellion was confined to the Egyptian Delta and lacked full Egyptian support. Hoglund (*Achaemenid Imperial Administration*, 163), however, contends that the rebellion was a major crisis in imperial control. Given the Levant's strategic importance as a land bridge to Egypt and access to the Mediterranean, he believes that the empire would naturally be concerned with its security and took "steps to consolidate its hold over territories imperiled by continuing Greek pressure."

17. Hoglund, *Achaemenid Imperial Administration*, 204.

18. Lipschits and Vanderhooft, "Yehud Stamp Impressions," 84.

even diverse stamps demonstrate an administrative apparatus in operation throughout the entire Persian period.

Hoglund also identifies other methods employed by the Persians to ensure ongoing imperial rule.[19] These include dissolving self-sufficient economic structures, incorporating local aristocracies into the governing system, and developing new and efficient means of communication. In particular, Hoglund believes that the concern for ethnic purity found in Ezra-Nehemiah coincided with long-standing imperial strategies of displacing populations and defining them in ethnic terms. He proposes that the missions of Ezra and Nehemiah were not rewards for loyalty but intended by the empire "to create a web of economic and social relationships that would tie the community more completely into the imperial system." He therefore suggests that the biblical author has submerged these social and historical factors in order to emphasize his theological interpretation.[20] If these books reflect growing tensions brought on by the presence of returnees, it would seem that such imperial strategies created conflict rather than consolidation. Jacob Wright also disagrees with Hoglund and maintains that Jerusalem occupied a central place not in the strategic plan of the empire, but rather in the ethnic and political consciousness of the Judean leaders.[21] Although Nehemiah presents himself as an imperial appointee, the account presents the rebuilding of Jerusalem as a communal project carried out at the behest of ethnic Judeans. If the rebuilding was initiated by ethnic repatriates, it might explain the hostility from regional neighbors. What is clear is that the imperial objectives were not identical with those of the local Judeans or returnees, and at all levels the interests of each group have to be navigated.

Although the political and cultural realities of the Persian Empire certainly influenced this composition, it is noteworthy that, as Blenkinsopp points out, Jewish texts present a favorable view of Persian rule in contrast to the growing opposition found in Greek texts. He declares that both, however, "were engaged, in their own ways, in defining their national identity over against the dominant power in the world at that time."[22] Nehemiah's own particular role, mediating between Persian rule and the local population, balancing the competing claims of the poor, the

---

19. Hoglund, *Achaemenid Imperial Administration*, 167.
20. Ibid., 244, 241.
21. Wright, *Rebuilding Identity*, 85.
22. Joseph Blenkinsopp, "The Nehemiah Autobiographical Memoir," in *Lan-

nobles, the priests, and the neighboring regions, influences the content of his memoir and how he portrays himself. The author draws on his own religious traditions and his imperial appointment to legitimate his efforts to rebuild and define his community in Jerusalem.

9.2. The Narrative of Nehemiah's Memoir

Williamson limits the Nehemiah memoir to Neh 1:1–7:5, 12:27–43, and 13:4–31.[23] Blenkinsopp accepts the same group of texts but also omits the prayer in 1:5–11a, the list of wall builders in Neh 3, and the third person narrative of 12:27–30.[24] Blenkinsopp's exclusion of the prayer and list is compelling, as the language and substance of each intrude into the ongoing narrative.

Narrative coverage of Nehemiah's twelve years (5:14) as governor is uneven.[25] The fifty-two days of wall building is the longest sustained account. The rest of his rule is treated summarily in chapter 5 plus a brief addendum in chapter 13 following an indeterminate absence from Judah (13:6–7). This final chapter describes actions to purify the temple, maintain the Sabbath, and eliminate mixed marriages thematically related to the covenant agreement in Neh 10. It is linked to the earlier section by "remember me" formulas (13:14, 22, 29, 31) also found in 5:19 and 6:14, but none of the formulas refers to the wall building.[26] Nehemiah 7:5–12:26, a lengthy insertion, divides the wall's completion (6:15; 7:1) from its dedication recounted in 12:27–43. Blenkinsopp, suggesting some reordering of the original material, believes that 5:14–19 with its invocation and recapitulation of Nehemiah's rule may have once been the memoir's conclusion.[27]

Labeling the first-person material in Nehemiah a memoir is a convenient but inadequate literary classification.[28] No exact parallels exist

---

guage, Theology, and the Bible: Essays in Honour of James Barr, ed. Samuel E. Balentine and John Barton (Oxford: Clarendon, 1994), 200.

23. Williamson, *Ezra, Nehemiah*, xxvi.
24. Blenkinsopp, *Ezra-Nehemiah*, 46.
25. Blenkinsopp, "Nehemiah Autobiographical Memoir," 203.
26. Williamson, *Ezra, Nehemiah*, xxviii. Blenkinsopp ("Nehemiah Autobiographical Memoir," 206) notes that Neh 6:14, an imprecatory prayer employing a remember formula directed against adversaries, refers to the wall construction. However, nowhere does Nehemiah ask God to remember *him* for the construction.
27. Blenkinsopp, *Ezra-Nehemiah*, 265.
28. Williamson, *Ezra, Nehemiah*, xxiv.

in other literature. Some of have noted similarities with inscriptions that commemorate the actions of kings or royal officials. Others have noted that the memoir shares similarities with votive prayers or psalms of lamentation that ask God to "remember" the author.[29] Blenkinsopp finds a close comparison especially with the Udjahorresnet autobiographical inscription, noting its apologetic tone and the author's position as a Persian collaborator sent back to his own country (Egypt) to resolve a national crisis.[30]

9.2.1. A Hero's Tale

Although not set at court, Nehemiah contains folk story elements such as those characteristic of Daniel or Esther.[31] Nehemiah holds an important position close to the king; he risks a breach of etiquette to ask the monarch for a favor on behalf of his people and is motivated by fidelity to his God. He takes action, often unilaterally, for the welfare of his people. Opponents counter his efforts through intrigue, threats, and accusations of disloyalty. Prayerful dependence upon God is integral to the narrative's successful conclusion. In a satirical move common to such literature, Nehemiah's foes are frequently controlled by their growing rage (2:10, 3:20; 4:7 [1 MT]) as they fruitlessly try to stymie the hero. The hero is also angered (5:6) but channels it into plans and actions that rectify unjust or religiously contaminated situations.[32] Susan Niditch observes that in Esther, concerned

---

29. Blenkinsopp ("Nehemiah Autobiographical Memoir," 204) suggests that the memoir "replicates the pattern of those psalms of lamentation which detail hostile accusations or actions against an innocent party, followed by trustful prayer and the prospect of a successful outcome enhanced by the discomfiting of the enemy (e.g. Pss. 7, 9, 54, 56, 59)."

30. Ibid., 210. Blenkinsopp ("The Mission of Udjahorresnet and Those of Ezra and Nehemiah," *JBL* 106 [1987]: 410) further notes that the inscription was probably written around 518 BCE and commemorates the Egyptian's efforts as a Persian collaborator "to carry out a thorough restoration of the cult at the dynastic sanctuary of Sais." His efforts included the expulsion of foreigners, the purification of the temple, and obtaining provisions from the Persian government.

31. Grabbe (*Ezra-Nehemiah*, 160) notes the similarity but only to suggest that it brings into question Nehemiah's close relationship to the king.

32. The citations mentioned here employ the terms רעע, "to be sad, evil, or displeased" (2:10), and חרה, "to burn or kindle in anger." Berquist (*Judaism in Persia's Shadow*, 163) observes that wisdom literature represents "a thought-centered mindset" that values thinking "though the problems of life and act[ing] on the basis of thought."

with insiders and outsiders, "violence rounds out a theme of just deserts."³³ Although sharing the underlying anxiety about boundaries, the conflict in Nehemiah is resolved through acts of restoration and cleansing; and physical violence is threatened but never actualized.

Categorizing the memoir as folk literature invites consideration of its purpose and how that is achieved. Kevin McGeough argues for wisdom elements within heroic narratives. He states that historicized wisdom tales were inherently didactic. Citing von Rad, he states, "Wisdom does not provide rules for behavior … but attempts to instill a type of understanding in the individual, who still retains final choice over his or her behavior."³⁴ Niditch contends that "the plot of the folktale, in which one knows all will turn out well for the heroes whether via their wisdom or 'some other source,' thus makes real suffering bearable and helps to bridge the gap between the way things are and the way they should be."³⁵ Nehemiah's heroic portrait is patterned on the human hero who risks everything (unlike a god) and one who demonstrates intellectual skill, judgment, and moral worth.³⁶ The narrative strategies of exaggeration or satire may be aimed at larger issues less easily addressed by straightforward accusations. These folklore elements muddle efforts to distinguish between history and fiction. Niditch suggests that in such literature "certain motifs may be included in a tale because such tales traditionally just go a certain way."³⁷

9.2.2. Literary Motifs

Several distinctive literary patterns play important structural and thematic roles in Nehemiah's memoir. In the first six chapters, adversaries "hear" (שמע) of the progress on the wall (Neh 2:10, 19; 4:1, 7, 15 [3:33; 4:1, 9 MT]; 6:1, 16). With each repetition, opposition escalates, as does Nehemiah's response, developing a contrast between Nehemiah and his opponents.³⁸ Blenkinsopp states that this contrast is "the most salient thematic

---

33. Susan Niditch, *A Prelude to Biblical Folklore* (Chicago: University of Illinois Press, 2000), 140.
34. Kevin McGeough, "Esther the Hero: Going beyond 'Wisdom' in Heroic Narratives," *CBQ* 70 (2008): 47.
35. Niditch, *Prelude to Biblical Folklore*, 145.
36. McGeough, "Esther the Hero," 52.
37. Niditch, *Prelude to Biblical Folklore*, 3.
38. Wright, *Rebuilding Identity*, 27.

and structural feature of this first section.... Beginning with his arrival in the province (2:9–10), and repeated seven times, it describes one stage in the progress of the work, its coming to the attention of his enemies ... their reaction to the news ... and Nehemiah's counter-measures (rebuttal, prayer, vigorous action)."[39] Twice Nehemiah will also "hear" news of his community that saddens or angers him (1:2 and 5:6). Whatever one hears appears to be bad news for the hearer. The response of the recipient underscores and characterizes his relationship to the community.

In the "Remember" refrains of the second half of the memoir, Nehemiah entreats God to remember him for actions taken on behalf of the community or the temple (5:19; 13:14, 22, 31). On two occasions he asks God to remember the mockery or threats of Tobiah, Sanballat, and others (6:14) or actions of the priestly family whose members married into Sanballat's family and "defiled the priesthood" (13:29). The litany draws contrasts between the actions of Nehemiah and those of his opponents. The repeated requests for divine approval invite the reader to concur with Nehemiah's evaluations of the various deeds.

A third motif is wordplay on good and evil, most noticeably in chapters 1 and 2.[40] The narrative begins with an announcement that the province is in "great distress" or "great evil" (רעה גדלה), and Nehemiah's sad or evil (רע) face and heart before the king mirror the state of the province (2:1–3). When Nehemiah makes his requests to the king, the term טוב ("good") as verb or noun is repeated five times (2:5–8). Repeatedly the monarch sees the cupbearer's plans as good, and Nehemiah concludes that the monarch's consent is due to "the good hand of my God upon me" (2:8). In 2:10, the news that someone has come to seek the welfare, "the good," of the people of Israel is greeted by Sanballat and Tobiah (whose name, "YHWH is my good," creates an ironic pun) as literally "evil, great evil" (ירע להם רע גדלה).[41]

This same language will occur once more in the final chapter. In 13:4–14, we learn that Eliashib was assigned responsibility for the chambers of the house of God and was related by marriage to Tobiah (13:4–5). Without

---

39. Blenkinsopp, "Nehemiah Autobiographical Memoir," 204.

40. Eskenazi, *In an Age of Prose*, 146. The roots for "evil" (רעע) and "good" (טוב) occur as nouns, verbs, and adjectives in these chapters.

41. The same language describes Jonah's reaction to God's decision not to bring "evil" (NRSV "calamity") upon Nineveh (Jonah 4:1). In both narratives, as good replaces evil for the people, evil begins to surround the characters opposed to their welfare.

the author directly identifying Eliashib as an opponent, references to evil and good, so prominent in Neh 2, recur. In this instance, it is Eliashib who does "evil" (NRSV "wrong") by providing rooms for Tobiah within the temple precincts (13:7). This takes place in Nehemiah's absence and is rectified by Nehemiah tossing out the *vessels* (כלי; most English versions translate "household goods" or the like) of Tobiah's *house* from the *house* of God, thus making room for the *vessels* (כלי) of God and the portions for the Levites (who had abandoned their posts to return to their fields in his absence). Eskenazi observes that the language indicates "Nehemiah's polarized views of reality. Nehemiah sees the world in terms of good or evil, friend or foe."[42]

Nehemiah enlists forms familiar from his community's mythology to construct an image of himself, his community, and his adversaries. Myths are a collectively appropriated product shared by the group as a whole (unlike ideologies that serve particular interests presented as universal).[43] However, like all symbolic systems, myth is an instrument for knowing and constructing the world. "Symbols are the instruments *par excellence* of 'social integration': as instruments of knowledge and communication … they make it possible for there to be a *consensus* on the meaning of the social world, a consensus which contributes fundamentally to the reproduction of the social order."[44] Forms of classification are not universal but "arbitrary (relative to a particular group) and socially determined."[45] By couching his story in folktale forms, Nehemiah can present himself as disinterested in his own gain and acting only for the good of the community. His cultural (religious), economic, political and even military capital are also recognized as resources essential to the success of his mission. The construction of Nehemiah as hero simultaneously creates an image of Judah as vulnerable to what lay outside the broken walls, with only Nehemiah capable of setting things right. The importance of his triumph over enemies is intensified through the added rhetoric of holy war.

---

42. Ibid., 146.
43. Bourdieu, *Language and Symbolic Power*, 167.
44. Ibid., 166.
45. Ibid., 164.

9.2.3. Holy War

9.2.3.1. Holy War Rhetoric

Holy-war ideology provides a thematic backdrop for the memoir. It consists of an all-encompassing assurance that YHWH is the people's champion who will hand their enemies over to them, striking foes with confusion and fear.[46] Common elements include divine deliverance of the oppressed, an inspired charismatic war leader, control of the land, and oppositions between order and chaos. Holy war builds on the tradition of a divine warrior reducing primeval chaos to order. The divine restoration of order became a paradigm for wars on earth and, as John Collins observes, gave nationalism "a mythological expression."[47] Early accounts perhaps began with an assumption of divine participation in battle but developed over time into the formalized accounts preserved in the Hebrew Bible.[48] Gwilym Jones believes that the ideology grew from the belief that YHWH granted Israel success against its enemies into a formula that emphasized YHWH wars were God centered and ultimately came to support the Deuteronomistic belief that the possession of Canaan was a gift from YHWH.[49]

---

46. Daniel E. Fleming, "The Seven-Day Siege of Jericho in Holy War," in *Ki Baruch Hu: Ancient Near Eastern, Biblical, and Judaic Studies in Honor of Baruch A. Levine*, ed. Robert Chazan, William H. Hallo, and Lawrence H. Schiffman (Winona Lake, IN: Eisenbrauns, 1999), 220.

47. John J. Collins, "The Mythology of Holy War in Daniel and the Qumran War Scroll: A Point of Transition in Jewish Apocalyptic," *VT* 25 (1975): 598. Collins observes that this mythology is particularly striking in Jewish apocalyptic, which evokes the old mythology of conflict between God and chaos and coincides with the turmoil of war and persecution under Antiochus Epiphanes. In Daniel, Israel's enemies are the patron deities of specific nations, and therefore chaos is identified in political terms (608).

48. Gwilym H. Jones, "The Concept of Holy War," in *The World of Ancient Israel: Sociological, Anthropological and Political Perspectives*, ed. R. E. Clements (Cambridge: Cambridge University Press, 1989), 306, 311. Jones provides a brief survey of various ancient Near Eastern examples of holy-war ideology and language. He argues that early narratives contain no fixed procedure for holy war and the whole concept of a YHWH war was not clearly expressed. He cites the accounts of Jephthah and Ehud in Judges as early examples. In particular, early evidence of חרם, the devotion of booty to God, is rare. Some biblical texts containing that element are of uncertain history while others are distinctly Deuteronomistic. See ibid., 309.

49. Ibid., 315.

Its use in prophetic oracles against nations (e.g., Amos 2:4–16; 5:1–27) suggests that it was a familiar concept.[50] Such mythology transforms "cultural values into a universal and natural value."[51] Holy war's resonance with community beliefs facilitates Nehemiah's representation of reality as unavoidable and natural.[52]

In general, holy-war narratives begin in a situation of oppression and distress. A leader arises who calls followers, and they engage in battle, which culminates with total victory over the enemies. Many of the distinct elements of holy war cataloged by von Rad have been identified by Blenkinsopp and Williamson in the growing conflict with Sanballat and Tobiah in Neh 4:1–15.[53] These include:

- enemies conspire together (4:8)
- the righteous call to God for help before arming themselves (4:9)
- the resources of the righteous and their numbers are limited (4:10)
- the righteous conscript a militia for battle rather than a standing army (4:13)
- the people are told God is with them therefore do not fear the enemy (4:14)
- the evil designs of the enemy are thwarted by divine intervention, and they are forced to acknowledge the hand of God (4:15)

Williamson, noting points of contact with Deuteronomic texts, observes that the meaning in this well-known tradition and its stereotypical language are "reinforced by the recollections it would evoke of the past victories of God for his people's sake."[54]

---

50. Ibid., 318. See also Susan Niditch, *War in the Hebrew Bible: A Study in the Ethics of Violence* (New York: Oxford University Press, 1993), 76.

51. Graham Allen, *Roland Barthes* (New York: Routledge, 2003), 37.

52. Graham Allen, *Intertextuality*, 2nd ed. (New York: Routledge, 2011), 87; cf. Roland Barthes, *S/Z*, trans. Richard Miller (New York: Hill & Wang, 1974), 206.

53. Gerhard von Rad, *Holy War in Ancient Israel*, ed. and trans. Marva J. Dawn (Grand Rapids: Eerdmans, 1991); Blenkinsopp, "Nehemiah Autobiographical Memoir," 205; Williamson, *Ezra, Nehemiah*, 224. Both Blenkinsopp and Williamson have drawn their lists from Ulrich Kellermann, *Nehemia: Quellen, Überlieferung und Geschichte*, BZAW 102 (Berlin: Töpelmann, 1967), 18. Kellermann contends that holy war displays not only the author's theological camp but "ensures the consistency and coherence of the text" (my translation)

54. Williamson, *Ezra, Nehemiah*, 227. Jones has argued that much of the holy-war

Holy-war ideology is not confined to Neh 4 but permeates the Nehemiah memoir. Nehemiah expresses the characteristic assurance of divine aid in his responses to mockery over efforts to rebuild the wall: "Then I replied to them, 'The God of heaven is the one who will give us success, and we his servants are going to start building'" (2:20; cf. 4:20). The enemies' fear upon seeing the completed wall embodies the conviction of divine mastery over the foe: "And when all our enemies heard of it, all the nations around us were afraid and fell greatly in their own esteem; for they perceived that this work had been accomplished with the help of our God" (6:16). Nehemiah departs from the customary claim that the Lord has given the land, the city, or the enemy into *Israel's* hand (cf. Josh 2:24; 6:2; 8:1, 18, etc.). Instead, God's hand is upon *Nehemiah* (Neh 2:8, 18), and his enemies simply lose heart when they recognize the completed wall as evidence of YHWH's aid (Neh 6:16).[55] In the holy-war narratives in Exodus, Joshua, or Judges, divine victory requires little from the Israelite army, thus diminishing the importance of Israel's contribution.[56] Jericho's walls fall before the Israelites even lift a sword; and in Exod 14:13, they are called upon to stand and watch as YHWH fights for them. In Nehemiah, the sustained attention to the community's efforts to build the wall affirms the importance of their participation to accomplish the divine will.

According to von Rad, holy war is initiated by mustering the people, usually with a trumpet blast.[57] Nehemiah invokes holy-war language to muster the builders (Neh 2:17–20), but a trumpeter (which never sounds) appears only in the last stages of construction as opposition grows (4:18, 20). Von Rad also asserts that in response to a misfortune, a ceremony of repentance and mourning typically precedes the call to arms, and in all cases requires an oracle confirming the divine decision. On this basis,

---

tradition was not a starting point but an editorial addition to earlier battle narratives. This opens the door to the possibility that Nehemiah's account employs language and theology produced by a more recent generation. See Jones, "'Holy War' or 'Yahweh War'?" *VT* 25 (1975): 655.

55. Josh 2:9–11 and 5:1 state that "hearts melted in fear" upon hearing of the arrival of the Israelites. Josh 10:10 and Judg 4:15 describe YHWH throwing the enemy army into confusion, leading to their defeat.

56. Von Rad, *Holy War in Ancient Israel*, 50. For a comparison of the use of holy war imagery in Joshua and Nehemiah, see Donna Laird, "Political Strategy in the Narrative of Ezra-Nehemiah," in *The Oxford Handbook of Biblical Narrative*, ed. Danna Nolan Fewell (Oxford: Oxford University Press, 2015), 276–85.

57. Von Rad, *Holy War in Ancient Israel*, 41.

the leader could proclaim that God has given the enemy into their hand.[58] Nehemiah responds to the misfortune that begins this book with appropriate repentance and mourning (1:4). Divine guidance is sought and recognized as the monarch approves his request, "And the king granted me what I asked, for the gracious hand of my God was upon me" (2:8). Nehemiah then declares the divine confirmation to the people, "I told them that the hand of my God had been gracious upon me, and also the words that the king had spoken to me" (2:18; cf. 2:20).

9.2.3.2. Jerusalem and Jericho

The wall narrative of Nehemiah has connections with the description of the conquest of Jericho in Joshua that go beyond a shared motif of holy war. Walls are of particular importance for both narratives. In Joshua, Rahab lives "in the wall" (Josh 2:15 NJPS, RSV) and the spies depart through the wall.[59] The battle in Joshua begins with a statement about Jericho's solid walls (Josh 6:1), and Nehemiah begins with a report on the broken walls of Jerusalem (Neh 1:3). In both accounts, the people circumnavigate the wall, and the final status of the wall marks the climax of each narrative. Preparations for action include secret nighttime inspections of the status of the cities. A secret scouting party spies out Jericho (Josh 2:1), and Rahab is warned not to tell their business (Josh 2:14). Similarly, Nehemiah goes at night to investigate the condition of Jerusalem's walls, and he pointedly tells no one his plans (Neh 2:12).[60]

The status of Jerusalem's walls is a touchstone for each episode in Nehemiah and could be considered a reverse image of the walls of Jericho. Jericho's walls begin the narrative as a solid construction: "Now Jericho was shut up inside and out because of the Israelites; no one came out and no one went in" (Josh 6:1). In the end, the walls fall (6:20), and the city is burned (6:24). In Nehemiah, the narrative begins with the walls broken

---

58. Ibid., 42.

59. If we include information in Neh 3, we find citizens who also live "next to" the walls.

60. Expeditions into enemy territory prior to battle and motifs of light and dark are common in accounts of holy war. Gideon makes a nighttime visit to the enemy camp and is encouraged by the description of a soldier's dream (Judg 7:10–15). Both Joshua and Gideon are encouraged by the information they collect. Nehemiah's circuit is more pragmatic as he assesses the wall's status.

down and the gates burned. This information is provided not once (Neh 1:3) but four times (2:3, 13, 17), and the situation is interpreted as a great reproach (1:3; 2:17; 4:2, 4 [3:34, 36 MT]). The constant reminder of the city with fallen walls and burned gates reverberates with the final status of Jericho. Jerusalem begins destroyed by fire, but it will end with a wall that has "no gap left in it" (6:1).

Many have perceived Nehemiah's intense mourning over burned city gates (Neh 1:4) as one of surprise and shock, making it especially puzzling if the condition of the gates is due to actions by the Babylonians a century earlier. This has led some to suggest a more recent historical cause for the gates' condition, but without much success.[61] Blenkinsopp notes, however, that "Nehemiah's reaction follows the conventions of postexilic piety … including sitting on the ground while in mourning."[62] The mourning is not necessarily extreme and is consistent with a response to a situation of national disgrace. Jacob Wright argues that the response also provides a positive example with which to compare the behavior of the antagonists.[63]

The multiple references to the burned gates associated with disgrace also provide a striking contrast with the completed wall. As construction continues, the growth of the wall becomes a recurring refrain (Neh 4:1, 6, 7, 11 [3:33, 38; 4:1, 5 MT]; 6:1, 15). By the end of the account, the wall with "no gap left in it" (6:1), with gates in place (7:1), now has guards (gatekeepers, singers, and Levites!), and Nehemiah orders the gates "not to be opened until the sun is hot" (7:3). At the dedication, the congregation circles the walls, giving thanks and offering sacrifices (12:31–43).[64] In a reverse scenario, Jericho begins shut up so "no one went in and no one went out" (Josh 6:1), and the gates are shut at night (2:5–7). The congregation circles the standing walls, surrounded by armed men and led by priests blowing trumpets in ritual confirmation of their obedience to God (6:3–4, 8–9, etc.). The repeated march around the walls anticipates their

---

61. Williamson (*Ezra, Nehemiah*, 172) comments, "A recent event, as yet unconfirmed must be intended." Blenkinsopp (*Ezra-Nehemiah*, 204) comments, "All we can say, then, is that some serious disturbance had taken place shortly before 445 B.C.E. the cause of which remains obscure."

62. Blenkinsopp, *Ezra-Nehemiah*, 207.

63. Wright, *Rebuilding Identity*, 29.

64. In Neh 12:30, the priests purify themselves, the people, and the walls. Whether this verse should be included in the memoir is a matter of debate. Without it, the priests have a more muted role in the celebration of thanks.

collapse (6:8–19). YHWH's victory is sealed as Israel devotes everything to destruction and burns the city and all that was in it (6:21, 24). In both narratives, the people of Israel carry out the will of YHWH (either to destroy in Joshua or to build in Nehemiah), and both cities end as spaces dedicated to God—one by חרם and one by restoration. Each narrative culminates in the city containing only what is holy and dedicated to the Lord.

Rituals of circumcision and Passover (Josh 5) precede the battle of Jericho and mark the Israelites as YHWH's people.[65] Such rites are reserved in Nehemiah until the wall is whole. However, evidence that the builders are YHWH's people develops in the cycles of conflict with Sanballat and Tobiah. Nehemiah's first riposte to Sanballat and Tobiah's accusation of sedition is to claim "you have no share or claim or historic right in Jerusalem" (Neh 2:20). Upon the next bout of mockery, Nehemiah prays, "Hear, O our God, for we are despised; turn their taunt back on their own heads, and give them over as plunder in a land of captivity" (4:4 [3:36 MT]). He seeks for them the same conditions he hopes to reverse for his own people. When confronted by further taunts, he encourages the nobles to fight "for your kin, your sons, your daughters, your wives, and your homes"— all couched in familial language (4:14 [8 MT]) and therefore excluding anyone outside that boundary. Confirmed by later rituals, the language describing the combatants also marks inclusion and exclusion as surely as the ritual of circumcision, confirmed by the successful battle against Jericho, defines membership in Joshua.

In both accounts, the concept of reproach has ties to captivity. At the beginning of Nehemiah, the Judeans are described as "brothers," but they are also escapees and those left from the captivity (הפליטה אשר־נשארו מן־השבי, Neh 1:2). Almost the same language, הנשארים אשר־נשארו, repeats in 1:3. In the book of Joshua, the phrase, "no one was left/he left no one remaining," is a recurring refrain after successful battles (Josh 8:17, 22; 10:28, 30, 37, 39, 40, etc.). Furthermore, the same combination of terms, "those who had escaped" and "[those who] survived," in Neh 1:2 also

---

65. Both accounts introduce a military aura prior to actions taken by Israel. Nehemiah refers to "officers" of the royal army who accompany him (Neh 2:9) prior to his inspection of the city wall. The same term, שר, is used later in Nehemiah for rulers but is used only once in Joshua, where it describes the "commander" of the Lord's army who meets Joshua just prior to the battle of Jericho (Josh 5:14). In both instances the officers, though clearly sympathetic toward the protagonist, are under the command of another.

describes the unfortunate condition of Ai's population in Joshua following that city's defeat, "no one was left who survived or escaped" (הִשְׁאִיר־לֹו שָׂרִיד וּפָלִיט, Josh 8:22). In Neh 1:3, the situation of the escapees is declared a state of great evil and reproach (חרפה), and Nehemiah assesses the broken walls as a reproach (Neh 2:17). In Joshua, the ritual of circumcision removes the reproach of Egypt prior to the conquest of Jericho (Josh 5:9). In Nehemiah, the Judeans remove their reproach by constructing the walls, even as Nehemiah prays that YHWH turn back on his enemies their reproach (taunt) (Neh 4:4 [3:36 MT]; 5:9). In both texts, the reproach of captivity and foreign power is removed through purifying ritual acts. In Joshua, these rituals signal divine support prior to the conquest of Jericho and the removal of its walls. In Nehemiah, the rituals celebrate and confirm divine assistance of the wall's construction. The final state of the city wall and the ceremonial acts confirm the claims that the shame of captivity and foreign rule has ended.

9.2.4. חרם

Von Rad states that הרם forms the high point and conclusion of holy war: "the consecration of the booty to Yahweh."[66] הרם is not limited to contexts of holy war. Niditch identifies two different (but contemporaneous) understandings of הרם. The first understands הרם as sacrifice, of giving God his due (Lev 27:21, 28–29).[67] In the second, הרם is justice. In the law, הרם is called for against anyone (Exod 22:20 [19 MT]) or any city (Deut 13:12–18 [13–19 MT]) that sacrifices to any God other than YHWH. Niditch observes that in Deut 13:12–18 (13–19 MT), הרם (ban) as justice is expressed in strongly covenantal terms: "To worship other gods and be faithless to Yahweh is to tear asunder the moral fabric of the Israelite world. It is to commit abomination (13:13 [v. 14 in the Hebrew]) as an ingrate to the God who has rescued and sustained his people."[68] הרם becomes the "means of rooting out … impure, sinful forces damag-

---

66. Von Rad, *Holy War in Ancient Israel*, 49. הרם occurs in the *hiphil* form of the verb.

67. Niditch, *War in the Hebrew Bible*, 29. Norbert Lohfink notes that this often involves the consecration of persons and objects for use in the temple ("הָרַם *ḥāram*; הָרֶם *ḥērem*," *TDOT* 5:194).

68. Niditch, *War in the Hebrew Bible*, 62–63.

ing to the solid and pure relationship between Israel and God."[69] Once the covenant is restored, the Lord expresses his compassion through an offer to make the people great, "as he swore to your ancestors" (Deut 13:17 [18 MT]).[70]

הרם as justice emphasizes purity through demands for separation from foreigners, it draws "a sharp line ... between us and them, between clean and unclean, between those worthy of salvation and those deserving elimination."[71] Deuteronomy 7:2–6 forbids mercy, covenants, or intermarriage with foreigners, for they lead "to contamination of the specially chosen, sacred people (see 7:3–4, 6)."[72] Louis Stulman contends that these offenses are related to a concern for the integrity of the community's boundaries and lead to the portrayal of exogamous contacts as extremely dangerous.[73] This reasoning provides logic and motivation for war "in order to purify the body politic of one's own group, to eradicate evil in the world beyond one's group, and to actualize divine judgment."[74] It is this understanding of הרם that informs and justifies the actions taken by Nehemiah and Joshua.[75]

In Joshua, the cities of Jericho (6:24), Ai (8:8, 19), and Hazor (Josh 11:11), and the family of Achan (7:15, 25) are all the objects of הרם and burned with fire. Once Jericho's walls fall, everything *inside* Jericho (except Rahab and her family) becomes הרם, or dedicated to the Lord. The only living survivors, Rahab and her family, will live outside the camp of Israel (Josh 6:23). A final oath seals the fate of Jericho as Joshua curses anyone who would rebuild the city. In particular, his curse touches on the city

---

69. Ibid., 56.
70. Ibid., 63.
71. Ibid., 77.
72. Ibid., 64. The inconsistency in this law, which excludes from marriage those that should already be dead, hints at the difficulty or unwillingness of the community to carry out such a slaughter. In Ezra-Nehemiah, הרם occurs only in Ezra 10:8 as a punitive measure for anyone failing to attend the assembly called to respond to the mixed marriages. In this instance, excommunication is threatened and the "forfeiture" or הרם of their property. This action employs הרם as sacrifice in a punitive way.
73. Louis Stulman, "Encroachment in Deuteronomy: An Analysis of the Social World of the D Code," *JBL* 109 (1990): 614.
74. Niditch, *War in the Hebrew Bible*, 77.
75. Niditch (ibid., 63) believes that the story of Achan contains both understandings of הרם. Achan withholds what is due God but then is devoted to destruction himself in an act of justice to purify the community.

walls and gates: "At the cost of his firstborn he shall lay its foundation, and at the cost of his youngest he shall set up its gates!" (Josh 6:26). Even as the curse extends the punishment beyond the immediate moment, it also testifies that reconstruction signals its end (cf. Deut 13:16 [17 MT]).

In Joshua, the purification of Israel does not end with the הרם of Jericho. It is followed by the story of Achan. A member of the clan of Judah, he brings items devoted to destruction into the camp of Israel and hides them.[76] Their presence makes the entire army vulnerable in their battle against Ai. Upon their defeat, Joshua pleads with YHWH, fearing that "the Canaanites and all the inhabitants of the land will hear of it, and surround us, and cut off our name from the earth" (Josh 7:9). YHWH informs Joshua that the people "have put [devoted things] among their own belongings" (7:11). The act is described as an act of deceit and a transgression of the covenant of the Lord (7:15). The presence of devoted things marks the entire community as הרם, and YHWH threatens to abandon Israel unless they "destroy the devoted things from among you" (7:12; cf. 7:13).[77] The slippage in these verses over what constitutes an object of הרם—Israel, stolen items, or Achan and his family—displays belief in, and anxiety about, the integrity of the community. Repair of the damage requires rituals of purification (קדש) for the community (7:13) and the הרם of Achan and his family.

In Ezra-Nehemiah, the inability to engage in warfare compels the author to reconfigure הרם. No one, and nothing, is devoted to physical destruction. Holy war and obedience to the law are recast as a construction project that protects the purity of the Jerusalem community, and "purity is quite clearly defined by separation from foreigners, as far as this is possible."[78] The community separates from the people "all those of foreign descent" (Neh 13:3). As in Joshua, people and objects that are the source of contamination are removed, beginning with Tobiah and his possessions (Neh 13:7). The governor orders the cleansing of temple chambers (13:9) and the Levites so they could guard the gates to keep the Sabbath

---

76. Achan is introduced with a significant lineage, "Achan son of Carmi son of Zabdi son of Zerah, of the tribe of Judah" (Josh 7:1). Such a lineage signifies a person of some importance.

77. In Josh 7:12–15, the term הרם is employed in a variety of ways. The text speaks of the people becoming הרם (7:12), removing הרם objects (7:13), the destruction of whatever is הרם, and the burning of the guilty by fire—an act of הרם (7:15).

78. Janzen, *Social Meanings of Sacrifice*, 194.

day holy (13:22). Nehemiah contends with those who married women of Ashdod, Ammon, and Moab, as he points to foreign women as the cause of Solomon's sin (13:25–26). The cleansing ends as he chases away the grandson of the high priest, Eliashib, who married the daughter of Sanballat the Horonite (13:28). He summarizes all his actions with the claim that he cleansed the priests and Levites "from everything foreign" (13:30).[79]

Like Achan, men of standing within Judah are accused of abetting the infiltration of dangerous "foreign" entities that threaten the community's status as a holy people. Unlike Achan, Eliashib is not punished for his involvement, despite making a room for Tobiah. However, his grandson, who had married the daughter of Sanballat, Nehemiah "chased away" (13:28). By cutting off his descendants from the community, Nehemiah restricts the influence of this family. These last episodes of purification culminate in the last two "remember" clauses. The priests are to be remembered for their impurity (13:29).[80] Nehemiah asks to be remembered "for good," which includes his steps to regulate and provide for the priesthood now purified by his own cleansing efforts (13:30–31). The reference to King Solomon (13:26) and the focus on the family of the high priest may indicate pockets of competition for Nehemiah. Those holding high economic or cultural capital may be making marriage alliances threatening to the governor's power. Thus his cleansing hides, in the guise of religious purity, efforts to limit the influence of others.

The exclusion of others as an act of obedience increases the wall's significance since it controls entrance to the site of worship. The newly rebuilt wall with its gates and guards separates the citizens of Jerusalem from outsiders as it denies merchants entrance on days of religious observance (Neh 13:13–22). Only Israel may sacrifice; outsiders who wish to

---

79. The chronological notices in this text create some uncertainty about the sequence. Narratively, Neh 13 begins with the people separating themselves from all those of foreign descent (13:3). However, 13:6–7 introduces a discussion of events that preceded this communal purification. It suggests that either the priest's actions *or* his actions *and* Nehemiah's cleansing preceded the separation recounted in 13:3. As it stands narratively, Nehemiah's actions are simply in keeping with the community's own commitment to the law to which the high priest was failing to adhere.

80. The verb גאל, here translated "defiled," also occurs in Neh 7:64, where a number of priests could not find their family names in the genealogical records and so were "excluded [from service] as impure." This passage shares a similar concern with this account for the genealogical purity of the priests.

participate and become part of Israel are problematic.[81] Nehemiah refers to the condition of the walls that began this account, a sign of הרם, to motivate the community to separate from surrounding people. He chastises the nobles, "Did not your ancestors act in this way, and did not our God bring all this disaster on us and on this city? Yet you bring more wrath on Israel by profaning the sabbath" (13:18), and calls on them to be vigilant in maintaining their separate identity. Exclusion of others from the temple (13:7–9) and from the city on the Sabbath are now the primary means of demonstrating obedience and loyalty to YHWH.

9.3. Symbolic Capital and Political Strategies

9.3.1. Holy War: Symbolic Language and Mobilizing a Group

Bourdieu comments that any ideological discourse is only operative inasmuch as it is able to make its addressees treat it the way it demands to be treated, namely, "with all due respect."[82] A symbolic strategy can never produce completely the conditions of its own success. It counts on the active complicity of those "who do not want to know that they are subject to it" and is always subordinate to whatever logic will mobilize the greatest number.[83] Ideas about the social world capable of engaging the classifications familiar to the audience are more able to produce groups.

The regulations put forth in this account gain traction by combining multiple familiar strands of ideology and social anxieties to motivate the hearers to embrace and act on the author's conception of the community. A doxic belief in a nationalistic, warring, patron deity is fused with historical traditions regarding covenant loyalty and developing religious conceptions of purity. Now, however, the maintenance of ritual purity is equated with ethnic boundaries. Demands of the covenant actualize, in Paul Hanson's words, *shalom*, "the realm where chaos is not allowed to enter, and where life can be fostered free from the fear of all which diminishes and destroys."[84] Yet now covenant loyalty is enacted through the enforcement of borders. Anxiety about chaos is linked to worries about communal boundaries, and devotional failure is tied to fears of

---

81. Janzen, *Social Meanings of Sacrifice*, 187.
82. Bourdieu, *Language and Symbolic Power*, 153.
83. Ibid., 164, 181.
84. Paul Hanson, "War and Peace in the Hebrew Bible," *Int* 38 (1984): 347.

subjugation. By joining religion and identity, the criteria for distinguishing order and chaos or purity and impurity become the same—national identity.[85] YHWH provides shalom only for those who are members of the covenant community. War and subjugation, as portrayed in Israel's now familiar history, result from refusal to live within the (narrowly defined) covenant.[86] The concerns addressed in holy-war accounts—apostasy, impurity, and the dangers of foreign influence—infuse this narrative, lending support to the order Nehemiah seeks for the community. Righteousness is defined in terms that exclude all rivals and reserve compassion exclusively for fellow members.[87]

In terms of economics and social alliances, these exclusivist strategies are counterproductive, yet this memoir appears to effectively mobilize people. Bourdieu suggests, "the power of a discourse depends less on its intrinsic properties [are its claims true] than on the mobilizing power it exercises—that is, at least to some extent, on the degree to which it is *recognized* by a numerous and powerful group that can recognize itself in it and whose interests it expresses (in a more or less transfigured and unrecognizable form)."[88] Clearly there were those who disagreed with Nehemiah's goals, his perspective on Tobiah or Sanballat, the evils of intermarriage, or the need to maintain the Sabbath.[89] Who, then, would share enough of this worldview to comply with its call to pursue this narrow definition of the community?

Niditch suggests "ban-as-God's-justice ideology is a way in which a group that fears loss of its identity attempts to define itself."[90] It is the "the world-view of a group not only distrustful of foreigners but of 'foreigners' in its own midst, enemies among former brethren."[91] The inability to insulate the community from outsiders makes this concern for outsiders unavoidable.[92] Groups such as this often seek a scapegoat and view the

---

85. Collins, "Mythology of Holy War," 599.
86. Hanson, "War and Peace," 349. Hanson argues that efforts to obtain order via the king were interpreted as a threat to the harmony of the community by ascribing to the king attributes properly belonging to God (361).
87. Ibid., 360.
88. Bourdieu, *Language and Symbolic Power*, 188.
89. In a later text, Neh 11:1–2, the people cast lots simply to populate the city, suggesting a lack of interest in living there.
90. Niditch, *War in the Hebrew Bible*, 74.
91. Ibid.
92. Stulman, "Encroachment in Deuteronomy," 613–32. Stulman identifies

world as fraught with danger and the community's survival in jeopardy. "Chaotic social forces—enemies, criminals, and indigenous outsiders—threaten to undermine its social and cosmic order."[93] Nehemiah's efforts to establish well-defined boundaries reflect such a complex social reality. Local indigenous people and kinsmen who make alliances with them are perceived as threats to the integrity of the community. (This focus on the community curtains off the danger such economic and political alliances pose to the standing of Nehemiah.)[94] The memoir melds religious rhetoric with ethnic anxiety in order "to produce a strong internal coherence and stability and to protect insiders and existing structures from dangerous indigenous outsiders."[95]

In the political competition for the control of nonprofessionals is a characteristic struggle between purists and those advocating compromise:

> on the one hand, [are] those who denounce the compromises necessary to increase the strength of the party (and thus of those who dominate it), but to the detriment of its *originality*, in other words, at the cost of abandoning its distinctive and original ... positions—those people ... advocate a return to basics, to a restoration of the original purity; and, on the other hand, [are] those people who are inclined to seek a strengthening of the party, in other words, a broadening of its clientele, even if this is at the cost of compromises and concessions or even of a methodical interference with everything that is too "exclusive" in the original stances adopted by the party.[96]

Those who denounce compromise can deprive the party of all temporal power, while "the latter group has on its side the logic of *Realpolitik*."[97]

Nehemiah's rhetoric denounces collaboration and compromise. He seeks to restore an original purity. Waging a purist, ideological war is the

---

concern for foreigners within the Deuteronomic tradition and comments that it is unavoidable because "Israel lacks the power to insulate itself from outsiders." He argues that the Deuteronomist "attempts to produce a program in which the integrity of Israel's internal boundaries is (re)established and clarified in order to protect insiders from potentially harmful outsiders" (614).

93. Ibid., 626.

94. Ibid., 632. Stulman identified a similar threat in the Deuteronomist, although he describes it only in religious terms.

95. Ibid.

96. Bourdieu, *Language and Symbolic Power*, 189.

97. Ibid., 190. *Realpolitik* is based on power rather than ideas.

most viable option if one lacks sufficient economic or coercive force to defeat competitors. So he symbolically demolishes them and in the process convinces his audience of the value of his call to purity. Nehemiah constructs his adversaries as purveyors of chaos through their threats, taunts, and subterfuge designed to halt the rebuilding of a wall that would remove the community's shame and protect its sanctity. He represents his project as essential to efforts to hold at bay forces of chaos and to create a defined space in which the community could live out shalom. He establishes himself as a hero, bringing order and purity to a community in need. In Neh 5, he rectifies economic injustice; and in Neh 6, he rejects kingship and so enhances his cultural capital as one whose primary concern is the good of the community.[98] In the war against the forces of chaos, the wall and his leadership are proven essential for the safety and good of the community.

Although the memoir is composed to influence a particular audience, the call for purity is fed, in part, by competition with opponents. Due to the duality of the fields of reference (the clients and competitors), the rhetoric must address, at the same time, internal and external struggles.[99] As he persuades his audience, Nehemiah must account for Persian power and contend with regional power brokers. Nehemiah values the goodwill of the monarch and validates Persian rule. Furthermore, to resist Persia would endanger the economic production of the region and his position. Hostile actions against local competitors would risk the ire of the satrap or monarch. Thus Nehemiah goes about his work (and his writing) without engaging in physical violence; but if any skirmish *were* to start, the narrative assigns blame squarely on the adversaries as instigators.

Despite Nehemiah's certainty regarding requirements for valid membership in the community, his account belies this clarity. For others, particularly those with whom Nehemiah vies for power, it is a matter of contention.[100] Compromise and collaboration, so useful for economic and political power, would lead to entrenched alliances with regional

---

98. Nehemiah will also remind the people that Solomon was a source of impurity for the nation (Neh 13:26)

99. Bourdieu, *Language and Symbolic Power*, 183. Bourdieu notes that this effort to address dual audiences often makes the discourse duplicitous, although not intentionally so.

100. People of standing are said to be related to Tobiah and Sanballat, others are bound by oath to Tobiah and report to Nehemiah good things about him (Neh 6:17–19). In particular, the priests throw in their lot with Tobiah.

powers. Resistance to this outcome produces Nehemiah's opposing call to purity, but with the caveat of collaboration with imperial rule. The highly polemical rhetoric of holy war paints Nehemiah's competitors as opponents to the good of the community, and alliances with them threaten the shalom of the community. If successful, Nehemiah's strategy creates a more cohesive community identity and secures his dominance within a smaller community.

9.3.2. Nehemiah's Capital

9.3.2.1. A Strategy of Condescension

To gain the approval of his audience, Nehemiah employs a tactic Bourdieu labels a *strategy of condescension*.[101] This strategy is possible

> whenever the objective disparity between the persons present … is sufficiently known and recognized by everyone (particularly those involved in the interaction, as agents or spectators) so that the symbolic negation of the hierarchy … enables the speaker to combine the profits linked to … hierarchy with those derived from the symbolic negation of the hierarchy.[102]

Nehemiah's self-presentation is filtered through the matrix of folktale and holy war. This folk hero introduces himself as someone "brothers" from Judah seek out with their news of Jerusalem. He claims a close relationship with Artaxerxes and expounds on the king's personal interest and concern for him.[103] The monarch provides letters to give safe passage during

---

101. Bourdieu, *Language and Symbolic Power*, 66–69. Bourdieu employs this description when discussing two speakers: an employer and employee or speakers of different languages when one language is generally associated with formal public speaking, turning an address to a community in their own tongue into a "thoughtful gesture."
102. Ibid., 68.
103. The monarch grants him leave to travel to Susa to repair the place of his ancestors' graves. When the monarch asks what he can do for Nehemiah, the cupbearer responds, "send me to Judah, to the city of my ancestors' graves, so that I may rebuild it" (Neh 2:5). Some have seen this request as an indication of separate and inconsistent sources from the rest of the account, since his concern stated elsewhere is for the people of Yehud and the city walls (Neh 1:2–3). However, Briant's description of Persian funerary practices (*From Cyrus to Alexander*, 94–96) indicates that the kings held ancestral graves in great regard. Lipschits (*Fall and Rise of Jerusalem*, 215)

travel, access to wood from the royal forests, and military support. Nehemiah presents himself as a devout person whose prayers for success are answered by the God of heaven (Neh 1:11; 2:4; 4:4–5, 9, 15 [3:36–37; 4:3, 9 MT]). This focus on prayer may be necessary to compensate for a lack of ordained religious capital. It may also explain why he draws on Joshua for inspiration—a military leader triumphs over enemies to take the city and purify the community for YHWH. Taken as a whole, whether historically accurate or not, Nehemiah claims an imperial commission and divine favor for his task (2:18).

These sources of cultural and political capital are necessary but not sufficient to lay claim on the labor of the Judeans or to motivate readers to accede to the social arrangements advocated in the account. Although Nehemiah never anticipates resistance from the Jerusalem community, we may note that the citizens of Judah never seek the help he brings to them. Even Hanani's report in Neh 1:3 is not framed as a request for aid but as a simple statement of fact. Nehemiah must convince them that his goals match *their* concerns, or, barring that, convince them that *his* intentions are for their good.

To that end, Nehemiah portrays the Judeans as desperate and in need, with the city devastated and desolate (Neh 1:3). The local population appears to lack the resources, leadership, and even awareness of their circumstances necessary to rectify the situation on their own. (Nehemiah must motivate them to begin labor by calling on them to *see* the evil they are in due to Jerusalem's broken walls and burned gates; 2:17). This image of need and dependence provides a sharp contrast with Nehemiah. He declares that he intends "to seek the welfare of the people of Israel" (2:10). He independently assesses the situation, formulates a plan, and pointedly refrains from informing the local leadership or community. Nehemiah matches his agenda, gifts, influence, and access to resources to the needs of the community. No edicts are needed and no archival searches are necessary to justify the project. Instead, Nehemiah operates with great personal freedom, with no need to justify his construction efforts except to the king himself. The disparity in social relations between the benevolent

---

comments that prior to the Babylonian invasion, "the boundary of the fortified part of the city [from the eighth and seventh centuries BCE] is defined principally by the many tombs that encircled it." This links the burned gates and the state of the tombs of Nehemiah's ancestors. Nehemiah's response capitalizes on the Persian attitudes toward ancestral graves.

Nehemiah and the Judeans produces an economic exchange, with profit derived from the power relations embedded in the social structure.[104] The unequal relations of power with his audience lend credence to his appeal for the social structure he describes.

The recognition accorded Nehemiah for the way he uses his superior capital in relation to others strengthens the social hierarchy. Nehemiah's efforts on behalf of the Judeans negate the social distance between them. At the same time, the distance (hierarchy) remains, giving Nehemiah growing legitimacy as the community and the reader accord him recognition. The strategy of condescension accumulates capital for future demands placed on the community by the hero, who, though separated by social distance, condescends to aid them.

9.3.2.2. An Effective Discourse

The efficacy of Nehemiah's discourse depends in part on linguistic competence but also on the group recognizing him as a legitimate representative of their interests. This requires signs and insignia that he is acting not in his own name or authority, thus explaining the importance of the details of his grief over the state of Jerusalem's wall, the hint of personal danger as he prepares to request leave to come to their aid, and his conviction that he carries out the divine will. His nuanced discourse shows he understands and anticipates the laws of the market and the sanctions through which they are manifested.[105] In this particular case, Nehemiah motivates his audience by employing extremely polemical linguistic forms grounded in concepts familiar to the community's national and religious traditions. This would not be effective if uttered by someone lacking legitimacy or if the polemics of the discourse were alien to the community. To be most effective, the expressions must achieve an optimum compromise between the intentions of the agent and censorship inherent in the social relationship between the parties.[106]

---

104. Bourdieu, *Language and Symbolic Power*, 67. "The linguistic relation of power is not completely determined by the prevailing linguistic forces alone; by virtue of the languages spoken, the speakers who use them and the groups defined by possession of the corresponding competence, the whole social structure is present in each interaction."

105. Ibid., 75, 78.

106. Ibid., 81.

Nehemiah takes issue with the state of the social order he finds in Yehud. His narrative lays out a new order to which he pins all his capital. Bourdieu states, "every group is the site of a struggle to impose a legitimate principle of group construction, and every distribution of properties … may serve as a basis for specifically political divisions or struggles."[107] Nehemiah's rhetoric denounces the "tacit contract of adherence to the established order" as he posits an alternative representation of the world.[108] By making conceivable and credible the possibility of changing the social world, he creates the collective representation that contributes to the production of a new social order—one that he is well suited to lead.

9.3.3. A New "Di-vision"

It seems clear, by the highly charged polemics of Nehemiah, that control over the loyalties of the Judeans was critical to Nehemiah's efforts to generate the social order beneficial to his interests. Bourdieu states,

> any attempt to institute a new division must reckon with the resistance of those who, occupying a dominant position in the space thus divided, have an interest in perpetuating a doxic relation to the social world which leads to the acceptance of established divisions as natural or to their symbolic denial through the affirmation of a higher unity (national, familial, etc.).[109]

At the same time, the most deprived people grant unlimited credit to the party of their choice, and those who dominate the party "find in the freedom they gain through their monopoly of … political interests, the possibility of imposing their own interests as the interests of those whom they represent.[110]

Nehemiah's account proceeds to shape how his opponents are viewed. Opposition, although local, is conceived of in terms of the "nations round about us." Adversaries are all identified by ethnic titles: Sanballat the Horonite, Tobiah the Ammonite official, and Geshem the Arab (Neh 2:10,

---

107. Ibid., 130.
108. Ibid., 127.
109. Ibid., 130.
110. Ibid., 175.

19).¹¹¹ However, these ethnic designations are problematic. Sanballat's referent is unclear, his sons have Yahwistic names, and according to 13:28 his daughter married into Jerusalem's high-priestly family. Tobiah also has a Yahwistic name and is given rooms in the temple in Nehemiah's absence. The title "Ammonite offical" likely indicates he was a servant of the king of Persia in residence in Ammon (e.g., a governor of Ammon).¹¹² In addition, his family is associated with Gilead, not Ammon.¹¹³ Since Nehemiah views Judah alone as "all Israel," he labels Tobiah as "foreign."¹¹⁴ This suggests that the insinuation of foreign association for these men is a literary construct and not a universally shared perspective.

Nehemiah adds to this alien portrait a dangerous component—opponents hostile to the community. The antagonists are angered that anyone should arrive "to seek the welfare of the people of Israel" (Neh 2:10), and each hostile action is countered by exclusionary statements by Nehemiah. As Knoppers observes, "the dialectic between protagonists and antagonists defines the ideological, ethnic, and religious boundaries of the community."¹¹⁵ Although scholars have posited that the conflict was due to political differences between regional governors, the biblical text refrains from providing a specific cause for their hostilities. Whatever the cause, the hostilities are couched as efforts to subvert the restoration of Jerusalem. Knoppers notes that the negative characterization is justified by descriptions of opponents engaging in intimidation (Neh 4:1–2 [3:33–34 MT]), obstruction (4:7–8 [1–2 MT]), and conspiracies against Nehemiah (ch. 6). Their foreignness is characterized as undesirable and dangerous, and the removal of Tobiah from the temple is couched in terms of pollution.¹¹⁶

---

111. H. H. Rowley (*Men of God* [New York: Nelson, 1963], 246) cites Horonaim in Moab or Beth-horon in Samaria or near Jerusalem as possibilities. E. Stern has suggested that the term means the first governor by that name ("Persian Empire," 150).

112. Carl Schultz, "The Political Tensions Reflected in Ezra-Nehemiah," in *Scripture in Context: Essays on the Comparative Method*, ed. Carl D. Evans, William W. Hallo, and John B. White, PTMS 34 (Pittsburgh: Pickwick, 1980), 232.

113. Ibid. However, other texts demonstrate that Gilead was a contested region between Ammon and Israel, e.g., Judg 10:17–18; and there is suspicion of the ethnicity of Gileadites apparent in the story of Jephthah in Judg 11.

114. Gary N. Knoppers, "Nehemiah and Sanballat: The Enemy Without or Within?" in Lipschits, Knoppers, and Albertz, *Fourth Century B.C.E.*, 319.

115. Ibid., 322.

116. Schultz, "Political Tensions," 312–14.

Nehemiah's extension of his list of foreign nations to include other Yahwists may have been met with resistance by some people of Judea. Hints of this can be seen in the support Tobiah has within the Judean community: he corresponds with them, people speak well of him to Nehemiah, and Nehemiah mentions Tobiah as a son-in-law of Shecaniah, the priest. This evidence indicates that Judeans may have "viewed marriages with Tobiah ... as strengthening pan-Israelite solidarity."[117] Knoppers argues that Sanballat viewed himself as an Ephraimite. He also notes that Nehemiah's imprecatory prayer against both men implies that they share the same God. This evidence indicates "two different and contradictory perspectives operating in Persian-period Judahite community." One advocated cooperation among regional neighbors, and another advocated maintenance of distinctions through separatist actions.[118]

In Nehemiah, the only returned exiles are Nehemiah and his "brothers." No exiles accompany his return nor are there resources donated by those in the Diaspora.[119] Ethnicity is "keyed to a certain but limited ancestral territory."[120] The only tribal territory mentioned is Judah, and terminology for the people differs from terms used in the Ezra memoir or Ezra 1–6. Nehemiah speaks of "the Judeans," "the people," "Judah," or "house of/children of Judah"—not "children of the exile" or "Judah and *Benjamin*," common elsewhere in these texts.[121] The Jerusalem wall provides a barrier to differentiate between the Judeans and those Nehemiah regards as non-Israel. Despite his assumption that ethnic categories are self-evident, the narrative indicates that boundaries are highly porous and contested.[122]

The new division of the social landscape and the effect it has on economic and political capital in the region provoke other governors or leaders to resist this reconfiguration. The more deprived Judean community (as portrayed by Nehemiah) becomes the site of struggle as competitors battle

---

117. Knoppers, "Nehemiah and Sanballat," 324.
118. Ibid., 329–30.
119. Only in Neh 1:2–3 is the exile mentioned. Jacob Wright (*Rebuilding Identity*, 62) contends that the reference to "remainder" and "escapees" in Neh 1:2–3 is different from the usage of the same terms in Ezra 1:4. Here it is not a reference to exiles but to those who were never exiled. Given the memoir's engagement with holy war, and its refrain of escapees from destruction as those who might have fled to safety, this is a likely reading of the text.
120. Knoppers, "Nehemiah and Sanballat," 309.
121. Ibid., 311.
122. Ibid., 316.

over the right to impose opposing principles of group construction so as to obtain group loyalty. Nehemiah's opponents' numerous relations with members of the community indicate that they possess significant influence. Notably, they accuse Nehemiah of disrupting the established local political order, as they affirm a higher unity linked to Persia (Neh 6:7).[123] This defense of the current order involves a reasonable offer to "confer together," a strategy Bourdieu attributes to dominant players.[124] This defense of the status quo and Nehemiah's appeals to separation and purity suggest that the opponents held dominant positions within the region.

Nehemiah's limited definition of the community is strategically couched in familial and religious language. His categorization is a social act, "which introduces by *decree* a decisive discontinuity in natural continuity" between spaces.[125] The symbolic power of the religious and ethnic categories grounded in group identity assures consensus and the durability of the community's adherence to his vision.[126] Nehemiah defines membership in terms favorable to himself, vaunts his personal resources (his capital), and displays his care for the community. If successful, he assures himself of a cohesive group and is able to monopolize their political capital and to impose his own interests as the interests of those whom he represents. If he fails, the community will be less integrated, more open to compromise, and less attuned to restrictive economic practices or the exclusion of regional power brokers who carry economic and political capital sufficient to undermine Nehemiah's dominant position within the community.

---

123. "You have also set up prophets to proclaim in Jerusalem concerning you, 'There is a king in Judah!' And now it will be reported to the king according to these words. So come, therefore, and let us confer together" (Neh 6:7). Nehemiah discounts their accusation, and it is mentioned only as evidence of hostility intended to discourage the builders.

124. Bourdieu, *Field of Cultural Production*, 83. He states, "Those in dominant positions operate essentially defensive strategies, designed to perpetuate the status quo by maintaining themselves and the principles on which their dominance is based. The world is as it should be, since they are on top and clearly deserve to be there; excellence therefore consists in being what one is, with reserve and understatement, urbanely hinting at the immensity of one's means by the economy of one's means, refusing the assertive, attention-seeing strategies which expose the pretensions of the young pretenders."

125. Bourdieu, *Language and Symbolic Power*, 221.

126. Ibid., 223.

10
Nehemiah 5: Economics and the State

> If you lend money to my people, to the poor among you, you shall not deal with them as a creditor; you shall not exact interest from them. (Exod 22:24)

> You shall not charge interest on loans to another Israelite, interest on money, interest on provisions, interest on anything that is lent. (Deut 23:19)

Taxes, debt, and economic disparity fuel a domestic conflict in Neh 5. Therefore it may be appropriate to begin with Bourdieu's discussion of the concentration of capital by the state and a brief survey of the evidence regarding political and economic circumstances in Jerusalem at this time.

Bourdieu describes state formation as the accumulation of various forms of capital and a growing control over the various fields, their specific capital, and the conversion rates between fields. He comments,

> The state is the culmination of a process of concentration of different species of capital: capital of physical force or instruments of coercion (army, police), economic capital, cultural or (better) informational capital, and symbolic capital. It is this concentration as such which constitutes the state as the holder of a sort of metacapital granting power over other species of capital and over their holders. Concentration of the different species of capital (which proceeds hand in hand with the construction of the corresponding fields) leads indeed to the emergence of a specific, properly statist capital (capital étatique) which enables the state to exercise power over the different fields and over the different particular species of capital, and especially over the rates of conversion

between them (and thereby over the relations of force between their respective holders).[1]

States must assert their physical force externally against other states (real or potential) and internally against rival powers and resistance from the dominated classes.[2] The Greek accounts of Persian military actions and court intrigues fixate on Persia's use of force in state formation, and archaeological research lends support to local military domination with evidence of the series of fortresses established in Yehud.[3] Both Nehemiah and Ezra note the use of armed personnel for travel (Ezra 8:33; Neh 2:9), and Nehemiah implies that regional leaders had their own military units as well (Neh 4:2, 23). Additionally, the monarch threatens physical force against those unwilling to obey Ezra's law (Ezra 7:26).[4] Yet these biblical books never mention any of Persia's recurring conflicts with Egypt or Greece. Imperial military power is mentioned only when useful to authorial interests.

Bourdieu notes that the concentration of physical force (armies and police) goes hand in hand with an efficient fiscal system and the unification of economic space.[5] During the Persian era, the use of weighed silver as a monetary system gradually gave way to minted coins and testifies to Persian economic consolidation.[6] Gold coins, minted only by royal mints, likely served both ideological and economic purposes.[7] The coins illustrated the king's power and prestige, and their circulation may have aided the imposition of an imperial monetary standard. Coins of smaller denominations were also minted locally. Even in Yehud, locally minted coins have been found containing the names of the local province and governors. This is clear evidence of local administrative structure, which Charles Carter suggests also indicates some autonomy.[8]

---

1. Bourdieu, *Practical Reason*, 41.
2. Ibid., 42.
3. Carter, *Emergence of Yehud*, 44.
4. "All who will not obey the law of your God and the law of the king, let judgment be strictly executed on them, whether for death or for banishment or for confiscation of their goods or for imprisonment."
5. Bourdieu, *Practical Reason*, 43.
6. Briant, *From Cyrus to Alexander*, 406.
7. Ibid., 409. The first evidence of royal coins comes from Darius's twenty-second year, 500 BCE, although they may have been minted as early as 512 BCE.
8. Carter, *Emergence of Yehud*, 279.

10. NEHEMIAH 5: ECONOMICS AND THE STATE

Briant notes that the payment of tribute also played an ideological purpose: "Within the dynamic of tribute, the ideological representations and the politico-economic realities were fused because, by means of tribute, gifts, and assessments, the Great King revealed and exercised his unshared authority not so much over the lands themselves as over the wealth they produced through the labor of his subjects."[9] Tribute was collected by satrapal authorities who retained some portion to pay for local expenses (e.g., cavalry garrisoned in Cilicia), and the rest would be kept in the royal treasuries. The complaints in Neh 5:4 cite loans required to obtain money (כסף) to pay the king's tax, and in 5:15 previous governors are accused of taking bread and wine in addition to "forty shekels." This corresponds with Briant's observation that the tribute system, like the military conscription in Persia, was maintained at the local level by the heads and leaders of the various peoples.

> Within each district, the satrap was responsible to the king for the raising and delivery of the general tribute that had been determined. But we may also presume that each "dynast" or "king" or "city" was individually responsible for raising the portion of the total tribute assessed to his *ethnos* in particular. It was his responsibility to parcel out the burden among the various subassemblies that made up the community that he represented before the satrapal authorities. This arrangement allowed the satrap to avoid becoming directly involved in the complications inherent in the internal distribution of the tribute payment among the various communities of his district. He would only intervene directly if the local authorities managed to evade their obligations.[10]

The actual burden imposed by tributes is difficult to assess. In fact, the only ancient text that quantifies this is the reference to forty shekels of silver in Neh 5:15. However, special payments for handling a state visit or double taxation for both civic and royal demands, or for the cost of garrisoning troops locally, would have burdened the people's resources. The strain on resources would be especially harsh if drought or blight coincided with these other demands.[11]

---

9. Briant, *From Cyrus to Alexander*, 471.
10. Ibid., 411.
11. Ibid., 810. David Hopkins ("Life on the Land: The Subsistence Struggles of Early Israel," *BA* 50 [1987]: 184) states that rainfall was "highly variable, both with respect to its distribution throughout the year and the achievement of average annual

Briant also challenges the commonly held view first promulgated by the ancient Greek historians that the great kings subjected their populations to unbearable financial burdens, and hoarded their wealth, leading ultimately to economic stagnation.[12] Briant argues that many regions of the empire were actually in a stage of expansion and population growth under Persian rule.[13] Archaeological evidence of Yehud during the Persian era supports this claim, although evidence of elite wealth seems limited to Samaria.

The nature and level of imperial involvement in Yehud changed during the Persian era. Ezra-Nehemiah asserts that exilic volunteers journeyed to Yehud and initiated the construction of temple and walls. Yet evidence from Elephantine and elsewhere describes municipal building projects requiring imperial permission. Persia itself engaged in local construction of citadels and administrative centers such as Ramat Raḥel. When such evidence is combined with the provincial stamped jar handles, it points to growing Persian military and administrative control over Yehud. Notably, Nehemiah's freedom to carry out his own policies contrasts with the later control exercised by Persia over the community evidenced in Ezra 1–6.

Nehemiah still governed under the weight of imperial demands for a portion of the proceeds from the area's produce, enforced by the presence of Persian garrisons and administrative centers. As an imperial appointee, he had the power to conscript labor for civil projects or military service. Yet he had to balance his demands on the local population with the need to let them generate enough money to pay their taxes and to maintain his own legitimacy with them. Otherwise he faced either dismissal (or worse) by the monarch or hostility and perhaps rebellion from the locals. The complaints in Neh 5 suggest problems over the tax burden, which may have been exacerbated if Nehemiah conscripted labor

---

accumulation. This variability is such that three years out of ten might not follow the expected pattern—for example, it might be very wet in the beginning of the season and very dry towards the end—so that there could be an agricultural drought even though the absolute total rainfall reaches the average."

12. Briant, *From Cyrus to Alexander*, 695, 801. In contrast, Briant contends that European colonial historians presented Alexander as generous and chivalrous and progressive, consistent with their view of colonial Europe. The theory of hoarding assumes that "the Great Kings, who were jealous for their power and authority more than anything else, had no interest in pursuing a policy that would develop the conquered countries, which were considered sources of revenue first and foremost" (804).

13. Ibid., 809.

for projects unrelated to agricultural production.[14] However, Nehemiah portrays the community's hostility directed toward the lending practices of other Judean nobles.

10.1. Nehemiah's Defense: A Literary Analysis

Nehemiah 5 divides into two separate pericopes. The first recounts the community's conflict over economic disparity (Neh 5:1–13). In the second, Nehemiah summarizes and defends his economic policies during his twelve-year rule (5:14–19). The chapter continues the previous chapter's first person voice and concludes with Nehemiah's characteristic "Remember me" formula (5:19). Yet its subject matter intrudes into the narrative of wall building. The tense scenario of hurried building while carrying swords and posting guards is suspended, only to be resumed in 6:1. This has raised questions regarding the historical accuracy and literary placement of Neh 5.[15] Rainer Albertz perceives this account as evidence of the beginning of a long-lasting and "severe social crisis" sparked by increased taxes in money and labor for the wall construction.[16] Philippe Guillaume has recently questioned the historicity of the crisis and argues that it existed mainly on paper.[17] He rejects claims that this chapter is about dire economic degradation. Instead, he posits that the complaints are simply three typical situations of economic duress, and the injustice of concern in 5:5 is not that children are forced to work but favoritism.[18]

---

14. Hopkins ("Life on the Land," 187–89) states attempts to lower risks associated with farming included terracing, spreading out risks by diversifying crops and planting times, and optimization of labor, by balancing demand and availability. Both terracing and coordinating labor required cooperation and exchange of labor forces. Increasing demands on the available workforce for other projects could jeopardize the ability of the community to move beyond "mere coping with risk to risk-reduction."

15. Williamson (*Ezra, Nehemiah*, 235) treats the events as a historical crisis closely tied to the period of the wall building. Blenkinsopp (*Ezra-Nehemiah*, 255) is more open to the possibility of the text having been relocated.

16. Rainer Albertz, *From the Exile to the Maccabees*, vol. 2 of *A History of Israelite Religion in the Old Testament*, trans. John Bowden, OTL (Louisville: Westminster John Knox, 1994), 495–97.

17. Philippe Guillaume, "Nehemiah 5: No Economic Crisis," *JHebS* 10 (2010): art. 8, p. 3, doi:10.5508/jhs2010.v10.a8.

18. Ibid., 4.

Although the historicity of Neh 5 may not be resolved definitively, we may still inquire as to why an account of economic crisis within the community occurs at this point in the narrative—especially since the surrounding narrative focuses on a brief and intense fifty-two day building program. Even if, as Williamson argues, these events are presented here because they happened at this point in time, historical sequence does not require the account be written in this particular order.[19] Nor does chronological succession explain the purpose for which they were recounted. What is apparent is that the author selected a highly tense narrative of conflict with outsiders into which he places another tense conflict among insiders.

The complaints in Neh 5 follow a common three-and-four sequence narrative pattern. This structure anticipates confrontation, raising readerly expectations for change, and is useful for persuasion as the situation is successfully resolved.[20] The complaints are concerned with creditors, debt, and economic loss. The final complaint gains a response and results in change. The drawn-out repetition inherent in this pattern creates exaggeration that leads to some humor.[21] One might wonder, after reading the first three complaints in 5:1–4, if things could get any worse—and in 5:5 they do!

The action begins as the people cry out to (or against) their "brothers the Judeans" (Neh 5:1, my translation). The first three complaints begin identically: ויש אשר אמרים (lit. "and there were those saying"; 5:2, 3, 4). The accusations concern food, survival, and family. The first complaint involves numbers—"With our sons and our daughters, we are many." The complainants posit a solution, "Let us take grain and let us eat, and let us live" (my translation). However, the source of grain is unspecified, and no action results. The request suggests there is a known source of grain that people might, if they had access to it, be able to take and eat and live.

The next two grievances center on people losing control over their land and produce. In the second complaint (5:3), the people state that due to a famine they have pledged their fields, vineyards, and houses in order

---

19. Williamson, *Ezra, Nehemiah*, 235.

20. Yairah Amit, *Reading Biblical Narratives: Literary Criticism and the Hebrew Bible* (Minneapolis: Fortress, 2001), 62. Amit cites, among other stories, the example of Delilah seeking Samson's secret to his strength.

21. David M. Gunn and Danna Nolan Fewell, *Narrative in the Hebrew Bible* (New York: Oxford University Press 1993), 148.

to "get [lit. 'take'] grain." Gregory Chirichigno states that pledges (people and nonmovable goods) were given at the beginning of a loan to the creditor until the debt was paid. If a person was pledged, he or she worked to pay the interest until the debtor paid back the principal.[22] The famine appears severe enough to leave these people without their own sources of food. Others in the community seem to have sufficient supplies to provide money in exchange for the peoples' pledges of their homes, their fields, and their vineyards; but the loans have left the people in worse financial straits. The third complaint (5:4) reiterates the loss of fields and vineyards (but not homes). This time it is in order to borrow money to pay the king's tax (למדת המלך). The people lacked the resources to pay the tribute from their produce, so loans were taken against their fields and vineyards.

The fourth complaint (5:5) begins with "now" (ועתה), which signals the narrative crisis; and Williamson suggests that it summarizes the previous causes rather than introducing a new concern.[23] Kinship relations between the two factions are stressed, followed by descriptions of children forced into slavery over which the complainants have no power, since their fields and vineyards belong to others. No new cause of debt is mentioned in this last complaint, but a demand is made that the growing crisis must be resolved.

Familial language begins and ends this pericope. The initial outcry is directed against (literally) "their brothers, the Yehudim." Then in 5:2 they assert "our sons and our daughters" are many. Familial claims are reiterated before the final complaint of poverty and oppression, "our flesh is our brothers' flesh, our sons—their sons" (5:5, my translation), and the problem is described in equally familial terms of the oppression of "our sons/our daughters." Each complaint begins with a different economic cause—too many mouths to feed, a famine, or taxes; but each ends at a similar place—debt to others. In the last complaint, upon the enslavement of their children, indignation and not only desperation is in the cry. Narratively this prepares the reader for the confrontation and persuasion to come. The language and content of the final complaint suggest that a different set of expectations feed this particular grievance, rather than simply an accumulation of economic woes.

---

22. Gregory Chirichigno, *Debt-Slavery in Israel and the Ancient Near East*, JSOTSup 141 (Sheffield: JSOT Press, 1993), 72.
23. Williamson, *Ezra, Nehemiah*, 238.

What assumptions lie behind these expectations? Why do the complainants submit to the king's tax but object to the behavior of their "brothers"? Bourdieu makes two important observations pertinent to these issues. The first is with regard to the power of the state to obtain submission. He claims that acceptance of and obedience to the state is generated by neither mechanical submission to force nor conscious consent to an order but is instead *doxic*.[24]

> Submission to the established order is the product of the agreement between, on the one hand, the cognitive structures inscribed in bodies by both collective history (phylogenesis) and individual history (ontogenesis) and, on the other, the objective structures of the world to which these cognitive structures are applied. State injunctions owe their obviousness, and thus their potency, to the fact that the state has imposed the very cognitive structures through which it is perceived.... The state does not have to give orders or exercise physical coercion in order to produce an ordered social world, as long as it is capable of producing embodied cognitive structures that accord with objective structures and thus of ensuring ... doxic submission to the established order.[25]

These verses in Nehemiah reflect this doxic acceptance of the state's order. The economic obligations of the state feel natural because they accord with individual and collective histories. This is most obvious in the failure to question the demand for tribute or taxes out of the produce of the people—whether they have the means or not. Neither Nehemiah nor the people who complain question the payment of taxes. Instead, Nehemiah chastises the local nobles for charging interest on loans to families who needed funds to make those payments.

Bourdieu's second point is, "Recognition of the legitimacy of taxation is bound up with the rise of a form of nationalism."[26] Consent to taxation is even more likely if the collection is associated with the interests of the country, particularly territorial defense.[27] While the text makes no explicit apology for taxes, the issue arises in the context of a larger narrative that intimates the need for good territorial defense. The community's involve-

---

24. Bourdieu, *Practical Reason*, 54.
25. Ibid., 55–56.
26. Ibid., 44. Bourdieu notes that the collection of taxes contributes to the perception of the state's legitimacy.
27. Ibid., 45.

ment in the wall's construction would make defensive spending accord with their collective history.

Funding for the temple would face challenges in this regard. It does not provide military protection. Nor, after years without a temple, would the local population necessarily find contributing to its maintenance part of their history. Thus motivation to provide for the temple would have to rely on the community embracing a compelling logic that suggests that the temple's deity was a source of protection, and that failure to remain loyal to the God and his temple would threaten their safety. This is, in fact, the nature of the claims in this book. The holy war language embedded in Nehemiah portrays YHWH as a warrior for his people, and the histories (Neh 9) and prayers describe or refer to the bitter consequences of human unfaithfulness.

In this narrative, the local structure also appears obvious and natural as the community directs its outcry toward immediate officials, and the author (Nehemiah?) assumes that the crisis is Nehemiah's to resolve. However, the complaint suggests that practices are not, in this matter, consistent with the cognitive structures held by the community. The familial language hints that economic actions are out of line with another order—that of the family, which appears as the most natural and fundamental social category. Bourdieu identified four properties that describe the concept people form when they refer to "family": (1) properties of an individual attributed to a group (a common life, will, unified thought, feeling, and action), (2) a separate social universe from the external world with a "sacred" interior, (3) a residence that is stable and enduring, and (4) a place "where ordinary laws of the economy are suspended, a place of trusting and giving, [it] designates the refusal to calculate; a place where interest … is suspended."[28] However, although the family is asserted as a body, it "still tends to function as a field," thus requiring the work of integration—for example, ritual and legal institutionalization—and feelings in each member that ensure its persistence as a unit.[29]

Bourdieu notes that small precapitalist pockets accompany the growth of the economy as an economy. This creates tension in these communities because the economic order of the family runs contrary to the wider econ-

---

28. Bourdieu, *Practical Reason*, 65. Struggles often occur over hierarchy or inclusion in social categories while all parties still agree on the underlying value of the overall category.

29. Ibid., 67.

omy. The market calculates, while economies based on kinship eschew practices such as lending to family members with interest. The family is united by land and name, but the land also divides the family, especially as the logic of the wider economic universe introduces calculation that undermines the logic of love. Precapitalist communities threatened by the market economy tend to respond by affirming explicitly their specific logic. Nehemiah 5 depicts "strategies of reproduction … [based upon] the unconscious desire of the family or the household to perpetuate itself by perpetuating its unity against divisive factors, and especially against those inherent in competition for the property that underlies family unity." So we see in Nehemiah this logic of familial love asserted against the influence of the wider economy and its calculation of interest.[30]

Nehemiah's response to the complaints builds on this logic of familial love. In 5:6–11, he claims first to be enraged, and then borrowing language from the court, he "brings charges" or "contends" with the nobles, accusing them of unfair economic practices (literally) "against your brothers." Verse 9 puts forward other motivations for ceasing these actions: "the fear of our God, to prevent the taunts [or 'reproach'] of the nations our enemies."[31] Nehemiah declares that to resolve the crisis, taking interest must halt and items that had been taken as collateral must be restored (5:10–11). The nobles agree to this, and Nehemiah makes them swear before the priests to do as they have said. The scene concludes as Nehemiah enacts a prophetic warning by shaking out his robes and threatening the loss of house and property of anyone failing to carry out his promise (5:13).

The term דבר, "word," plays a key role in structuring this passage. The *words* of the community initiate the drama, inciting Nehemiah to anger (5:6). The nobles and officials "could not find a *word* to say" (5:8), while the *word* ("thing") they are doing is deemed "not good" (5:9). In 5:12, Nehemiah makes them promise (literally) "to do as this *word*" (NRSV "to do as they had promised"). In 5:13, Nehemiah warns the community against failing to keep "this *word*" (NRSV "promise"), and the episode concludes with the statement that the people "did according to this *word*" (NRSV "did as they had promised"). This literary structure, the use of court language, allusions to Levitical law, the fear of God, prophetic judgment, and oaths combine to support the complaint of the community against the actions of

---

30. Ibid., 104–7.
31. Williamson, *Ezra, Nehemiah*, 240. The fear of God is twice cited in Leviticus as motive for not charging interest to kinsmen or treating debtors harshly (Lev 25:36, 43).

10. NEHEMIAH 5: ECONOMICS AND THE STATE

the leadership. Nehemiah stands above the fray as he provides the solution (the words) agreed to by everyone that restores communal harmony.

The exact nature of this problem is complicated by difficulty making sense of the terms employed to describe the nobles' actions.[32] The verb נשא and its related noun form משא occur five times in 5:7–11.[33] The two forms are partnered in 5:7, משא איש־באחיו אתם נשאים, and could be literally translated, "interest each against his brother you are extracting." The phrase has been variously translated, "Each of you are acting as creditor against his brother" (Williamson), "ye lend upon pledge" (JPSV), "you are exacting usury" (NIV, NASB), or "you are all taking interest" (NRSV). Carl Gross has suggested that משא refers not to interest but instead to pressing claims for repayment. He translates the phrase, "Claims for repayment by each against his fellow—you are pressing these claims."[34] The participle translated "creditors" or "pressing claims" (נשאים) carries the sense of exaction (e.g., in 1 Kgs 8:31 an oath is exacted from a person). Guillaume comments that the ambiguity in meaning opens a range of possible translations. The problem, he states, "is not these standard practices but their use in financial dealings with brothers."[35]

---

32. The phrase in question reads, משא איש־באחיו אתם נשאים (Neh 5:7).

33. Carl D. Gross, "Is There Any Interest in Nehemiah 5?" *SJOT* 11 (1997): 271. Gross posits two closely related verbal roots, נשא and נשה. *HALOT* (2:728) and Bibleworks treat them as one. A third term in Neh 5:4, לוינו, means "we borrowed," and appears in Exod 22:25 (24 MT); Deut 28:12, 44; etc. The noun מַשָּׁא, translated "interest," occurs only in Neh 5:7, 10, and 10:31 (32 MT). In Neh 10:31 (32 MT), it occurs in the phrase ומשא כל־יד, which many translate, "exaction of every debt." A more common term for interest, נשך (Exod 22:25 [24 MT]; Lev 25:36; Deut 23:19 [20 MT]; Ezek 18:17; 22:12), is not found in Nehemiah, but its usage parallels the context described—charging interest within the community, especially to the poor. Exod 22:25 (24 MT) reads, "If you lend money to my people, to the poor among you, you shall not deal with them as a creditor; you shall not exact *interest* [נשך] from them." In Deut 23:19 (20 M), it occurs three times in the noun form and twice in verbal form: "You shall not *charge interest* on loans to another Israelite, *interest* on money, *interest* on provisions, *interest* on anything that is *lent*." In Leviticus and Ezekiel, it is paired with תרבית and together they are translated variously, "advance interest and accrued interest" (NRSV), "interest and profits" (NASB), "usury and excessive interest" (NIV). Perhaps it is this prohibition against taking interest that prompts the author to use an alternative word in Neh 5, particularly since Nehemiah acknowledges that he too has been a creditor, נשא (5:10).

34. Gross, "Is There Any Interest," 274.

35. Guillaume, "Nehemiah 5," 5.

Guillaume also argues that land was of less value than its produce and the labor to work it, and he points out that the practice of making money by offering loans, such as our modern banking system employs, did not exist in the ancient world.[36] Interest rates were determined by custom rather than the market, and creditors were interested in a predetermined portion of a yield. Seizing debtors and their property would have defeated the whole point of lending. He suggests instead that this is a case of an antichretic loan where the borrower gives the creditor use of his property as interest on the loan.[37]

> Therefore, the return imposed by Nehemiah involved assets mortgaged to secure loans serviced through predetermined portions of yields. There is no transfer of ownership back to the previous owners. Repayment is deferred or the interest abandoned. By adding the demonstrative pronoun to *maššāʾ* (5:10) (המשא הזה] it is fairly clear that the relief measure is a one-off instance. Nehemiah proposes to stop the clock until the forthcoming grape, olive, and grain harvest so that the burden does not accrue during the famine.[38]

Guillaume suggests that taxpaying at the local level was a "bitter game." Taxpayers systematically complained that they were fleeced, and the satrap may have had to contribute from his own funds to make up for missing revenue. Governors like Nehemiah were compelled to "steer a course between exigencies of maximum tax extraction and social peace to preserve their positions and their lives."[39]

What purpose might it serve to replay this crisis in this text? What benefit accrues to Nehemiah? Not only does Nehemiah present himself as incensed by the practices of the nobles (even though he acknowledges he and his brothers and his servants, or "lads," have also made loans, 5:10), he calls a great assembly and in that context expresses his outrage. Before the congregation, Nehemiah declares the situation to be one of selling brothers into slavery: "We have been buying back our brothers, the Judeans, who had been sold to the nations as much as we are able, and

---

36. This goes against many biblical scholars who assume that the text refers to the forfeiture of land.

37. Bourdieu attests to a similar practice of loaning animals in exchange for future services in his ethnographic study of the Kabyle in Algeria (*Outline*, 179).

38. Guillaume, "Nehemiah 5," 6.

39. Ibid., 14.

10. NEHEMIAH 5: ECONOMICS AND THE STATE 241

you, you will sell your brothers and they must be purchased by us?" (my translation).[40] Four times reference is made to the selling and purchasing of brothers, with Nehemiah always aligning with those reacquiring the brothers sold. In response to the accusation, the nobles "were silent and could not find a word to say" (5:8). The problem, as described by Nehemiah, is not identical to any of the previous complaints described—indeed, it is much worse, and made so by his use of the language of "brothers." He accuses the nobles of directing economic calculation not only toward the *land* held by the family but at the family *members* themselves—charging interest now equates to selling relatives. To undo the damage requires a second bailout by the community. Nehemiah's complaint draws a stark picture of the divide created in the community by the increasing influence of the larger economy.

The dramatic and immediate confrontation has led Williamson to observe that if Nehemiah had not taken immediate action, "it is likely at best that he would have lost the service of many of his workers, and at worst that civil unrest would have developed."[41] This observation points to the linkage between symbolic and economic capital. Bourdieu states "that symbolic capital, which in the form of the prestige and renown ... is readily convertible back into economic capital, is perhaps *the most valuable form of accumulation* in a society in which the severity of the climate (the major work—ploughing and harvesting—having to be done in a very short space of time) and the limited technical resources (harvesting is done with the sickle) demand collective labor."[42] He acknowledges that this can be viewed as "a covert exaction of corvées." However, he argues that "this appropriation of services lies in the fact that it can only take place in the disguise of ... the voluntary assistance, and that ... implies ... a conversion of material capital into symbolic capital itself reconvertible into material capital." The acquisition of a clientele "implies considerable labor devoted to making and maintaining relations, and also substantial material and symbolic *investments*, in the form of political aid against attack, theft, offence, and insult, or economic aid, which can be very costly, especially in times of scarcity. As well as material wealth, *time* must be invested, for the

---

40. The purchase of "brothers" from debt-slavery to "resident aliens" is in keeping with Lev 25:47–49.
41. Williamson, *Ezra, Nehemiah*, 235.
42. Bourdieu, *Outline*, 179.

value of symbolic labour cannot be defined without reference to the time devoted to it."[43]

This entire chapter (and its context of corvée labor needed for wall construction) displays such conversions between material capital and symbolic capital. The inefficiency of the means of production and the social mechanisms inclining agents to repress or disguise economic interest combine to make only symbolic capital the recognized, legitimate form of accumulation and prohibit the accumulation of material capital. Wealthy members must contend with collective pressure because they draw their authority from it. Their ability to mobilize the group requires that they pay the largest share of the cost of ceremonial exchanges, and make the biggest contributions to the maintenance of the poor, the lodging of strangers, and the organization of festivals. "Above all, wealth implies duties."[44] Nehemiah's ability to mobilize his community requires devoting his energy toward building and maintaining relations. When a crisis arises, he can then mobilize the accumulated capital to turn the collective pressure toward those whose accumulation of material capital the group may view as excessive, particularly if they fail to carry out the duties that wealth implies.[45]

In Neh 5:14–19, the account leaves the resolution agreed upon by the community and moves to a description and defense of Nehemiah's overall policies. This paragraph is generally viewed as having been added at a later stage.[46] In these verses, Nehemiah claims a number of state-authorized powers and resources only to then enumerate his sacrifice of those interests on his part and on the part of his men. He begins by contrasting his economic policies with previous governors, pointing out that he never (literally) "ate the bread of the governor." Previous governors, he states, not only took from the people bread and wine, but also forty shekels of silver and allowed their servants to oppress the people. Briant believes that the refusal to accept the bread of the governor was largely symbolic.[47] But Nehemiah goes further: he partners devotion to the work on the wall with the information that he acquired no land, and his servants were "gathered there for the work" (5:16). His abundant table and international

---

43. Ibid., 179–80.
44. Ibid., 180.
45. Ibid.
46. Williamson, *Ezra, Nehemiah*, 235.
47. Briant, *From Cyrus to Alexander*, 585.

guests (5:17–18) contrast with the hunger and economic injustices just resolved; however, he declares that he refused the food allowance of the governor, "because of the heavy burden of labor on the people" (5:18). His beneficence, couched in terms reminiscent of royal largesse with the large number of guests, the amount of food, and the international visitors partnered with his refusal to take what was his due, becomes evidence of his selfless concern for the good of the community. It supersedes all others before him, including the current crop of nobles, with whom he has taken strong measures.

Nehemiah's show of generosity is not without value. His access to and control over valuable state resources is endangered unless he convincingly portrays himself as legitimate in his monopoly. Bourdieu links the monopolization of resources by the state with representations of universal concerns:

> The unification and universalization associated with the emergence of the state has for counterpart the monopolization by the few of the universal resources that it produces and procures.... However, this *monopoly of the universal* can only be obtained at the cost of a submission (if only in appearance) to the universal and of a universal recognition of the universalist representation of domination presented as legitimate and disinterested.[48]

Nehemiah must at least appear to sacrifice for the benefit of all even as he gains control over physical and symbolic violence. He presents himself as neutral and devoted to the public good. Commissioned officials "vested with a mission of general interest and invited to transcend their particular interests in order to produce universal propositions … constantly have to labor … to constitute their point of view into a legitimate one, that is, as universal, especially through use of the rhetoric of the official."[49] Thus the wall building is portrayed as sacrificial work for the benefit of the whole community in contrast with the purchase of others' fields (5:16). In response, "collective judgment cannot but perceive, and approve, [such] an expression of recognition of the value of the group."[50] This move, submission to the universal (the value of the group), produces

---

48. Bourdieu, *Practical Reason*, 59.
49. Ibid.
50. Ibid., 59–60.

symbolic profits. Nehemiah's emphasis on his own public service (the loaning of food to those in need) and public order (correcting economic abuse, the building of the wall) dissociates him from dynastic or personal interests. This discourse of "disinterested loyalty" in turn provides justification for his position. A growing autonomous order (as opposed to coerced order or order to serve dynastic interests) is "capable of imposing ever more widely the submission to its functions and to its functioning and the recognition of its principles."[51] This neutral discourse also imposes itself on state functionaries who must increasingly value (or appear to value) the point of view of society in lieu of their personal interests. The official norm of submitting to the universal (sacrificing one's particular point of view on behalf of society) is often at odds with reality. Thus Nehemiah has no trouble itemizing the offenses by other Judeans and previous governors and their representatives even as he obscures his personal interests and benefit from his control over society.[52]

Nehemiah's self-presentation can be evaluated in terms of the various fields and agents involved. Guillaume comments, "Nehemiah's claim that he and his entourage lent money and grain is essential to his presentation as an active member of the corporation and it shows that he was not 'above the fray' of contending parties."[53] Bourdieu states, "The sacrifice of selfish (especially economic) interests is universally recognized as legitimate."[54] Even as he holds economic capital, Nehemiah contends that he sacrifices it for the good of the community. Nehemiah 5 seems to be an effort to defend Nehemiah's legitimacy to an audience not completely convinced he has their best interests at heart.

10.2. The Memoir: A Consolidation of Capital

Even as Nehemiah contends that he exercises his power in the interests of the community, he consolidates various forms of capital in his small corner of the world. He exhibits great benevolence and great resources—political, economic, military, and religious. Bourdieu notes that this concentra-

---

51. Ibid., 58.
52. The cracks in his defense have been highlighted by Eskenazi (*In an Age of Prose*, 141–44), who compares his actions with those of Ezra, who, in her mind, provides a more inclusive leadership and therefore represents universal interests.
53. Guillaume, "Nehemiah 5," 19.
54. Bourdieu, *Practical Reason*, 59.

tion of material and symbolic resources allows the regulation of different fields through financial intervention in the economic field, symbolic support for institutions in the cultural field, and juridical intervention that can regulate the organization or behaviors of individual agents.[55] In that vein, we see Nehemiah pointedly use his capital to restore the community physically, purify it spiritually, and protect its members from economic abuse through the use of his position and personal resources. Using his capital for public service allows him to accumulate symbolic capital and garner the political loyalty of the community. This allows him to put his own stamp on the definition of the community and exclude others from imposing social organizations conducive to the advancement of their own positions. As a result, his symbolic labor will garner him economic capital when he calls upon his clients.

His strong defense of his economic policies and his narrative's charged language suggest that neither his political achievements nor his definition of the community were easily maintained. The memoir is therefore intended to prove that this particular social order is beneficial and necessary, and the alternatives are dangerous. His competitors are portrayed as antagonistic but ineffective outsiders. Nehemiah is careful to demonstrate his humane treat of others in Neh 5 as he compels the wealthy to modify their lending practices to avert a crisis and details his own financial sacrifices for the sake of the community.

In the final chapters, Nehemiah counters actions of the priests (Neh 13), encroaching on their sphere of influence as he warns that they are the source of continuing impurity. Indeed, it is Nehemiah who leads the celebration of thanksgiving (12:31, 38), and the priests are reduced to marginal roles in the procession. The ordination of priests or the attention to the sacrificial calendar, important elsewhere in Ezra-Nehemiah, are absent from the memoir, and at the conclusion of the book it is Nehemiah who appoints the priests and Levites to their tasks and arranges for the wood and offerings for sacrifices (13:30–31). His management of the clerics and their absence as significant players in his narrative suggest that the priests were contenders for the community's loyalties and resources. Nehemiah could not simply dismiss them as outliers, as he does Sanballat and Tobiah; yet he may be countering their influence by marking their behavior as disloyal to the good to the community. Nehemiah takes pains to justify each

---

55. Ibid., 33.

new form of capital that he consolidates into his care in terms of the universal good. The preservation of this text testifies to at least his partial success at creating a social order that he controlled yet was compelling enough to gain the loyalty and support of Judeans in Jerusalem.

11
Penitential Prayers

Ezra-Nehemiah contains three of the clearest examples of penitential prayers in the Hebrew Bible: Ezra 9:6–15, Neh 1:5–11, and Neh 9:6–37.[1] Although other prayer forms make an appearance, the space allotted to penitential prayers in these two books far exceeds other forms.[2] In addition, penitential rituals and language are incorporated into other portions of the text (Ezra 8:21–24). Indeed, mourning seems so endemic that people weep when they rejoice (Ezra 3:12), and leaders must tell the people when *not* to mourn (Neh 8:9). In this chapter I will treat the prayers in Nehemiah, while I will treat Ezra 9 in conjunction with Ezra 7–10.

Rodney Werline defines penitential prayers as "a direct address to God in which an individual, group, or an individual on behalf of a group confesses sins and petitions for forgiveness as an act of repentance."[3] Penitential prayers link to, and perhaps replace, the communal lament.[4] These two prayer forms share similar language: second-person vocatives, a request accompanied by a motive clause, descriptions of internal anguish or external predicaments, and the use of historical overviews. Both seek divine aid

---

1. Other notable penitential texts include 1 Kgs 8:33–39, 46–54; Dan 9:4–19; and Ps 106.

2. Nehemiah seeks divine aid, requests God to remember him for good (or his enemies for their actions), and throughout the text are acts of worship (Ezra 3:11; Neh 12:36–43) or words of praise or confidence (Ezra 7:27).

3. Rodney Werline, "Defining Penitential Prayer," in *The Origins of Penitential Prayer in Second Temple Judaism*, vol. 1 of *Seeking the Favor of God*, ed. Mark J. Boda, Daniel K. Falk, and Rodney A. Werline, EJL 21 (Atlanta: Society of Biblical Literature, 2006), xv.

4. Dalit Rom-Shiloni ("Socio-ideological Setting or Settings for Penitential Prayers?" in Boda, Falk, and Werline, *Origins of Penitential Prayer*, 64) challenges the diachronic explanation for the differences, noting the exilic context of both prayer forms. He argues instead for theological diversity among contemporaries.

and share a common setting of fasting, mourning, or distress. However, penitential prayers lack the typical questions of lament, "Why?" and "How long?"[5] Instead, they praise God for his constancy, justice, and steadfast love (e.g., Ezra 9:9, 15; Neh 9:32–33).[6] Both forms of prayer call on God to remember the covenant promises; the penitential prayers replace accusations against the Deity with self-critical confession.[7] The penitential prayers in Ezra-Nehemiah are narratively connected to acts of renewal: Neh 1 with the construction of Jerusalem's wall, and Ezra 9 and Neh 9 with covenant ceremonies that renew the community's commitment to maintaining the law (Ezra 10:3; Neh 9:38).[8]

William Morrow and Bernard Williams suggest that penitential forms grew from a consciousness of human responsibility due to a historical development of a sense of disjunction between the everyday and a universal deity.[9] Yet both biblical corporate laments and penitential prayers arose in the aftermath of the fall of Jerusalem and the destruction of the state. Laments question the trauma and God's response. Boda suggests that penitential prayers reflect a shift in perspective regarding these events. "They have moved from a place where there is ambiguity over the cause of the predicament to one where there is certainty; the people now believe they are implicated and God is exonerated."[10] A second stage leaves behind disorientation to embrace certainty about the cause for the predicament and the outcome for the petitioner's request.[11] Alternatively, Rom-Shiloni,

---

5. Mark J. Boda, "Form Criticism in Transition: Penitential Prayer and Lament, Sitz im Leben and Form," in Boda, Falk, and Werline, Origins of Penitential Prayer, 184.

6. Rom-Shiloni, "Socio-ideological Setting," 60, 63.

7. Boda, "Form Criticism in Transition," 185.

8. Ibid., 188. Textual links to confession include ידה in the hithpael stem, e.g., Ezra 10:1; Neh 1:6; 9:2–3; and Dan 9:4, 20.

9. William Morrow ("The Affirmation of Divine Righteousness in Early Penitential Prayers: A Sign of Judaism's Entry into the Axial Age," in Boda, Falk, and Werline, Origins of Penitential Prayer, 101–6) relates these changes to an Axial Age (800–200 BCE), which "heralded fundamental and revolutionary changes in human social, religious, and intellectual history." Bernard Williams (Shame and Necessity [Berkeley: University of California Press, 1993], 16) rejects an evolutionary process and sees the (concurrent) development of Greek tragedy as the product of a particular historical development, coming about at a particular time.

10. Boda, "Form Criticism in Transition," 188. Most scholars treat these different prayer forms as a diachronic change true for the community as a whole.

11. Prayers of confidence could also fit within this second stage as they lack the bewilderment of laments.

noting the exilic context for both prayer forms, contends that penitential prayers were responses by orthodox sources (priests and prophets) to non-orthodox communal laments.[12] Ultimately, he argues, the orthodox line of thought gained dominance and the communal lament form vanished.[13] Like Weber's "carrier groups," those with the resources (cultural, political, and economic capital) to articulate and gain legitimacy for their claims win the ideological battle.[14]

Penitential prayers build on the older Deuteronomic tradition that God will punish sin by scattering Israel; but if the people repent and pledge obedience, God will restore them.[15] Confessional prayer is understood as essential to this process.[16] The prayers contrast God's faithfulness with the infidelity of the people and define "the people of the God of Israel" in relationship to the land and obedience (or not) to the covenant and law. Sin is violation of the law and equated with personal rejection of the Lord (Neh 1:7).[17] These ideas—land, covenant, and law—are adjusted to the new status of the people as "a remnant in the midst of powerful nations."[18] The law is used to bolster authority but also interpreted to apply to the new situation.[19]

Priestly traditions contribute to the concept of unfaithfulness (מעל), which led to the exile (Neh 1:8) and "demanded a penitential confession to restore covenantal relationship."[20] Meanwhile, the Deuteronomic tradition contributes a concern for "return" (שוב) to the observance of Torah as covenant (Neh 1:9; 9:29; cf. Ezra 9:14; Neh 9:26, 28).[21] In general, unfaithfulness was understood to have serious corporate consequences.[22] Boda

---

12. Rom-Shiloni ("Socio-ideological Setting," 64) contends that the two sources differed over commitments to the covenant taken on by humans or God (58).
13. Ibid., 67.
14. Weber, *Sociology of Religion*, 118–32.
15. Rodney Werline, *Penitential Prayer in Second Temple Judaism: The Development of a Religious Institution*, EJL 13 (Atlanta: Scholars Press, 1998), 18.
16. Boda, "Confession as Theological Expression: Ideological Origins of Penitential Prayer," in Boda, Falk, and Werline, *Origins of Penitential Prayer*, 27.
17. Ibid., 42, 46.
18. Boda, "Confession as Theological Expression," 45.
19. Ibid., 45.
20. Ibid., 34. "If you are unfaithful, I will scatter you among the peoples" (Neh 1:8)
21. "If you *return* to Me and keep My commandments and do them, though your outcasts are under the farthest skies, I will gather them from there and bring them to the place at which I have chosen to establish my name." (Neh 1:9)
22. Boda, "Confession as Theological Expression," 34. Cf. Lev 26:39–40 and Amos

states, "Penitential prayer, therefore, relies heavily upon the foundational notions of corporate guilt that link the present generation of the pray-ers with the past generation of guilt. This leads to the consistent articulation of the sinfulness of Israel as something related to both past and present generations (Ezra 9:6; Neh 1:6; 9:32–37; cf. 9:2…)."[23] Berlinerblau identifies this ancient Near Eastern assumption of corporate guilt as doxic. Although it moves people toward certain actions, the assumption is unrecognized—it is "what everyone in a social body 'knows.'"[24] Thus, although lacking the intent of ideology, it plays a role in assigning guilt.

Penitence became an essential ingredient in the religious thinking of the Persian period.[25] Ideas circulating in the wider world and the collectively remembered trauma of Jerusalem's destruction influenced the religious understanding of the Jewish people. To understand and give order to their new realities, they turn to their own religious texts and traditions. Boda suggests the prayers were intended to bring an end to the devastating effects of the fall of the state: either to captivity, oppression, or the sorry condition of Palestine.[26] Yet we might ask why, after the punishment of exile, penitence was embraced to facilitate this goal?

11.1. The Function of Penitential Prayer

Shame and guilt are central motivators in penitential prayer. Defining and differentiating between them is difficult and requires "a clear perception of their linguistic and social context."[27] The multiple terms translated as "shame" in the Hebrew Bible add to the difficulty.[28] In Ezra-Nehemiah, of the three terms for shame analyzed by Martin Klopfenstein (בוש, כלם,

---

1–2. Typical of such thinking is punishment threatened by Achan's theft of devoted items that implicated all Israel (Josh 7:1; cf. Josh 22:20) and punishment extended to Achan's family.

23. Ibid., 39.

24. Berlinerblau, "Ideology," 203.

25. All prayers identified as penitential contain historical references or terms in keeping with the Persian era.

26. Mark J. Boda, *Praying the Tradition: The Origin and Use of Tradition in Nehemiah 9*, BZAW 277 (Berlin: de Gruyter, 1999), 28.

27. Michael Herzfeld, "Honour and Shame: Problems in the Comparative Analysis of Moral Systems," *Man* 15 (1980): 348.

28. Yael Avrahami ("בוש in the Psalms: Shame or Disappointment?" *JSOT* 34 [2010]: 303) has posited that בוש may more accurately be translated *disappointment*.

and הרף), two occur only in the penitential prayer in Ezra 9 (בוש and כלם) and are paired in 9:6, "I am too ashamed and embarrassed to lift my face to you."²⁹ In 9:6–7, these expressions of shame surround a confession of guilt (עון), clearly linking the two concepts, although not necessarily equating them. The term הרף (variously translated as "taunting," "despise," "shame," "disgrace," or "reproach") permeates the Nehemiah memoir as the governor contends with antagonists he describes as outsiders.³⁰ The penitential prayers in Nehemiah confess offense, unfaithfulness, sin, and rebellion but do not employ shame terminology. Yet reproach (הרף) sets the stage for Nehemiah's first prayer (Neh 1:3), and guilt (עון) describes the ancestors in Neh 9:2 prior to the actual prayer. "Honor" (כבד) does not appear in Ezra-Nehemiah, nor does its opposite, "dishonored, disgraced" (קלה).³¹ In addition, John Chance reminds us that "texts composed for didactic or inspirational purposes, such as those of the Bible, generally tend to emphasize the normative point of view," in contrast with actual practice.³² Analysis is made all the more difficult because the social context can only be reconstructed, not observed.

Scholars have applied both anthropological and psychological lenses to analyses of shame. Both approaches recognize the importance of social relations in the experience of shame and have generally differentiated between shame and guilt (see below).³³ Psychological studies explore the emotional component of shame and define it as "an emotion focused on the vulnerability and conspicuousness of one's self-image … in terms of a

---

She notes that both shame and disappointment emerge from a gap between expectations and reality.

29. Martin Klopfenstein, *Scham und Schande nach dem Alten Testament: Eine begriffsgeschichtliche Untersuchung zu den hebräischen Wurzeln bôš, klm und ḥpr*, ATANT 62 (Zurich: TVZ, 1972). In Ezra-Nehemiah, the term כלם occurs only in Ezra 9:6 as "embarrassed." Elsewhere it is often translated "humiliated" (e.g., NASB in 1 Chr 19:5; Jer 22:22; 31:19).

30. The noun חרפה occurs in Neh 1:3; 2:17; 4:4 (3:36 MT); 5:9; the verb חרף, "to taunt," in 6:13.

31. All three terms examined by Klopfenstein occur in Isa 54:4. The term כבד occurs in Neh 5:15, 18 to describe the weight of taxes on the people. Typical of the honor/shame opposition is Isa 3:5, והנקלה בנכבד, "the base [insolent] to the honorable."

32. John K. Chance, "The Anthropology of Honor and Shame: Culture, Values, and Practice," *Semeia* 68 (1994): 146.

33. Lyn M. Bechtel, "Shame as a Sanction of Social Control in Biblical Israel: Judicial, Political, and Social Shaming," *JSOT* 49 (1991): 49.

perceived ideal."[34] Anthropological studies identify shame and honor as opposing social values and locate them as core values in cultures where individual identity is determined by group membership.[35] A careful analysis shows how these affective dimensions of a culture's value system contribute to its structure.[36]

11.1.1. The Social Implications of Shame

Julian Pitt-Rivers defines honor as "the value of a person in his own eyes, but also in the eyes of his society. It is the estimation of his own worth, his *claim* to pride, but it is also the acknowledgement of that claim, his excellence recognized by society, his *right* to pride."[37] Frank Stewart has suggested that honor is a "right to respect" within a group that follows the same code of honor. Honor can be lost; to retain it one must follow certain rules deemed to be "of cardinal importance in judging a person's worth."[38] Alternatively, shame is "a claim to worth that is publicly denied and repudiated."[39] Pitt-Rivers states that shame is "what makes a person sensitive to the pressure exerted by public opinion but also the reputation earned in consequence."[40]

---

34. Johanna Stiebert, *The Construction of Shame in the Hebrew Bible: The Prophetic Contribution*, JSOTSup 346 (Sheffield: Sheffield Academic, 2002), 3.

35. In his introduction, J. G. Peristiany states, "Honour and shame are the constant preoccupation of individuals in small scale, exclusive societies where face to face personal, as opposed to anonymous, relations are of paramount importance" (*Honour and Shame: The Values of Mediterranean Society* [London: Weidenfeld & Nicolson, 1965], 11). In the same volume, Bourdieu states, "The point of honor is the basis of the moral code of an individual who sees himself always through the eyes of others, who has need of others for his existence, because the image he has of himself is indistinguishable from that presented to him by other people" ("The Sentiment of Honour in Kabyle Society," 211).

36. Chance, "Anthropology of Honor and Shame," 142.

37. Julian Pitt-Rivers, *The Fate of Shechem, or the Politics of Sex: Essays in the Anthropology of the Mediterranean* (Cambridge: Cambridge University Press, 1977), 1.

38. Frank H. Stewart, *Honor* (Chicago: University of Chicago Press, 1994), 145–46.

39. Joseph Plevnik, "Honor/Shame," in *Handbook of Biblical Social Values*, ed. John J. Pilch and Bruce J. Malina (Peabody, MA: Hendrickson, 1993), 107.

40. Pitt-Rivers, *Fate of Shechem*, 20.

Honor and shame are "high context" terms that require localized definition.[41] Pitt-Rivers states that what is perceived as honorable varies "from one period to another, from one region to another and above all from one class to another."[42] However, evidence of honor and shame as a shared value in Mediterranean culture has led biblical scholars to adopt it as a basic working model.[43] In this context, "men vie with each other for honor in an agonistic fashion and women are acutely sensitized to shame as a mechanism for preserving their honor."[44] Jane Schneider argues that the values of honor and shame complement institutional distribution of power and social order. She suggests that these were localized means of social control adapted to the conflict created by the coexistence of pastoral and agricultural communities in the absence of state control.[45] However, "even if we describe the rules or structures of society, this would not explain why [members] follow the rules or how many of them actually do."[46]

11.1.2. The Psychology of Shame, Guilt, and Corporate Trauma

Weber has argued that when a deity is conceived by analogy to living persons, the god can be coerced into service of the person. By "attributing to the gods the human behavior patterns appropriate to a mighty terrestrial potentate, whose freely disposed favor can be obtained by entreaty,

---

41. Plevnik, "Honor/Shame," 108. See also Herzfeld, "Honour and Shame," 339.

42. Pitt-Rivers, *Fate of Shechem*, 1. Plevnik ("Honor/Shame," 107) identifies the "value cluster" of honor as strength, courage, daring, valor, generosity, and wisdom. However, what constitutes each of these or when they are deemed appropriate can only be understood in context.

43. Chance, "Anthropology of Honor and Shame," 142. See also Plevnik, "Honor/Shame," 106. For problems with the Mediterranean culture paradigm, see W. R. Domeris, "Shame and Honour in Proverbs: Wise Women and Foolish Men," *OTE* 8 (1995): 86–102.

44. Stiebert, *Construction of Shame*, 16; Pitt-Rivers, *Fate of Shechem*, 78. Bourdieu states, "one of the fundamental categories of this system is the division of the world into complementary and opposing principles, masculine and feminine" ("Sentiment of Honor," 226); he also details the separate male and female social contexts as well as challenge and riposte between men (221–25, 199–208).

45. Jane Schneider, "Of Vigilance and Virgins: Honor, Shame and Access to Resources in Mediterranean Societies," *Ethnology* 10 (1971): 3. She observes that this way of life constantly requires all adults, and particularly heads of households, to make important economic and political decisions (5).

46. Chance, "Anthropology of Honor and Shame," 147.

gifts, service, tributes, cajolery, and bribes," the deity's favor may then "be earned as a consequence of the devotee's own faithfulness and good conduct in conformity with the divine will."[47] With this understanding, supplication takes on "a purely business-like, rationalized form that sets forth the achievements of the supplicant on behalf of the god and then claims adequate recompense therefore."[48] Weber notes that under these circumstances sacrifice can be viewed as tribute (such as the firstfruits offering) or as a self-imposed punishment (such as the sin offering) that averts the wrath of the god before it falls upon the sacrifice.[49] This same logic may be operational in penitential prayer—self-blame averts the wrath of God and becomes a form of self-protection. However, in these books, punishment (at least for past sins) has already occurred in the exile. The prayers, therefore, suggest anxiety over a return to the conditions of punishment. These prayers preserve God's prestige by explaining the exile as punishment for the failures of the people. The people "had not honored their god sufficiently ... they neglected him in favor of other gods."[50]

Helpful for understanding these prayers is some definition of shame and guilt as well as their relationship to trauma and corporate responsibility. Through a study of Greek texts, Bernard Williams explores shame and guilt in ancient Greek society. He states, "The basic experience connected with shame is that of being seen, inappropriately, by the wrong people, in the wrong condition."[51] The experience of shame is connected to nakedness, but "the root of shame lies in exposure in a more general sense, in being at a disadvantage ... a loss of power. The sense of shame is a reaction of the subject to the consciousness of this loss."[52] Fear over the prospect of shame motivates people to act. He maintains that shame is not just about "being found out" (e.g., Jer 2:26, the thief who is discovered is shamed), but "for many of its operations the imagined gaze of an imagined other will do."[53] The reaction to shame is self-protection—to cover oneself or to hide—and people naturally take steps to avoid the situations that call

---

47. Weber, *Sociology of Religion*, 25.
48. Ibid., 26.
49. Ibid., 27.
50. Ibid., 33.
51. Bernard Williams, *Shame and Necessity* (Berkeley: University of California Press, 1993), 78.
52. Ibid., 220.
53. Ibid., 82.

for it. Williams contends that shame is neutral with regard to moral and nonmoral qualities. We can be mortified or disgraced on a failure of prowess as easily as a failure of generosity or loyalty.[54] "What arouses shame … is something that typically elicits from others contempt or derision or avoidance."[55] The expression of shame is not just the desire to hide but the wish to be gone. This sense of personal humiliation may also lead to attempts to reconstruct or improve oneself.[56]

In contrast to the visual exposure associated with shame, Williams suggests that guilt is more associated with hearing "the sound in oneself of the voice of judgment, it is the moral sentiment of the word."[57] "What arouses guilt in an agent is an act or omission of a sort that typically elicits from other people anger, resentment, or indignation. What the agent may offer in order to turn this away is reparation; he may also fear punishment or may inflict it on himself."[58] This also indicates that forgiveness, with the associated suspension of punishment, speaks more effectively to guilt than to shame. However, it has less power to repair one's sense of self.[59]

Lenore Terr has considered the difference between shame and guilt with regard to victims of trauma who experience a profound loss of control over their lives.[60] Like Williams, Terr associates shame with the gaze of the other. She differentiates shame from guilt by their operation in public or private spheres:

> Shame comes from public exposure of one's own vulnerability. Guilt, on the other hand, is private. It follows from a sense of failing to measure up to private, internal standards. When others "know" that you once were helpless, you tend to feel ashamed. *They* know. If, on the other hand, you feel you caused your own problems, you cease feeling so vulnerable and blame yourself, instead, for the shape of events. *You* know. But you are the only one.[61]

---

54. Ibid., 89, 91.
55. Ibid., 90.
56. Ibid.
57. Ibid., 89.
58. Ibid., 90.
59. Ibid.
60. Lenore Terr, *Too Scared to Cry: How Trauma Affects Children … and Ultimately Us All* (New York: Basic Books, 1990), 112.
61. Ibid., 113.

Terr maintains that victims take on guilt to cover over humiliation. "Rather than thinking that something wrong 'just happened,' trauma victims seem to prefer believing that they caused or contributed to the events—that they were responsible."[62] Guilt becomes a defense mechanism from the identity-destroying effects of shame associated with traumatic and public vulnerability. In particular it defends against the shame of being "less-than-human," which is often one's experience as a victim of violence.[63]

All three penitential prayers concern themselves not only with failures by the community but also failures by the ancestors. Nehemiah 1:6 confesses the sins of the people of Israel, Neh 9 details the nation's entire history as failure to obey the law and to respond to God's repeated mercy, and Ezra 9 confesses the sin of the present community at a particular moment but treats it as a continuation of past failures (Ezra 9:13–14).[64] Farid Abdel-Nour claims that for a person's responsibility to extend to past generations, it requires "a credible account of continuity between persons whose actions have brought about a bad state of affairs in the distant past and others from whom a response is appropriately elicited in the present."[65] This would require a person to "actively associate herself in a very specific way with these actions."[66] A sense of personal guilt over historic acts by previous generations requires members to conceive of the nation as a stable and continuous organism, something of which individual members are integral parts, having a past, a future, a consciousness, often imagined as having emotions, a memory, and will.[67] It is often evidenced in language such as "*we* have prevailed" or, as in the biblical texts, "*we* have been deep

---

62. Ibid.

63. Ibid., 116–17. When describing the guilt a woman felt over events that occurred when she was a toddler, Terr states, "Charlotte's guilt was worn like a cloak. It covered up something even worse than guilt.... Without guilt, Charlotte would be left with an overpowering sense of inferiority, of vulnerability, of shame. She might not be fully able to face the world of humans."

64. "You, our God, have punished us less than our iniquities deserved and have given us such a remnant as this, shall we break your commandments again and intermarry with the peoples who practice these abominations? Would you not be angry with us until you destroy us without remnant or survivor?" (Ezra 9:13–14).

65. Farid Abdel-Nour, "National Responsibility," *Political Theory* 31 (2003): 698.

66. Ibid., 694.

67. Ibid., 698.

in guilt" (Ezra 9:7) or "*we* have acted wickedly" (Neh 9:33) and "*our* sins" (Neh 9:37) when describing the ancestors' failures.[68]

Taking *pride* in the achievements of others renders the idea of national responsibility (or guilt) intelligible. Through pride in one's nation, an agent identifies with the actions of others.[69] When a causal link is established between a bad state of affairs and actions associated with one's national pride, "a *potential* path of responsibility between oneself and the bad state of affairs in question is established."[70] The logic of penitential prayers is predicated on a narrative of national success embedded in a covenantal relationship as God's chosen people (Ezra 9:10; Neh 1:10; 9:7–9). Former measures of success—the achievements of the historic kings and the grandness of the Jerusalem temple—now are the primary evidence of national failure. One might reasonably demand a response by those whose actions caused this state of affairs. But a feeling of national responsibility due to one's national pride cannot meaningfully lead to punishment; rather, it leads to national guilt or shame.[71] By sharing a group identity now mixed with national failure, the individual is compelled to reassess who he or she is.[72]

Williams, Abdel-Nour, and Terr agree that guilt carries a sense of debt that demands some form of punishment, such as restitution or reparations. According to Abdel-Nour, it demands "an appropriate act that substitutes for the impossible task of undoing the deed."[73] Shame requires a different response. Because Terr concerns herself with victims of trauma, she notes the destructive aspect of shame and the tendency by victims to substitute guilt for shame. However, Williams and Abdel-Nour, who consider shame due to other causes, offer a more positive role for it. Williams suggests that the more deeply felt sense of shame gives "a sense of who one is and of what one hopes to be" and so mediates between ethical demands and the rest of life.[74] Similarly Abdel-Nour states that national shame involves an

---

68. Ibid., 699.
69. Ibid., 702.
70. Ibid., 703.
71. Ibid.
72. Larry May, "Metaphysical Guilt and Moral Taint," in *Collective Responsibility: Five Decades of Debate in Theoretical and Applied Ethics*, ed. Larry May and Stacey Hoffman (Lanham, MD: Rowman & Littlefield, 1991), 242.
73. Abdel-Nour, "National Responsibility," 708.
74. Williams, *Shame and Necessity*, 102.

idealized image of *who one is* and an audience (real or imagined) by whom one is not fit to be seen as one is.[75] It can lead to hate or disgust with oneself, but it can also become an occasion for growth and development into someone who is not shameful. Since shame is self-directed, that is, about one's character, it is associated with a "call for greater self-consciousness on the part of members of the nation."[76] Where one carries pride in national accomplishments, one is then open to national responsibility. This may lead members of the community to take on the task of responding to the effects of (historic) guilt or shame.

Williams argues that ancient Greek culture lacked the differentiation we make today between guilt and shame, and even today both can be experienced toward the same action. "*What I have done* points in one direction towards what has happened to others, in another direction to what I am."[77] Williams perceives guilt as more isolated than shame from other elements of one's self-image. It can direct one toward those who have been wronged and demand reparation. "But it cannot by itself help one to understand one's relations to those happenings, or to rebuild the self that has done these things and the world in which that self has to live. Only shame can do that, because it embodies conceptions of what one is and of how one is related to others."[78]

What then can we say about the relationship of corporate and national identity and its relationship to guilt and shame in these biblical prayers? Much like the trauma victims studied by Terr, those confessing guilt are the ones harmed by the actions of the ancestors. They attribute their current sad state to the actions of previous generations, yet their sense of national solidarity leads them to claim responsibility for those actions. The confessions conceive of the Deity as the offended party—we have harmed God and deserve the punishment we received. External groups are mentioned only as tools of the Deity to discipline and punish the offending community or as threats to the integrity of the community. The confessions of iniquity, guilt (Ezra 9:6, 7, 13), offense, failure, sin (Neh 1:6–7), rebellion, evil, and stubbornness (Neh 9:26–29) counter the sense of shame acknowledged in the surrounding narratives. Terr contends that acceptance of blame by victims ("It's my fault, I was wrong, they were right") are often lies. The lie

---

75. Abdel-Nour, "National Responsibility," 708.
76. Ibid., 711.
77. Williams, *Shame and Necessity*, 92.
78. Ibid., 94.

removes the feeling of helplessness and reasserts a sense of control.[79] The guilt expressed in these prayers is an empowering response by those who experience the shame of trauma. It directs attention away from identity and the exposure associated with shame. This opens the door to making reparations or seeking forgiveness (or both) as means of rectifying the situation and reclaiming an honorable identity.

It is too simplistic to argue that the Babylonian invasion of 587 BCE directly traumatized the generation of Nehemiah or Ezra in 458–445 BCE. Yet these prayers indicate that the community has processed this event as a trauma. "Trauma" is not a guaranteed result of a group experiencing pain—even genocide. Rather, a community must process the event and represent it as trauma. According to Jeffrey Alexander, this requires collective actors deciding "to represent social pain as a fundamental threat to their sense of who they are, where they came from, and where they want to go."[80] He states, "Traumatic status is attributed to real or imagined phenomena, not because of their actual harmfulness or their objective abruptness, but because these phenomena are believed to have abruptly, and harmfully, affected collective identity."[81]

To claim something as cultural trauma involves the construction of a new master narrative. It requires a "compelling framework of cultural classification."[82] A successful narrative requires an identification of the nature of the pain—what happened and to whom? Furthermore, the relation of the trauma victim to the wider audience must be articulated as

---

79. Terr, *Too Scared to Cry*, 112.

80. Jeffrey C. Alexander, "Toward a Theory of Cultural Trauma," in *Cultural Trauma and Collective Identity*, ed. Jeffrey C. Alexander (Berkeley: University of California Press, 2004), 10.

81. Ibid., 9.

82. Ibid., 12. Alexander identifies several necessary conditions that influence whether an event becomes the focus of cultural trauma: members of the social group must make claims about the shape of social reality and there must be a carrier group that gives voice to these claims. This group would have ideal and material interests within the social field and "particular discursive talents for articulating their claims … in the public sphere" (11). The group employs symbolic resources available in the particular historical context to further these claims and makes use of the constraints and opportunities provided by institutional structures. Alexander references Weber's carrier group concept. See in particular Weber's description of the priesthood (*Sociology of Religion*, 118–32) as the chief carrier of literature, intellectualism, and religion.

well as an attribution of responsibility—who was the perpetrator?[83] In this case, all three prayers bind "the suppliant together in solidarity with his forefathers' guilt" (Neh 9:32–37; Ezra 9:6–7; Neh 1:6–7).[84] In doing this, the prayers unite the audience (the listening community) with the trauma victims. They are united not only by their shared sense of trauma but also by a shared sense of responsibility. In contrast to the sorrowful questioning of communal laments, the historic trauma of the exile is understood in these prayers as deserved; "Yahweh's actions are viewed as justified due to the rebellion of his people."[85]

Trading on the cultural values of honor and shame, the prayers explain the shame of defeat as the trespass of "divinely inspired ethics and sacred law."[86] The ideology provides a framework for the social (re)construction of the community. The community's own religious traditions of Deuteronomy and Priestly sources are enlisted to frame the issue and legitimate this interpretation of the exile. Each prayer is narratively presented as a first step toward removing the problems facing the community.[87] As aesthetic productions, the participatory nature of the prayers and their associated ceremonies provide an effective channel for producing identification and emotional cleansing.[88]

11.2. Nehemiah 1:5–11: Removing Shame

11.2.1. Literary Analysis

At first glance, the prayer in Neh 1:5–11 appears poorly connected to its narrative setting. Although Nehemiah mourns and prays for *days* (Neh 1:4) over the troubles of Jerusalem, the prayer is quite brief. So, as Clines notes, "The prayer is thus a literary construction, not a record or reminiscence."[89] The prayer concludes with a request for success for

---

83. Alexander, "Theory of Cultural Trauma," 13–14.
84. Boda, *Praying the Tradition*, 9.
85. Ibid., 26.
86. Alexander, "Theory of Cultural Trauma," 15.
87. Werline, *Penitential Prayer*, 2.
88. Alexander, "Theory of Cultural Trauma," 16.
89. Clines, "The Nehemiah Memoir: The Perils of Autobiography," in *What Does Eve Do to Help? and Other Readerly Questions to the Old Testament*, JSOTSup 94 (Sheffield: JSOT Press, 1990), 129.

Nehemiah and mercy before the king, but it does not lament the conditions of the walls or people—the news of which prompted his prayers. Instead, it contains a generic confession that the people have sinned, that "I and my family" have sinned, and all have offended God deeply (1:6–7). The confession of sin lacks content—there is no history describing past sin as in Neh 9 and no present behavior in need of reform as in Ezra 9. It appears especially at odds with the rest of Nehemiah's self-presentation as a hero who wishes to be remembered "for good" (and on occasion someone who would not sin even when threatened; Neh 6:10–13). Further, the prayer requests that God remember his word to gather "your outcasts" and "bring them to the place at which I have chosen to establish my name" (1:9). The return of exiles goes without mention throughout the rest of the memoir—the single returnee is Nehemiah. Two expressions in this prayer are also uncharacteristic of Nehemiah. The divine name, YHWH (1:5), is used within the memoir only in 5:13 and elsewhere in Nehemiah only in chapters 8–10; and the expression "sons of Israel" (1:6) contrasts with Nehemiah's preferred "Judeans."[90] The prayer "is a mosaic of earlier biblical phrases" that Williamson suggests incorporates well-known liturgical language "thoroughly familiar to Nehemiah."[91] Given these differences, it is unlikely that the prayer was composed at the time of the narrative.[92] Its presence reflects on, and realigns, the memoir into which it is placed.

Deuteronomistic thought and language lace the prayer. Among many parallels, Williamson notes that both Neh 1:8 and Deut 4:27 refer to being "scattered among the peoples."[93] Blenkinsopp also draws attention to vari-

---

90. "Sons of Israel" occurs within material associated with the memoir only in Neh 2:10; 13:2, 18, 26; and two of these uses are preexilic historical references.

91. Williamson, *Ezra, Nehemiah*, 172. Blenkinsopp (*Ezra-Nehemiah*, 208–9) suggests that the prayer is a late expansion of an earlier, briefer prayer.

92. Eep Talstra ("The Discourse of Praying: Reading Nehemiah 1," in *Psalms and Prayers: Papers Read at the Joint Meeting of the Society of Old Testament Study and Oudtestamentische Werkgezelschap in Nederland en Belgie*, ed. Bob Becking and Eric Peels, OTS 55 [Leiden: Brill, 2007], 220–21) comments, "The outcome of textual reconstruction in several commentaries does not reveal much about praying as such. Rather one reaches the conclusion that the prayer in Neh 1 is just piling up pious phrases from deuteronomistic stock about the sins of Israel, which results in a prayer that hardly seems fit for Nehemiah's actual situation." See also Williamson, *Ezra, Nehemiah*, 167.

93. Williamson, *Ezra, Nehemiah*, 172.

ous correspondences, especially the correlation of Neh 1:8–9 with Deut 30:1–5.[94] Both texts promise a return and restoration to the land despite how distantly the people are scattered. The prayer also draws heavily on idioms found in Solomon's inaugural temple prayer found in 1 Kgs 8 and 2 Chr 6. The table below charts some of the concepts or phrases Nehemiah's prayer in 1:5–11 shares with these other texts.

Nehemiah	Deuteronomy	1 Kings	2 Chronicles
"the great and awesome God" (1:5; 4:14 [8 MT])	7:21; 10:17	8:23	6:14
"the God who maintains [שמר, 'keeps/observes'] covenant loyalty with those who love him and keep his commandments (who walk before him)" (1:5)	7:9		
people keeping [שמר] commandments (1:5, 7, 9)	4:6, 9, 23, etc.	8:58, 62	7:17, Solomon alone
"let your ear be attentive and your eyes open" (1:6; cf. 1:11)		8:52; cf. 8:29	6:40
"the commandments, the statutes, and the ordinances" (1:7)	5:31; 6:1; 7:11; 26:17	8:58	
"your servant Moses" (1:7)	34:5	8:53, 56	
"unfaithful [מעל]" (1:8; cf. 13:27; Ezra 9–10)	not in Deuteronomy; cf. Josh 7:1; 22:16–31		1 Chr 2:7; 10:13; 2 Chr 28:19

---

94. Blenkinsopp, *Ezra-Nehemiah*, 209. See also Clines, *Ezra, Nehemiah, Esther*, 138–39.

"the place at which I have chosen to establish my name"; "the city that you have chosen and the house that I have built for your name" (1:9)	12:11; 14:23; 16:2, 6, 11; 26:2	8:44, 48	6:6, 34; 7:12, 16
the strong hand (of God) (1:10)	3:24; 7:19; 11:2; 34:12	8:42	6:32
"your servant/s" (1:6, 11)	3:24	8:28, 29, 30, 52	6:19, 20, 21

* Some parallels are gleaned from Williamson, *Ezra, Nehemiah*, 172; Blenkinsopp, *Ezra-Nehemiah*, 84; Talstra, "Discourse of Praying," 229.

Although the prayer makes no direct reference to the temple or altar, it draws heavily in both its structure and language from Solomon's temple dedication prayer in 1 Kgs 8. In so doing, it constructs allusions between the two rulers.[95] Gordon Davies comments that Nehemiah lays claim to the promise in Solomon's prayer that YHWH would hear a sincere supplicant in a foreign land.[96] Each leader prays for God to be attentive to his petitions on behalf of the people. Both employ the language of Deut 7:9 to address YHWH as the God of the heavens who "keeps covenant and steadfast love" (Neh 1:5; 1 Kgs 8:23). Solomon asks God to hear the confession of people in exile, "if they come to their senses … and repent, and plead with you … saying, 'We have sinned, and have done wrong; we have acted wickedly' … then hear in heaven … and forgive your people" (1 Kgs 8:47–50). Echoing Solomon's language, Nehemiah confesses on behalf of the scattered people of Israel, "We have sinned against you. Both I and my family have sinned. We have offended you deeply [acted corruptly against you], failing to keep the commandments, the statutes, and the ordinances that you commanded your servant Moses" (Neh 1:6–7). The prayer in Nehemiah now enacts the confession anticipated by Solomon and for which he has requested God to respond with forgiveness.

---

95. Boda (*Praying the Tradition*, 209) suggests that Solomon's temple dedication prayer delineates the agenda for all penitential prayers.
96. Davies, *Ezra and Nehemiah*, 92.

The term מעל ("unfaithful") is the only expression that Neh 1 shares exclusively with 2 Chr 6. All other links can be accounted for by the Chronicler's dependence on 1 Kgs 8.[97] In Neh 1:8, being scattered or driven into foreign lands is the result of *unfaithfulness*.[98] In the Deuteronomic warning about exile, the people are warned not to *forget* the covenant (Deut 4:27–30).[99] Significantly, מעל is used five times in Josh 7:1 and 22:16–31 to describe the sin of Achan and Israel—a narrative that bears some thematic correspondence with the Nehemiah memoir. In Joshua, unfaithfulness poses an immediate threat for anyone convicted of it and an extended threat for the community if it fails to contain it. While not associated with exile, it does pose a threat for the community in its efforts to possess the land. The Chronicler also cites the faithlessness of Achan (1 Chr 2:7) and ties the faithlessness of leaders to consequences for the people (2 Chr 28:19).[100] In Ezra 9:2, 10:2, and Neh 13:27, intermarrying with the women of the land constitutes unfaithfulness that threatens to recreate the condition of exile. In each instance, faithlessness begets anxiety about life in the land.

Talstra organizes the prayer's structure by a series of inclusions.[101] The prayer begins and ends with a request for divine attention (1:5, 11). A second set of enclosures concern commandments that people confess they have failed to keep or are encouraged to keep (1:6–7, 9–10), and the focal point is a request that God remember the word commanded to Moses with respect to Israel.[102]

---

97. Blenkinsopp, *Ezra-Nehemiah*, 209.

98. This is true also in the prayer of Daniel (Dan 9:7).

99. Elsewhere in Deuteronomy, the people are warned not to forget the Lord (e.g., 6:12; 8:11, 14, 19). Only in Deut 4 is the community explicitly warned not to forget the covenant (cf. 26:13). Deut 28:58 warns the people to "diligently observe" the words of the law. Deut 29:25 anticipates abandoning the covenant.

100. "For the Lord brought Judah low because of King Ahaz of Israel, for he had behaved without restraint in Judah and had been faithless to the Lord" (2 Chr 28:19).

101. Talstra, "Discourse of Praying," 226. See his detailed analysis on 225.

102. This organizational scheme has led Talstra (ibid., 226–27, 230) to question labeling it as a penitential prayer. He notes that the central request is to "remember" (not to forgive), and he argues that it makes no reference to the petitions for forgiveness from 1 Kgs 8. However, his schema tends to elide the confession of 1:6–7, which seems to be a necessary prerequisite to the request.

A   1:5–6a O YHWH God of heaven … let your ear be attentive and your eyes open to hear the prayer of your servant that I now pray before you day and night for your servants
   B   1:6b–7 Confessing the sins.… We have offended … failing to keep the commandments … that you commanded your servant Moses
      C   1:8 Remember the word that you commanded your servant Moses, "If you are unfaithful, I will scatter you"
   B'   1:9–10 If you return to me and keep my commandments,… I will gather them.… They are your servants … whom you redeemed
A'   1:11 O Lord, let your ear be attentive to the prayer of your servant and to the prayer of your servants who delight in revering your name. Give success to your servant today.

Talstra argues that the central request, "Remember the *word* that you commanded your servant Moses," "stresses the contrast between the *commandments* given *through* Moses (7) and the *word* given *to* Moses (8)."[103] First Kings 8:52–53 also refers to the word given to Moses. There the word that God speaks or promises to Moses refers to God separating Israel to be his people, "just as you promised [דבר] through Moses, your servant." In 1 Kgs 8:56, playing on the root דבר, Solomon blesses God for having "given rest to his people Israel according to all that he *promised*; not one *word* has failed of all his good *promise*, which he *spoke* through his servant Moses." On this basis, Solomon asks that God not leave them or abandon them (8:57). The word of Moses, the servant of God, holds out a promise of renewal and provides a basis for the petition for success and mercy of this new servant, Nehemiah (Neh 1:11).[104] This word to Moses is different from the commandments that the people failed to keep. It is a promise that overrides the consequences of unfaithfulness. The "good word" of rest in the land also provides a larger framework for Nehemiah's later requests to be "remembered for good."[105]

Gordon Davies contends that that through allusions to past leaders (specifically Moses and Solomon) the words of Ezra and Nehemiah "reval-

---

103. Ibid., 226 (italics mine).
104. Ibid., 227.
105. Ibid.

idate tradition, but each in his own fashion."[106] Combined with the disappearance of one leader after another within Ezra-Nehemiah, the allusions create a "complex statement about leadership and heritage in post-Exilic Israel."[107] In this text, Nehemiah, like Moses and Solomon, intercedes for the people (Neh 1:6). The parallels place these leaders into theological discourse. Just as Solomon prayed for the forgiveness of the exiles at the dedication of the temple, so Nehemiah prays for exiles as he begins the reconstruction of Jerusalem's wall. The prayer concludes with a request that God be attentive to "the prayer of your servants who delight in revering your name" and that he make Nehemiah successful (Neh 1:11). These final requests bear a notable resemblance to Moses's assurance in his final discourse in Deuteronomy, "Therefore diligently observe the words of this covenant, in order that you may succeed in everything that you do" (Deut 29:9 [8 MT]).

Eskenazi maintains that, in contrast to Ezra, who throws himself upon God's mercies, Nehemiah

> casts himself in the line of the worthies—the true servant of God.... Nehemiah speaks from the perspective of one who belongs to the circle of those who love God and keep God's commandments and is therefore deserving of God's attention and support.... The premise of his prayer is the righteousness of the one who now approaches God.[108]

This assessment is true regarding the Nehemiah memoir. However, with the insertion of this prayer, Nehemiah begins his work with a confession that he and his house have sinned (Neh 1:6-7) and concludes with a request for mercy (1:11). The forward placement of this confession indicates that it is a critical step toward the righteousness needed to approach God. This prayer, on the lips of Nehemiah, adds a level of legitimacy to his actions that later editors may have felt was absent without the confession.

Rodney Werline notes that in Third Isaiah (65:8-16; 66:2) "servants" are those who are penitent. Only they seek God and will receive YHWH's salvation. The term "servants" functions as a legitimating descriptor and

---

106. Davies, *Ezra and Nehemiah*, 93.
107. Ibid.
108. Eskenazi, *In an Age of Prose*, 145. Eskenazi prefers the character and methods of Ezra to those of Nehemiah, finding in Nehemiah a foil for the more exemplary scribe.

"as a line of social demarcation."[109] This usage may lie behind Nehemiah's request in 1:11 that God hear the prayers of "*your servants* who delight in revering your name." By incorporating servant terminology and language from Solomon's prayer, Nehemiah positions his community among those who come to their senses and return to the Lord. By the end of the prayer, Moses, Nehemiah, and the people all share equal standing as servants of God. In Ezra 1–6, returning exiles are lent legitimacy in part by portraying their journey to Jerusalem as the exodus.[110] In Nehemiah, the people in dire straits *in the land* are given hope when Jerusalem is reclaimed and rebuilt by those who keep the covenant of Moses and seek mercy after the pattern of Solomon.

11.2.2. Reframing Destruction: Shifting from Shame to Guilt

In Nehemiah, concern for shame surrounds this prayer. Nehemiah declares that rebuilding Jerusalem's walls will end the community's disgrace and silence his adversaries' mockery (Neh 1:3; 2:17; 3:36).[111] The reconstructed wall reverses the shame of Jerusalem's broken state. The addition of this prayer provides a different framework for interpreting the events that follow in the memoir. It removes shame by confessing sin and petitioning God for the return of exiles. Shame, originally removed by Nehemiah's deeds of honor (building the wall, combating local opponents, and resisting sin), is now purged by confession of guilt and dependence on divine mercy. It claims returned exiles are now evidence of the fulfillment of the divine promise, and Nehemiah's achievement becomes a fruit of successful confession. The tradition of penitential prayer repurposes Nehemiah's lament over the walls. The shame of broken walls is now unmistakably linked to sin and requires confession. No room is left for a lament's accusation against God. Penitential prayer appropriates the narrative of wall construction for new meaning.

The prayer anticipates the gathering of the exiles, and its theology relies on the word of Moses, which harkens back to texts explicitly concerned with God listening to penitential exiles. These cultural values

---

109. Werline, *Penitential Prayer*, 43.

110. H. G. M. Williamson, "The Concept of Israel in Transition," in *The World of Ancient Israel: Sociological, Anthropological and Political Perspectives*, ed. R. E. Clements (Cambridge: Cambridge University Press, 1989), 157.

111. It also motivates walking "in the fear of our God" (Neh 5:9).

(embodied and reproduced by means of habitus) likely emerged among exiles prior to any return to Jerusalem. Those in exile who maintained a shared national identity could do little to rectify the shame they felt due to their national losses except to exchange it for the less identity-threatening option of guilt. This cultural value is transferred to a new environment, and "without either explicit reason or signifying intent, [appears] to be none the less 'sensible' and 'reasonable.'"[112] The developing exilic tradition of confession overwrote shame over their national trauma with guilt. The ritual enables the cultural symbolic system to be brought to bear on these events.[113] Guilt can be assuaged by acts of reimbursement or restitution toward the offended party. By identifying God as the offended party and channeling penitence toward their Deity, restoration became a sign of divine forgiveness. The prayer reinforces the exile as an important communal identity marker but allows the petitioner to distance himself and his community from responsibility for their shameful condition.

Nehemiah's motivations for his program are not identical to the motivations contained in the penitential prayer. Nehemiah is motivated by the social experience of shame and believes that God is "with him" to carry out the construction and so undo the shame. He responds to shame much as a warrior who retaliates. There is no distinction between moral and nonmoral motivations. In the prayer, on the other hand, action is rooted in satisfying ethical categories.[114] Honor is regained by embracing a sense of responsibility for the situation through expressions of self-abasement. This is also an empowering response that counters the sense of shame acknowledged in the surrounding narrative and associated with exile. It reasserts a sense of self-control and directs attention away from the exposure associated with shame.[115] God has not predetermined their fate. They have only to confess their sin, keep God's commandments, and revere his name. Then God will forgive, have mercy, and give success. As a result,

---

112. Bourdieu, *Outline*, 79.
113. Bell, *Ritual*, 77.
114. Williams, *Shame and Necessity*, 42–43. Williams contends that in the archaic writings of Homer, assumptions regarding fate, the gods, and social expectations served to shape the world. Although in the Homeric world it was understood that people could deliberate and decide, only in Plato's writing are actions explained in terms that get their significance from ethics.
115. Bechtel, "Shame as a Sanction," 50.

they can reclaim an honorable identity. Nehemiah's completed wall now validates the effectiveness of this confession.

11.3. Nehemiah 9–10: A Response to Corporate Trauma

11.3.1. Literary Context: Nehemiah 8–10

Scholars often view Neh 8–10 as the climax of the work of Ezra and Nehemiah and a defining moment for the postexilic community.[116] Within these chapters the community composes a written agreement that defines the contours and character of the reestablished community. The missions of Ezra and Nehemiah converge here for the first time, as do several narrative motifs: the assembly of the people, Torah, prayer, and temple.[117]

Eskenazi titles this section "Consolidation according to Torah" and observes that the chapters demonstrate how the written text governs communal life.[118] Three separate gatherings for the reading of Torah are narrated in these chapters. In Neh 8:1, all the people gather; in 8:13, the leadership gathers to study Torah; and in 9:1–3, the people of Israel separate from foreigners, confess their sins, and gather to read the book of the law of YHWH. After each reading the community responds with either celebration or confession. The entire passage concludes with a written agreement (9:39) signed by leaders of the community to adhere to the law of God (10:28). Specific laws detailed in the agreement include refraining from intermarrying with foreigners, refraining from business on the Sabbath, and financial commitments for the maintenance of the temple and its functionaries (10:30–39). The narrative displays "an incremental progression, with an ever intensifying display of commitment by the community."[119] The thematic thread of Torah highlights the community's

---

116. Michael W. Duggan, *The Covenant Renewal in Ezra-Nehemiah (Neh 7:72b–10:40): An Exegetical, Literary, and Theological Study*, SBLDS 164 (Atlanta: Society of Biblical Literature, 2001), 67; Williamson, *Ezra, Nehemiah*, 330; Eskenazi, *In an Age of Prose*, 95.

117. Duggan, *Covenant Renewal*, 67.

118. Eskenazi, *In an Age of Prose*, 95.

119. Ibid., 97. Williamson (*Ezra, Nehemiah*, 276) states that reading the law, confession, and covenant renewal is a threefold structure shared by other texts. So, for example, Josiah mourns when he hears the law and calls on the people to agree to a covenant in response (2 Kgs 22:11–23:3). Blenkinsopp (*Ezra-Nehemiah*, 294) states that the assemblies in Neh 8 and 9 bear some striking parallels, e.g., each is convened

commitment to the law as a crucial component of their renewal, while agreement to particular laws clarifies the religious piety that is to characterize and define the community.

Although Neh 9 shares motifs with surrounding texts, it also displays inconsistencies with them.[120] A joyful celebration of the Festival of Booths in Neh 8 ends on the twenty-second day of the month. Two days later, in Neh 9, on the twenty-fourth day, the community separates from foreigners and proceeds to mourn. As Grabbe observes, it "feels as if one has come into a film part way through."[121] A more logical order would place the confession in Neh 9 prior to the festival, on the Day of Atonement, the tenth day of the month. The separation from foreigners would also have made more sense prior to Neh 8 (cf. the separation prior to Passover in Ezra 6:21). In addition, after Ezra's prominent leadership in Neh 8, he is absent from Neh 9 and the community is led by Levites.[122] Williamson comments, "Coming where it does, however, it strongly suggests that the gathering described was quite independent of any preceding celebration."[123] Furthermore, the prayer fails to even once mention the temple. In contrast, commitment to the law in Neh 10 identifies numerous obligations assumed by the people for temple support.

---

for the reading of the law led by Levites. He suggests that Neh 9:1–5a incorporates a parallel version of 8:1–12—but with the conspicuous absence of Ezra.

120. The inconsistencies have led scholars to posit alternative initial placement of this chapter. For example, Williamson (*Ezra, Nehemiah*, 310) suggests that Neh 9 is a natural sequel to Ezra 9–10. Neh 9 and Ezra 9–10 both involve separation from foreigners, "holy seed," fasting, and a confessional prayer. Noting a possible fit of dates with Ezra, he argues for an original placement of this text after Ezra 10:9. However, as Blenkinsopp (*Ezra-Nehemiah*, 295, 301) observes, Ezra 9 focuses on foreign women, and here the reference is to foreigners in general. He also draws attention to the generic description of the law, "with the sole exception of sabbath, references to the law and its nonobservance are quite unspecific.… If it had originated as part of the Ezra material … we might have expected some allusion to foreign marriages as a prominent example of infidelity." Clines (*Ezra, Nehemiah, Esther*, 199), noting that the list in Neh 10 contains Nehemiah's name but not Ezra's, suggests placing the covenant ceremony of Neh 10 after Neh 13. Its current context presents the reforms initiated as the spontaneous response of a repentant community, and Nehemiah's reforms in Neh 13 become dependent on this communal decision.

121. Grabbe, *Ezra-Nehemiah*, 55.
122. Williamson, *Ezra, Nehemiah*, 309.
123. Ibid.

The prayer, Neh 9:6–37, also shows some disconnect from its introduction in 9:1–5. In the Masoretic Text, 9:6 follows without interruption from the call to praise and the blessing of the holy name issued by the Levites in 9:5. However, as Blenkinsopp notes, the words of the blessing in 9:5, "bless the LORD your God from everlasting to everlasting. Blessed be your glorious name, which is exalted above all blessing and praise," normally belong "not to the beginning but to the end of a liturgical psalm (see especially Pss. 41:13 [14]; 106:48 …)."[124] The Septuagint inserts Ezra at this juncture, separating the blessing from the historical narrative. Williamson argues that if Ezra had led this confession, he would have been introduced in the introductory narrative (Neh 9:1–5) instead of the double reference to Levites who lead the congregation.[125] Thus the Septuagint's inclusion of Ezra at this juncture suggests a recognized break between the narrative introduction and the prayer. This originally independent prayer provides an explanatory history prior to the commitments made in Neh 10.[126]

11.3.2. Nehemiah 9: Literary Structure and Context

Nehemiah 9 is a skillfully constructed literary argument that consists of an introduction (9:1–5), a historical narrative (9:6–31), and a concluding plea (9:32–37). The introduction begins as the congregation separates from foreigners. They stand, confessing their sin and the iniquity of their ancestors (9:2). This dual confession corresponds to requirements found in the Holiness Code for exiles (Lev 26:40–42).[127] Again they stand and read the law, which is followed by more confession and worship (Neh 9:3). Only then are leaders introduced. The role of leaders is more limited

---

124. Blenkinsopp, *Ezra-Nehemiah*, 296. Ps 41 ends, "Blessed be the LORD, the God of Israel, from everlasting to everlasting" (41:13 [14 MT]). Ps 106 concludes with, "Blessed be the LORD, the God of Israel, from everlasting to everlasting. And let all the people say, 'Amen.' Praise the LORD!" (106:48).

125. Williamson, *Ezra, Nehemiah*, 304.

126. Ibid., 276.

127. Duggan, *Covenant Renewal*, 152. "But if they confess their iniquity and the iniquity of their ancestors, in that they committed treachery against me and, moreover, that they continued hostile to me—so that I, in turn, continued hostile to them and brought them into the land of their enemies; if then their uncircumcised heart is humbled and they make amends for their iniquity, then will I remember my covenant with Jacob; I will remember also my covenant with Isaac and also my covenant with Abraham, and I will remember the land" (Lev 26:40–42).

here than in Neh 8, and Duggan observes that the Levites in Neh 9 do not initiate actions.[128] As a consequence, the assembly appears more unified and bears greater responsibility for the ritualized reading and prayer. This lends greater weight to the chapter's practices and theological assertions.

The historical recital explains the origins of the community's distressing circumstances and provides a pattern for restoration.[129] Like the prayer in Neh 1, it incorporates various biblical traditions. Deuteronomistic influence is predominant, although in sections the Priestly tradition is apparent, as is the influence of the prophetic book of Ezekiel.[130] Scholars divide it at different points; however, most agree on the following general movement:

- Neh 9:6–8: Creation and the Abraham covenant provide foundational traditions.
- Neh 9:9–21: The exodus and wilderness underscore God's ongoing mercy despite sin.
- Neh 9:22–31: The conquest and life in the land introduces a cycle of disobedience alternating with measures of divine discipline and restoration.

The final two historical episodes contain similar structures: God's grace, the people's rebellion, and continuing divine mercy.[131] The appeal at the close of the prayer rests on the history's evidence of God's grace, "you did not make an end of them or forsake them, for you are a gracious and merciful God" (9:31).

Psalm 106 also employs a historical recollection as a basis for confession and plea for aid.[132] The psalm's brief initial declaration that God is good and his steadfast love endures forever (106:1) contrasts with the extended focus on the ancestors' rebellion and sin. The ancestors' sins are concrete and detailed, beginning with rebellion the moment they cross the Red Sea (106:7). Each successive transgression in the wilderness is met with a direct disciplinary response (106:15, 17, 18). Only Moses's intervention prevents their complete destruction (106:23). Nehemiah 9 dwells

---

128. Ibid., 145, 156. He notes that the Levites only redirect actions in Neh 9.
129. Boda, *Praying the Tradition*, 31.
130. Duggan, *Covenant Renewal*, 224.
131. Williamson, *Ezra, Nehemiah*, 308.
132. Ibid., 307. Duggan (*Covenant Renewal*, 227) also compares these prayers.

more fully on God's unreserved care in the wilderness, and sin intrudes only at the construction of the calf at Sinai (Neh 9:18).[133] Only in the land do they experience negative consequences. Furthermore, God's discipline is mediated as he gives the people into the hands of enemies, and he responds in mercy to their suffering.

The history begins with God's first great act of creation placed in parallel with God's election of Abraham and the covenant to give the land to his descendants (Neh 9:6–8).[134] These divine acts conclude with the emphatic declaration, כי צדיק אתה, "for you are righteous." The formula is repeated once more at the conclusion of the prayer: Israel is in great distress but God is righteous (9:33; NRSV "you have been just"). "Covenant" occurs only here with regard to God's pledge of the land, identifying the land as a key concern.[135] The use of covenant also establishes God's commitment to this promise despite evidence to the contrary.[136] "Land" is mentioned fourteen times in the prayer, "four times in conjunction with the promise to the ancestors" (9:8, 15, 23, 36).[137] God creates the land (or "earth," 9:6), makes a covenant to give the land of Canaan to Abraham (9:8), and commands the people to go into the land (9:15). Life in the land is threatened by the people's rebellion, and ultimately hardship in the land is the chief concern of the final petition.

As divine care and provision alternate with episodes of human rebellion, the character of God and the people diverge over the issue of faith-

---

133. Reference to this is delayed until after the law is given in Neh 9:13–14.

134. Rolf Rendtorff, "Nehemiah 9: An Important Witness of Theological Reflection," in *Tehillah le-Moshe: Biblical and Judaic Studies in Honor of Moshe Greenberg*, ed. Mordechai Cogan, Barry L. Eichler, Jeffrey H. Tigay (Winona Lake, IN: Eisenbrauns, 1997), 115. He notes that the history in Ps 106 makes no mention of Abraham and jumps from creation to the exodus. This is the only text that speaks of God "choosing" Abraham. In Isa 41:8–9, the exiles are Abraham's offspring; and in Ezek 33:24, nonexiles claim to be Abraham's offspring. For a discussion on this, see Duggan, *Covenant Renewal*, 202.

135. Moses provides commandments, statutes, and laws but not a covenant. See Blenkinsopp, *Ezra-Nehemiah*, 303.

136. Ibid.

137. Judith H. Newman, "Nehemiah 9 and the Scripturalization of Prayer in the Second Temple Period," in *The Function of Scripture in Early Jewish and Christian Traditions*, ed. Craig A. Evans and James A. Sanders, JSNTSup 154 (Sheffield: Sheffield Academic, 1998), 113.

fulness.[138] In Neh 9:6–15, God's care is free and uninterrupted. God is the covenant maker (9:6–7), the righteous promise keeper (9:8), the God who sees the distress of the ancestors (9:9) and makes a name for himself as he miraculously rescues them from the "presumptuous" pharaoh—a name that "remains to this day" (9:10).[139] God sustains them in the wilderness and provides them with the law by the hand of Moses (9:12–15). Except for the Sabbath, the law is described in four generalized legal terms, "right ordinances and true laws, good statutes and commandments" (9:13).[140] The people are passive recipients of all these gifts.

In the wilderness tradition in Neh 9:16–21, God's acts grow increasingly "qualified by the accounts of rebellion."[141] Yet in this context God remains patient.[142] Once the people are commanded to enter the land, they "acted presumptuously" (a term that previously described Pharaoh and his servants, Exod 18:11); they stiffen their necks, refuse to obey, do not remember God's wonders, and determine to return to their slavery in Egypt (Neh 9:16–17).[143] Yet God remains faithful, "ready to forgive, gracious and merciful, slow to anger and abounding in steadfast love, and you did not forsake them" (9:17). When the people cast an image of a calf, God remains merciful, refusing to forsake them (9:18–19).[144]

---

138. Williamson, *Ezra, Nehemiah*, 313–15; Boda, *Praying the Tradition*, 77.

139. "Saw the distress [עֳנִי] of our ancestors in Egypt" reflects Exod 3:7, "Then the Lord said, 'I have observed the misery [עֳנִי] of my people who are in Egypt'" (Exod 3:7). "Signs and wonders" repeats language from Exod 7:3.

140. Only the Sabbath law is specifically mentioned (Neh 9:14). Ezek 20 also displays a concern for the Sabbath. The legal terminology is used elsewhere only in the historical recitals of 2 Kgs 17:37 and 2 Chr 19:10, which also pairs punishment with disobeying the law.

141. Williamson, *Ezra, Nehemiah*, 313. Boda notes that the prayer reverses the order of the law at Sinai and provision of manna and water. In the Pentateuch, the provisions precede the giving of the law. Additionally, the prayer makes no mention of the rebellion that accompanied these gifts (*Praying the Tradition*, 77).

142. Boda, *Praying the Tradition*, 84–85.

143. The character of the people also contrasts with Abram. God brings him out of Ur, makes a covenant with him, and promises him the land. God takes similar but more wondrous steps to bring the people out of Egypt. They reject the covenant, forget the wonders, and determine to return to slavery.

144. Boda (*Praying the Tradition*, 87) observes that in the Pentateuch, the demarcation between divine patience and divine discipline occurs at Sinai. In Neh 9, it occurs after the conquest of the land.

Despite the wilderness generation's refusal to enter the land, God gives their descendants the same opportunity.[145] Once they are in the land, rebellion does have repercussions as God gives the people into the hands of enemies (Neh 9:22–31). The word "land" clusters in these verses as the people take the land and subdue the people of the land. Its bounty and goodness are described at length, yet delight in God's goodness is immediately followed by rebellion (9:26). Rebellion lacks specificity but is cast as a general rejection of the law and sins against God's ordinances (9:26, 28, 29). Williamson observes that in 9:26–29 the law "can stand virtually alongside God himself: to reject the one is to reject the other (vv 26a, 29), while to return to the one is to return to the other (vv 26b with 29a)."[146] To reject God or the law has consequences for life in the land.

The account clearly reflects the cyclical narrative from Judges (see particularly the proleptic summary in Judg 2:12–18). Three times a cycle of rebellion is described, and three times God hands the people over to their enemies, who make them suffer (Neh 9:26–30). On each occasion the people receive and fail to heed divine and/or prophetic warnings (9:26, 29, 30, 34). In the first two cycles, cries for help gain a reprieve as God sends saviors who deliver them from their oppressors (9:27, 28). The final episode of rebellion and punishment extends to the Babylonian exile as God turns them over to the peoples of the lands (9:30).[147] The cycle interprets the losses and suffering as self-inflicted and suggests that divine punishment seeks repentance from the people, providing a pattern for renewal for the present generation.[148] Penitence now becomes essential for restoration.

The final petition (Neh 9:32–37) unites the themes of covenant and land. It begins with a familiar description of God, "the great and mighty and awesome God, keeping covenant and steadfast love" (9:32).[149] However, the covenant is now contextualized, since the only covenant mentioned is the promise of the land to Abraham. The petitioners confess that

---

145. Ibid., 78.
146. Williamson, *Ezra, Nehemiah*, 316.
147. Ibid., 315.
148. Boda, *Praying the Tradition*, 85, 87. Boda argues this model explains why the people have lost the land. But the prayer only states the people are handed over to the peoples of the land and the current petitioners complain they are slaves in their own land, perhaps suggesting a nonexilic origin.
149. This is nearly identical to the beginning of the prayer in Neh 1:5.

their ancestors failed to serve God in the "land that you set before them" (9:35), leading to the petitioners' condition of being slaves in *their* land, the land of the covenant.[150] Having confessed sin, the assembly now enacts the missing cry for help; their petition that God not let their hardship be small before him (9:32) now awaits divine mercy.

The prayer's narrative contends that God is righteous because he has remained faithful to the covenant, and the people were unrighteous because they were unfaithful.[151] Control of the land is now tied to faithful obedience. The petition appeals to a contradiction between the community's character, their present circumstances, and their expectations of God.[152] Unlike the rebellious ancestors who threw God's law behind them, they are like faithful Abraham, worthy of receiving the promise of the land. They are committed to keeping Torah, which is portrayed as the key to control of the land. They maintain that by distancing themselves from their ancestors' stiff necks, stubborn shoulders, and rebellion, they ought to be able to enjoy the fruit of the land.[153] They immediately make a firm written agreement to keep the law (Neh 9:38). Based on God's great mercy in the past and the renewed commitment to the law, the petitioners now seek to be saved from their oppressive situation. Signing the covenant becomes proof of their loyalty to God, even in adversity.[154] The strategy empowers "the community to take charge of its destiny even as it calls for trust in God."[155]

---

150. Manfred Oeming ("'See, We Are Serving Today' (Nehemiah 9:36): Nehemiah 9 as a Theological Interpretation of the Persian Period," in Lipschits and Oeming, *Persian Period*, 579, 582) maintains that this language is polyvalent. The petitioners are claiming that, unlike the ancestors who refused to be God's servants, they are, in fact, God's servants in the land. The confession and petition therefore express concern about once again rejecting Torah. This reading retains the cohesiveness of the wider book in its view on Persian rule and directs the text toward exclusively religious concerns. It does not account for the prayer's repeated association of foreign rule with sin and discipline and oppression.

151. Boda, *Praying the Tradition*, 63. In Neh 9:8, blessings are extended because Abraham is faithful, but in 9:33 the people are cursed for their wickedness. God remains faithful in both contexts.

152. Williamson, *Ezra, Nehemiah*, 319.

153. Tamara C. Eskenazi, "Nehemiah 9–10: Structure and Significance," *JHebS* 3 (2001): art. 9, pp. 2.14, doi:10.5508/jhs.2001.v3.a9.

154. Ibid., 4.1.

155. Ibid., 3.6.

11.3.3. Social Context, Cultural Capital, and Symbolic Language

Perhaps this prayer began as a communal lament written during a time of military aggression. Yet references to the exile are muted at best. There are no details of deportation, the destruction of Jerusalem or the temple, or life outside the land.[156] According to Judith Newman,

> The reason for the de-emphasis would seem to lie with the author's desire to establish an inalienable claim to the land, a claim writ large in this prayer. How better to establish such a claim than to mitigate the aspect of the Exile having to do with the loss of the land as punishment? Here the punishment for disobedience lies in the fact that the Israelites were put under foreign rule.[157]

However, the exile may not be prominent because the prayer was first composed by those who remained—not by exiles, thus explaining its concern for foreign rule. Adam Welch first posited a northern (but preexilic) origin for the prayer. He cites evidence that includes the reference to the slaying of prophets, which recalls the policy of King Ahab in 1 Kgs 19; the beginning of the catastrophe dated to the Assyrians (Neh 9:32) (which fits the northern kingdom history); the failure to mention the exile and restoration; and silence regarding David and Solomon.[158] Gary Rendsburg and Waldemar Chrostowski also advocate for a northern origin, dating it after the fall of the northern kingdom.[159] Rendsburg suggests that the prayer represents the literary remains of an Israelite community that "continued uninterruptedly in the regions of Samaria and Galilee, regardless of the occupation of their land by Assyrians and Babylonians."[160] Chrostowski

---

156. Judith H. Newman, *Praying by the Book: The Scripturalization of Prayer in Second Temple Judaism*, EJL 14 (Atlanta: Scholars Press, 1999), 99.

157. Ibid., 99–100.

158. Adam C. Welch, "The Source of Nehemiah IX," *ZAW* 47 (1929): 134.

159. Gary A. Rendsburg, "The Northern Origin of Nehemiah 9," *Bib* 72 (1991): 348. He supports this claim through a linguistic analysis and offers eight lexemes that he attributes to a northern context and five Late Biblical Hebrew features that date it to the postexilic period. Williamson ("Concept of Israel in Transition," 152) seems to concur with this context. Waldemar Chrostowski ("Examination of Conscience by God's People as Exemplified in Neh 9:6–37," *BZ* 34 [1990]: 258) notes also the prayer's emphasis on deeds of old.

160. Rendsburg, "Northern Origin of Nehemiah 9," 366.

believes that the prayer "was recited by those who had seen in the domination of foreign rulers the punishment of God against their nation."[161] Its incorporation in Ezra-Nehemiah, a text filled with anxiety over the surrounding communities, suggests an early, closer relationship with those very people, a relationship that involved shared religious practices.

This prayer constructs a (new) master narrative that confesses the nation's history as a traumatic corporate failure. All of God's actions (the covenant with Abraham, the exodus, the laws of Moses, and even his punishments) are deemed good and just, but the disastrous actions of the ancestors are repudiated and condemned. They are responsible for the present community's servitude under foreign rulers. The community's recitation of this history (abetted by extensive reappropriation of religious texts) fosters a sense of inclusion in this national story as a valid explanation of the community's current distress. The corporate responsibility generates a need to rectify the consequences of the ancestors' disobedience.[162]

The linkage of the ancestors' behavior with adversity in the land prompts the current generation to dissociate themselves from those who rebelled and failed to keep the law. The prayer guides the hearers to believe that it is within their power to forge a new path out of their oppressive circumstances. They are faithful, like Abraham, and committed to the law, like Moses. God's unfailing mercy in response to suffering prompts the final plea. The surrounding narrative invites the hearers to go even further, to model their actions after the petitioners who sign an agreement to walk in God's law (Neh 10:29).

The prayer straddles the line between lament and penitential forms. Laments conceive of people devoted to God who beseech God to honor his obligations toward them.[163] This is consistent with the petitioners'

---

161. Chrostowski, "Examination of Conscience," 258. He contends that the prayer's emphasis on deeds of old, its silence about David, and its strong condemnation of the ancestors show affinities with Ezekiel. The prayer "was composed in the circles directly connected with the prophet Ezekiel, perhaps with his disciples and followers." He suggests that Neh 9:6–37 "is a careful interpretation of the prophetic oracle preserved in Ez 20" (259).

162. Newman ("Nehemiah 9," 115) comments, "The purpose of this reappropriation [of biblical texts] … was to make the character praying self-consciously associate him- or herself with the ongoing history of Israel…. Indeed, the people as a whole was constituted in part by shared historical memory, in particular, memories of God's promises and actions on their behalf in the past."

163. Rom-Shiloni, "Socio-ideological Setting," 62.

self-portrayal.[164] In addition, the prayer ends very much like a lament as it describes the desperate straits of the people. Yet the dissonance of their situation and God's goodness is resolved in a way more consonant with penitential prayers. God is declared just, while the ancestors are repeatedly faulted for disobedience and failure to remain loyal to God.[165] However, *only* the ancestors are implicated in this. The present-day petitioners stand innocent of wrongdoing, and remain faithful to God and his covenant as they await divine renewal from a faithful God.[166] The line drawn between past and present resolves these binary expectations of covenant obligations.

Liturgical practices (Torah reading, a formalized covenant) and language surround the confession and affirm its effectiveness. The self-abasement of the confession empowers the dominated community to rectify what the ancestors failed to get right and avert God's wrath. It suggests that vigilance is necessary lest such behavior reoccur and these dire straits continue unabated. The agreement that follows (Neh 10) specifies the necessary commitments to ensure that they can enjoy the fruit of the land. The names of legitimate community officials, Levites, and priests are added to seal the agreement. The added names not only validate the measures but benefit those who carry out such symbolic work—the community will need its priests and Levites to fulfill these functions in its quest to regain its honor and autonomy.

11.3.3.1. Ritual, Legitimation, and the Creation of Boundaries

Through a recitation of history and confession, the penitential prayer in Neh 9 disconnects the community from a past rebellious identity and provides the motivation for the rite in Neh 10 that will reincorporate them into a new social order. The new identity the ritual imposes creates certain

---

164. Chrostowski ("Examination of Conscience," 255) suggests that 9:33–34, which now read, "we have *acted wickedly*; our kings, our officials, our priests, and our ancestors have not kept your law," originally read, "we *condemn* our kings, our officials, our priests...." This alternative translation would accurately reflect the *hiphil* form of the verb and account for the definite direct object marker that precedes "kings" in the following line. He argues that the standard translation assumes that the verb's meaning reflects a Late Biblical Hebrew usage, and the definite direct object marker is understood as an indicator of the nominative case.

165. Rom-Shiloni, "Socio-ideological Setting," 65.

166. Ibid., 60.

limits—"to do what it is one's essence to do, and not something else."[167] If one is to regain the land, one must be part of the community that observes the Sabbath, supports the cult, and remains distinct from those labeled foreign (9:2; 10:31). This is ceremonially confirmed as they (literally) "cut the agreement" and write the names of the leadership on the sealed document (9:38).

As a solemn act of categorization, ritual does not constitute a new group but changes the perception of the social order. "The categories according to which a group envisages itself, and according to which it represents itself and its specific reality, contribute to the reality of this group."[168] The community's defining criteria of land, religion, and a myth of a common origin facilitate ethnic maintenance. The prayer's creation of a shared cultural trauma now reinforces these criteria. Both insiders and outsiders are hindered from crossing the established boundary. In deference to solidarity, individual economic prosperity is sacrificed by curtailing trade on the Sabbath and forbidding the construction of familial ties with foreigners.

An effective ritual requires the right social conditions for people to grant it recognition, and the right liturgical conditions that communicate that those acting do so not on their own authority but in their capacity as delegates.[169] In these chapters, individual leaders are nearly invisible, and the community acts as one to proclaim their commitment to the law, "*we* make a firm agreement," and on the sealed document are the names of "*our* officials, *our* Levites, and *our* priests" (Neh 9:38). The names of officials on the written agreement add legitimation as they consent to the community's commitments.[170] The right actions begin with the reading of Torah and confession and end with written documents and adherence to codified law. The literary aspects of these rituals requires scribes to document the community's newly incorporated status. The record of these

---

167. Bourdieu, "Rites as Acts of Institution," in *Honor and Grace in Anthropology*, ed. J. G. Peristiany and Julian Pitt-Rivers, trans. Roger Just (Cambridge: Cambridge University Press, 1992), 83. For example, noblemen must act nobly in keeping with their social position.

168. Bourdieu, *Language and Symbolic Power*, 133.

169. Ibid., 115. Bourdieu further states, "The symbolic efficacy of the ritual will vary … according to the degree to which the people for whom the ritual is performed are more or less prepared, or more or less disposed, to receive it" (125).

170. The community's leadership in these chapters has been noted by numerous scholars; see esp. Eskenazi, *In an Age of Prose*, 97–104.

measures benefits those who carry out such symbolic work as it testifies to their value in the community's quest to regain its honor and autonomy.

In these chapters, the community employs ritual to reshape their cultural environment.[171] The confession develops a sense of crisis resolved by the covenant agreement in Neh 10. The narrative of trauma represents the victims narrowly—as the storytellers' own ancestors—and creates a sense of self-pity that Jeffrey Alexander states "reinforces rather than mitigates ... particularistic hatreds ... earlier hatreds are reproduced, not overcome."[172] Over time the religious practices enumerated in Neh 10 solidify the community's boundaries through the acquisition of lasting predispositions— the basis for defining others as foreign. Bourdieu states that this involves naturalizing difference and turning it into second nature through inculcation and incorporation as a set of habits.[173] The practice of Sabbath (given prominence in both the prayer and the agreement [9:14; 10:31]) and the regularity of the offerings enumerated in 10:32–39 inculcate practices that foster a sense of distinction that naturalizes difference from nonparticipants. Claims about the identity and character of the community are now ritually constituted. This written account of the community's agreement now provides a basis for the same commitments for the readers.

11.3.3.2. Cultural Production and the Field of Power

This prayer provides a countervision of the current political and economic situation for an economically deprived community. Out of a sense of solidarity with the economically and culturally dominated classes, cultural producers use their skills and "the power conferred on them, especially in periods of crisis, to mobilize the potential strength of the dominated classes and subvert the order prevailing in the field of power."[174] The offer contained in this prayer coincides with a sense of honor associated with disprivileged classes. It rests on "some guaranteed promise for the

---

171. Bell, *Ritual*, 76.
172. Jeffrey C. Alexander, *Trauma: A Social Theory* (Malden, MA: Polity, 2012), Kindle edition, 2147–50.
173. Bourdieu, *Language and Symbolic Power*, 85.
174. Bourdieu, *Field of Cultural Production*, 44. Bourdieu states that the "homologies between the fundamental opposition which gives the [cultural] field its structure and the oppositions structuring the field of power and the field of class relations" provide a basis for alliances.

future.... What they cannot claim to *be*, they replace by the worth of that which they will one day *become*."[175] However, the prayer's logic also affirms the more economically enfranchised belief that material wealth, enjoying the fruit of the land, is a sign of divine reward for virtuous human action.[176] This makes foreign subjugation problematic, and the prayer constructs it as shameful in both overt and subtle ways. Nehemiah 9:6 begins, "you are the Lord, you alone," the same language used by Hezekiah when faced with being overpowered by the Assyrians (2 Kgs 19:15, 19).[177] Every act of divine punishment is linked to foreign rule. It culminates with the cry, "we are in great distress," because of the power of the kings God has set over them (Neh 9:37). The presence of foreigners in the land remains a constant reminder of the consequences of failure to obey the law; their removal signals forgiveness. In contrast to the more benign perception of foreign rule elsewhere in Ezra and Nehemiah, here there is little room for accommodation. Only with the removal of foreign rule will the current generation be sure of once again being in God's good graces, creating a motivation for ethnic boundaries.

The prayer champions a transformation of the people from a passive, subordinate "object" to an empowered community regaining control over its homeland.[178] It reasons that religious obedience will result in the removal of foreign rule. YHWH now offers not only forgiveness but independence. This gives greater significance to the priests and Levites as they offer the community a path to exchange shame for guilt, and servitude for autonomy. Coincidentally, obedience demands faithful maintenance of the temple and the priests and Levites who serve there (Neh 10:32–39).

Religious texts are not the creation of a disinterested, isolated religious scholar, but neither are they consciously produced with entirely external and material interests at heart.[179] Bourdieu argues that external influences challenge the autonomy of cultural producers, compelling them to become subject to ordinary laws of the economic field.[180] The fallow-year law and

---

175. Max Weber, *Economy and Society: An Outline of Interpretive Sociology* ed. Guenther Roth and Claus Wittich, trans. Ephraim Fischoff, 2 vols. (Berkeley: University of California Press, 1978), 2:490.
176. Ibid., 491.
177. Boda, *Praying the Tradition*, 94.
178. Smith, "Politics of Culture," 720.
179. Bourdieu, *Field of Cultural Production*, 34.
180. The newly defined community requires separation from "the peoples of the

debt forgiveness (Neh 10:31b) generate support for the community from the economically oppressed and thereby undergird community cohesion.[181] Hefty support for the temple is required, specifically obligating offerings of "our" fruits and livestock (10:35–36), commodities controlled by the king in 9:36–37.[182] These measures would shift economic power to the religious leadership of the community, who could then ostensibly wield it to offset the power held by those deemed outsiders. Bourdieu comments, "The most disputed frontier of all is the one which separates the field of cultural production and the field of power."[183] In this prayer, the holders of religious capital fight to legitimate their religious traditions and are drawn into a debate over the economy of the community. In so doing they stand toe-to-toe against the Persian Empire.

Boundaries that limit individual economic advancement and increase commitments for the temple would have to appeal to issues of great value, such as identity. Thus foreign rule is framed as "a fundamental threat to their sense of who they are, where they came from, and where they want to go."[184] The confession removes shame and forges a new sense of honor and destiny through the covenant ceremony. It provides a grand vision of reclaiming the land achieved by the community's own initiative in making the agreement. That this portrait of the community's future is made with confession, ritual, and signed agreements suggests that the argument needed to be compelling to contend with the realities of larger forces.

---

lands" (Neh 10:28, 30). The Sabbath law also reinforces this boundary: "and if the peoples of the land bring in merchandise or any grain on the sabbath day to sell, we will not buy it from them on the sabbath or on a holy day" (10:31).

181. "We will forego the crops of the seventh year and the exaction of every debt" (Neh 10:31). Duggan (*Covenant Renewal*, 288) also recognizes the unifying effect of these laws.

182. Ibid., 289.

183. Bourdieu, *Field of Cultural Production*, 42.

184. Alexander, "Theory of Cultural Trauma," 10.

12
Ezra 7–10: (De-)Constructing a Community

A plain reading of Ezra 7–10 places Ezra's arrival in 458 BCE under Artaxerxes I, prior to Nehemiah. However, as Hoglund points out, scholars question this on two counts. The dating would have the missions of Ezra and Nehemiah overlap (Nehemiah was most likely governor from 445 to 433 BCE), but the narrative places them together on only two occasions (Neh 8:2 and 12:36), both of which appear to be harmonistic insertions.[1] In addition, Nehemiah returns to address the problem of intermarriage without reference to an earlier reform by Ezra (Neh 13:23–29). Thus some are inclined to date Ezra to the reign of Artaxerxes II (405–359 BCE). However, the community structure portrayed in these chapters lacks the priestly led hierarchical structure and temple rituals one might associate with this later date. Perhaps the accounts of Ezra and Nehemiah represent divergent but contemporary traditions and only later were incorporated into a historical sequence. Together the two narratives imagine the same community tackling issues of self-definition but with significantly different methods and leadership.

These chapters expound one of the most troubling social rearrangements in the Hebrew Bible: the divorce and removal of wives with their children. This action is deemed a necessary purification to avert a grave danger to the Judean community's identity. Ethnicity, expressed as the "the holy seed" (9:2), is understood as the determining factor for inclusion or expulsion. Ritual and religious purity language permeate the text as it gives shape to the ethnic representation of the community. We will begin with a brief overview of the literary character of these chapters prior to treating how symbolic language operates in this text.

---

1. Hoglund, *Achaemenid Imperial Administration*, 43. See also Clines, *Ezra, Nehemiah, Esther*, 16–17; and Williamson, *Ezra, Nehemiah*, xliv, 368.

12.1. The Literary Composition of Ezra 7–10

Ezra 7–10 introduces Ezra into the ongoing narrative of the restoration of Jerusalem. It begins simply, "Now after these things" (Ezra 7:1a NASB), following the account of the temple's construction during the reign of Darius. This suggests that Ezra's arrival is the next formative step in the restoration. However, as Williamson notes, this leaps over approximately fifty-seven years until Ezra arrives in the seventh year of the reign of Artaxerxes I (465–425 BCE).[2] The narrative then recounts events spaced out over the course of a single year. It begins in the first month of the seventh year of King Artaxerxes (7:8) and ends with actions taken on the first day of the first month of the following year (10:17). Within that time frame, the preparations for the journey to Jerusalem are recounted over nearly two chapters, but the five-month journey is summarized in two short verses.[3] Likewise, once Ezra arrives, additional spans of several months are passed over in silence.[4] The schematic nature of this account suggests that its primary purpose is to create a particular perception of the past in order to validate social, religious, or political arrangements in the author's present.

In brief, after Ezra gathers Levites from the place of Casiphia, he travels with others to Jerusalem carrying gifts for the beautification of the temple. He holds a mandate from the king to appoint judges and to teach the law of his God and to enforce the law of God and king. Upon arrival in the fifth month, he presents the money and gifts to the temple priests and the company of travelers offer burnt offerings (Ezra 8:33–35). If Neh 8 is placed here, then in the seventh month he reads the law to the community, and they celebrate the Festival of Booths. In the ninth month, leaders approach Ezra to inform him of the mixed marriages, which, all involved agree, is a transgression of the law. A prayer of repentance follows (Ezra 9:6–15), and three days later the people assemble (10:7–9) and are ordered to divorce foreign wives. The decree is not easily enacted, and a committee of leaders is appointed to "investigate

---

2. Williamson, *Ezra, Nehemiah*, 91.

3. "Then we left the river Ahava on the twelfth day of the first month, to go to Jerusalem; the hand of our God was upon us, and he delivered us from the hand of the enemy and from ambushes along the way. We came to Jerusalem and remained there three days" (Ezra 8:31–32).

4. These time spans involve intervals between the fifth and seventh months, the seventh and ninth months, and the first month of the following year.

the matter" (10:16 NASB). The account ends with a list of those who married foreign wives.

These chapters, particularly Ezra 7–8, contain a variety of literary styles and evidence of editorial activity. There is a mixture of first-person and third-person narrative into which is inserted a rescript from Artaxerxes in Aramaic (7:12–26), a list of returnees (8:1–14), a penitential prayer (9:6–15), and a second list of men associated with the marriage infraction (10:20–43). In addition, it is highly likely that the ceremonial reading of the law and the Festival of Booths that stand now in Neh 8 originally followed Ezra 8.[5] It provides a fitting conclusion for the arrival of the scribe who came to teach the law of God. However, it provides no clear motivation for the divorce measures in Ezra 10. With its removal, the divorces are initiated unprompted by leaders of the community who seem to already know the law that Ezra was to teach when he arrived. The addition of the prayer in Ezra 9 now provides explicit motivation for these actions. The book concludes with a garbled final verse, making it difficult to establish the actual outcome of the judicial decision.[6]

Literary Forms in Narrative Sequence (Ezra 7–10)

7:1–10	third-person narrative: Ezra's lineage and travel to Jerusalem
7:11–26	Aramaic letter of Artaxerxes commissioning Ezra
7:27–28	first-person narrative: a prayer of thanks
8:1–14	list of returnees
8:15–32	first-person narrative: gathering the Levites of Casiphia
8:33–36	third-person narrative: delivering goods and sacrifices at temple
9:1–5	first-person narrative: officials report mixed marriages to Ezra
9:6–15	first-person penitential prayer

---

5. Jacob Wright ("Writing the Restoration," 27 n. 87) argues against this, noting especially that "the Ezra of Nehemiah 8 fully neglects the Altar and the Temple. The Ezra of Ezra 7–8, in contrast, is completely focused on the Altar and Temple." For his evaluation of the transposition arguments see his monograph *Rebuilding Identity*, 321–30.

6. For a careful analysis of the compositional development of these chapters see Pakkala, *Ezra the Scribe*.

10:1–19   third-person narrative: actions taken by assembly
10:20–43   list of offending families
10:44   third-person concluding statement

The editorial process continues to be a subject of debate, yet identifying the interests behind various editorial insertions hint at changing social contexts or competing ideologies during the Persian period. In Pakkala's diachronic evaluation of these chapters, he argues for four major stages of editorial activity in Ezra 7–10 and Neh 8. He believes that the original text of Ezra 7–8 began with a simple introduction of Ezra the scribe, a description of his departure from Babylon, and his arrival in Jerusalem.[7] This was heavily edited and expanded in numerous stages.[8] He suggests that Ezra's mission was to teach Torah, and intermarriage provided a serious example of the consequences of neglecting the law but was not the main issue.[9] Ezra's prayer (Ezra 9:6–15) then interprets the Ezra story using Deuteronomistic conceptions and raises mixed marriages to a more prominent role. Pakkala identifies further additions by golah editors in Ezra 9:4 and 10:6–8 that represent a changed self-understanding: Israel now consists only of returned exiles.[10] Levitical editors, for whom intermarriage ceased to be a central issue, added a final update in which priests and Levites were assigned key roles in the account. In 10:5, they lead the community in dissolving mixed marriages but also in taking foreign wives. The expansions added drama to Ezra's journey and suggest to Pakkala that "the author

---

7. Ibid., 74. Pakkala posits the following original text from Ezra 7: "In the reign of King Artaxerxes of Persia, Ezra son of Seraiah (Ezra 7:1) went up from Babylonia. He was a scribe skilled in the law of Moses that the LORD the God of Israel had given (Ezra 7:6). He came to Jerusalem in the fifth month, which was in the seventh year of the king (Ezra 7:8)."

8. Ibid., 73. See also Wright, *Rebuilding Identity*, 256. He maintains that the text was composed during Hellenistic times and therefore provides no information about events in the fourth century BCE.

9. Juha Pakkala, "Intermarriage and Group Identity in the Ezra Tradition (Ezra 7–10 and Nehemiah 8)," in *Mixed Marriages: Intermarriage and Group Identity in the Second Temple Period*, ed. Christian Frevel, LHBOTS 547 (New York: T&T Clark, 2011), 82.

10. Ibid., 83, 85. Pakkala suggests that perhaps later generations would have identified with the exiles to the point of assuming the entire community was from the exile (87).

regarded Ezra as a great hero."[11] Whether or not Pakkala's reconstruction is entirely correct, his analysis does suggest that editors with different concerns but a shared respect for Ezra contributed to the account as we now have it.[12]

12.2. Ezra 7: The Commission of Ezra, the Priest and Scribe

Ezra is introduced with a priestly lineage (Ezra 7:1b–5) that links him to Aaron and establishes his ancestral roots in the land.[13] Perhaps Ezra is being written into the influential Zadokite priesthood (7:2). Yet when his lineage is compared with the list of priests in 1 Chr 5:27–41, scholars have noted that Ezra lacks a series of names most closely associated with the Zadokites.[14] Alice Hunt contends that the list "seems intentionally to avoid, or at least to be unconcerned with, priests known from the deuteronomistic historian's accounts."[15]

Some believe that the genealogy indicates that Ezra was a high priest. Mark Leuchter observes that Ezra is unmistakably portrayed as a priest of consequence; in these books only he appears to hold the pedigree and influence of a high priest. Yet Ezra is never called "high priest," and "upon reaching Jerusalem there is little to point to Ezra's incorporation into the

---

11. Ibid., 75.
12. Ralf Rothenbusch suggests that Neh 8 originally fell after Ezra 10, providing a climax to the book. He also argues that Ezra 9–10 is the oldest section and believes that those chapters originally made no mention of Ezra. See Ralf Rothenbusch, "The Question of Mixed Marriages between the Poles of Diaspora and Homeland: Observations in Ezra-Nehemiah," in Frevel, *Mixed Marriages*, 67.
13. Gary N. Knoppers, "Ethnicity, Genealogy, Geography, and Change: The Judean Communities of Babylon and Jerusalem in the Story of Ezra," in *Community Identity in Judean Historiography*, ed. Gary N. Knoppers and Kenneth A. Ristau (Winona Lake, IN: Eisenbrauns, 2009), 151. The genealogy is similar to 1 Chr 6:3–8, 12–14 (5:29–36, 38–40 MT). However, if Ezra dates to 457 BCE, his father cannot have been the Seraiah who was high priest at the fall of Jerusalem in 587 BCE. See Williamson, *Ezra, Nehemiah*, 91. This genealogy is likely composed by a later editor.
14. Alice Hunt, *Missing Priests: The Zadokites in Tradition and History*, LHBOTS 452 (New York: T&T Clark, 2006), 101.
15. Ibid. Hunt suggests that the Zadokite priestly line is a postexilic development and contends that if there had been a dominant Zadokite priesthood, it would be more apparent in the biblical literature (123). Her argument has found little support among other scholars.

active temple priesthood."[16] His reading of Torah occurs beyond the precincts of the temple.[17] He is missing from any other biblical list of priest or high priest.[18] Williamson finds it "inexplicable that [the editor] should either have omitted Ezra from the list of high priests in Neh 12:10–11 or that he should not have included Jeshua the high priest … at this point [in Ezra]" had he intended to claim Ezra as a high priest.[19] Blenkinsopp finds the pedigree improbable but suggests that it "is a fiction designed to convey the message that Ezra's function with respect to the law and the cult continued that of the preexilic priesthood."[20] Pakkala suggests that the editor had a high regard for Aaronide priests and notes that in the exilic families listed in the following chapter, the priestly lines are listed prior to the Davidic (8:2).[21] Knoppers states,

> The point of the genealogist is … unmistakable. The priestly pedigree of Ezra was as strong as that of any of the high priests of Judah. The fact that Ezra's particular family line had been absent from the land for several generations had no negative bearing on his suitability for assuming a position of leadership in his homeland. In the context of the work, his priestly training, scribal expertise and exilic pedigree are all presented as positives.[22]

Knoppers's assessment indicates that providing an extensive (and probably fictitious) lineage was added for polemical reasons and, as Hunt has suggested, developing lineages was an expedient method of legitima-

---

16. Mark Leuchter, "Ezra's Mission and the Levites of Casiphia," in Knoppers and Ristau, *Community Identity in Judean Historiography*, 175. Leuchter assumes that the Zadokites were a powerful priesthood in the Second Temple era (176).

17. Ibid., 176.

18. Hunt, *Missing Priests*, 100.

19. Williamson, *Ezra, Nehemiah*, 91.

20. Blenkinsopp, *Ezra-Nehemiah*, 136.

21. Pakkala, *Ezra the Scribe*, 79. He comments, "The reference to the Davidic line implies that the royal line still had a role in the Israelite society, although its placement after the priestly line and the lack of any prominent figure … suggest political insignificance."

22. Gary Knoppers, "Exile, Return, and Diaspora: Expatriates and Repatriates in Late Biblical Literature," in *Texts, Contexts and Readings in Postexilic Literature: Explorations into Historiography and Identity Negotiation in Hebrew Bible and Related Texts*, ed. Louis Jonker, FAT 2/53 (Tübingen: Mohr Siebeck, 2011), 40. Knoppers charts priestly genealogies found in 1 Chr 5, Josephus, and Neh 12:10–11, 22; and Ezra's is second only in length to the list in 1 Chronicles.

tion to validate efforts to create a new social order.[23] The lineage may validate Ezra in face of questions regarding his qualifications, as Knoppers suggests, or, conversely, a priestly lineage for the esteemed Ezra validates the priesthood, particularly for those priestly houses descended from families in exile. In the future, those within these priestly lines can rightfully execute functions similar to Ezra. This lineage may also reflect "a scribal assault on Zadokite exclusivity" similar to that identified by Leuchter in Deuteronomy.[24] In this case the incorporation of Ezra into this lineage subordinates the priestly program to the theology and agenda of the Ezra narrative—most likely representing the view of scribes and Levites.[25]

Having established his priestly lineage, the narrative begins with Ezra the *scribe*, whose skill in the law of Moses results in "the hand of the LORD his God [being] upon him" (Ezra 7:6). Twice in 7:6–10 the divine hand of favor is paired with Ezra as scribe, and in 7:6 God's care explains why the king responds favorably to all of Ezra's requests. Ezra 7:9–10 reiterates this same judgment, and the grammar suggests that divine favor is extended in response to scribal skill. Ezra came to Jerusalem, "for [כ] the gracious hand of his God was upon him. For [כ] Ezra had set his heart to study [to seek] the law of the Lord, and to do it, and to teach the statutes and ordinances in Israel." Ezra's exceptional skill in Torah leads to God's favor manifest in royal benevolence and a successful journey to Jerusalem.

Despite the narratorial claim that the king gives Ezra all he asks for (Ezra 7:6), there is no record of Ezra's request (unlike the account of Nehemiah). Indeed, if one compares Ezra's purpose for the return (7:10) with the royal letter, the king appears to have clearer reasons for the return than Ezra—including lavish provisions for the temple! Ezra's commission goes well beyond "teaching and doing the statutes and ordinances of Israel." The king delegates to Ezra imperial responsibilities and power as he gives him access to the provincial treasury and the right to appoint judges and

---

23. Hunt, *Missing Priests*, 190. Hunt identifies the combined effects of commercialization, trade issues, empire shifts, and life upheavals as possible sources of rapid change.

24. Mark Leuchter, "Zadokites, Deuteronomists, and the Exilic Debate over Scribal Authority," *JHebS* 7 (2007): art. 10, p. 12, doi:10.5508/jhs.2007.v7.a10.

25. Leuchter (ibid., 7) makes a similar argument with regard to written texts: "These groups were responsive, feeding off of each other's earlier accomplishments for the sake of advancing their specific ideologies to the exclusion of the other, often making overt references to each other's written texts, but primarily for the purposes of subordination or condemnation."

enforce the law in keeping with his own God. Ezra gives thanks that God put this "in the heart of the king" (7:27–28). His language suggests that the king is unaware of the divine inspiration that leads him to deputize Ezra and provide contributions for the journey. The king plays a more limited role than Cyrus in 1:2. He is a means to carry out the divine will—not a partner with God.

The Nehemiah memoir also attributes royal benevolence to divine inspiration. "And the king granted them to me because the good hand of my God was on *me*" (Neh 2:8c). Unlike the royal decree in Ezra 1, or the implied request in Ezra 7, Nehemiah's personal request is essential to the royal bequest. The language in Nehemiah is strikingly similar to Ezra 7:6.[26] However, the narrative suggests uncertainty about the royal response. Nehemiah's personal commitment to the people of Yehud, his close personal relationship with the monarch (Neh 1:11), and his boldness in making the request combine to suggest that it is Nehemiah's *own character and actions* that garner royal support. Each account makes the doxic assumption that kings are divinely inspired—that favorable decrees have a divine origin. However, each expresses the nature of this relationship among God, emperor, and exiles in a way uniquely suited to the particular concerns of the author.

In Ezra 7, the study of Torah is essential to gain divine and royal support. Ezra does not seek the monarch's permission like Nehemiah, nor does a royal edict prompt his decision to make the journey. Rather, the king's letter follows logically after Ezra's decision to journey to Jerusalem (Ezra 7:6). Commitment to Torah translates into divine favor, a royal grant, and a successful outcome. Indeed, the hand of God alone is sufficient protection when Ezra, the scribe of the Torah, "goes up" (aliyah) bearing gifts to Jerusalem.

Artaxerxes's letter (Ezra 7:12–26) is primarily concerned with gifts and financial support for the temple (7:15–23), sharing themes of the temple and aliyah found in Ezra 1–6.[27] Ezra is to bring with him "any of the people of Israel or their priests or Levites in my kingdom who freely offers to go to Jerusalem" (7:13; cf. 1:3). The rescript employs incredible numbers (e.g., 100 talents of silver).[28] In fact, "most of the royal edict consists of an

---

26. Williamson, *Ezra, Nehemiah*, 92.
27. Pakkala, *Ezra the Scribe*, 28.
28. Knoppers ("Exile, Return, and Diaspora," 51) notes that according to Herodotus the royal income from the entire province was 350 talents of silver annually.

itemization of all the extravagant gifts, grants and concessions the imperial monarch bestows upon the Jerusalem shrine" (cf. 1:6–7).[29] The tendency to exaggerate can be seen even in the royal order that forbids taxing temple personnel (7:23–24), which has little to do with Ezra's mission and goes beyond what may be realistically expected.[30] However, Ezra is given two other duties to discharge unique to this rescript. He is ordered "to make inquiries about Judah and Jerusalem according to the law of your God, which is in your hand" (7:14), and to appoint judges and magistrates who will judge all the people of the province (7:25). These duties also reflect a high level of exaggeration. The judges and magistrates "may judge all the people in the province Beyond the River who know the laws of your God" (7:25), and Ezra is given great power to enforce his laws: death, banishment, confiscation, and imprisonment (7:26).

The rescript is filled with religious terminology, and the list of offerings in 7:17 corresponds to other biblical lists (Num 29; 1 Chr 29:21), including Ezra 6:9, 16–18, and 8:35. Pakkala argues that it contains an Aramaic dialect more common in Palestine than in the royal capital.[31] It is poorly integrated into the surrounding material: its interest in the temple is completely absent from Ezra 9–10, and despite the double reference to Ezra as priest, he performs no priestly functions in the earliest portions of the text or in Ezra 9–10.[32] The addition of 7:25–26 also exaggerates Ezra's administrative role and significance. He is the supreme judge of the province, personally appointed by the king, and his counselors are "responsible for instating the law and the judges in the satrapy."[33] This does not correspond to his localized actions that follow. This editorial activity buries

---

29. Ibid., 50.
30. Pakkala, *Ezra the Scribe*, 36.
31. Ibid., 36, 47–50. He contends that the rescript was composed in the late Persian period after the reign of Artaxerxes and does not derive from the Achaemenid administration but from a Judean source (40–42). The letter provides no reason why the king should have intervened in the local affairs of this small region, leading Pakkala to suggest that there was no imperial authorization for Ezra's mission. This claim counters the theory of imperial authorization put forth by Peter Frei (48, 75). Others are less inclined to treat the entire rescript as a late addition. Blenkinsopp (*Ezra-Nehemiah*, 147), for example, finds Ezra's mission credible and argues that restoring the Jerusalem cult and instituting a firm basis for Jewish law would promote peace and stability in the province. See also Knoppers, "Exile, Return, and Diaspora," 51 n. 79.
32. Pakkala, *Ezra the Scribe*, 42.
33. Ibid., 38.

Ezra's more modest role as a scribe in the service of grander priestly and political interests in the final text of Ezra 7–8.[34]

The rescript is followed by a prayer (Ezra 7:27–28) that thanks God for prompting the king to beautify the temple and for extending toward Ezra "steadfast love before the king and his counselors, and before all the king's mighty officers" (7:28). The prayer draws attention once again to Ezra's close connection with king and Deity. As Ezra gathers the *leaders* (ראשים) to go up with him, the prayer leads easily into the list of "their family *heads*" (ראשי אבתיהם, lit. "heads of their fathers").[35]

12.3. Ezra 8: The Role of Levites

Ezra 8:1–14 lists by patronym those who "went up" to Jerusalem. Beginning with Parosh (8:3), the sequence of twelve family names are also contained in the longer list of Ezra 2, and many occur in the same order.[36] This repetition of exactly twelve patronyms may indicate an ideological motive for this list, perhaps indicating completeness or patterning Ezra's journey after the twelve tribes of the exodus.[37] However, while the list in Ezra 2 concludes with priests and temple personnel, Ezra 8 gives primacy to priestly names, even before Hattush of the house of David (8:2).[38]

Ezra 7:7 includes Levites among those who traveled with Ezra from Babylon. Yet in this first-person account, Ezra reports that he delays the

---

34. Ibid. He suggests recognizing the secondary nature of Ezra as priest removes problems plaguing the composition, e.g., the contrast between Ezra the priest in these chapters and Ezra the scribe in Ezra 9–10 (74).

35. Pakkala (*Ezra the Scribe*, 56) notes that the change from "heads" to "heads of their fathers" may signal two sources. "Heads of the fathers" occurs regularly in Ezra 1–6, but in Ezra 8–10 "heads" is used exclusively, except here (8:1) and in 10:16.

36. Parosh, Pahath-moab, Zattu, and the last five names in 8:10–14 follow the same order as the names in 2:10–14. Nearly all of them also recur in Neh 10:14–16 as signatories of the covenant.

37. Pakkala, *Ezra the Scribe*, 57. Other connections to the exodus include Ezra's lineage linking him to Aaron, the date for the outset of the journey from Ahava, "the twelfth day of the first month" (8:31), coincides with Passover, which corresponds with the exodus (Exod 12:1–2; Num 9:1–3). The hand of God on Ezra (7:6, 9, 28; 8:18, 22) alludes to the strong hand of God that accompanied the Israelites out of Egypt (Exod 13:3, 14). Blenkinsopp (*Ezra-Nehemiah*, 139) suggests that the overall text creates an image of a "new beginning, a replica of the first exodus to be followed, then as now, by the giving of the law."

38. Blenkinsopp, *Ezra-Nehemiah*, 161.

journey to take inventory at the river Ahava and discovers he has no Levites (8:15). To rectify this, he sends emissaries to the priest Iddo at Casiphia (8:16), and they obtain thirty-eight Levites to accompany him.[39] The recruits are from the Levitical houses of Mahli and Merari (Ezra 8:18–19), which are also listed in Numbers, and their descendants are identified in Num 10:17 as those who carried the tabernacle.[40] The search process is couched in terms of wisdom. Emissaries to Ahava are noted for their discernment (מבינים, 8:16), and due to divine guidance they return with Sherebiah, a man of discretion or insight (שכל, 8:18). Williamson suggests that the attention to Levites at this point may have been dictated by a desire to create further connections with the original exodus, when Levites carry the tabernacle and its furnishings.[41] Leuchter suggests that finding Levites of Casiphia "after his departure allows them to qualify as Levites consecrated during the ritualized second period of wilderness wandering."[42]

All these narrative details (the halt in the journey, exodus allusions, the wise emissaries, divine guidance, and the understanding attributed to Sherebiah) coalesce to frame Levites as essential to Ezra's program and thus to anticipate their importance for the community. Their contingent of two hundred and twenty temple servants "whom David and his officials had set apart to attend the Levites" (Ezra 8:20) heightens their prestige—it is hardly a description of minor temple functionaries needed to carry temple equipment. Three of the Levites are named, and two of those play prominent roles elsewhere in Ezra-Nehemiah. Sherebiah and Hashabiah are among the priests who transport the temple gifts (Ezra 8:24), lead the confession in Neh 9 (9:5), sign the covenant in Neh 10 (10:11–12), and lead the Levites (12:24).[43] Furthermore, Sherebiah assists in the teaching

---

39. Five of these emissary names also occur in the list of those who married outside the community (Ezra 10), and Meshullam is named as an opponent of Ezra's measures (10:15); see Blenkinsopp, *Ezra-Nehemiah*, 165. The list of eleven emissaries may contain dittography. It consists of Eliezer, Ariel, Shemaiah, Elnathan, Jarib, Elnathan, Nathan, Zechariah, and Meshullam, who were leaders, and Joiarib and Elnathan (Ezra 8:16). The name "Elnathan" occurs three times, and Jarib and Joiarib may be the same as well.

40. Num 3:17, 20, 33–36; 26:57–58.

41. Num 1:50–51. See Williamson, *Ezra, Nehemiah*, 116.

42. Leuchter, "Ezra's Mission," 179.

43. Hashabiah is likely referenced in Neh 9:5 among the Levites leading the confession, although the name there is "Hashabneiah." This Hashabiah, the *Levite*, should not be confused with the Hashabiah of the house of *Israel* who is listed among those

of Torah (8:7). The concentrated attention upon Levites as crucial members of *Ezra's* entourage now links Levitical legitimacy to Ezra and to an exilic heritage.

Ezra 8:21–23 describes arrangements for the safe transport of temple gifts and introduces the text's only doubt about a successful journey. *Seeking* (בקשׁ) God recurs three times in these three verses, signaling appropriate appeals to God as essential to success. Ezra declares a fast so "that we might humble ourselves before our God, to *seek* of Him a straight way, for us" (Ezra 8:21 JPSV). In 8:22, Ezra admits he was too ashamed to ask the king for soldiers and cavalry to protect them (8:22) "because we had spoken unto the king, saying: 'The hand of our God is upon all them that *seek* Him, for good'" (8:22 JPSV). In 8:23, he states, once again, that they fasted and *sought* (NASB) God. The proper rituals, fasting and humbling themselves, are enacted to ensure divine help. At the conclusion of the entire section, Ezra confirms, "the hand of our God was upon us, and he delivered us from the hand of the enemy and from ambushes along the way" (8:31). Williamson suggests that "the initial unlikelihood of success in the venture" highlights the providence of God.[44] The refusal of a military escort establishes that ritualized seeking of divine aid as carried out by Ezra's company can ensure protection equal to a Persian guard.

In Ezra 8:24–34, Ezra sets apart twelve priests (earlier and elsewhere identified as Levites) and carefully measures money and implements for the temple into their hands to transport to the temple. (If the hundred talents of silver in Artaxerxes's rescript is an exaggeration [7:22], this makes the 650 talents of silver and 100 talents of gold listed here staggering!) This list reflects, on a smaller scale, the many temple vessels and bowls familiar from the inventory in 1:9–11. Ezra advises the priests that they are holy, as are the vessels, and declares the gold and silver a freewill offering to the Lord. He warns them to guard and keep the goods until they are once again weighed out "before the chief priests and the Levites and the heads of families in Israel at Jerusalem, within the chambers of the house of the Lord" (8:29). Upon arrival, the valuables are once again carefully weighed out to the (named) priests and Levites who receive delivery (8:33). The description takes on a ritual-like quality as those assigned to carry materi-

---

with foreign wives (Ezra 10:25) and who aided the construction of the wall and was ruler "of half the district of Keila" (Neh 3:17). Levites are consistently grouped separately and identified separately from the laity in Israel.

44. Williamson, *Ezra, Nehemiah*, 123.

als are "set apart" or "separated" from others (8:24), items are inventoried, and priests and vessels are declared holy. Then Ezra issues a command to keep all safe until arrival. The journey (8:31–32) becomes a cipher for the transition of these holy items from Babylon to active service in the temple. The actions and commands surround and safeguard the holy priests, holy vessels, and freewill offerings for YHWH. The refusal of military protection may also emphasize a boundary between Persia and the temple furnishings. Even though resources flow from exile, they arrive in Jerusalem purified and untainted.

Williamson has suggested that the actions taken in preparation for the journey (e.g., prayer, fasting, and refusing a military escort) demonstrate that God's grace operates through human channels.[45] Conversely, it also indicates that such practices are necessary to receive divine aid. They also provide a proleptic summary of Ezra's leadership. Ezra anticipates a danger to the exiles from "the enemy on the way" and refuses outside aid because, as he tells the king, "the hand of our God is gracious to all who seek him, but his power and his wrath are against all who forsake him" (Ezra 8:22).[46] The refusal of aid suggests that even offers of help carry danger. Then he and all those with him fast and pray, and God listens to their entreaty. These practices occur again in 9:3–5 and become crucial components to Ezra's strategy when he again perceives danger from outsiders.

The narrative stresses the value and exilic origins of the Levites. They are sought after by Ezra, who sends a named delegation of leaders and two wise men to obtain the Levites. Their town, Casiphia, and their leader, Iddo, are identified. These details suggest that if Ezra's religious personnel come from Casiphia in Babylon, then others from there should also be held in esteem. Their character is proven absolutely reliable when everything they carry to Jerusalem is counted and weighed upon arrival. In Ezra's reading of the Torah (Neh 8), the Levites, trained in exile, perform prominent roles. As "orthodox Yahwists qualified to undertake the leadership of their community," they become the standard by which others are measured.[47] They are fit for their roles by training "in orthodox Yahwism preserved in Diaspora."[48] The lines to the exilic community are firmly drawn as Ezra

---

45. Ibid., 124.
46. Upon arrival, Ezra will confess that the people have forsaken God's commandments (Ezra 9:10), which indicates that God's gracious hand should not be anticipated.
47. Kessler, "Diaspora in Zechariah 1–8," 134.
48. Ibid.

journeys to Jerusalem. The narrative gives legitimacy to particular religious personnel and a form of Yahwism. By incorporating Levites, Torah study, adherence to ritual purity, and provisions for the temple, the text melds together two different perspectives on religious practices.

12.4. Contesting Leadership?

Leuchter suggests that the Levites of Casiphia were "selected due to their association with an intellectual and sacral tradition fostered among Levite circles … that Ezra wished to have represented within his delegation."[49] The historical roots of these Levites were grounded in opposition to a centralized cult, "which threatened their traditional loci of power."[50] Leuchter believes that the rift between centralizing Zadokites and the Levites "only broadened during the course of the exile."[51] He suggests, "the scribal process itself became a potent devotional act during the exile," offering an alternative to foreign cultic practices and "an avenue away from the discourse that still placed the Zadokite priests at the top of the pecking order."[52]

Scholars associate the Levitical tradition with Deuteronomy and Jeremiah, a tradition "openly concerned with the status of Levites" and of notable influence in Ezra-Nehemiah.[53] Stephen Cook suggests that the aim of Deuteronomy "was to temper centralized monarchic power."[54] He identifies within it "a multipronged plan for overcoming Levitical disenfranchisement.… It included rotating country Levites into the capital to serve as interpreters of the covenant at the palace, to hear legal cases within appeals courts, and to serve as altar priests at the temple."[55] The Jeremianic tradition provides a model for a viable life "without the need

---

49. Mark Leuchter, "The Levites in Exile: A Response to L. S. Tiemeyer," *VT* 60 (2010): 589. Some scholars have argued that, by and large, Levites were not exiled. The small number of Levites in the list of Ezra 2 is often provided as evidence (584).

50. Stephen L. Cook, "Those Stubborn Levites: Overcoming Levitical Disenfranchisement," in *Levites and Priests in Biblical History and Tradition*, ed. Mark Leuchter and Jeremy M. Hutton, AIL 9 (Atlanta: Society of Biblical Literature, 2011), 157.

51. Leuchter, "Ezra's Mission," 181.

52. Ibid.

53. Leuchter, "Levites in Exile," 589. Leuchter also identifies Deuteronomistic language in Ezra 7–8 ("Ezra's Mission," 184–85).

54. Cook, "Those Stubborn Levites," 169.

55. Ibid., 159.

for a temple (Jer 29:5–7) through an emphasis on study, text and exegesis (Jer 31:31–34)."[56] Evidence of this Levitical tradition can be identified in the Ezra memoir in the double reference to the Levitical city of Casiphia as "the place" (8:17), the use of Deuteronomistic language and logic in the confession of Ezra 9, and the convening of the community for a covenant ceremony rather than for temple sacrifices.[57]

The redactors of this text still retained temple-centered concerns but made Ezra an ideological colleague of the Levites, and Leuchter suggests that the editors were perhaps a mediating party between Zadokites and Levites.[58] Ezra's original scribal role pertained to imperial administration, and the "early stratum of material in the Ezra corpus casts him in the same role that Moses plays in P—a facilitator of the Zadokite cultic and theological system—only now, this system is empowered as much by Artaxerxes as by YHWH (Ezra 7:26)."[59] This portrait was taken over by later redactors, transforming "the earlier image of Ezra as a P-type Moses into a D-type Moses: an exegete, teacher, covenant mediator, and lawgiver."[60] The result is a composite Ezra who bridges both priestly traditions.[61]

This text may testify to a resurgence of Levitical influence and to efforts to broaden the group's appeal. Bourdieu states, "The strategies which one group may employ to try to escape downclassing and to return to their class trajectory, and those which another group employs to rebuild the interrupted path of a hoped for trajectory, are ... one of the most important factors in the transformation of social structures."[62] In these books, scribal practices and ceremonies operate without recourse to temple rituals, and Leuchter argues that the text targets "the Zadokite priesthood active in the Jerusalem temple."[63] However, the text does not simply reject all that is associated with the Zadokites or the singular importance of the temple. Instead, it "supports an argument for a broader scope of political

---

56. Leuchter, "Levites in Exile," 590.
57. Leuchter, "Ezra's Mission," 182, 191.
58. Ibid., 189.
59. Ibid., 193.
60. Ibid.
61. Ibid., 194.
62. Bourdieu, *Distinction*, 147.
63. Leuchter, "Ezra's Mission," 194.

and religious leadership, one in which Zadokite theology has to function in tandem with other literary and exegetical methods and values."[64]

The redactors perform a careful dance in this text. They must navigate the cultic and centralizing pull of the priesthood, the administrative requirements of the Persians, and account for their own social trajectory as they vie to distinguish themselves to the community—they are not operating in isolation.[65] The Zadokite doctrines "threatened to marginalize the Deuteronomists' impact in exilic society and religious thought."[66] The Levitical response was to attack the Zadokite exclusivity. So, in these chapters, it is the Levites who are essential to a successful journey, and wise and conscientious in their duties. It is Ezra the *scribe* who receives the honor and power of an imperial commission and divine blessing. The portrait lends legitimacy to the actions taken in the next chapter when the community looks to the Levitical leadership to carry out their reform.[67]

But even more shrewdly, the authors incorporate and rework the concepts and language of their opponents into their account. A great disparity between the priests and Levites might have silenced the Levitical discourse, but instead it fosters strategic modifications. The categories by which the Levites are described have roots in history, but the text reinforces and symbolically favors certain aspects of those categories while ignoring others.[68] Their specific capital is set at the top of the hierarchy, yet the language employed to recognize excellence is taken at least in part from (the dominant) priestly concepts of purity. Taking their cue from the standards for legitimacy of the dominant producers, the group is purified, devout, and identified by lineage. Yet purity is achieved without sacrifice.[69] After prayer and fasting, Ezra sets apart the Levites (8:24) and declares them holy (8:28).[70] Attaining purity without temple rituals retains purity as a shared value but marginalizes the most significant area in which Levites

---

64. Ibid.
65. Leuchter ("Zadokites," 8) points out that Ezekiel is the product of the Zadokites, who have appropriated a prophetic tradition that "had largely been Levitical in the past."
66. Ibid., 10.
67. Bourdieu, *Language and Symbolic Power*, 111–12.
68. Ibid., 133.
69. In Num 8:21, a priestly atonement is made for the Levites in addition to their own acts of purification.
70. This is more in line with guidance given to Aaron in Leviticus than in Numbers. See Lev 10:10 and 20:24–26.

hold less capital than the priests. Relations with competitors mediate the way the Levites relate to the wider community.[71] Thus the Levites are not opponents to Jerusalem priests but benefactors of the temple and committed to purity. Their facility with the law opens Persian coffers and promises the institution of the law of God. These chapters portray an essential role for the Levites among the leaders in Jerusalem. The text then becomes a means to educate others in the Levitical vision and increase their authority and influence.[72]

For the Levites to grow in influence requires members of the community to give credence to their representation of the group. Thus the anticipated response of the community determines, at least in part, the content of this discourse.[73] A distinguishing aspect of the Ezra memoir is the limitation that Ezra and the leaders place on their own power so as to act as executors of the will of the people.[74] This gains the support of the greatest number of citizens and at the same time ensures that the leaders hold positions that allow them to wield power.[75] Yet Bourdieu points out that the interests of these representatives do not necessarily coincide with those they represent. Indeed, "They serve the interests of their clients in so far (and only in so far) as they *also* serve themselves."[76] Attention to the empowerment of the laity indicates that, for the Levites, power was grounded in the social capital accorded them by the community—capital contested by alternative visions of the community.

---

71. Bourdieu, *Language and Symbolic Power*, 183.
72. Ibid., 174.
73. Ibid., 76–77, 192.
74. Bourdieu states, "They turn the masses into the leaders and turn themselves into the executive organs of the conscious action of the masses" (ibid., 174).
75. Ibid., 181.
76. Ibid., 183.

13

Ezra 9–10: Israel and "Foreign Wives"

The mood in Ezra 9–10 shifts suddenly from marking the successful completion of Ezra's return (8:35–36) to great sorrow over unfaithfulness in 9:1.[1] As the narrative stands, the faithlessness identified in the first-person account of 9:1–5 seems to be replayed in the third-person in Ezra 10. Both chapters begin by informing Ezra of the same problem, that the people married foreign women from the peoples of the land (9:2; 10:2). Pakkala argues that Ezra 9 is dependent on Ezra 10, with the prayer the main reason for its addition.[2] The prayer provides an explanation or defense for the actions taken in Ezra 10. It may also be that the editors felt that a penitential prayer was a necessary ritual prior to initiating the reform.

13.1. Ezra 9: The Confession of the "Holy Seed"

13.1.1. Confessing Community Guilt

Laments ask, "Why?" Penitential prayers *know* why—it is our fault and we have offended God.[3] Penitential prayers express this by combining the priestly language of unfaithfulness with the Deuteronomic concern for a return to the Torah as covenant. Resting on a doxic belief in corporate guilt, the trauma of the exile is understood as a consequence of unfaithfulness (Ezra 9:13; Neh 1:8). The prayer in Ezra equates exogamous marriages with unfaithfulness. The contention is that the present community is continuing in the sinful footsteps of the ancestors and must rectify the

---

1. Wright, *Rebuilding Identity*, 252.
2. Pakkala, *Ezra the Scribe*, 92.
3. For a fuller discussion of penitential prayers, see §11.2 above.

situation to avoid the fate of their predecessors (Ezra 9:7, 14).[4] The confession begins this process as it constructs these unions as a source of guilt and guides the community to the inevitable conclusion that the marriages must be eradicated to assure the continuation of divine favor.

Ezra 9:1–5 anticipates the confession with a theologically laden description of the community's actions. Officials inform Ezra, "The people of Israel, the priests, and the Levites have not separated [בדל] themselves from the peoples of the lands with their abominations [תועבה]" (9:1). "Separate" is a commonly used term when differentiating between clean and unclean.[5] Abominations are normally associated with idolatrous practices (Deut 17:1–4). In Ezra 9, abominations cling to the peoples of the lands and are linked to uncleanness and impurity—terms most often used to describe sexual transgressions, menstrual blood, or touching corpses.

The polluting effect of the abominations and the danger this poses to the community continue to be developed within the prayer (9:11, 14).[6] Ezra declares that the people have forsaken God's commandments given "by your servants the prophets," who warn, "the land which you are entering to possess is an *unclean* [נדה] *land* with the *uncleanness of the peoples of the lands*, with their *abominations* which have filled it from end to end and with *their impurity* [טמא]" (9:11 NASB).[7] The evil of idolatry is blended with sexual impurity. Now the punishment historically imputed for the worship of foreign gods (e.g., Deut 31:16–18) threatens again due to these "foreign" marriages (Ezra 9:14).

The officials confess that by marrying the women of these people, "the *holy seed* has mixed itself with the peoples of the lands" (Ezra 9:2). *Holy seed* occurs only here and in Isa 6:13. In Isaiah, after the judgment of exile, God promises renewal through the holy seed.[8] Similar usage of זרע ("seed") occurs elsewhere in Isaiah; God promises to bring forth "a seed"

---

4. The penitential prayers in Neh 1 and 9 recall the sin of the ancestors but maintain the petitioners' distance from past sins.

5. See its use in Lev 10:10; 11:47; 20:24–26; Ezra 6:21; 8:24; 10:8, 11, 16.

6. Ezra 9:14 is most often translated, "the people who *practice* these abominations." However, the Hebrew lacks a verb. It is a noun construct that literally reads, "the people of these abominations."

7. There is no exact Torah reference for this. Lev 18:24–25 expresses similar ideas but uses טמא throughout rather than נדה.

8. "Then I said, 'How long, O Lord?' And he said, 'Until … the Lord sends everyone far away, and vast is the emptiness in the midst of the land. Even if a tenth part remain in it, it will be burned again, like a terebinth or an oak whose stump remains

from Jacob" and that "the seed" will be blessed (65:9, 23 JPSV; cf. 66:22). The concept of holy *people* is found in Deut 7:6, "you are a people holy to the LORD your God; the LORD your God has chosen you out of all the peoples on earth to be his people." In that text, being *holy people* provides the basis for the ban on marriages with the indigenous peoples and the destruction of their sites of worship (Deut 7:1–5). Ezra's preference for holy *seed* combines the notion of Israel as holy with a hereditary basis for membership in the community.[9] The theologically potent terminology divides the two groups: holy and remnant versus pollutions, abomination, and unclean. The division rests on religious and ethnic categories of great import to the community (and the reader), yet what specifically makes the present-day peoples of the lands unacceptable remains obscure. The confession warns twice that failure to maintain God's commandments (9:10, 14) will permanently end any divine favor; yet only the commandment that forbids relations with people in the land is cited, "Do not give your daughters to their sons, neither take their daughters for your sons, and never seek their peace or prosperity" (Ezra 9:12).[10]

The prayer forms a chiastic structure that begins and ends with an acknowledgment of guilt and shame (9:6, 15). At the center of the prayer are contrasting statements. One describes God's faithfulness (9:8–9), and the second, the people's failure (9:10–12). These are surrounded by confessions of guilt and ensuing punishment for the past (9:7) and the present (9:13–14).

The Prayer's Structure

9:6: Ezra confesses guilt and sin. Too shamed to lift his face to God
    9:7: confession of the ancestors' guilt and sin resulting in punishment

---

standing when it is felled.' The holy seed is its stump" (Isa 6:11–13). Davies (*Ezra and Nehemiah*, 67) reads the Isaiah usage as a reference to those who remain in the land.

9. Katherine Southwood ("The Holy Seed: The Significance of Endogamous Boundaries and Their Transgression in Ezra 9–10," in *Judah and the Judeans in the Achaemenid Period: Negotiating Identity in an International Context*, ed. Oded Lipschits, Gary Knoppers, and Manfred Oeming [Winona Lake, IN: Eisenbrauns, 2011], 199) notes that the language also unites these concepts with the injunction against mixing seeds in Lev 19:19.

10. See Deut 7:3–4.

9:8–9: details of God's favor and steadfast love for people
9:10–12: details of the commandments forsaken by the people
9:13–14: God would be right to punish us for doing this again
9:15: God is just, we are before you in our guilt, we cannot face you.

The twin themes of shame (9:6, 7, 15) and guilt (9:6, 13, 15) are woven throughout the confession. Williams describes shame as a sense of exposure linked to something that elicits contempt or derision.[11] Unlike shame, which carries a sense of helplessness before others, guilt carries a sense of responsibility and control, so people feel less vulnerable.[12] Guilt can become a defensive mechanism to avert identity-destroying shame by eliciting reparation or self-punishment to restore one's standing.

Ezra begins the confession by stating, "O my God, I am too *ashamed and embarrassed* [בשתי ונכלמתי] to lift my face to you, my God, for our iniquities have risen higher than our heads, and our guilt has mounted up to the heavens" (Ezra 9:6). Jeremiah 6:15 employs the same combination of shame and embarrassment, "They acted *shamefully* [בוש], they committed abomination; yet they were *not* ashamed [בוש], they did *not* know how to blush [or '*be embarrassed*'; הכלים]." They treated the abominations of the people lightly and faced disaster "because they have not given heed to my words; and as for my teaching, they have rejected it" (Jer 6:19). In contrast, Ezra demonstrates he *does indeed* know how to blush over iniquity and guilt. He takes the moral high ground, giving heed to God's word and accepting condemnation. It provides a model for the response sought for the community in Ezra 10.

After the opening confession, a single verse styles the entire history of the people as a continuation of (literally) "great guilt" that continues "to this day." Past sin led to captivity, exile, and shame (9:7). Though they are now "slaves" (9:8–9), God is not at fault—indeed, God has shown them favor and has not forsaken them but "extended to us his steadfast love before the kings of Persia, to give us new life" (9:9). On the contrary, the people are held responsible for failing to keep God's commandments by marrying the people who live in the land and jeopardizing their brief moment of divine favor (9:11–12). Three rhetorical questions lead to the

---

11. Williams, *Shame and Necessity*, 90. Ezra 9:15 does not use the word בוש ("shame") but does describe the sense of exposure associated with shame when it states, "no one can face you because of this."

12. Terr, *Too Scared to Cry*, 112.

conclusion that God would be right to punish the community for their failure (9:10, 14).[13] In fact, says Ezra, we received less than we deserved (9:13). The prayer ends with Ezra and his community standing in guilt before a just God (9:15).[14] Although the prayer lacks an appeal for mercy, the acceptance of guilt becomes a means of averting the wrath of God.[15]

13.1.2. The Peoples of the Lands

Ezra 9:1 incorporates "the peoples of the lands" into a standard litany of peoples whose influence is blamed for the ruin of Jerusalem and the destruction of the First Temple: "the Canaanites, the Hittites, the Perizzites, the Jebusites, the Ammonites, the Moabites, the Egyptians, and the Amorites."[16] This represents "an advanced level of exegetical reflection on several legal texts."[17] In Deut 7:1–6, the Israelites are warned away from indigenous peoples because their religious practices pose a threat to exclusive worship of YHWH. The three groups added to the list of excluded marriage partners are the Ammonites, Moabites, and Egyptians. The exclusion of Ammonites and Moabites appears to be drawn from Deut 23:3, but the people are commanded *not* to abhor the Egyptians in Deut 23:7–8 and to allow the third generation of their children into the congregation.[18] Their exclusion in Ezra may reflect anti-Egyptian rhetoric as a show of solidarity with Persia in light of Egypt's rebellion in the early fourth century BCE.[19]

---

13. "And now, our God, what shall we say after this?" (Ezra 9:10). "Shall we break your commandments again and intermarry with the peoples who practice these abominations? Would you not be angry with us until you destroy us without remnant or survivor?" (9:14).

14. In contrast, the prayer in Neh 1:5–11 reiterates God's promise to gather his people and asks God to be attentive to Nehemiah's prayer. The confession in Neh 9 asks God not to treat lightly all their hardship (9:32).

15. Weber, *Sociology of Religion*, 26.

16. Blenkinsopp, *Ezra-Nehemiah*, 175. The most common listing includes the Canaanites, the Hittites, the Amorites, the Perizzites, the Hivites, and the Jebusites (Exod 3:8; Deut 7:1; Josh 9:1; 12:8; etc.).

17. Williamson, *Ezra, Nehemiah*, 131.

18. Williamson (ibid.) notes that Deut 23 says nothing about marriage. He also notes that 1 Esdras has "Edomites" instead of "Amorites." "No Ammonite or Moabite shall be admitted to the assembly of the Lord. Even to the tenth generation, none of their descendants shall be admitted to the assembly of the Lord" (Deut 23:3).

19. Fantalkin and Tal ("Canonization of the Pentateuch," 208, 212) have argued that the exodus narrative represents such a response to that event.

Lining up the current population with past foreign enemies generates a correspondence that invites negative assessments without having to articulate clear lines of connection. Similarly, the text equates the exiles with the community of the exodus poised to take possession of the land (9:11–12) and so ensures the exiles' privilege. Eskenazi notes that the accusation against the peoples of the lands refers to them doing "as" or "according to" the abominations of these people (9:1).[20] This makes the ethnic identity of the targeted women ambiguous (9:2). Are they nonexiled Judahites, members of foreign nations, or from Judahite families in the land with different practices and beliefs?[21]

Ezra 9:2 equates marriage with these people with *faithlessness* (מעל). In Ezra 9–10, מעל is used six times to characterize intermarrying with the women of the land (9:2, 4, 6; 10:2, 6, 10). (This same usage is also present in Neh 13:27.) Ezra 9:7 links unfaithfulness to guilt and iniquity that led to sword, captivity, and the shame of exile. Ezra 9:10–11 employs language from Deuteronomy to warn that this unfaithfulness is an act of disobedience.[22] While other texts share this concern over intermarriage, each cites religious practices as the inherent danger: worshiping other deities or appropriating practices alien to the Israelite cult.[23] In those texts, God's statutes and ordinances are contrasted with the practices of the inhabitants, and the Israelites are warned that they too could be vomited out if

---

20. In the Pentateuch and the Deuteronomistic History, the term "people of the land" refers to Israelites. The plural construction, "peoples of the lands" (or "peoples of the land") in these chapters creates differentiation between Israel and others.

21. Tamara C. Eskenazi and Eleanore P. Judd, "Marriage to a Stranger in Ezra 9–10," in *Second Temple Studies 2: Temple and Community in the Persian Period*, ed. Tamara C. Eskenazi and Kent H. Richards, JSOTSup 175 (Sheffield: JSOT Press, 1994), 269.

22. This is introduced with language found in Deut 7:1 and the blessings and curses of Deuteronomy, "The land that you are entering to possess" (Deut 28:21, 63; 30:16).

23. Deut 7:2–6 calls on Israel to defeat and utterly destroy the people, make no covenant with them, and refuse to marry them. However, it cites the danger of worshiping other gods as the reason for such drastic actions. Exodus 23:32–33 issues similar commands for similar reasons, "make no covenant with them and their gods … they will make you sin against me." Exodus 34:11–16 runs through the list of people in the land, followed by a warning not to covenant with them because it will lead the Israelites to eat the sacrifices to their gods and marry their daughters who might "make your sons also prostitute themselves to their gods" (Exod 34:16). Lev 18:24–30 enumerates the practices of the nations for which God cast them out of the land.

they follow suit and defile the land.²⁴ In Ezra, there is no mention of worship of other gods, or incorporating pagan practices into worship. Marriage to indigenous people is the sole threat to the community's existence in the land.

13.1.3. The Confession as Social Alchemy

Otto Maduro states that religion transforms the socially lived into the socially thought and "will define, for certain social groups, the thinkable and the unthinkable, the desirable and the undesirable, the possible and the impossible, the useful and the harmful … the forbidden, the permitted, and the obligatory."²⁵ Religion "limits and orientates the behavior of the believing groups."²⁶ The prayer in Ezra 9:6–16, and indeed the entire chapter, creates a portrait of the community to control how the marriages are to be perceived, or in Bourdieu's terminology, *recognized* (or misrecognized). The prayer defines, for this group, what is thinkable, what is possible, what is desirable, and what is harmful. Richard Bautch observes that in the prayer, members of the community are indicted for taking foreign women as wives in "Priestly terms for deliberate, high-handed offences so serious that they cannot be forgiven."²⁷ Furthermore, these actions are interpreted as threatening the community's existence. Transgressors are kept at odds with God, making "the subsequent program of forced divorce … all the more imperative."²⁸ Their stake in God's holy place, tenuous as it is, is a sign of divine favor that is in danger of being lost through a return to sword, captivity, and plundering (9:13).

The accusation that the people have not separated from the peoples of the lands "sets the parameters for discussion and interpretation of these groups."²⁹ Ancient ethnic boundaries "are reinvoked to symbolically

---

24. Deut 28:2, 15, 63; 30:16.
25. Maduro, *Religion and Social Conflicts*, 116.
26. Ibid.
27. Richard J. Bautch, "The Formulary of Atonement (Lev 16:21) in Penitential Prayers of the Second Temple Period," in *The Day of Atonement: Its Interpretations in Early Jewish and Christian Traditions*, ed. Thomas Hieke and Tobias Nicklas, TBN 15 (Boston: Brill, 2012), 38. He particularly notes the uses of מעל and עון as evidence of this categorization of offense.
28. Ibid., 39.
29. Southwood, *Ethnicity*, 141.

dichotomize between the *Golah* and the 'people of the land.'"[30] Although the prayer, in keeping with its sources, condemns all foreign marriages, the narrative identifies only the women as problematic. To avert God's wrath, a single acceptable action is proposed—the removal of the women and their children. Failure to do so will jeopardize the future of the community. The language and selective history of the prayer create a sense of doom and urgency. The transgression is described in language of significance, spoken with certitude, and attached to a figure of such repute that the judgment appears legitimate and natural, thus diminishing the probability that the logic will be reflected on and criticized.[31] No other solution is considered; indeed, none even seems possible. Nor is it possible that the women are not a danger.

This confession is an act of ideological alchemy that transfigures social relations into supernatural relations.[32] Through a sleight of hand, social relations are delegitimized in religious terms that define the very nature of the people: *holy seed, unclean, foreign, abomination*, and *guilt*. The confession also performs an explanatory role.[33] It declares what is to be valued and why, and it justifies Ezra's mourning and the future demands that he will make of the assembly (Ezra 10:11). It creates a religious equation that turns admonitions against religious apostasy into sanctions against current marital practices and then insists on obedience to these newly interpreted commandments as an act of religious fidelity. The religious language and ritualized mourning then consecrates or validates this perspective.

Bourdieu argues that religious wars are both theological quarrels and material class interests at once. Religious alchemy transforms "social barriers ... into logical, eternal, necessary limits."[34] Therefore this social conflict is couched in religious terms even if the issue is not, at its core, a religious one. Indeed, these women are likely less foreign than the text

---

30. Ibid., 142.

31. Robin Celikates, "Systematic Misrecognition and the Practice of Critique: Bourdieu, Boltanski and the Role of Critical Theory," in *Recognition Theory and Contemporary French Moral and Political Philosophy*, ed. Miriam Bankowsky and Alice Le Goff (Manchester: Manchester University Press, 2012), 169.

32. Bourdieu, "Genesis and Structure," 5.

33. Bourdieu (ibid., 14) states that an explanation "transmutes the *ethos* as a system of implicit schemes of action and appreciation into *ethics* as a systematized and rationalized ensemble of explicit norms."

34. Ibid., 15.

claims, and the issue is just as much a matter of politics and economics. Evidence to support this may be seen in the complaint that "in this faithlessness the officials and leaders have led the way" (Ezra 9:2). Those with the most marital options are accused of being the primary offenders. To stave off such arrangements and their associated external influence, the confession transfigures an exilic ethos of endogamous marriage that arose out of necessity into an ethical demand, and then legitimates it through a sophisticated interpretation and application of religious texts.

To gain adherence, those identified as the elect must be persuaded to accept the sacrifices necessary to retain their positions of privilege. Bourdieu observes that a party that tends toward asceticism must "reckon with the temptations of nature or of counter-culture." He goes on to say, "The strategy universally adopted to combat any temptation not to behave according to one's rank consists in naturalizing difference and in turning it into a second nature through its inculcation and incorporation as a set of habits."[35] By identifying the differences between people as (super-)natural and linking this with a set of familiar and durable habits (Torah study, rituals of mourning, and confession), the author justifies strict adherence to ethnic segregation as a distinctive property of those who include themselves among "the holy seed," or more specifically the returnees.[36] It naturalizes this arbitrary limit and inclines people to maintain their social position.

The practices of confession and mourning that permeate these chapters turn what was perhaps the *necessity* of asceticism into a *virtue* of self-abasement. These rituals depict the exiles as extremely pious. They reinforce the returnees' symbolic strength and lend legitimacy to their definition of the community. Holiness, now attached to economic and political limits, is no longer "just a matter for the cult and priests" but is embodied by the people.[37] Notably, temple-centered worship practices provide a setting for Ezra's mourning but do not factor as motivation for the rituals or purity practices advocated. Nor are cultic sacrifices necessary for restor-

---

35. Bourdieu, "Rites as Acts of Institution," 88. Similarly, see Bourdieu, *Language and Symbolic Power*, 122.

36. The technical vocabulary that marks the identity of the community, e.g., "the exile" or "the congregation of the exiles" (Ezra 10:8), is not used outside these texts. See Hoglund, *Achaemenid Imperial Administration*, 35.

37. Davies, *Ezra and Nehemiah*, 72.

ing purity. Instead, the exilic practices of confession and maintenance of community boundaries restore the holiness of the people.

13.2. Ezra 10: Resetting Boundaries

Ezra 10 consists of a narrative (10:1–17) and a list (10:18–44). It begins as a very great assembly of men, women, and children respond to Ezra's confession with bitter weeping (10:1). The image of the entire community in mourning signals their growing involvement and anticipates Shecaniah's announcement (10:2) that "we have acted faithlessly" (my translation) by dwelling with foreign women. Both here and in 9:1–5 the news of the community's unfaithfulness leads Ezra to ritually mourn before the evening sacrifice (9:4) and in the chamber of the high priest (10:6). Just as those who "trembled at the words of the God of Israel" gathered around Ezra in chapter 9, so here the whole community is ordered to assemble, and they too are trembling or shaking (רעד) "because of this matter and because of the heavy rain" (10:9).[38] In his first public statement, Ezra declares them guilty, and they agree to remove the foreign wives (10:12). The growing size of the assemblies over the course of the narrative communicates "the growing cohesion of the audience."[39] The narrative then describes the steps taken to investigate the matter, and the chapter concludes with a list of those who sent away their wives.

13.2.1. Ezra 10:1–17: The Assembly and the Agreement

In Ezra 10:1–5, Shecaniah informs Ezra that "we have broken faith with our God and have married [ישב, or 'dwelled with'] foreign women" (Ezra 10:2). This alternate term for marriage, rather than the more frequent "take" (לקח) (cf. Gen 24:3), casts a suspicious light on these relationships.[40]

---

38. רעד occurs elsewhere only in Ps 104:32 and Dan 10:11. Daniel shivers for similar reasons. A man in a vision speaks to Daniel saying, "'Daniel, greatly beloved, pay attention to the words that I am going to speak to you. Stand on your feet, for I have now been sent to you.' So while he was speaking this word to me, I stood up trembling."

39. Davies, *Ezra and Nehemiah*, 68.

40. Ezra 10:2, 10, 17, 18; Neh 13:23, 27. In Ezra 9:2, the officials state they "took wives." Williamson (*Ezra, Nehemiah*, 150) notes that in Proverbs a "foreign woman" is synonymous for "harlot" and that Solomon is faulted for loving foreign women (1 Kgs 11:1; Neh 13:26).

It insinuates a less than legal arrangement, implying that separation from these women is not tantamount to divorce. Shecaniah then suggests, "Let us make a covenant with our God to send away all these wives and their children, according to the counsel of my lord and of those who tremble at the commandment of our God; and let it be done according to the law" (Ezra 10:3).[41]

He then enjoins Ezra, "Take action, for it is your duty, and we are with you; be strong, and do it" (Ezra 10:4). This echoes holy war language from Josh 1:9, "I hereby command you: Be strong and courageous; do not be frightened or dismayed, for the LORD your God is with you wherever you go."[42] In both books, leaders are to carry out their actions "in accordance with all the law" (Josh 1:7–8)/"according to the law" (Ezra 10:3). Joshua is encouraged to carry out his duty because *God* is with him. But Ezra is encouraged to be strong and do his duty because the *people* are with him. The divine support for Joshua is supplanted in Ezra with the support of the community. In both situations, the people promise obedience to their leader's words (Josh 1:16–18; Ezra 10:5).[43] Those who fail to obey are threatened with death in Joshua (Josh 1:18) or banishment and loss of property in Ezra (Ezra 10:8). The military language gives a sense of urgency to Ezra's commands, and obedience to his orders is equated with obedience to God (Ezra 10:11). Its nuanced usage and the prominent role of the community indicate the importance the author places on community involvement and cohesion.

After he makes the leaders swear agreement with Shecaniah's proposal, Ezra withdraws to mourn in "the chamber of Jehohanan son of Eliashib, [the high priest],[44] where he spent the night. He did not eat bread or drink

---

41. Only here in Ezra-Nehemiah do the people make a covenant. Elsewhere God is faithful to his covenant (Neh 1:5; 9:8, 32) or, in Neh 13:29, the priests are accused of defiling the covenant of the priests and Levites. See Williamson, *Ezra, Nehemiah*, 150.

42. Similar language occurs in Deut 20:1, where the people are commanded not to fear when entering into battle because "the Lord your God is with you." Williamson (ibid., 151) sees parallels with an "installation genre" found in Deut 31:23; 1 Chr 22:11; 28:10, 20. However, there is no element of succession in office in this text.

43. The people respond to Joshua with, "Whoever rebels against your orders and disobeys your words, whatever you command, shall be put to death. Only be strong and courageous" (Josh 1:18).

44. Although not granted the title of high priest in this chapter, Eliashib is elsewhere clearly identified as such (Neh 3:1; 12:10; 13:28). Neh 12:10–11 list the high priest genealogy: "Jeshua was the father of Joiakim, Joiakim the father of Eliashib,

water, for he was mourning over the faithlessness of the exiles." The chamber is almost certainly within the temple precincts.[45] Ezra's night in the rooms of the high priest's son shares an affinity with Samuel's night-time divine encounter with the priest Eli in 1 Sam 3.[46] In both cases, judgment is announced the next day.[47] Samuel informs Eli of the judgment against his house. Likewise Ezra informs the exiles of their sin, "You have trespassed and married foreign women, and so increased the guilt of Israel" (Ezra 10:10). The recipients of each judgment accede to the divine will.[48] Like Samuel, Ezra steps into leadership with words of judgment that translate into a critique of previous leadership. Though not directed exclusively at priests, Ezra's accusation does create a subtle judgment against them.

At this point, Ezra's portrait takes on a priestly cast. In the first six verses of chapter 10, Ezra has no title linked to his name (10:1, 2, 5, 6). At the moment he finally speaks to the community, he becomes "Ezra *the priest*" (10:10, 16) who commands the people to "separate" from the peoples of the land, and he "selects" or "separates" leaders to conduct the investigation. The officials and elders threaten to "forfeit" (חרם) the belongings of any who refuse to participate and to ban or separate (בדל) them from the community.[49] When the people assemble in Jerusalem, they sit in the open square before the house of God, shaking, "because of this matter and

---

Eliashib the father of Joiada, Joiada the father of Jonathan, and Jonathan the father of Jaddua." Eliashib is criticized in 13:4 for being related to Tobiah (without detail) and providing him with a chamber in the temple for his personal use. Furthermore, Nehemiah "chased away" his son, Joiada, because he was the son-in-law of Sanballat (13:28).

45. Ezra had been praying "before the house of God" (10:1), and evidence elsewhere indicates that rooms in the temple court were not only for storage but for personal use of temple personnel. See, e.g., Jer 35:4, "I brought them to the house of the Lord into the chamber of the sons of Hanan son of Igdaliah, the man of God, which was near the chamber of the officials, above the chamber of Maaseiah son of Shallum, keeper of the threshold." Cf. Neh 13:4–5, 8–9; Jer 36:10.

46. Eli's sons are accused, among other things, of sleeping with women who served at the entrance to the tent of meeting (1 Sam 2:22). God informs Samuel that he will punish the house of Eli because Eli knew of his sons' sin but failed to restrain them (1 Sam 3:13).

47. Likewise, Isaiah's temple vision results in a message of judgment (Isa 6:11–13).

48. Eli responds with, "Let him [the Lord] do what seems good to him" (1 Sam 3:18). Ezra orders the people to make confession and separate from the peoples of the land and the foreign women, and the congregation responds, "It is so; we must do as you have said" (Ezra 10:12).

49. Calling this assembly is the only example of the use of power given to Ezra in

because of the heavy rain" (10:9). Ezra issues his judgment and orders the people to "make confession" (or "give thanks") and separate (בדל) from the foreign wives.[50] The assembly responds with a loud voice, "It is so; we must do as you have said." Rain soaks everyone as they stand in the open before the house of the Lord; the twin references to rain frame the assembly's covenant to separate (בדל) from the peoples of the lands. The technical language of *covenant, separation,* and חרם combines with the imagery of the shaking community being washed (purified) in the temple court to portray this agreement as a purifying act. "The community initiated and executed its own purification, assisted by Ezra."[51]

Despite this wholehearted endorsement, the rain and the large number of transgressors prompt the community to request a longer time frame in which to conduct their investigation (10:13). Plans are made to carry out the inquiry but interjected into this is the notice that two men, supported by two Levites, "opposed this" (lit. "stood on this," עמדו על־זאת; 10:15).[52] The wording leaves it unclear whether they opposed the covenant or perhaps opposed the delay.[53] Williamson prefers the latter option, arguing that they are not listed among those having foreign wives and therefore they have no reason to oppose it. He suggests that their Levitical status tips the balance in favor of them taking a more rigorous line than was adopted.[54] However, efforts to construct the temple and build the wall faced opposition; so, as a plot device, opposition to the covenant should not be unexpected. Given the focus on the make-up of the community, it is well within reason to expect resistance to come from within.[55] (Their silent opposition is noted but passed over without response.) The investigation takes three months to complete, and the list of transgressors con-

---

the king's letter. See Mary Douglas, "Responding to Ezra: The Priests and the Foreign Wives," *BibInt* 10 (2002): 4.

50. In Ezra-Nehemiah, בדל, the term for "separate," occurs nine times, seven of which are for separation from people deemed foreign (Ezra 6:21; 9:1; 10:8, 11; Neh 9:2; 10:28 [29 MT]; 13:3; see also Ezra 8:24; 10:16).

51. Eskenazi, *In an Age of Prose*, 70.

52. The LXX states they were the only ones that stood *with* Ezra on this. In 1 Esd 9:14, they implement the decision assisted by the other two.

53. The sentence begins with אך, which almost always emphasizes that what follows is in contrast with previous ideas.

54. Williamson, *Ezra, Nehemiah*, 156.

55. The listing of the names of these four men would then either stand as a testimony to their dedication to the law or as a censure for their unwillingness to comply.

tains only 113 names. The note of opposition in 10:15 and the slow pace of the investigation indicate that enacting the measure was contentious. The removal of wives and children was no small matter even when couched in terms of holiness, covenant, and divine anger.

13.2.2. Ezra 10:18–43: The List of Names

This list, enumerating all those who have married foreign women, like the list in Ezra 2, "gives the feeling of national unity,... ascribes importance to each individual, [and] it gives the people a more central role than their leaders or the Temple."[56] Despite the claim that "many of us have transgressed in this matter" (10:13), the three-month investigation came up with only 113 names, even though the entire congregation was committed to carrying out Ezra's orders (10:12). Was the project less successful than the narrative suggests? Might this explain the necessity to address this again in Neh 13:23–28?[57] Ezra 10:19 states that priests included on the list pledged to send away their wives. This statement and the summary in 10:44 suggest that the list is restricted to only those who made such a pledge rather than all those found in breach of the agreement.[58] This leaves open the possibility of other offenders who opted not to embrace the reform.

The list of transgressors begins with the priests, who, in addition to the pledge to send away their wives, also made an offering (אשמה) for their guilt (10:19).[59] "Guilt" is repeatedly cited as the source of shame in the confession (9:6, 7, 13, 15) and as the negative result of these marriages (10:10). To remove guilt for the priests requires not only the dismissal of wives but the extra step of an offering. Following the priests are Levites, singers, and gatekeepers (10:23–24), and then Israel (10:25) grouped by family names. It does *not* delineate the lower classes such as we find in the list in Ezra 2.[60] Notably, Jehiel, from the family of Elam (10:26), is included. He may be the

---

56. Angel, "Literary Significance," 146.
57. Ibid., 147.
58. Blenkinsopp, *Ezra-Nehemiah*, 198. Blenkinsopp wonders if this should be considered identical with all who were identified as having transgressed.
59. The priests are from the line of Jeshua, the high priest prominent in Ezra 1–6, *not* from the Aaronide line associated with Ezra (7:2–5). References for Jeshua son of Jozadak are Ezra 2:2; 3:2–8; 4:3; 5:2.
60. Williamson, *Ezra, Nehemiah*, 157.

father of Shecaniah (10:2), who initially posited the divorce proceedings. If so, Shecaniah is either suggesting his own excommunication or (more likely) the possibility that his father has married twice.[61]

Mary Douglas contends that inheritance was at issue. She suggests a polygamous situation and argues that a mother would be following precedent if she "persuades her husband to nominate one of her own children as his heir." If sons of other mothers feared being excluded by their half-siblings, then "the demand that the children be sent away (disinherited), along with their mothers" becomes more understandable.[62] This may be true, especially if the earlier threat to confiscate property for failure to participate in the assembly was a move to keep land from passing into the hands of "foreigners" who would have preferred not to participate.[63] However, the author does not introduce inheritance into the text, which suggests that he prefers to base his argument on religious grounds for its greater symbolic legitimacy and avoid accusations of greed.[64]

The incoherent final verse in the Masoretic Text is commonly translated, "the wives and children were sent away." This corresponds to 1 Esd 9:36. Other translators choose to conclude with the statement, "All these had taken foreign wives; and some of them had wives by whom they had children."[65] Regarding the negative tone of this conclusion, Lester Grabbe observes that it draws our attention to "the plight of the wives and children of those who repudiated their marriages."[66] He suggests that for an ancient reader the willingness to sacrifice family for faith and obedience could be read positively, but "the negative effect still hovers over the passage."[67] H. Zlotnick-Sivan suggests that the references to the children of mixed marriages (10:3, 44) "serve as a silent testimony to the length of the mar-

---

61. Ibid., 150.
62. Douglas, "Responding to Ezra," 12.
63. Fewell, private communication, 22 September 2012.
64. The land is referenced in Ezra 9 only as a divine inheritance bestowed on the community, not in terms of family holdings. Nor is inheritance an issue in Neh 13 or even in Neh 5, where children and land tenure are central concerns.
65. E.g., JPSV; cf. NASB, ESV. Commentators have suggested that the vagueness of this verse either hides a failure of the strict anti-assimilationist policy (Blenkinsopp, *Ezra-Nehemiah*, 200) or, as Grabbe (*Ezra-Nehemiah*, 36) posits, reflects an unwillingness to focus on the hurt and so detract from the main issue.
66. Grabbe, *Ezra-Nehemiah*, 38.
67. Ibid.

riage between their foreign mothers and the Jewish fathers."[68] For today's reader the account ends on a note of poignancy that remains unresolved.

13.2.3. The List as Symbolic Confirmation of Group Definition

Core markers of ethnicity consist of kinship, commensality, and a common cult. When those markers are not available in social interaction, other surface features stand for the index features.[69] These secondary markers must be related in determinate ways to the basic elements of blood, substance, or cult. This list in Ezra 10:16–44, like the list in Ezra 2, operates with a doxic belief in kinship as criteria for determining inclusion. The names are grouped by family, and "of the sons of X" is a recurring refrain. Despite this, the list affirms and testifies to the breakup of families in order to reconfigure the community's boundaries. The children, blood relations to those named in the list, are no longer recognized as kin in order to concretize new standards for membership. The secondary marker of exilic status now surfaces to supersede this more fundamental marker of ethnicity.

Niditch has argued that record keeping developed in stages, and administrative lists, even in the medieval era, were not created for utilitarian purposes, but "rather they [were] pledges to posterity and an assurance of the continuity of institutions under God's providence."[70] In the discussion on Ezra 2, I established that the list of returnees in that chapter performed a new function, to authenticate the Jewish identity of members based primarily on their exilic history.[71] The list in Ezra 10 provides a conclusion to the covenant ceremony. It is a roster of those whose exilic status and kinship ties were at odds. To be reintegrated into the community required cutting relations with those of nonexilic descent. Their own exilic status is not in question—but the nonexilic history of their spouses is conceived as a threat to the community. The primary marker of ethnicity, kinship, is abandoned with the children in exchange for a shared history.[72] The written list legitimates this arbitrary basis for determining

---

68. H. Zlotnick-Sivan, "The Silent Women of Yehud in Ezra 9–10," *JJS* 51 (2000): 16.
69. Nash, *Cauldron of Ethnicity*, 11.
70. Niditch, *Oral World and Written Words*, 42. She states, "Making records for administrative use, keeping them as records, and using them again for references were three distinct stages of development which did not follow one another immediately."
71. See section 4.2.1 above.
72. Nash, *Cauldron of Ethnicity*, 5.

membership. It becomes a persuasive testimony of those willing to sacrifice for membership in the community and a road map for reintegration into the community. Indeed, Bourdieu maintains that "people's adherence to an institution is directly proportional to the severity and painfulness of the rites of initiation."[73] The record becomes the "society's legacy, proof of their status and history."[74] If there are more pragmatic motivations for the divorces (e.g., land claims by the returnees), they are obscured by the framework of religious logic.

13.3. The Community: The Holy Seed in Other Words

Even with the arrival of the imposing personage of Ezra, the community remains the major thematic interest in Ezra 9–10. Not only is the integrity and purity of the "holy seed" a primary focus, but the assembly performs key roles in the plot, and a variety of leaders actively participate in carrying out the agreement. In these chapters, restoration is centered on the community—not on rebuilding the temple or reconstructing city walls.[75]

While "holy seed" has garnered attention because of its uniqueness and theological implications, four other terms for "community" are more commonly used in these chapters: (*the people of*) *Israel*, *the* (*sons of the*) *exile(s)*, *congregation*, and *people*. "The people of Israel" continues a pattern from Ezra 1–6. It denotes those in Babylon who may wish to "go up" with, or contribute to, Ezra's journey.[76] In 9:1, "the people of Israel" are faulted for failure to separate from the peoples of the lands, and in 10:1–5 an assembly "from Israel" gathers before Ezra in sorrow over this issue. There is yet hope for Israel (10:2) once Israel swears an oath to put away foreign women (10:5).[77] Ezra declares marrying foreign women has increased "the guilt of Israel" (10:10). To be Israel is to be separate from the

---

73. Bourdieu, *Language and Symbolic Power*, 123.
74. Niditch, *Oral World and Written Words*, 42.
75. Eskenazi, *In an Age of Prose*, 62.
76. Ezra 7:7, 13, 28; 8:25; cf. 2:59; 4:3; 6:21. In Ezra 1–6, the use of "Israel" for the people most commonly occurs as "sons of Israel." This is used also in Ezra 7:7 and Neh 8:14, 17. However, in Ezra 7–10 "Israel" more often stands alone as a referent for the people.
77. In Ezra 10:5, "Israel" appears to be a designation for the laity separate from the priests and Levites.

surrounding people. Placing "Israel" and "foreign" in opposition symbolically separates the women from the community.

"The exiles" (הגולה) or "the sons of the exile" (בני הגולה) continues a usage found frequently in Ezra 1–6, particularly 6:16–20. The latter phrase occurs three more times: 8:35, 10:7, and 10:16. "The exiles" refers to the initial returnees in 1:11 and 2:1. In 10:6–8, the term is clustered in a section concerned with the faithlessness of the community. A shift in 10:5–6 from "Israel" to "exiles" likely marks an editorial seam, yet taken together the usage equates Israel with the exiles.[78] Having these titles indicates relative status and moral worth, especially through the use of associated purity language.[79] Foreigners now are simply those whose ancestors never left. A historical connection to the region is insufficient for membership. In fact, membership requires one's link to the land be broken by a history of exile.

Two other terms designate the community: *congregation* and *people*. "Congregation" (קהל) occurs ten times in Ezra-Nehemiah. Four of those occur in Ezra 10:1–14 as the people gather to discuss the mixed marriages; twice it is partnered with either "Israel" (10:1 JPSV, KJV) or "the exiles" (10:8). Although קהל can refer to assembling for a meeting, it also refers to the community from which one can be excluded.[80] The term עם, "people," also occurs with frequency, usually modifying other identifying terms such as "congregation" or "Israel." However, it also occurs alone, setting the people apart for special scrutiny or attention. Ezra reviews "the people and the priests" (8:15); the governors of the province aid "the people and the house of God" (8:36). If we include Neh 8, "the people" assemble and call Ezra to bring the book of the law and then celebrate Passover. Eskenazi notes that in that chapter "the people" are mentioned thirteen times

---

78. Ezra exacts an oath from everyone in Ezra 10:5 to resolve the issue, but in 10:6 he again begins to mourn the situation. This too supports this claim of an editorial seam. Juha Pakkala ("The Exile and the Exiles in the Ezra Tradition," in *The Concept of Exile in Ancient Israel and Its Historical Contexts*, ed. Ehud Ben Zvi and Christoph Levin, BZAW 404 [Berlin: de Gruyter, 2010], 97) argues that Ezra 10:6–9 is a golah addition to an older text.

79. Nash, *Cauldron of Ethnicity*, 9.

80. קהל also occurs twice in Neh 8. The congregation consists of "all those who could understand" the Torah when read (8:2) or those who returned from exile (8:17). People are threatened with exclusion from the congregation either for failure to attend the assembly regarding marriages (Ezra 10:8), or due to their foreign ethnicity (Neh 13:1).

in twelve verses as both actors and subjects.[81] Both terms occur in Ezra 10:1 as the congregation gathers around Ezra and the people join him in weeping. The level of responsibility taken on by the people presents them with a measure of control over their social organization. The "assembly" (קהל) may agree to Ezra's demands, but they set the time and conduct a systematic review led by their own family heads (10:12–13).

The community's composition is the central issue in these chapters. Exilic history is necessary for membership and to assure the purity of Israel and the congregation in Jerusalem. The variety of communal labels is summed up in the title, "The Holy Seed." The text steadfastly refrains from giving voice to any competing construction. Religious, communal, ethnic, and historical categories are all enlisted to dissociate the community of the exiles from the polluting "peoples of the land(s)."

13.4. Leadership and Change

A comparison of the community in Ezra 7–10 with the Judeans in the Nehemiah memoir affords evidence of greater agency by the community in Ezra. The people feature prominently in Nehemiah's account of the wall building in Neh 4 and the economic crisis in Neh 5. However, in both cases, the people are portrayed as dependent and vulnerable to the stratagems of outsiders and even their own officials (5:7). In Neh 5, the dominated members of the economically divided community are limited to complaining about their circumstances as they seek Nehemiah to intervene and alleviate their hardship. The community takes little initiative. The people either follow Nehemiah's lead or serve as audience to Nehemiah's public shaming of others. The uncomplicated social order and clearly defined leadership suggests that Nehemiah encountered a society that initially had a single specific class structure (and a religion suited to that structure).

In contrast, the people in Ezra 7–10 are complicit in and held responsible for sin rather than being victimized by others. They mourn their *own* actions and provide advice for handling the situation and identify their own representatives to handle the investigation.[82] While the people remain important to the purposes of both books, their differing levels of

---

81. Eskenazi, *In an Age of Prose*, 97.
82. This contrast holds true even for their presentation in the confessional prayers. The prayer in Neh 9 portrays the people as victims of the ancestors' sins (Neh 9:37). In Ezra 9, the guilty party are the people themselves (9:10, 14).

agency suggest different structural dynamics. In Ezra, the community as a whole agrees to the decision and identifies representatives from among their ranks to oversee the process (10:12, 14). Further evidence of a collective local political organization is found in the variety of leaders who play key roles in Ezra 7–10.[83] In 7:25, the king issues a sweeping decree that empowers Ezra to "appoint magistrates and judges who may judge all the people in the province." He adds that "you" *plural* are to teach any who do not know these laws. Even if hyperbolic, this decree anticipates Ezra delegating authority to others. As Ezra prepares for his journey, he selects "leaders" (ראשים) to accompany him (7:28); he sends nine of these leaders (all named) and two men "who were wise" to Casiphia to recruit more Levites (8:16–17).[84]

The concern over the marriages is voluntarily raised first by *officials* (השרים) of the community (Ezra 9:1). In 10:1, as Ezra and the assembly weep, Shecaniah son of Jehiel not only apprises Ezra of the dilemma but offers a solution (10:2–3) and prompts Ezra to take action (10:4). Only then does Ezra stand and issue commands. In 10:7–8, the community is summoned to appear within three days not by Ezra but "by order of the officials and the elders [הזקנים]."[85] The two categories of leaders act jointly; and when a plan is put in place to decide matters, the assembly decides to conduct its investigation by enlisting their officials, plus "the elders and judges of every town" (10:14). The narrative suggests that the officials/chiefs hold positions of wider influence in the community and that elders held genealogically and geographically specific roles. Ezra then appoints "heads of fathers' houses," laity who hold leadership within their particular extended families, to investigate the marriages (10:16 JPSV). The various actors and leaders indicate a field with significantly more diverse sources of authority than the community portrayed by Nehemiah (although Nehemiah's self-interest may have led him to minimize the role of local leaders).

---

83. One influential group, "those who tremble" (9:4; 10:3), is discussed below in the treatment of Ezra's character (section 13.5.1).

84. The phrase ראשי האבות, "heads of families" (lit. "heads of the fathers"), is also used twice in these chapters to introduce genealogical lists. However, in Ezra 1–4 and in Nehemiah, this phrase refers to leaders of the community (e.g., Ezra 1:5; 3:12; 4:2–3). It is used this way also in Ezra 10:16.

85. Williamson, *Ezra, Nehemiah*, 154.

The variety of titles for leaders and their overlapping responsibilities suggest that the text reflects an earlier mode of production and a social organization in the process of reorganizing. Pakkala suggests that later additions to these chapters emphasize the golah (Ezra 10:6–9) and introduce priests and Levites into the deliberations (10:5b, 15b, 18, 20–44). He argues that these changes indicate challenges to the leadership structure of "officials, "elders," and "heads of households," as well as the assembly implied in the older text.[86] The influx of Babylonian immigrants would have placed in forced relationship two systems that were oriented to different social and economic conditions. Persian rule also influenced relations, introducing greater stratification as Persia's administrative organization and economic demands grew, particularly as Judah became a border territory in the conflict with Egypt.[87] In the process, the older structure is "subjected to a restructuring, directed toward a new class division corresponding to the current dominant mode of production."[88] Evaluating the effect of colonization in Central America, Maduro observes, "Even where traditional structures were partially preserved, a new social relationship was imposed from without in the form of a relationship of subordination."[89] Likewise the account in Ezra attests to shifts in social hierarchy that subordinated earlier arrangements to those imposed by the imperial appointees and exilic community.

The effects of this greater stratification and new class divisions lead to strategies to acquire power, maintain dominance, or demand reform. The particular course adopted by actors (or class fractions) depends on their social position and trajectory. This conflictive dynamic between social classes imposes "new limitations and orientations upon religious functioning."[90] As a result, the orientation and practices of a religion will vary, and the competing forces will cause its transformation.[91] The decision to abolish previously recognized marriages is part of such adjustments in the religious field due to the restructuring of society.

---

86. Pakkala, *Ezra the Scribe*, 125.
87. Fantalkin and Tal, "Canonization of the Pentateuch," 202.
88. Maduro, *Religion and Social Conflicts*, 62.
89. Ibid.
90. Ibid., 64.
91. Ibid., 71.

13.5. Ezra's Capital, Representation, and Symbolic Power

Ezra's titles and attributes make his importance for the entire work unmistakable. He is introduced with an extensive priestly genealogy of fourteen generations linked to Aaron (Ezra 7:1–5).[92] The narrator states that he is a skilled scribe who receives from the king all he asks because God's hand is on him (7:6). He is often identified by the joint titles "priest" and "scribe" (7:11, 12, 21; Neh 8:9). On two occasions, he is "Ezra the priest" (Ezra 10:10, 16).[93] Even when his only title is "Ezra" (10:1, 2, 5, 6), he leads the entire assembly, giving orders to the leading priests, Levites, and all Israel (10:5, 10–11). Artaxerxes's letter (7:12–26) shows great confidence in him; the king entrusts him with money and gifts for the temple, granting him authority to appoint judges according to his "God-given wisdom," and to enforce the law.[94] Narrative allusions to the exodus add to Ezra's standing—he becomes a second Moses as he leads the journey to Jerusalem.[95] The author enhances Ezra's esteem by weaving together multiple voices into univocal praise of his character. The narrator, the people, the king, and even Ezra's own statements affirm his integrity, his piety, his skill, and his leadership.[96]

Yet, as Ezra's figure develops, his actions challenge the reader's expectations.[97] Grabbe observes that Ezra is presented "as if he had the power of the governor or even the satrap of the entire region.… Yet when it comes time to exercise all this power, he is at a loss."[98] Ezra's initiative is limited to acts of mourning and confession. The laity initiate further action (10:2) and, more importantly, resolve the individual cases of foreign marriages (10:16). They even have to prod Ezra into taking further steps (10:4). Both Williamson and Eskenazi view Ezra's lack of initiative

---

92. Blenkinsopp (*Ezra-Nehemiah*, 136) calls the genealogy a fiction. He suggests that the genealogy conveys Ezra's function with respect to the law and cult and continues that of the preexilic priesthood.

93. Neh 8–12 shows similar treatment: "scribe" and "priest" (8:1–2, 9; 12:26); "scribe" alone (8:4, 13; 12:36); "Ezra" alone (8:5, 6; 9:6).

94. Eskenazi, *In an Age of Prose*, 63.

95. Williamson, *Ezra, Nehemiah*, 94.

96. In contrast, Eskenazi (*In an Age of Prose*, 150–51) notes that at times the narrator undermines Nehemiah's claims (Neh 12:44, 45, 47).

97. Ibid., 62.

98. Grabbe, *Ezra-Nehemiah*, 153. He especially notes a difference between the Ezra of chs. 7–8 and his portrayal in chs. 9–10.

positively. Williamson suggests that Ezra does not directly coerce the community, but encourages "the people to see the problem for themselves and so formulate their own response."[99] Eskenazi argues that, although Ezra is uniquely qualified, he exemplifies the proper use of power and responsibility by transferring these to the community.[100]

Because Ezra embodies a great quantity of cultural capital, his power sharing is more noteworthy.[101] By yielding the authority his capital might command, he negates the hierarchy. Bourdieu refers to this as a strategy of condescension. When the speaker and audience are cognizant of the hierarchy created by disparate quantities of capital, "the speaker [is able] to combine the profits linked to … hierarchy with those derived from the symbolic negation of the hierarchy."[102] Such nobility invites others to approve Ezra's leadership, which sustains the social hierarchy and translates into greater influence for Ezra and those who possess similar capital.

Ezra's relationship with the forms of capital is nuanced in ways that advance authorial interests and values. His relationship to economic capital is carefully controlled. Ezra arrives bearing some weighty gifts for the temple. However, he is never personally identified as a donor. Instead, the silver, gold, bronze, and utensils are gifts of "the king, his counselors, his lords, and all Israel [in Babylonia]" (Ezra 8:25; cf. 7:15–16, 20). Ezra's responsibility entails safely transporting these goods to the Jerusalem temple. The itemization of donations demonstrates that Ezra is a conscientious custodian of resources. His responsible transport of these assets justifies the imperial mandate that gives him license to determine how monetary gifts are spent (7:15–16, 18) and to make further demands on the provincial treasury (7:20–21). Ezra has responsibility for, but not ownership of, financial resources provided by the Persian government or contributed by those in exile. Most importantly, Ezra never personally gains economically from these resources. In Bourdieu's schema, disinterest in economic gain coincides with increasing cultural capital—the capital upon which this portrait of Ezra is centered. Carrying enormous wealth all the way to Jerusalem on behalf of others stresses Ezra's disinterest in economic capital.

---

99. Williamson, *Ezra, Nehemiah*, 133.
100. Eskenazi, *In an Age of Prose*, 62.
101. Ibid., 64.
102. Bourdieu, *Language and Symbolic Power*, 68.

Ezra's cultural capital falls into two related areas; the first is expertise in Torah. He is a "skilled" scribe; he can interpret and teach the law of king and Deity. Because of this expertise, the imperial mandate grants Ezra exaggerated political powers. He is commissioned to appoint judges and magistrates over the entire province to teach the laws of his God to any who do not know his law. He is also granted extensive powers of enforcement, from the confiscation of goods up to the death penalty (7:26). He also knows how the religious laws of the community should be understood and employed within the community. His commitment to the Torah is stated repeatedly (7:6, 10, 14, 25–26), and his penitential prayer (9:6–16) exemplifies his facility with its interpretation. Thus Jerusalem officials seek his expertise regarding the mixed marriages, and "all who trembled at the words of the God of Israel" gather to him (9:4). When Ezra declares the marriages to foreign women to be sinful, his word becomes law. The fullborn acceptance by king and community of Ezra's legal competence translates into great political power and draws the reader to embrace society as mandated in the narrative.

Second, Ezra is pious. His rituals of piety and confession are narratively linked to divine blessing. Ezra proclaims a fast and humbles himself prior to the aliyah (8:21–23). Upon hearing news of the foreign marriages, he ritually mourns and confesses (9:3–6). His prayers, weeping, confession, fasting, and all-night vigil (9:3–4; 10:1, 6) repeatedly exemplify his pious stance. When he finally commands the community to do God's will, it begins with confession (10:11).[103] Ezra's actions exemplify humility as the proper response to God's provision and demonstrate repentance as a necessary precursor to petition on behalf of those guilty of faithlessness. Ezra's piety obtains and protects goods destined for the temple and protects the community from incurring divine wrath.[104] It is also the model for those seeking to know God's will. The ability to gain blessing, avert

---

103. The demand for a confession, תנו תודה ליהוה, could also be translated, "Give thanks to YHWH." However, it is framed by the accusation, "You have trespassed and married foreign women, and so increased the guilt of Israel" (Ezra 10:10), and Ezra's demand that they separate from the peoples of the land and the foreign wives (10:11). This language is nearly identical to that in Josh 7:19. There Joshua commands Achan to "give glory to the Lord God of Israel and make confession [or 'give thanks'] to him. Tell me now what you have done." It too is preceded by a declaration of sin (Josh 7:11) and followed by actions to cleanse the community of foreign influence. In both texts, pollution is introduced through the agency of a community member.

104. If we include Neh 8 in our consideration, then Ezra's personal piety extends

punishment, and receive divine wisdom convey that these acts of self-denial are virtuous and beneficial.

In these chapters, prestige and political influence are directly linked to expertise in religious law and personal piety distinguished by practices of confession and self-denial. Although Ezra is repeatedly referred to as a priest, rituals requiring priestly oversight are not detailed as they are in other portions of these books (e.g., Ezra 3, 6, or Neh 12:35–47). Instead, these chapters display religious practices most at home in the absence of temple rituals. The community is restructured in Ezra 7–10 not by embracing the temple cult but by embracing a penitential mind-set that concerns itself with the community's boundaries.

13.5.1. Ezra's Followers Are "Those Who Tremble"

Ezra and his piety are associated closely with "those who tremble at the words [or 'commandment'] of the God of Israel." They are the first to gather around Ezra when he mourns (9:4), and their counsel contributes to the decision of the community (10:3). Isaiah 66:2–5 refers to this same body. Isaiah 66:2 confers on them divine approval, but 66:5 acknowledges that those who tremble are not well received by their community, "Your own people who hate you and reject you for my name's sake." The situation leads Isaiah to equate temple sacrifices and offerings "with murderous and abominable acts."[105] Because of the prophet's lack of specificity, there is debate over the identity of the parties involved.[106] Some suggest that the prophet condemns the temple, others that people are performing cultic acts while engaging in violence or forbidden rites. Still others contend that the critique is leveled against the Jerusalem priests. Even if the temple is being attacked, this conflict over worship signals that there are parties contesting control over the community. Isaiah declares that those who call for

---

to the ritualized reading of the law. Notably, this reading of the law leads to congregational weeping (Neh 8:9).

105. Paul D. Hanson, *Isaiah 40–66*, IBC (Louisville: John Knox, 1995), 250.

106. See Hanson (ibid.) for his argument that the debate is over the temple. For arguments centered on those who offer sacrifices, see Wim Beuken, "Does Trito-Isaiah Reject the Temple? An Intertextual Inquiry into Isa. 66:1–6," in *Intertextuality in Biblical Writings: Essays in Honour of Bas van Iersel*, ed. Sipke Draisma (Kampen: Kok, 1989), 54, 57; or Alexander Rofé, "Isaiah 66:1–4: Judean Sects in the Persian Period as Viewed by Trito-Isaiah," in *Biblical and Related Studies Presented to Samuel Iwry*, ed. Ann Kort (Winona Lake, IN: Eisenbrauns, 1985), 212.

joyful worship are those who reject God's name (66:5). Instead, like Ezra, Isaiah promotes austere practices centered on the reading of Torah—practices so deeply ingrained in the habitus of those who tremble at God's word that other practices are denied validity.

Rejoicing, singing, and praise led by priests are part of the celebrations associated with the temple in Ezra 3:11, 6:20–22, and Neh 12:43. In Ezra 7–10, there is no mention of joy or celebration in relation to religious practices. Although grounded in a priestly theology, the ritualized self-denial and Ezra's frequent posture of mourning and confession reflect the ascetic practices and commitments of *those who trembled*.[107] Blenkinsopp concludes that Ezra "appears to have found his principal support among a prophetic-eschatological group which espoused a rigorist interpretation of the law and which was out of favor with the religious leadership in the province."[108] The absence of temple rituals but the inclusion of priestly understandings of rituals—interpretations centered on separation and purity—are evidence of Levitical editors reworking Zadokite theology to extend priestly categories to the community as a whole.

Bradford Verter states, "Personal piety may be viewed as a matter of taste—in other words, as a product of social relations—and thus as a marker of status within struggles for domination in a variety of contexts. Spiritual knowledge, competencies, and preferences may be understood as valuable assets in the economy of symbolic goods."[109] Throughout this narrative, Ezra's spiritual competence accrues political and material capital. With this wealth of capital his leadership is unchallenged. The text then uses the character of Ezra to champion the marriage reforms and to advocate for the religious practices associated with him. These narrative strategies legitimate the worldview presented in this text and facilitate the modification of the worldview of the reader. For, as Bourdieu states, religious power is measured by the authority "to modify, in a deep and lasting fashion, the practice and world-view of lay people."[110] In this case

---

107. Fewell (private communication, 23 September 2012) notes the priestly theology. If Neh 8 is included as part of the Ezra memoir, even those celebrations are disconnected from sacrificial practices. People celebrate understanding the word of the law, share portions (Neh 8:12), and dwell in booths (Neh 8:17).

108. Blenkinsopp, *Ezra-Nehemiah*, 179.

109. Bradford Verter, "Spiritual Capital: Theorizing Religion with Bourdieu against Bourdieu," *Sociological Theory* 21 (2003): 152.

110. Bourdieu, "Legitimation and Structured Interests," 126.

it sanctifies political limits by converting them into divine law and legitimates forms of piety held by a specific group.[111]

13.5.2. Written Texts and Authority

Eskenazi identifies the authority of written texts as one of three major themes within Ezra-Nehemiah.[112] Yet Niditch reminds us that in the ancient world "the world of orality frames and colors a world of writing," and as a consequence the written word was respected and even "valorized as validating religious practice and belief."[113] Yet it also necessitated interpretation and scribes to give its meaning. The records, documents, and written law, though recognized as communication, were beyond the average person's ability to access.[114] This created a context in which "writing is often believed to have magical transformative qualities and in which writing has symbolic and monumental significance."[115]

Written communication such as letters, lists, or royal edicts continue to play a role in Ezra 7–10 much as they do in Ezra 1–6. But in these final chapters of Ezra, law takes center stage and is referenced in multiple ways.[116] Ezra brings the law from exile in order "to teach the statutes and ordinances in Israel" (7:10–11).[117] His skill and devotion to the study of law explains God's good hand on Ezra and therefore the king's generosity to him.[118] Ezra's reverence for the law translates into respect for Ezra and his

---

111. Bourdieu, "Genesis and Structure," 14.
112. Eskenazi, *In an Age of Prose*, 40. She also identifies themes of community and the house of God.
113. Niditch, *Oral World and Written Words*, 107.
114. Ibid., 143.
115. Ibid., 108.
116. Law would have an even greater role if the reading of the law in Neh 8 is included. The reading of Torah would be a motivation for the penitential prayer and divorce proceedings of Ezra 9–10. Blenkinsopp (*Ezra-Nehemiah*, 153) observes the many allusions to law in the text: "the law [Torah] of Moses" (Ezra 3:2; 7:6) or "the law of God/YHWH/God of heaven" (e.g., 7:10, 12), in addition to "the words" (9:4), and commandments, statutes, and ordinances (7:11; 9:10).
117. Pakkala, "Exile and the Exiles," 96.
118. In Deut 4:27–31, Moses states that if exiled people seek God he will not abandon them. Ezra in exile, setting his heart to seek the law, may be alluding to this text (cf. 1 Chr 28:8).

actions.¹¹⁹ Similarly, Ezra's prestige lends gravitas to those who continue to enact rules for the community based on the study of the Torah of God.

The word translated "study" (דרש) in Ezra 7:10 is one of several terms that refer to *seeking* in Ezra-Nehemiah. It is translated "worship" in Ezra 4:2 and 6:21 but is also associated with seeking the peace of others (9:12) or examining the list of those married to foreign women (10:16). Pakkala points out that the entire phrase, "he set his heart to seek," occurs elsewhere only in 2 Chr 12:14, 19:3, and 30:19 and refers to seeking *God*.¹²⁰ Ezra, however, sets his heart to seek the *Torah* of YHWH. By recycling the phrase, Ezra's study of the law is now equated with seeking God. In 2 Chronicles, seeking God (or not) is linked to religious faithfulness (or apostasy) and is the genesis for Hezekiah's reform. The language thus anticipates Ezra's coming reorganization. The Aramaic term בקר (found only in Ezra) refers to searches of official archives or histories in Ezra 4–6. In 7:14, the king sends Ezra "to make *inquiries* about Judah and Jerusalem *according to the law of your God, which is in your hand*."¹²¹ The law in Ezra's hand is mostly likely a reference to *written* laws. The connection between investigating the community based on written texts of divine law lays the groundwork to legitimate Ezra's assessment of the community's composition.

Law is a recurring theme within Artaxerxes's letter. The king sends Ezra, "the scribe of the law [דת] of the God of heaven" (7:12), "to make inquiries [lit. 'to seek'] about Judah and Jerusalem according to the law of your God" (7:14). Five times the letter refers to the "law" of either the God of heaven or of Ezra. Magistrates and judges are to judge all "who know the laws of your God; and … teach those who do not know them" (7:25). In 7:26, the king orders all who fail to obey the law of God and the law of the king to be punished. Eskenazi observes that these laws, divine and human, work together as the king's edict supports the law of God.¹²² As a result,

---

119. Eskenazi, *In an Age of Prose*, 76.

120. Pakkala, *Ezra the Scribe*, 31. "He [Rehoboam] did evil, for he did not set his heart to seek the LORD" (2 Chr 12:14). "Nevertheless, some good is found in you [Jehoshaphat], for you destroyed the sacred poles out of the land, and have set your heart to seek God" (2 Chr 19:3). "But Hezekiah prayed for them, saying, 'The good LORD pardon all who set their hearts to seek God, the LORD'" (2 Chr 30:18b–19).

121. A third term is בקש. In Ezra 7–10, it is used three times in three verses and always with regard to petitioning God (8:21–23; cf. 2:62). It occurs elsewhere in Neh 2:4, 10; 5:12, 18; 7:64; 12:27.

122. Eskenazi, *In an Age of Prose*, 75, 77.

in this narrative, all that transpires does so in keeping with the written law. By granting Ezra the authority to administer official policy, the king's letter allows Ezra's social policy to trump the authority of his superiors.[123] Ezra then uses his mandate and position as license to give new shape to the structure of the community—something completely absent from the imperial correspondence.

What are the implications of Ezra's relationship with the written law for the political and social organization of the Judeans? Mark Christian observes that the distribution of power at any one time depends upon the complex network (or field) in which it operates.[124] The Ezra nemoir shifts the power of the king into the hands of Ezra. The scribe chosen by the monarch and Deity to promulgate the law becomes a conduit for the central authority.[125] Ezra adapts the official memorandum with which he is entrusted to exercise his own power. He also employs his Torah knowledge as a means to ensure the loyalty of the members of his community and gain their support for his program.[126]

If Ezra (or this text) is to modify the worldview of others, the line of reasoning must coincide with the epistemological categories of the recipients (a product of their habitus), and new practices must resonate with ones already familiar to the audience. A different understanding regarding the marriages comes into being through religious language, rituals, social networks, and institutions with which the audience is already conversant. At the same time, the new rulings "find a stable place within an epistemological system whose existing elements undergo adaptation in order to accept them, making the 'incoming' components compatible."[127] Appeals to traditional religious concepts and familiar community values give Ezra's definitions discursive power to enact changes in the community's institutions. The law provides a legal basis for Ezra's ruling, and its authority sanctions this new social boundary.

---

123. Mark A. Christian, "Priestly Power that Empowers: Michel Foucault, Middle-Tier Levites, and the Sociology of 'Popular Religious Groups' in Israel," *JHebS* 9 (2009): art. 1, p. 47, doi:10.5508/jhs.2009.v9.a1.

124. Ibid., 52.

125. Christian (ibid.) argues for evidence of a similar expansion of Levitical power in the requirement to provide a copy of the law for the Judean king. The king's revelatory monopoly decreases, and he is no longer the scribe chosen by the Deity.

126. Ibid., 60.

127. Ibid., 66.

Ezra's prayer demands an increased level of devotion to YHWH by community members and defines this primarily in terms of family marriage arrangements. As the events play out in these chapters, the power to adjudicate is given into the hands of the local leadership, the officials.[128] But in turn, their decisions are grounded in the interpretive skills of the scribe of the Torah, Ezra. The king and the community agree to place deliberative powers into the hands of the Levite-priest-scribe. This scenario requires that Ezra maintain a balance between the various poles of influence. He must balance the desires of the king with his political (and coercive) capital against the social capital of the community and those with cultural and economic capital with whom he contends.

Those with the ability to read and interpret the law would have been in a position to reshape their own traditions and then deploy these written texts in service of new purposes. The oral cultural context gave the newly cast written law a numinous quality. The record of these events, incorporated into a religious text, contributes to the standardization and normalization of the behaviors according to the new categories espoused through Ezra's prayer. This contested new knowledge slowly insinuated "itself into the broader epistemological framework of Israel."[129] "By virtue of being written down and through the prestige of authoritative status as a text which interprets and enforces the 'law' … the ethnic boundaries which the text promotes are able to be perpetuated, and strengthened, in later Jewish literature and practice."[130]

13.6. Mixed Marriages

Frevel and Conczorowski state that the arguments against marriage to foreign women in Ezra 9–10 and Neh 13:23–24 "represent the most extensive and sophisticated anti-exogamy texts in biblical writings."[131] Roland Boer calls them xenophobic.[132] They are not the only texts in

---

128. Christian (ibid., 55) treats legal material in Deut 17, but his work provides the impetus for ideas employed here.
129. Ibid., 71.
130. Southwood, *Ethnicity*, 2.
131. Christian Frevel and Benedikt J. Conczorowski, "Deepening the Water: First Steps to a Diachronic Approach on Intermarriage in the Hebrew Bible," in Frevel, *Mixed Marriages*, 16.
132. "The act of preserving the community by expelling some is nothing other

Ezra-Nehemiah concerned with foreignness, but they are the only ones that treat it exclusively as a problem involving foreign *women*.[133] The ethically suspect breakup of these marriages raises a number of questions. What circumstances would motivate such an action? How is religious rationale complicit in these actions? Why are women the primary targets of the endogamous marriage reforms? Bourdieu's theories lend weight to some recent proposals regarding the role of ethnicity in these chapters and help to clarify how these texts functioned in their social context.

13.6.1. Marriage and Divorce in the Ancient Near East

We know of marriage and divorce practices in the fifth century BCE from a variety of sources, including seven marriage contracts from Elephantine. These contracts were composed as agreements between the groom and the bride's father or family member (although there is wide variety in this regard). Unlike the Deuteronomic divorce legislation, both wife and husband were equals "as far as the power of unilateral divorce."[134] Edward Lipiński notes that marriage involved the payment of a bride-price to the head of the bride's family but argues that this was undergoing significant developments in Western Asia and the payment was becoming part of the wife's dowry, which she would receive upon her husband's death or divorce.[135] He suggests that written contracts would more likely be used among the literate classes of Jewish society.

---

than xenophobic." So Roland Boer, "No Road: On the Absence of Feminist Criticism of Ezra-Nehemiah" in *Her Master's Tools? Feminist and Postcolonial Engagements of Historical-Critical Discourse,* ed. Caroline Vander Stichele and Todd Penner, GPBS 9 (Atlanta: Society of Biblical Literature, 2005), 238. He argues, however, that the expulsion may be related to broader issues of economics and power.

133. Several other texts concern separation from foreigners but do so with less regard to gender (Ezra 4:1–3; 6:21; Neh 9:2; 10:28–30; 13:1–3). Only Ezra 6:21 accommodates the incorporation of nonexilic people. Foreignness is also used to negatively depict Sanballat and Tobiah (Neh 2:10, 19; 4:3), yet both seem to have been legitimate partners for Judean officials. They have close family ties to the high priest, they communicate with them, and members of the community are bound by oath to them (Neh 6:17–19).

134. Edward Lipiński, "Marriage and Divorce in the Judaism of the Persian Period," *Transeu* 4 (1991): 66.

135. Ibid., 67.

Divorces required certainty and publicity.[136] The Pentateuch speaks only of men divorcing their wives, formalized by a bill of divorcement for the wife. Elephantine, on the other hand, recognizes both husband and wife having the right to divorce but cites no document; instead, "the proper divorce formula had to be spoken by the husband or the wife 'in the congregation,' a procedure that satisfied the need for certainty and that for publicity."[137] The congregation had no judicial role except as witnesses to the transaction. On this basis Lipiński contends that the court in Ezra 10:14 could only state whether the marriage was endogamous or not—they had no power to dissolve the marriages. That was up to the husbands. The decision to divorce could have been financially costly. He states,

> divorce had pecuniary consequences and the party taking the initiative was normally bound to pay the "divorce money" stipulated in the marriage contract. Besides, the husband was obliged to return the dowry and, according to Ezra 10:19, he was supposed in this particular case to bring a ram from the flock as a guilt-offering for the ritual sin that had consisted in his marriage with a "foreign" woman. All these obligations would probably restrain the large majority of ordinary people from divorcing their "foreign" wives.[138]

This cost may suggest a reason for the threat to confiscate property in Ezra 10:8. The members are threatened with the loss of *all* their possessions if they fail to cooperate. If they divorce, they retain their own holdings, even though the wife would leave with her dowry.

13.6.2. Membership or Marriages

Conczorowski observes that biblical texts employ various strategies to justify the prohibition of certain marriages: moral devaluation, fear of apostasy, and the dichotomy of pure versus impure or holy versus profane.[139] All are evident in Ezra 9–10. The author "applies priestly terminology to

---

136. Ibid., 70.
137. Ibid.
138. Ibid., 71.
139. Benedikt J. Conczorowski, "All the Same as Ezra? Conceptual Differences between the Texts on Intermarriage in Genesis, Deuteronomy 7 and Ezra," in Frevel, *Mixed Marriages*, 108.

the topic ... and constructs an exclusive ideal of the community as holy and pure."[140] This is interwoven with the Deuteronomistic fear of apostasy that links intermarriage with sin, pollution, shame, and guilt.[141] A series of mutually reinforcing boundaries (exilic history, Yahwism, and ethnic labels) are then enlisted to form "a deeply exclusive sense of community and results in the overly suspicious interpretation of outsiders."[142]

This textual strategy is aided by nuanced terminology. Southwood concludes that the account lacks any formal divorce document or formal divorce pronouncement (e.g., Deut 24:1–4). Nor is there mention of financial compensation, division of property, or restoration of the bride-price.[143] The divorce language from Deuteronomy, "he sends her out" (ושלחה), is not used here. Instead, women and children are to be "cast out" (להוציא), the language used elsewhere to terminate unions in which the woman's sexual purity is compromised.[144] Southwood observes that this language would coincide with a claim that the "foreign wives" are "impure, and therefore without legal standing."[145] The wording indirectly stigmatizes the character of the women by associating them with sexual transgression. The insinuation coincides with an established aversion to foreign women and so erodes their legal standing, delegitimizing what otherwise would be legal marriages. This justifies their removal without the formality of divorce proceedings. It also makes suspect all future marriages that transgress the defined boundaries.

"Foreignness" is problematic throughout Ezra, but Pakkala argues that only in later editorial additions is foreignness a matter of nonexilic history.[146] This displaces other more common means of demarcating ethnic groups. Ancient societies most often recognized someone's citizenship through relevant landownership and participation in communal activities,

---

140. Ibid.
141. Frevel and Conczorowski ("Deepening the Water," 16) identify both an antiapostasy and a cultic-related tradition in Neh 13:23–29.
142. Southwood, *Ethnicity*, 184.
143. Ibid., 177–78.
144. Ibid., 180. See Deut 22:21–24; Gen 38:24. She also notes that the language is used for Lot's daughters when offered to the men of the city (Gen 19:8).
145. Ibid., 181.
146. Pakkala, "Exile and the Exiles," 95. He states the oldest layers of the Ezra material assume that intermarriage is a sin committed by Jews who remained in the land (94, 97).

for example, shared cult, warfare, and communal assemblies.[147] Sanballat and Tobiah would easily qualify as citizens using these criteria. They have Yahwistic names; they are landholders; Sanballat is a governor in the area; and Tobiah's use of rooms in the temple suggests shared cultic practice. These criteria would also likely apply to the women. Yet the text insists that these influential men from the province and wives taken from the local population are "foreign." Prohibitions against intermarriage and exclusion from the cult "prevent the common activities that lead to integration."[148] Other avenues of recognition are cut off, leaving only an exilic history as the sole marker for membership.

Efforts to understand these heavily drawn boundaries have led scholars to explore possible structural explanations. Wolfgang Oswald examines Greek assemblies and maintains that, in contrast to monarchies that would benefit from foreign marriage alliances, marriage laws were "a common device [to control citizenship] in societies which are organized as associations of persons."[149] Oswald contends that, when compared with evidence from Greek texts (the citizenship law of Pericles, an inscription and court proceeding from Thasos), the assemblies found in Ezra and Nehemiah conform to the political organization of these Greek citizen states. In particular, the communities controlled their own affairs according to their laws, and the assemblies had legislative functions rather than merely providing auditoriums for royal edicts or trials more typical of assemblies in Mesopotamia.[150] He contends that the marriage crisis in Ezra was not a "crisis" associated with a specific occasion or certain period of time. Instead, he believes that the account reflects conflict over a structural issue—the nature of the community's organization "demanded certain regulations of this type."[151] He argues that prohibitions against marital ties (Deut 7:1–5; Exod 34:15–16) and expulsion from an institutional body as we find in Ezra 9–10 and Neh 13 "attests that the actors defined themselves politically as an association of persons."[152] Yehud's structure as a nonmonarchic state constituted by its assembly of citizens and its partici-

---

147. Wolfgang Oswald, "Foreign Marriages and Citizenship in Persian Period Judah," *JHebS* 12 (2012): 15, doi:10.5508/jhs.2012.v12.a6
148. Ibid., 16.
149. Ibid.
150. Ibid., 6, 14.
151. Ibid., 14.
152. Ibid., 5.

patory political system made it "necessary to control membership permanently and not only occasionally."¹⁵³

Fried questions whether the Judean community shared the drive toward democracy associated with the Greek assemblies, noting that the assemblies under the Babylonians, Assyrians, and Persians were always tyrannies.¹⁵⁴ She points out that, for aristocratic families, exogamous marital alliances "provided a power base outside of the *polis* … which could threaten [the city's] autonomy and supremacy."¹⁵⁵ She argues that the efforts to control foreign marriages reflect a desire to "limit the influence of these families."¹⁵⁶ Zlotnick-Sivan compares the community with the Roman reconceptualization of its early history. In both cases, family and community loyalties are at odds. She underscores the way in which men of the community in Ezra are compelled to eschew familial relations in order "to demonstrate their attachment to the community.… Patriarchy and patriotism assert themselves … at the expense of foreign women."¹⁵⁷

These comparative models draw attention to the important role of structural systems in fostering exclusion. However, Bourdieu compares the logical relations constructed in this way (even when nuanced for context) to mapping "all possible routes for all possible subjects," which is not the same as "the network of pathways that are really maintained and used."¹⁵⁸ He warns that the "map" puts theoretical relationships on the same footing with practical ones and can lead to "projecting into reality what only exists on paper."¹⁵⁹ Bourdieu proposes that habitus can assist in identifying which tracks are actually utilized because it brings attention to the role of practical beliefs in making practices sensible.¹⁶⁰ He argues that practices can "only be accounted for by relating the social

---

153. Ibid., 14.
154. Lisbeth Fried, "The Concept of 'Impure Birth' in 5th Century Athens and Judea," in *In the Wake of Tikva Frymer-Kensky*, ed. Steven Holloway, JoAnn Scurlock, and Richard Beal (Piscataway, NJ: Gorgias, 2009), 135.
155. Ibid., 137.
156. Ibid.
157. Zlotnick-Sivan, "Silent Women of Yehud," 14. The Roman example requires only that newly married women renounce their families of origin rather than requiring men to abandon their wives and children.
158. Bourdieu, *Logic of Practice*, 35.
159. Ibid., 36.
160. Ibid., 69. He contends that practical belief is not an arbitrary adherence to a set of instituted dogmas or state of mind but is a "state of body." He states, "Practical sense,

conditions in which the *habitus* that generated them was constituted, to the social conditions in which it is implemented."[161] Even an agent's conscious adjustments or actions "presuppose mastery of a common code."[162] Furthermore, to successfully mobilize the community requires "concordance between the *habitus* of the mobilizing agents (prophet, leader, etc.) and the dispositions of [the audience]."[163] Ezra's xenophobic outlook and exclusionary practices are driven not only by a reasoned response to external structures but by an internalized and embodied history that has found some concordance with new conditions.

A compelling explanation for the imposition of endogamous marriages in Ezra 9–10 has been suggested by Southwood, who analyzes the text informed by a wide range of ethnic theory. She states that rapid social changes, especially those associated with the experience of forced migration, are commonly perceived as threatening for the groups that experience them. This often results in the development of a sense of ethnicity and the "buttressing of, and increased emphasis on, established forms of exclusivity."[164] She further maintains that those who experience forced exile create an idealized view of the homeland. It is to this mythic homeland the exiles from Babylon imagined returning. Meanwhile Yehud underwent changes in population, landownership, and political structure. The clash between expectations and reality generated a sense of estrangement and alienation for the returnees.[165] This disjunction compounded awareness of ethnicity in this new context as "the 'people of the land' now function[ed] almost like surrogate foreigners against whom ethnic identity [could] be redefined."[166]

Southwood notes the preference for בני הגולה, "sons of the golah," rather than "holy seed" as an expression for the community. She contends

---

social necessity turned into nature, converted into motor schemes and body automatisms, is what causes practices … to be *sensible*, that is, informed by common sense."

161. Ibid., 56.
162. Ibid., 59.
163. Ibid.
164. Southwood, *Ethnicity*, 197.
165. Ibid., 203.
166. Ibid., 206. Southwood comments, "in order to create a sense of group membership, a group must fabricate an 'Other,' perceived as a binary opposite, external to the boundaries. However, we also recognized in the discussion of 'proximate Others' that distinctions made by ethnic actors are often not between binary opposites (as perceived), but between those groups sharing a degree of similarity" (188). See also 205.

that it reflects an awareness of being outsiders as well as acting as a "boundary-marking, self-isolation device."[167] The preference for "sons of the golah" may also be related to ongoing relations with those who remained in exile. This is hinted at in the provision for financial needs of those who make the journey. These texts reflect an acceptance of the Diaspora (no longer in a forced exile) as a fact of life.[168] Each major movement of return in these books is initiated in exile. Gifts from the Diaspora enrich the temple, while Levites, trained and living in exile, must be sought to accompany Ezra and teach the law. Knoppers points out that the return does not translate into a critique of those who choose to remain behind.[169] In fact, he argues, these actions reverse the normal homeland-diaspora relationship. Jerusalem is the community in need and dependent (much as a colony might be) on the strength and privilege of those living abroad.[170] These ongoing relations with the diasporic community hindered the returnees from full integration in Yehud by "providing them with the economic and social power to diminish the need for successful reassimilation."[171] Continued ties with the Diaspora would also have reinforced cultural practices associated with exilic identity and therefore "a greater propensity towards ethnic exclusivity."[172] One consequence is that those outside the group are conceived as inappropriate marriage partners. In this context, those "within the in-group who have selected partners from outside … [are] considered as deviants and coerced or forced to relinquish such partners."[173]

This reconstruction meshes with the operation of habitus. Southwood speaks of "functionally autonomous ethnic behaviors" developed in exile that stand behind the author's need for rigid ethnic boundaries in the new context of Yehud.[174] For Bourdieu, these "durable dispositions" "generate and organize practices and representations that can be objectively adapted

---

167. Ibid., 208.
168. Knoppers, "Exile, Return, and Diaspora," 48.
169. Ibid.
170. Ibid., 49. Rom-Shiloni (*Exclusive Inclusivity*, 87–89) also argues for a center-periphery relationship between Babylonian exiles and Jerusalem repatriates.
171. Southwood, *Ethnicity*, 201.
172. Ibid., 202.
173. Ibid., 185.
174. Ibid., 205. Bourdieu (*Logic of Practice*, 62) states that, in new contexts, groups "persist in their ways, due … to the fact that they are composed of individuals with durable dispositions that can outlive the economic and social conditions in which they were produced."

to their outcomes without presupposing a conscious aiming at ends."[175] Bourdieu observes that habitus gives weight to early experiences that make it resistant to change and protects itself from critical challenges by rejecting new information "capable of calling into question its accumulated information, if exposed to it accidentally or by force, and especially by avoiding exposure to such information."[176] Ezra 9–10 describes a community avoiding exposure to alternative practices and those who might introduce them. Ezra responds with shock to the foreign marriages because they are so alien to (his) normative practice. Furthermore, the persistence of habitus explains the retention of practices that are "objectively ill-adapted to the present conditions because they are objectively adjusted to conditions that no longer obtain."[177] The community persists in its exclusionary ways even when those ways outlive the economic and social conditions in which they were produced.[178]

13.7. Conclusions

As the book of Ezra closes, families are painfully torn apart, professedly to restore and protect the community. Couched as an essential action, it is attributed to the venerated Ezra and the entire early Jerusalem community. Claudia Camp states that in this narrative "foreignness" is a construct assigned to the people of the land as the exiles form their own identity by rejecting foreign women, "with all the rhetorical baggage of perverse sexuality they bring along."[179] She maintains that this is a textual trope that is part of a discourse on identity rather than an account of a historical reality.[180] Camp contends that the widespread metaphor of strange women implies a male gender identity issue and reasons, "The

---

175. Bourdieu, *Logic of Practice*, 53.
176. Ibid., 60.
177. Ibid., 62.
178. Ibid.
179. Claudia V. Camp, "Feminist- and Gender-Critical Perspectives on the Biblical Ideology of Intermarriage," in Frevel, *Mixed Marriages*, 305, 306.
180. Ibid., 304–5. Camp points to the narrative embellishments in the text as evidence of its theoretical character, e.g., Ezra brings back unrealistic amounts of silver to Yehud, the "fairytale quality" of his announcement calling all the men of Judah and Benjamin to Jerusalem within three days, the alacrity with which they agreed to divorce their foreign wives (Ezra 10:7–12), and the "heroic" accretions to the character of Ezra.

anti-marriage ideology is a surface manifestation of … deeper struggles with the construction of identity, all hinging on the androcentric construction of gender."[181] Her observation points to the fact that this discourse shapes (and is shaped by) its cultural context as well as social tensions between the author, his competitors, and the recipients of the text.

Underlying the narrative's undisguised interest in defining collective boundaries there operates a doxic conviction that the entire community shares responsibility for purity and enacting the reforms. This is potentially empowering for people who identify with the narrative community as they "come to play a substantive role in the reconstituting of the Israelite nation."[182] Several forms of capital are enlisted to lend credence to the community's actions. The critique of the marriages is shrouded in religious piety; Ezra's legal expertise and imperial appointment grant him authority to compel compliance. Rooting such practices in the commitments of the early community invalidates alternative practices—to belong means to conform. Advocates for a more open community now find the founding community arrayed against them.

Both Pakkala and Knoppers observe that in Ezra 7–10 one social formation is unmade and a new one constructed "according to mores developed and cultivated in the Diaspora."[183] This is accomplished "by producing, reproducing or destroying the representations that make groups visible for themselves and for others."[184] Familiar priestly classifications (holiness, purity) are set in opposition to the concept of the strange woman. Correspondences are then created between these and the objective divisions of society (the exiles as Israel versus the peoples of the lands).[185] Through these classificatory schemes, the author seeks to reconfigure (re-represent) the community. This necessitates a break with the previous order and producing a new common sense that integrates "within it the previously tacit or repressed practices and experiences of an entire group, investing

---

181. Ibid., 314.

182. Christian, "Priestly Power that Empowers," 73.

183. Knoppers, "Ethnicity, Genealogy, Geography, and Change," 149; Pakkala, "Intermarriage and Group Identity," 85.

184. Bourdieu, *Language and Symbolic Power*, 127.

185. Bourdieu (ibid., 134) states that the principles of division, the ability to favor certain aspects of reality and ignore others, are more powerful "when the divisions of thought correspond to real divisions."

them with the legitimacy conferred by public expression and collective recognition."[186]

Bourdieu argues that the question of legitimate social definition "arises only if a competing group lays claim to membership."[187] The existence of foreign marriages suggests alternative social constructions that represent a "heretical discourse." They disrupt the correspondence between mental representations and objective structures that form the basis of adherence to the "world of common sense."[188] Their existence produces a competing category of perception regarding group membership and identity and lays bare the arbitrariness of the social order. The public expression and collective recognition of these marriages makes this alternative social construction conceivable and credible.[189]

Ezra 9–10 embodies a dominant group's reactionary discourse against this alternative social order. In the struggle over what distinctive properties will characterize the members of the group, the social order espoused in the text is portrayed as obvious and necessary. It is naturalized by using "the language of nature" and sustained through "language of propriety and decency."[190] It becomes common sense that the holy seed is in danger of becoming polluted through the undesirable mixing with foreign women. The language and logic mark as valid internalized dispositions such as "Israel" and "purity," and it makes these exist as a social difference and presents them as "universal interests shared by the group as a whole."[191] Alternative sources of influence or social constructions are silenced or rejected as means to gain favored status.

Formalizing this construction of the community based on distinctive properties shifts what was a practical group to being an instituted group. Not only do certain traits now characterize members, but the act of institution annuls other properties "which might serve as a basis for other

---

186. Ibid., 129.
187. Bourdieu (*Outline*, 164) states that practical taxonomies (upon which this belief is constructed) are the product of the social order. "The adherence expressed in the doxic relation to the social world is the absolute form of recognition of legitimacy through misrecognition of arbitrariness, since it is unaware of the very question of legitimacy, which arises from competition for legitimacy, and hence from conflict between groups claiming to possess it" (168).
188. Bourdieu, *Language and Symbolic Power*, 129.
189. Ibid.
190. Ibid., 131.
191. Ibid., 167.

constructions."[192] This requires expressing the interests of a large segment of the community and monopolizing the "legitimate principle of division of the social world."[193] It deploys whatever instruments of power are most capable of making people see and believe and so ensure the support of the citizens. Religious ritual and language enunciate and dramatize classifications that are then recorded as a written record of agreement. Members can mobilize against the arrangement only if "they question the categories of perception of the social order which, being the product of that order, inclined them to recognize that order and thus submit to it."[194] This power to impose a vision of the social world translates into the ability to make and unmake groups.[195] Religion contributes uniquely to the imposition of this vision because "its system of practices and representations ... presents itself as the natural-supernatural structure of the cosmos."[196] The social and political structure, "objectively founded on a principle of political division," now becomes "God's will."[197]

For the men who embrace the identity expressed in Ezra 9–10, the text also informs each of them "of what he is and what he must be."[198] The division that identifies the men as members of a distinguished class leads to the reduction of those outside that boundary. What were once economically and politically astute marriages are now liabilities. The prayer frames these relations as jeopardizing the entire community's moment of favor (9:8) and provoking God to destroy them (9:14). More importantly they also endanger the men's identity as "Israel" and chosen people. The sense of importance and purpose for those so designated now hinges on adopting all that Ezra declares makes them worthy of the title.

Ezra commences his journey to Jerusalem with fasting and prayer for a safe journey "for ourselves, our children, and all our possessions" (Ezra 8:21). Despite prayers for the safety of family, the narrative does not end safely for all. To avoid the forfeiture of property, "the sons of the exile" attend an assembly (10:7–8). But, for 113 men, the cost of membership is the loss

---

192. Ibid., 130.
193. Ibid., 181.
194. Ibid., 131.
195. Ibid., 221.
196. Bourdieu, "Genesis and Structure," 5.
197. Ibid.
198. Bourdieu, *Language and Symbolic Power*, 121.

of their wives and sons.[199] The commitment to families created with wives acquired after the return is given over to the demands of the community.

---

199. The children who gather as part of the assembly that addresses the foreign marriages, are the ילדים. The term includes both genders, but the children of those wives are "sons" (בנים). Sons could inherit and control property and inherit their father's position within the structure of the assembly.

14
Conclusions

> The culture of a people is an ensemble of texts, themselves ensembles, which the anthropologist strains to read over the shoulders of those to whom they properly belong.
> —Clifford Geertz

Ezra-Nehemiah is an ensemble of texts composed by various authors at different times and knitted together by later editors. At each stage contributors wrote to persuade an unconvinced and perhaps resistant readership to modify their view of the social world in accordance with the values and social order each felt essential for the community. The particulars of the discourse provide data to construct a context for its production: sources of competition, the authors' positions within the community, and the social backdrop against which appeals to the audience are deployed. In the preceding analysis, I offer insights into how the ancient authors navigated their social world and how that context shaped their argumentation.

These books are a cultural production, operating in a field that uses an inverse logic to the economic field. Legitimation and power are achieved by means that eschew money or coercive power. The authors compete not only with other cultural producers but also against economic inducements or threats directed at their audience. At stake is the definition of the community and, with that, the author's position and influence within it as well as in the wider world. By token of their literary expertise, the authors already hold a dominant position within the cultural field and operate essentially defensive strategies, designed to perpetuate social and political arrangements beneficial to their own positions. They employ their capital to limit the influence of those entering the field and to shape the structure of the cultural field in ways beneficial to their particular forms of capital. Each of the three major sections of these books displays different symbolic strategies, different forms of capital associated with the authors, and changing social contexts. At the same time, each piece contributes to an overall rhetoric that furthers a developing definition of the community that suits the cultural producers at the time of the latest textual production.

14.1. The Date of Writing

Behind the rhetoric of the three major narrative episodes of Ezra-Nehemiah lie unique historical realities. Later compilers, wrestling with their own circumstances, reshaped these accounts and obscured the initial narratives and original concerns. Assigning dates for this material is difficult due to the reuse of lists, edicts, and prayers as well as the rearrangement of earlier material. Even so, there remain distinctive rhetorical strategies and themes that testify to the separate historical contexts of each narrative.

The earliest narrative, portions of the Nehemiah memoir, dates to the latter years of Artaxerxes I (465–424 BCE). Nehemiah is believed to have arrived in Jerusalem in 445 and composed his memoir some fifteen or more years later. In the memoir, controversy is largely between Nehemiah and fellow political appointees. His actions and rhetoric display a level of autonomy that is not shared by the latest portions of these books. Notably, Nehemiah is concerned with establishing boundaries; but identifying legitimate community members is not a matter of debate, indicating a more cohesive community than is attested in later texts.

According to the Ezra memoir (Ezra 7–10; Neh 8), Ezra arrived in Jerusalem prior to Nehemiah, but the conflict over establishing communal membership corresponds with a later, growing community of repatriots. The matter is framed in terms of ethnicity, but the determining categories for inclusion are obedience to Torah and exilic history. Levites who arrive from exile are portrayed as teachers and scholars of religious texts. This suggests that the memoir is a product of an established literary elite associated with the exilic community. By placing the temple in the background and pressing the case for Levites, the text testifies to a contested situation over power among the temple leadership. The twin concerns, community purity and Levitical power, may reflect two distinct accounts composed at different times. That an earlier version has been broken apart and rearranged makes dating this section difficult, but one could still place its completed form sometime after the Nehemiah memoir but before the addition of Ezra 1–6 (possibly during the reigns of Darius II, 423–405; or Artaxerxes II, 405–360).

14. CONCLUSIONS

The narrative of Ezra 1–6 dates to the last decades of Persian rule, between 410 and 333. Its placement at the beginning of Ezra-Nehemiah marks the temple and its priesthood as an essential starting point and centerpiece for the author and his community. This defense of the Jerusalem temple perhaps reflects competition from the temple in Samaria, temples elsewhere, or economic adversity.[1] These chapters more delicately thread the needle between Persian authority and local autonomy, grounding the community in distinctive religious practices centered on the Jerusalem temple as a balance to increased Persian influence. The use of Aramaic and attention to paper shuffling are further indicators of tightening bureaucratic control by Persia.

The various lists, letters, and prayers are earlier compositions now repurposed within Ezra-Nehemiah. In their new setting, they take on new significance. In particular, the penitential prayers (Ezra 9, Neh 1:5–11, and Neh 9) draw on earlier compositions and were added as late as the reigns of Artaxerxes II and Artaxerxes III (359–338) or even during Ptolemaic rule. They contain a reasoned theology that interprets the exile or foreign domination as a national trauma rooted in divine judgment against Israel. Corporate responsibility for the past generates a sense of control over the future. Yet it also warns against the present tenuous status of the community. The recitation of these prayers galvanizes the hearers to embrace exclusionary ethnic and religious practices so as to maintain divine favor.

The community's membership and character remain a primary concern throughout these books. Although seemingly settled in one section of the account, the same matters persist throughout the entirety of these books. Thus Nehemiah physically controls access to Jerusalem as a means to contain external influences. Ezra will demand the expulsion of women and their children to halt foreign influence. The priests in Ezra 1–6 offer a green card but require holders to separate themselves from the nations. Responses to the significant issue of membership continue to evolve over the course of Persian rule.

---

1. We know of correspondence seeking support for the Yahwistic temple at Elephantine in 410 BCE.

14.2. Behind the Text: The Social Context

Evidence within Ezra-Nehemiah suggests that, in the Persian period, relations between returnees and the surrounding communities were more ambiguous than the overall narrative indicates. The adversaries in Ezra 4 claim to seek the same God as the exiles, and the list of returnees in Ezra 3 and Neh 7 is organized in part by towns in Benjamin—the area where population continued throughout the Babylonian era. Members of the community are married to people from the region, Tobiah has rooms in the temple, and the high priest's son is married into his family. Prophetic and prayer traditions of both exiles and those who remained in the land are incorporated into the text.[2] Nehemiah refers to the Judeans, not exiles, and his imprecatory prayer to God (Neh 4:10–12 [4–6 MT]) seems to assume that Sanballat and Tobiah pray to the same deity.[3] The text could have employed this common ground to legitimate the temple and worship for audiences from these disparate backgrounds. Shared religious traditions and geographic proximity could have provided a basis for inclusion in the community, yet these are rejected in these texts. Despite the available building blocks for a more inclusive community, the authors repudiate broader constructions and opt instead for a community with an exclusive and exilic character.

The text testifies to a growing divide between new arrivals and the local population. The preexilic historical and legal traditions are nuanced and used to justify dividing those who belong from "others." Readers are invited to embrace distinctive practices that segregate participants from others (e.g., Sabbath keeping, the Festival of Booths, and worship at the Jerusalem temple). Hostilities against outsiders grow from Nehemiah's conflict with regional rulers to more generalized rejection of entire communities and the removal of women newly identified as foreign. To avoid being perceived as outsiders and opponents, members commit themselves to support the temple, adhere to Torah, and maintain ethnic boundaries built primarily on shared religious practices and exilic history.

Throughout these books imperial influences are under constant and nuanced negotiation. Persia's royal largesse and support for the commu-

---

2. Ezra 1–6 uses Jeremiah and Haggai/Zechariah prophecies, which present opposing "signet ring" language, and the penitential prayer of Neh 9 reflects a nonexilic outlook.

3. Knoppers, "Nehemiah and Sanballat," 329–30.

nity is an ongoing theme. Each stage of return begins with imperial permission. Kings authorize the construction of the temple and city walls and grant access to materials necessary for the task. Nehemiah highlights his close personal relationship with the monarch as a source of personal cultural capital. However, he carries out his building campaign and institutes his social reforms without recourse to imperial provisions, despite opposition from others. Ezra, too, enjoys the prestige of a royal appointment, but once he delivers the king's commission to the satraps and governors, he never again mentions the king. The steps taken to shape the community in Ezra 9–10 are done without any outside interference. In Ezra 1–6, royal consent is a contested commodity and key to the resumption of the project. The monarch is credited for his support, and prayers may be said on his behalf, but the account avoids assigning him the role of temple builder—that is reserved for the local community.

Although the presentation of Persian rulers and representatives is carefully controlled, it appears that over time Persian involvement in local bureaucracy increases. Nehemiah's independent actions of restoration are replaced in Ezra 1–6 with repeated correspondence between local representatives and the monarch. Whether the details of the correspondence are accurate or not, they likely replicate government practices familiar to the author of Ezra 1–6. While giving ground to the power of kings, the authors keep them at arm's length with regard to the community's organization. Only *local* powerbrokers are problematic, and any negative imperial decision is attributed to the influence of these regional competitors.

Persian rule is a reality the local leadership can use to their advantage. Royal patronage legitimates each successive exilic leader and provides for the temple and affirms its validity. However, Persian rule also circumscribes options available for self-definition, and so the text promotes certain choices while ignoring those lost due to imperial rule. There would be no Judean king, there would be no national state, and taxes would be paid into Persian coffers. Local conflicts would at times have to defer to imperial decisions. These circumstances produce a definition of the community using criteria of kinship, worship, shared history, and commensality—criteria disconnected from political or geographical boundaries. The specific character of these criteria is shaped by exilic experience. The evolving definition of the community is validated by familiar rituals that cement a particular definition of the community.

This literary production was generated in the context of a confluence of opportunity and obstacles. Exiles returned with an idealized concept of their former land only to be confronted by a region populated by people with their own claims on the land and their own cultural practices. They had to contend with economic hardship and other sites of worship and adjust to Persian hegemony. Additionally, even among the exiles there was not a consistent theology, as evidenced by the priestly and Levitical additions to these books, nor a shared perspective on relations with locals. These realities complicated claims regarding the temple's centrality and efficacy. The defense of the temple, particularly by the author of Ezra 1–6, suggests that influence over the community relied heavily on the temple retaining an active stake in the cultural field.

Efforts to form a more cohesive community also faced challenges. Exilic and nonexilic Judeans were separated by distinct histories and their associated traumas and practices. The repatriates' ties to the Diaspora reduced the need to integrate with the local economy and society and continued to reinforce cultural practices associated with exilic identity. Economic hardship and class distinctions created further tension. Each factor complicated the simplistic definition of membership and weakened the social utility provided by a more unified and cohesive community. The rhetorical force of Ezra-Nehemiah mitigates the fracturing of the community by strengthening a cohesive and exclusionary worldview. The rhetorical strategies adopted in these texts compel obedience. This bolsters both the temple's value (its cultural capital) and the prestige and coherence of the community, but is achieved at the expense of other worship sites, practices, and peoples. The limitations placed on membership also limit the community's economic possibilities.

14.3. In the Text: A Response to the Times

Narrative strategies in each portion of the text engage ideals or motifs familiar to the ancient audience. Ezra 1–6 constructs its narrative around a temple building account and recasts the journey of the repatriates as a second exodus. The account undermines the conventional representation of the king as temple builder as it substitutes the exiles as the primary protagonists. The creation or inclusion of imperial edicts and letters and the many lists all lend an air of authenticity to the narrative that produces a formal legitimacy. The three penitential prayers provide essential starting points to reform, reflecting an important practice developed in response to the destruction of Judah by the Babylonian army. They interpret the destruction and deportation as a trauma that produced a profound sense of national shame. The confessions absolve the Deity of fault and attribute blame to the community. This cedes responsibility to the community to make amends and restore its standing before the Deity and the world. In the Nehemiah memoir, holy war rhetoric links Nehemiah with heroes of the past. The reproach of captivity and foreign power is removed through the reconstruction of the wall and purifying ritual acts. In the final half of Nehemiah, the familiar customs of Torah reading and Sabbath keeping are instituted and associated with the maintenance of purity now equated with ethnic boundaries. The varied religious rhetoric in these texts builds legitimacy into the actions of the protagonists and ensures the durability of the community's adherence to the authors' vision for society.

Consistent with efforts by the dominant class to defend doxa or, failing that, to establish orthodoxy, the text rhetorically exerts pressure on its audience to conform—and attaches penalties to deviance.[4] This imposes greater demands on those whose membership or identity is insecure. Alternative social constructions are soundly rejected by associating them with opposition, threats, and conflict. Limiting collaboration and excluding opponents overwrites competing claims with regard to legitimate worship and definitions for the community. Describing outsiders as opponents (or opponents as outsiders) also repudiates any alternative forms of worship or social arrangements that come from those quarters. Only Ezra 7–10 lacks contesting voices. The community is unified in its commitment to purify itself. The women identified as foreign speak no words and make no claims, and no opposition is voiced to the community's plan despite the personal and economic cost of adhering to the narrowly defined ethnic parameters. In a narrative composed for a later generation, the heightened religious motivation for these marital rearrangements testifies to a contested situation, one that required considerable symbolic capital to gain compliance and then maintain it.

14.3.1. Forms of Capital

In each of the three major narratives in these books, different forms of cultural capital are in play. In Ezra 1–6, the ordained priesthood is given a central role. The resumption of temple ritual requires an official priesthood, and the ritual performance in Ezra 3 marks the people as distinc-

---

4. Bourdieu, *Outline*, 169.

tive (and the priests even more so). The priesthood is reserved for members with particular family lineages, and this limitation provides a basis for hierarchy within the community. Their presence and purification are essential elements to the successful institution of the temple altar and the celebration of Passover. In Ezra 4–6, scribal expertise defeats the opposition's own scribal efforts to halt construction. The author weaves examples of textual production—lists, edicts, and letters—into his narrative. The text is composed in two languages, demonstrating the value of facility in official discourse and official language, and success hinges on archival searches. The need for such expertise to successfully construct the temple attests to the value of those holding these specialized skills.

Although Ezra is given a priestly genealogy and title in Ezra 7–10, he is renowned for his skill and devotion to Torah. This dedication seems to garner him a governmental role to enforce laws and appoint judges and magistrates. His heightened prestige grants him unquestioned authority in the narrative community, but the account shifts from an interest in Ezra's personal cultural capital in Ezra 7–8 to a focus on the community. Ezra's leadership style is markedly organic. He makes public confession but waits for community members to raise issues, suggest solutions, and carry out decisions. Even the covenant that limits membership in Ezra 10 is enacted by the community. Each member is ritually instituted as a custodian of the limits of the assembly.[5] The group acting in concert achieves what the actions of an individual leader alone cannot—a definitive and enforced boundary. By establishing a monopoly over marital exchanges, the community is constituted of homogeneous individuals "in all the pertinent respects in terms of the existence and persistence of the group."[6] The social relationships produced are perceived as necessary, with durable obligations and institutionally guaranteed rights. Such a cohesive social group becomes useful for securing material or symbolic profit.[7] The narrative encourages the endless reproduction of this definition of the community as it invites readers to recognize it as essential. This social capital, now embedded in the text, becomes one more source of legitimation for the structure of the field that suits the author's position.

---

5. Bourdieu, "Forms of Capital," 250.

6. Ibid.

7. Ibid., 249: a useful social network is the "product of an endless effort at institution." In these circumstances, contingent relationships are deemed necessary and elective and obligations are "either subjectively felt or institutionally guaranteed."

Like Ezra, Nehemiah is also portrayed as a favorite of the Persian monarch. Unlike Ezra, he must galvanize the narrative community to action and convince them and the readers that, indeed, he has their best interests in mind. Portrayed in the heroic manner of Joshua, he completes the wall and resolves economic injustice, putting his skills and his benevolent intentions on display. At no point are documents, scribal skills, or priests essential to his success. Nehemiah does not contend with a crowd of ill-defined foreigners but with individual leaders who wield forms of capital similar to his own. Nor does Nehemiah require lay elders or priests to lend support to his policies: all bow to the force of his capital. Nehemiah's character advances his position by means of condescension and acts of disinterested loyalty. He has the means and the power to rule, but at each step demonstrates his commitment to the community's good over his personal gain. His story becomes a testimony to the essential role a Persian appointee can play to counter unwanted influences seeking control over the city of Jerusalem. It also communicates that physical control over the city creates a space in which the community can define itself as evidenced in the rituals and reforms that follow the wall's construction.

In each major episode of Ezra-Nehemiah, the intended goal is achieved: the temple is completed, the walls are repaired, and the community purified against the threat of divine punishment. All this is accompanied by a growing definition of the character and boundaries of the community. The combination accrues recognition for people holding the forms of capital utilized by the narrative heroes and lends legitimacy to similar boundaries, actions, or beliefs regarding the community. Yet Neh 13, the final conclusion, reveals a distressing failure to maintain the community's center (the temple) or boundaries. Taken as a whole, Ezra-Nehemiah issues an invitation and a warning. The audience is called upon to give generously to the temple, to accept Persian rule, and to maintain boundaries against the wider population. The community that takes these actions achieves distinction, but failure to maintain vigilance over its boundaries endangers its existence. Readers are motivated to conform to these arrangements through identification with the narrative community.

14.3.2. The Representation of the Social Field

In all three portions of Ezra-Nehemiah, definition of the various agents and communities is problematic. The text employs stereotypes of both members and nonmembers of the community. These form an important dimension of classification and identification but do not provide clarity about how distinctions are made.[8]

The terms used for outsiders either lack specificity or, conversely, are unequivocally clear about a character's identity. These "others" are vaguely grouped as "peoples of the lands" or individually identified with a foreign state, Tobiah *the Ammonite* or Gershom *the Arab*. Not only are they foreign but they are dangerous opponents. In Ezra 1–6, people claim to seek the same God as the exiles, but before they even speak they are introduced as people to be feared (3:3) and as adversaries (4:1); and by their own admission, their history is different from "Israel." In Ezra 7–10, women and their children, already part of the community, are removed on the basis of being "foreign," their continuing presence linked to divine punishment. In Nehemiah, in response to reading the Torah, the community again separates itself from all those who are foreign (Neh 9:2) or "mixed" (13:3 KJV). The book concludes with Nehemiah still admonishing the community about a failure to separate from foreign women (13:26–27). Both books clearly express anxiety about foreignness, but what constitutes "foreignness" is not made explicit.

Those negatively stereotyped have their cultural capital, specifically their religious capital, invalidated, limiting their ability to compete with the author on those terms. In Ezra 1–6 and Nehemiah, they therefore turn to the wider economic and political powers to engage the community. The anxiety over these "others" indicates alternative constructions of the community that would accommodate a more inclusive definition of the community are perceived as threats to the community and to the author's interests. The use of stereotypes combines with purity language and ritual to advocate for, and enforce, a community defined by ethnic, religious, and historical criteria.

---

8. Scholars vary over whether the "foreign" label in these texts reflects a truly different origin for those so labeled or is a polemical usage designed to create difference. Two rather different historical contexts can be imagined: either the "people of the land" are descendants of foreigners or, as I believe, they are non-exiled Judeans. In the absence of the temple the Judeans would have developed new religious practices different from those that arose in exile; however, this would not constitute an ethnic difference. The trio of Tobiah, Gershom, and Sanballat exemplify a greater ethnic and religious diversity and partnering with them would represent more collaborative relations within the wider region.

Terms referring to members of the community are equally varied and ill-defined. Lists of returning exiles, ostensibly organized by family, include groupings by local towns and non-Israelite personal and family names. Judah and Benjamin are used to refer to the community (Ezra 1:5; 4:1; 10:9; Neh 11:31, 36) but are used interchangeably as geographic and tribal references and equated with the exiles (Ezra 4:1). Prior to his return, Nehemiah asks about "the Jews that survived" in Judah (Neh 1:2) and refers to them as "Israel" (Neh 2:10).[9] Most commonly the Jerusalem community is called *Israel* or (literally) *sons of the exile*. *Israel* links them to the monarchical Judah, while the title *sons of the exile* links them to the community of the Diaspora. Although exilic status appears to be an essential ingredient to membership, nowhere is this directly posited as the basis for participation. This lack of definition may be an example of doxa; certain things are known by agents without having to articulate how it is known. However, it also is an indication of changing conditions. In Nehemiah, the local population is "Israel." By the time Ezra is composed, that title belongs to the exiles alone.

Social structure and leadership within the community lack consistent representation. In Ezra 1–6, Jeshua the high priest shares leadership with Zerubbabel, and priests perform an essential role in the dedication of the temple, while the contribution of Levites is limited. As a result, priests benefit from the greater allocation of symbolic capital for their positions. The laity is distinguished by their inclusion in the community and identification as those who returned from exile, and their prestige is enhanced by limiting membership. The accident of birth or history is treated as determinative for membership. These arbitrary norms of determining membership or selecting priests are legitimated by their inclusion in this literary production. The existence of these books with their clashes over participation and detailed membership lists now disqualifies those who may have been included based on other criteria.

In Ezra 9–10, the active participation of lay leadership reduces Ezra's role to one of public mourning and calling on the people to carry out their own decisions (10:5, 10–11). The community is led by officials, heads of the fathers, and elders. In these chapters, the group is represented not by a single individual but by a variety of agents who represent the assembly and

---

9. Within the wider literary context, one might contend that this refers to earlier returnees, but the account does not use the same language or make the same distinction between residents as we find elsewhere in these accounts.

act in its name. However, the situation requires the "'great' to step forward and defend the collective honor" by forcing the expulsion of the embarrassing individuals.[10]

While great attention is given the acquisition of Levites from Casiphia in Ezra 8, their key role of teaching Torah is displaced to Neh 8. Their close association to Torah and instruction suggests an alternative religious leadership in competition with the Jerusalem priesthood. This may explain the attention given their skills with the law and teaching, and even suggests a desire to add to their legitimacy by highlighting their leadership in the Festival of Booths. In Nehemiah, the festival needs no formal temple rituals but becomes a response to the ritualized reading of the law presented with all the trappings of an act of worship. The use of lineage as the criterion for priestly ordination and Levitical status excluded Levites from supreme temple leadership but helped maintain well-educated members of this class as a select body. The Levites' ability to draw upon written sources to validate or explain religious or social actions provided a further avenue to cement their place within the community.

Throughout Nehemiah, snapshots of the community hint at variety and structure in the local lay leadership. Nehemiah 2:16 refers to "the Jews, the priests, the nobles, the officials, and the rest." Yet in the first six chapters no one but Nehemiah exercises leadership.[11] Nehemiah prays for them and prods them to construct the wall. When threatened by Sanballat and Tobiah, "Judah" complains to Nehemiah, who motivates the people to continue working and complete the project. In later chapters, nobles and priests take actions that invariably contravene Nehemiah's actions on behalf of the larger community. In Neh 5, he intervenes in a conflict between nobles and the people. In Neh 6, the nobles send messages to Tobiah (6:17), and Nehemiah remonstrates with them for trading with the Tyrians on the Sabbath (13:17). Likewise in Neh 13, he takes on the high priest who has made accommodations for Tobiah in the temple. In this account, the leaders do little to aid Nehemiah's efforts of reconstruction or reform, and the narrative undermines their influence in the community to the benefit of Nehemiah. Nobles and officials are of little help against opponents, and priests are less protective of the sanctity of the temple than is Nehemiah. The internal organization of the community is of little

---

10. Bourdieu, "Forms of Capital," 251.

11. Nobles, as a class, occur in the Hebrew Bible almost exclusively in Nehemiah and not at all in Ezra.

concern in the Nehemiah memoir. It is most concerned with Nehemiah's peers, competitors with economic or cultural capital, in or outside the community. Each is handled in ways that advance the author's standing before the general public. As a result, the image we gain casts all possible leaders as suspect and prone to advancing "outside" influences for economic gain and personal advancement. One thing, however, that is not present in these chapters is a dichotomy between exiles and nonexiles. In the memoir, local Judeans are threatened, not by nonexilic "people of the land," but by individual leaders with ties to the neighboring states of Ammon, Samaria, and Arabia.

Throughout Ezra-Nehemiah there is a consistent drive to separate the community from a variety of groups or people deemed outsiders. Purity language justifies the existence of the laity as occupants of a distinguished position in the world. The language grounds the dignity of the community in a conviction of their own excellence.[12] By being labeled as alien, competing claims or beliefs are disqualified, and this maintains the community's superiority in propaganda.[13] The temple creates a focal point for this community, while language, kinship, exilic status, and shared history mark the boundaries allowing participation in worship. The author employs his own pen and his access to written Torah to guide the ritual and social life of the community and to mediate the distance between king and people.[14] In employing and elevating his communication skills, he maintains the political and social hierarchies of his world. The penitential prayers, the public reading and ritualized responses of commitment to Torah, and the calls to purity appeal to the reader to embrace the community created by these symbolic acts and to identify themselves with the textual community's commitments of ethnic (or more specifically exilic) difference.

The text constructs classifications to produce a distinctive community. It transforms a practical group into an instituted group. This requires producing a new common sense that integrates within it previously tacit practices and experiences and investing them with legitimacy.[15] The classifications are enunciated and dramatized in religious language and ritual

---

12. Bourdieu, "Legitimation and Structured Interests," 125.
13. Weber, *Sociology of Religion*, 70.
14. On the use of written texts in an oral culture, see Niditch, *Oral World and Written Words*, 106. On mediating social distance, see Bourdieu, *Language and Symbolic Power*, 167.
15. Bourdieu, *Language and Symbolic Power*, 129.

that strengthen them against alternatives. The text motivates the reader to embrace the definition of the group by the claim to distinction. It also encourages a sense of responsibility by combining the fear of divine wrath with shame over the alternative. Not only do certain traits now characterize members, but the acts of institution annul other properties "which might serve as a basis for other constructions."[16]

14.4. The Readers: Perspective and Influence

The author appeals to the reader to embrace membership in an ethnically bounded, temple-centered community—one that is led by those most skilled to meet their ideological or religious needs and most able to navigate the political landscape. However, the legitimacy of such claims rests not on social utility but on the extent to which the people's beliefs converge with the purposes for which the leadership exercises authority. The more the proffered construction conforms to the people's values or satisfies their normative expectations, the more likely it is to be given consent as legitimate.[17] This suggests that the reinforcement of boundaries described in the text connected with readers' tacit practices. It may also indicate that worship of the reading audience is most likely enlisted as a basis for the accounts of worship in Ezra-Nehemiah. The connection of the audience's practices with the first returnees, the premonarchic past, and obedience to Torah consecrates their ongoing practices. It encourages them to perceive themselves as distinguished through association with the historical returnees, who perform the same rituals, embrace the same boundaries, and enforce them with the same social strategies. These practices are now intertwined with an increasingly rigid definition of the community. This linkage invites recognition of the associated claims as also legitimate.

In each narrative movement, the actors express the value of the community and protagonists sacrifice for the good of the community. They give of their wealth, they relinquish wives and children, and they endure ridicule and opposition in order to create the community now constituted by the reading audience. The steps taken to create the community involve a host of attitudes and actions: giving tithes and donations to the temple, forgoing interest on loans within the community, enforcing social

---

16. Ibid., 130.
17. Beetham, *Legitimation of Power*, 11.

boundaries through exclusionary measures (sacrificing wives and children, ejecting those labeled as foreign), sacrificing time and wealth for public construction such as the temple or wall, collective expressions of penitence, adhering to the content of the agreement and covenant that define the community membership and community responsibilities. To emulate these sacrificial actions constitutes honorable commitments. Bourdieu comments that "collective judgment cannot but perceive, and approve, an expression of recognition of the value of the group and of the group itself as the fount of all value."[18] However, to be certain, at every step royal edicts, rituals, and theological statements articulate and affirm the group's sense of their own worth. Benefits that accrue to particular positions within the community are obscured or made acceptable as they are seen to result from acts in service of the greater good.

The redefinition of the community continued over a long period of time. Changing circumstances were met with changing tactics and were accompanied by a move toward greater exclusionary practices. Authors adopted different strategies due to their different forms of capital as they competed with opponents over the ability to modify the worldview of the audience. The early heroic tale of Nehemiah, the Persian appointee, is concerned primarily with removing the shame of destruction. That he records his exploits with a mind to ensure his own legacy skews the account so the value of his own capital is on display.

The remigration of exiles complicates the definition of the community. In Ezra 7–10 and Neh 8, another hand takes up the pen and creates a community grounded in practices from the exile: the reading of Torah and signing covenants to maintain practices of boundary maintenance such as Sabbath keeping and endogamous marriage contracts. Levites now assume a prominent teaching role, but the community relies on elders and fathers and officials who share responsibility to lead the community as they carry out agreed-upon commitments.

Ezra 1–6, the youngest layer of the text, is placed at the beginning of the account, establishing the temple as the central component of the community. Priests take the lead in communal worship, but the overall leadership is held jointly by the high priest and the governor. Most obvious at this point is the need to navigate Persian bureaucracy and local opposi-

---

18. Ibid., 59–60.

tion; thus a case is made to join together or risk losing control over their sacred institution.

The persuasive discourse throughout these books is reacting to a stressful, contested context of a changing and growing population, increasing imperial influence, economic activity from external sources, and contested leadership at the local level. Although its definition of group identity is clearly exclusionary in terms of ethnicity, the text makes accommodations to certain realities. The readers are never asked to reject Persian rule, to act in ways detrimental to Persian rule or to the community's standing before the king. The community is not confined by geography or state borders. The boundaries advocated here allow inclusion that accommodates distant exilic communities throughout the empire. Only those who lack this history are the target of exclusion. It is unlikely that all readers adopted the strategies advocated here. The argument for exclusivity is made with great force, suggesting resistance to such stringent interpretations of Israel's practices or boundaries.[19] The text itself acknowledges that repeated efforts were needed to gain conformity. However, the text is retained; and as Southwood observes, those who write the literature "retain the power to establish and to perpetuate self-designations and classifications of Others."[20] Yet other preserved texts dispute the boundaries drawn here, and even within Ezra-Nehemiah there is mute testimony to the permeable boundaries of the congregation.

By using Bourdieu's theories, I have in this study demonstrated that in this text a cultural ethos of a particular class is carefully transfigured into a religious ethical requirement for the entire community. Religious language in this text systematizes and rationalizes an ensemble of explicit norms impacting societal relations. It then consecrates and validates the perspective advanced. Bourdieu's work allows us to observe how pragmatic motivations for land, power, or prestige can be obscured by religious logic and how this rhetoric influences the reader by engaging with their doxic values.

---

19. Katherine Southwood, "An Ethnic Affair? Ezra's Intermarriage Crisis against a Context of 'Self-Ascription' and 'Ascription of Others,'" in Frevel, *Mixed Marriages*, 59.

20. Ibid., 46.

14.5. Reading over the Shoulder

To read over the shoulders of those who originally possessed a text is problematic. Bourdieu argues that the one "looking over the shoulder" does not hold the same perceptual and evaluative schemata of agents in the original culture and therefore perceives and evaluates the culture using different criteria.[21] This is in part because we do not share the same social structures. He invites us to engage in what he terms "reflexive sociology"—to be aware of one's own perceptions and appreciations, one's habitus. Our point of view always owes something to our situation in a field.[22] Bourdieu identifies three types of biases that blur the sociological gaze: the social origins of individual researchers, their position within the academic field, and their intellectualist bias.[23] Reflexivity involves the exploration of these "unthought categories of thought [because they] delimit the thinkable and predetermine the thought."[24]

Investigations that focus on issues of dating, historical veracity, and compositional sequence are concerns born of the Enlightenment and tend to view the biblical text as a report of reality rather than recognizing that they are "implicated in the work of reality construction."[25] The text's heated polemics often appear as an obstacle to such investigations. This intellectual bias, construing the world as something to be interpreted rather than as concrete social problems to be solved, "can lead us to miss entirely the … [specific] logic of practice." I hope that, by employing a Bourdieuian lens, this study has demonstrated how the text's voice engages with the ancient social situation. Recognizing the specific logical and polemical adjustments made in the text to solve concrete social problems provides an avenue to understand the text within its social world.

For religious laity, the blurred gaze involves taking material from these books to address present-day issues of leadership and perseverance in the face of opposition or difficulties.[26] Because these two books are part

---

21. Wacquant, in Bourdieu and Wacquant, *Invitation to Reflexive Sociology*, 12.
22. Ibid., 39.
23. Ibid. This involves "viewing the world as a spectacle, a world to be interpreted rather than a concrete problem to be solved practically."
24. Ibid., 40.
25. Ibid., 41.
26. For example, Warren Wiersbe, *Be Determined (Nehemiah): Standing Firm in the Face of Opposition* (Colorado Springs: Cook, 2009); Gene A. Getz, *Nehemiah:*

of a sacred canon, it is often assumed that they provide helpful models to apply to communities today. (This assumption is an outgrowth of the modern-day doxic perspective on reception of a sacred text.) Often these studies accept on face value the text's evaluation of others as adversaries and foreign and rightfully silenced. This fails to provide a thorough treatment of the ramifications of such labels and outcomes. Moreover, a selective focus on these topics ignores or excuses the more problematic aspects of these texts. Rarely, if ever in such instances, are issues of domination, oppression, or ethnic exclusion explored and evaluated. Nor are the issues of guilt and shame, important motivations in the prayers, considered with regard to the role they play in the self-definition of the community or the members' relations with others. Ethical issues surrounding the strategies and outcomes in these narratives also are lost in the rush to praise the success of the builders.[27] These treatments tend to strip the text of the objective reality of its material world and the social reality constructed and addressed by the actors.

Writing about leadership is most likely a topic of interest to those who hold a certain amount of social capital. Studies composed by and consumed by this class focus on how to gain control, how to maintain it, and how to deploy it. They may also be drawn to examples of how to motivate a social group to buy into a particular project and therefore to contribute funds to support the effort. A more self-reflexive treatment of these texts would require an assessment of one's habitus and recognizing how it shapes the issues and the questions one is inclined to see and address. Using these same biblical texts, the focus of study could be shifted to examine the books with an eye toward a different position within one's social field. One could explore how the forms of capital, ideology, and social history interact in a specific social context and contribute to the effects of power. The texts could be evaluated for ethical issues associated with leadership strategies or social organization and the findings then turned toward assessing the social structure of one's own community.

Becoming a Disciplined Leader (Nashville: Broadman & Holman, 1995); Raymond Brown, *The Message of Nehemiah* (Downers Grove, IL: InterVarsity Press, 1998); James M. Boice, *Nehemiah: An Expository Commentary* (Grand Rapids: Baker Books, 2006). Many organizations (accessible online) concerned with leadership or rebuilding of families or cities also incorporate Nehemiah into their names.

27. The prayers could be studied with attention to how a society evolves the capacity to direct its own development.

14. CONCLUSIONS

A further treatment that might draw our attention away from the elite and issues of personal power is to explore how social organization relates to issues of identity construction in changing circumstances. Within these books, responses to these realities, such as the boundary maintenance strategies, can be both problematic and helpful. These strategies could be further explored from various perspectives, such as nonelite members of the community or those targeted as foreign, rather than only from the standpoint of leaders or of the community as a whole. As already observed, ethnicity and issues such as exile, imperial control, and return migration change the conversation about identity, create new forms of worship, and generate new debates about what markers are critical to retain a sense of continuity and identity. Class, economics, and even geography also contribute to the material and ideological context and generate new criteria and motives for membership and practices.

The account of Ezra-Nehemiah, read through the lens of Bourdieu's social theories, provides a moving picture of the dynamic interaction of social, political, cultural, and economic forms of capital over time, in a particular place, among particular people. The authors, galvanized by contested social and political arrangements, appropriate historic traditions in new ways to advance their causes. The political reality of the destroyed city and temple coupled with Persian rule generates an increasing rationalization of theology in order to validate and shore up support for a reconstructed temple. The authors explain and temper imperial rule by designating it as the means of fulfilling the divine will and as a source of legitimacy for the temple. The tragedy of Jerusalem's destruction is acknowledged in penitential prayers, but blame is laid at the feet of the ancestors. The logic enables the current generation to confess guilt over the national disgrace while distancing themselves from the cause. It also prompts the community to adopt ethnically differentiated communal boundaries as marks of purity so as to avoid a recurrence of the disaster. Familiar rituals generated in exilic contexts or earlier times are appropriated and reconfigured to lend legitimacy to both exclusionary practices and internal hierarchy. Each adjustment and the various forms of capital deployed in the narrative are engaged to address and construct a new community.

The theology, worship, methods of leadership, and constructions of the community found in these texts are not generated in a social vacuum. Each flows from a need to adjust to or to contest concrete factors, competitors, or other competing constructions of the field. To grasp fully the content, methods, and logic of these texts demands attention to the social genesis and purposes of the claims and actions within these accounts. By doing so we can more fully understand the theology, social constructions, and leadership styles contained within these pages. Attention to these issues clarifies the many particular ways that this textual production is constructed to address its own social reality. When combined with a self-reflexive attention to one's own social context and habitus, reading in this manner will produce for today's audiences a more thoughtful, and more ethical appropriation of these accounts.

Bibliography

Abdel-Nour, Farid. "National Responsibility." *Political Theory* 31 (2003): 693–719.

Ackroyd, Peter. "The Jewish Community in Palestine in the Persian Period." Pages 130–61 in *Introduction; The Persian Period*. Vol. 1 of *The Cambridge History of Judaism*. Edited by W. D. Davies and Louis Finkelstein. Cambridge: Cambridge University Press, 1984.

Albertz, Rainer. *From the Exile to the Maccabees.* Vol. 2 of *A History of Israelite Religion in the Old Testament*. Translated by John Bowden. OTL. Louisville: Westminster John Knox, 1994.

———. "The Thwarted Restoration." Pages 1–17 in *Yahwism after the Exile: Perspectives on Israelite Religion in the Persian Era*. Edited by Rainer Albertz and Bob Becking. STAR 5. Assen: Van Gorcum, 2003.

Alexander, Jeffrey C. "Toward a Theory of Cultural Trauma." Pages 1–30 in *Cultural Trauma and Collective Identity*. Edited by Jeffrey C. Alexander. Berkeley: University of California Press, 2004.

———. *Trauma: A Social Theory*. Malden, MA: Polity, 2012. Kindle edition.

Allen, Graham. *Intertextuality*. 2nd ed. New York: Routledge, 2011.

———. *Roland Barthes*. New York: Routledge, 2003.

Allen, Leslie C. "'For He Is Good…': Worship in Ezra-Nehemiah." Pages 15–34 in *Worship and the Hebrew Bible: Essays in Honour of John T. Willis*. Edited by M. Patrick Graham, Rick R. Marrs, and Steven L. McKenzie. JSOTSup 284. Sheffield: Sheffield Academic, 1999.

Alt, Albrecht. "Die Rolle Samarias bei der Enstehung des Judentums." Pages 316–37 in vol. 2 of *Kleine Schriften zur Geschichte des Volkes Israel*. 3 vols. Munich: Beck, 1953–1959.

Amit, Yairah. *Reading Biblical Narratives: Literary Criticism and the Hebrew Bible*. Minneapolis: Fortress, 2001.

Angel, Hayyim. "The Literary Significance of the Name Lists in Ezra-Nehemiah." *JBQ* 35.3 (2007): 143–52.

Arnold, B. T. "The Use of Aramaic in the Hebrew Bible: Another Look at Bilingualism in Ezra and Daniel." *JNSL* 22.2 (1996): 1–16.

Arnold, William R. "The Passover Papyrus from Elephantine." *JBL* 31 (1912): 1–33.

Avrahami, Yael. "בוש in the Psalms: Shame or Disappointment?" *JSOT* 34 (2010): 295–313.

Barstad, Hans. "After the 'Myth of the Empty Land': Major Challenges in the Study of Neo-Babylonian Judah." Pages 3–20 in *Judah and the Judeans in the Neo-Babylonian Period*. Edited by Oded Lipschits and Joseph Blenkinsopp. Winona Lake, IN: Eisenbrauns, 2003.

Barth, Fredrik. "Introduction." Pages 9–38 in *Ethnic Groups and Boundaries: The Social Organization of Culture Difference*. Edited by Fredrik Barth. Boston: Little, Brown, 1969.

Barthes, Roland. *S/Z*. Translated by Richard Miller. New York: Hill & Wang, 1974.

Bautch, Richard J. "The Formulary of Atonement (Lev 16:21) in Penitential Prayers of the Second Temple Period." Pages 35–45 in *The Day of Atonement: Its Interpretations in Early Jewish and Christian Traditions*. Edited by Thomas Hieke and Tobias Nicklas. TBN 15. Boston: Brill, 2012.

Bechtel, Lyn M. "Shame as a Sanction of Social Control in Biblical Israel: Judicial, Political, and Social Shaming." *JSOT* 49 (1991): 47–76.

Becking, Bob. "Do the Earliest Samaritan Inscriptions Already Indicate a Parting of the Ways?" Pages 213–22 in *Judah and the Judeans in the Fourth Century B.C.E.* Edited by Oded Lipschits, Gary N. Knoppers, and Rainer Albertz. Winona Lake, IN: Eisenbrauns, 2007.

———. "'We All Returned as One!': Critical Notes on the Myth of the Mass Return." Pages 3–18 in *Judah and the Judeans in the Persian Period*. Edited by Oded Lipschits and Manfred Oeming. Winona Lake, IN: Eisenbrauns, 2006.

Bedford, Peter R. *Temple Restoration in Early Achaemenid Judah*. JSJSup 65. Boston: Brill, 2000.

Beetham, David. *Legitimation of Power*. Atlantic Highlands, NJ: Humanities Press International, 1991.

Bell, Catherine M. *Ritual: Perspectives and Dimensions*. Oxford: Oxford University Press, 1997.

Berlinerblau, Jacques. "Ideology, Pierre Bourdieu's *Doxa*, and the Hebrew Bible." *Semeia* 87 (1999): 193–214.

———. "Toward a Sociology of Heresy, Orthodoxy, and *Doxa*." *HR* 40 (2001): 327–51.

Berman, Joshua. "The Narratological Purpose of Aramaic Prose in Ezra 4:8–6:18." *AS* 5 (2007): 165–91.

Berquist, Jon L., ed. *Approaching Yehud: New Approaches to the Study of the Persian Period*. SemeiaSt 50. Atlanta: Society of Biblical Literature, 2007.

———. *Judaism in Persia's Shadow: A Social and Historical Approach*. Minneapolis: Fortress, 1995.

Betlyon, John Wilson. "The Provincial Government of Persian Period Judea and the Yehud Coins." *JBL* 105 (1986): 633–42.

Beuken, Wim. "Does Trito-Isaiah Reject the Temple? An Intertextual Inquiry into Isa. 66:1–6." Pages 53–66 in *Intertexuality in Biblical Writings: Essays in Honour of Bas van Iersel*. Edited by Sipke Draisma. Kampen: Kok, 1989.

Bickerman, Elias J. "The Edict of Cyrus in Ezra 1." *JBL* 65 (1946): 249–75.

———. "The Generation of Ezra and Nehemiah." Pages 299–326 in *Studies in Jewish and Christian History: Part Three*. AGJU 9. Leiden: Brill, 1986.

Blenkinsopp, Joseph. "Benjamin Traditions Read in the Early Persian Period." Pages 629–45 in *Judah and the Judeans in the Persian Period*. Edited by Oded Lipschits and Manfred Oeming. Winona Lake, IN: Eisenbrauns, 2006.

———. *Ezra-Nehemiah*. OTL. Philadelphia: Westminster, 1988.

———. "The Mission of Udjahorresnet and Those of Ezra and Nehemiah." *JBL* 106 (1987): 409–21.

———. "The Nehemiah Autobiographical Memoir." Pages 199–212 in *Language, Theology, and the Bible: Essays in Honour of James Barr*. Edited by Samuel E. Balentine and John Barton. Oxford: Clarendon, 1994.

———. "Temple and Society in Achaemenid Judah." Pages 22–53 in *Second Temple Studies*. Edited by Philip R. Davies. JSOTSup 117. Sheffield: JSOT Press, 1991.

Boda, Mark J. "Confession as Theological Expression: Ideological Origins of Penitential Prayer." Pages 21–50 in *The Origins of Penitential Prayer in Second Temple Judaism*. Vol. 1 of *Seeking the Favor of God*. Edited by Mark J. Boda, Daniel K. Falk, and Rodney A. Werline. EJL 21. Atlanta: Society of Biblical Literature, 2006.

———. "Form Criticism in Transition: Penitential Prayer and Lament, *Sitz im Leben* and Form." Pages 181–92 in *The Origins of Penitential Prayer in Second Temple Judaism*. Vol. 1 of *Seeking the Favor of God*. Edited by Mark J. Boda, Daniel K. Falk, and Rodney A. Werline. EJL 21. Atlanta: Society of Biblical Literature, 2006.

———. *Praying the Tradition: The Origin and Use of Tradition in Nehemiah 9*. BZAW 277. Berlin: de Gruyter, 1999.

———. "Redaction in the Book of Nehemiah: A Fresh Proposal." Pages 25–54 in *Unity and Disunity in Ezra-Nehemiah: Redaction, Rhetoric and Reader*. Edited by Mark J. Boda and Paul L. Redditt. HBM 17. Sheffield: Sheffield Phoenix, 2008.

Boer, Roland. "No Road: On the Absence of Feminist Criticism of Ezra-Nehemiah." Pages 233–52 in *Her Master's Tools? Feminist and Postcolonial Engagements of Historical-Critical Discourse*. Edited by Caroline Vander Stichele and Todd Penner. GPBS 9. Atlanta: Society of Biblical Literature, 2005.

Boice, James M. *Nehemiah: An Expository Commentary*. Grand Rapids: Baker, 2006.

Botterweck, Johannes G., Helmer Ringgren, and Heinz-Josef Fabry, eds. *Theological Dictionary of the Old Testament*. Translated by John T. Willis, Geoffrey W. Bromiley, David E. Green, and Douglas W. Stott. 15 vols. Grand Rapids: Eerdmans, 1975–2011.

Bourdieu, Pierre. *Distinction: A Social Critique of the Judgement of Taste*. Translated by Richard Nice. Cambridge: Harvard University Press, 1984.

———. *The Field of Cultural Production: Essays on Art and Literature*. Edited by Randal Johnson. New York: Columbia University Press, 1993.

———. "The Forms of Capital." Pages 241–58 in *Handbook of Theory and Research for the Sociology of Education*. Edited by John G. Richardson. New York: Greenwood, 1986.

———. "Genesis and Structure of the Religious Field." *CSR* 13 (1991): 1–44.

———. *Language and Symbolic Power*. Edited by John B. Thompson. Translated by Gino Raymond and Matthew Adamson. Cambridge: Harvard University Press, 1991.

———. "Legitimation and Structured Interests in Weber's Sociology of Religion." Pages 119–36 in *Max Weber, Rationality and Modernity*. Edited by Scott Lash and Sam Whimster. Translated by Chris Turner. London: Allen & Unwin, 1987.

———. *The Logic of Practice*. Translated by Richard Nice. Stanford, CA: Stanford University Press, 1980.

———. *Outline of a Theory of Practice*. Translated by Richard Nice. London: Cambridge University Press, 1977.

———. *Practical Reason: On the Theory of Action*. Stanford, CA: Stanford University Press, 1998.

———. "Rites as Acts of Institution." Pages 79–89 in *Honor and Grace in Anthropology*. Edited by J. G. Peristiany and Julian Pitt-Rivers. Translated by Roger Just. Cambridge: Cambridge University Press, 1992.

———. "The Sentiment of Honour in Kabyle Society." Pages 191–232 in *Honour and Shame: The Values of Mediterranean Society*. Edited by J. G. Peristiany. London: Weidenfeld & Nicolson, 1965.

———. "The Social Space and the Genesis of Groups." *Theory and Society* 14 (1985): 723–44.

Bourdieu, Pierre, and Loïc J. D. Wacquant. *Invitation to Reflexive Sociology*. Chicago: University of Chicago Press, 1992.

Briant, Pierre. *From Cyrus to Alexander: A History of the Persian Empire*. Translated by Peter T. Daniels. Winona Lake, IN: Eisenbrauns, 2002.

Brown, Raymond. *The Message of Nehemiah: God's Servant in a Time of Change*. Downers Grove, IL: InterVarsity Press, 1998.

Camp, Claudia V. "Feminist- and Gender-Critical Perspectives on the Biblical Ideology of Intermarriage." Pages 303–15 in *Mixed Marriages: Intermarriage and Group Identity in the Second Temple Period*. Edited by Christian Frevel. LHBOTS 547. New York: T&T Clark, 2011.

Carter, Charles E. *The Emergence of Yehud in the Persian Period: A Social and Demographic Study*. JSOTSup 294. Sheffield: Sheffield Academic, 1999.

Cataldo, Jeremiah. "Persian Policy and the Yehud Community." *JSOT* 28 (2003): 131–43.

Celikates, Robin. "Systematic Misrecognition and the Practice of Critique: Bourdieu, Boltanski and the Role of Critical Theory." Pages 160–72 in *Recognition Theory and Contemporary French Moral and Political Philosophy*. Edited by Miriam Bankowsky and Alice Le Goff. Manchester: Manchester University Press, 2012.

Chance, John K. "The Anthropology of Honor and Shame: Culture, Values, and Practice." *Semeia* 68 (1994): 139–51.

Childs, Brevard S. *Introduction to the Old Testament as Scripture*. Philadelphia: Fortress, 1979.

Chirichigno, Gregory. *Debt-Slavery in Israel and the Ancient Near East*. JSOTSup 141. Sheffield: JSOT Press, 1993.

Christian, Mark A. "Priestly Power that Empowers: Michel Foucault, Middle-Tier Levites, and the Sociology of 'Popular Religious Groups' in Israel." *JHebS* 9 (2009): art. 1, pp. 2–81. doi:10.5508/jhs.2009.v9.a1.

Chrostowski, Waldemar. "An Examination of Conscience by God's People as Exemplified in Neh 9:6–37." *BZ* 34 (1990): 253–61.

Clines, D. J. A. *Ezra, Nehemiah, Esther*. NCBC. Grand Rapids: Eerdmans, 1984.

———. "The Nehemiah Memoir: The Perils of Autobiography." Pages 124–64 in *What Does Eve Do to Help? and Other Readerly Questions to the Old Testament*. JSOTSup 94. Sheffield: JSOT Press, 1990.

Cohen, Margaret. "Leave Nehemiah Alone: Nehemiah's 'Tales' and Fifth-Century BCE Historiography." Pages 55–74 in *Unity and Disunity in Ezra-Nehemiah: Redaction, Rhetoric and Reader*. Edited by Mark J. Boda and Paul L. Redditt. HBM 17. Sheffield: Sheffield Phoenix, 2008.

Collins, John J. "The Mythology of Holy War in Daniel and the Qumran War Scroll: A Point of Transition in Jewish Apocalyptic." *VT* 25 (1975): 596–612.

Conczorowski, Benedikt J. "All the Same as Ezra? Conceptual Differences between the Texts on Intermarriage in Genesis, Deuteronomy 7 and Ezra." Pages 89–108 in *Mixed Marriages: Intermarriage and Group Identity in the Second Temple Period*. Edited by Christian Frevel. LHBOTS 547. New York: T&T Clark, 2011.

Connerton, Paul. *How Societies Remember*. Cambridge: Cambridge University Press, 1989.

Coogan, Michael D. *West Semitic Personal Names in the Murašû Documents*. HSM 7. Missoula, MT: Scholars Press, 1976.

Cook, Stephen L. "Those Stubborn Levites: Overcoming Levitical Disenfranchisement." Pages 155–70 in *Levites and Priests in Biblical History and Tradition*. Edited by Mark Leuchter and Jeremy M. Hutton. AIL 9. Atlanta: Society of Biblical Literature, 2011.

Dandamayev, Muhammad A. "Neo-Babylonian and Achaemenid State Administration in Mesopotamia." Pages 373–98 in *Judah and the Judeans in the Persian Period*. Edited by Oded Lipschits and Manfred Oeming. Winona Lake, IN: Eisenbrauns, 2005.

Dandamayev, Muhammad A., and Vladimir G. Lukonin. *The Culture and Social Institutions of Ancient Iran*. Translated by Philip L. Kohl and D. J. Dadson. Cambridge: Cambridge University Press, 1989.

Davies, Gordon F. *Ezra and Nehemiah*. Berit Olam. Collegeville, MN: Liturgical Press, 1999.

Davies, Philip R. "Defending the Boundaries of Israel in the Second Temple Period: 2 Chronicles 20 and the 'Salvation Army.'" Pages 43–54 in *Priests, Prophets and Scribes: Essays on the Formation and Heritage of Second Temple Judaism in Honour of Joseph Blenkinsopp*. Edited by Eugene Ulrich, John W. Wright, Robert P. Carroll, and Philip R. Davies. JSOTSup 149. Sheffield: JSOT Press, 1992.

Dianteill, Erwan. "Pierre Bourdieu and the Sociology of Religion: A Central and Peripheral Concern." *Theory and Society* 32 (2003): 529–49.

Dillon, Michele. "Pierre Bourdieu, Religion, and Cultural Production." *CSCM* 1 (2001): 411–29.

Domeris, W. R. "Shame and Honour in Proverbs: Wise Women and Foolish Men." *OTE* 8 (1995): 86–102.

Douglas, Mary. "Responding to Ezra: The Priests and the Foreign Wives." *BibInt* 10 (2002): 1–23.

Duggan, Michael W. *The Covenant Renewal in Ezra-Nehemiah (Neh 7:72b–10:40): An Exegetical, Literary, and Theological Study*. SBLDS 164. Atlanta: Society of Biblical Literature, 2001.

Dyck, Jonathan E. "Ezra 2 in Ideological Critical Perspective." Pages 129–45 in *Rethinking Contexs, Rereading Texts: Contributions from the Social Sciences to Biblical Interpretation*. Edited by M. Daniel Carroll R. JSOTSup 299. Sheffield: Sheffield Academic, 2000.

———. "The Ideology of Identity in Chronicles." Pages 89–116 in *Ethnicity and the Bible*. Edited by Mark G. Brett. BibInt 19. Leiden: Brill, 1996.

Edelman, Diana. *The Origins of the "Second" Temple: Persian Imperial Policy and the Rebuilding of Jerusalem*. London: Equinox, 2005.

Eidheim, Harald. "When Ethnic Identity Is a Social Stigma." Pages 39–57 in *Ethnic Groups and Boundaries*. Edited by Fredrik Barth. Boston: Little, Brown, 1969.

Eshel, Hannan. "The Governors of Samaria in the Fifth and Fourth Centuries B.C.E." Pages 223–34 in *Judah and the Judeans in the Fourth Century B.C.E.* Edited by Oded Lipschits, Gary N. Knoppers, and Rainer Albertz. Winona Lake, IN: Eisenbrauns, 2007.

Eskenazi, Tamara C. "From *Exile and Restoration* to Exile and Reconstruction." Pages 78–93 in *Exile and Restoration Revisited: Essays on the Babylonian and Persian Periods in Memory of Peter R. Ackroyd*. Edited by Gary N. Knoppers and Lester L. Grabbe with Deirdre Fulton. LSTS 73. London: T&T Clark, 2009.

———. *In an Age of Prose: A Literary Approach to Ezra-Nehemiah*. SBLMS 36. Atlanta: Scholars Press, 1988.

———. "Nehemiah 9–10: Structure and Significance." *JHebS* 3 (2001). art. 9, pp. 1–19. doi:10.5508/jhs.2001.v3.a9.

Eskenazi, Tamara C., and Eleanore P. Judd. "Marriage to a Stranger in Ezra 9–10." Pages 266–85 in *Second Temple Studies 2: Temple and Community in the Persian Period*. Edited by Tamara C. Eskenazi and Kent H. Richards. JSOTSup 175. Sheffield: JSOT Press, 1994.

Fantalkin, Alexander, and Oren Tal. "The Canonization of the Pentateuch: When and Why?" *ZAW* 124 (2012): 1–18, 201–12.

Finkelstein, Israel. "Jerusalem in the Persian (and Early Hellenistic) Period and the Wall of Nehemiah." *JSOT* 32 (2008): 501–20.

Fleming, Daniel E. "The Seven-Day Siege of Jericho in Holy War." Pages 211–28 in *Ki Baruch Hu: Ancient Near Eastern, Biblical, and Judaic Studies in Honor of Baruch A. Levine*. Edited by Robert Chazan, William W. Hallo, and Lawrence H. Schiffman. Winona Lake, IN: Eisenbrauns, 1999.

Frei, Peter. "Persian Imperial Authorization: A Summary." Pages 5–40 in *Persia and Torah: The Theory of Imperial Authorization of the Pentateuch*. Edited by James W. Watts. SymS 17. Atlanta: Society of Biblical Literature, 2001.

Frevel, Christian. "Introduction: The Discourse on Intermarriage in the Hebrew Bible." Pages 1–14 in *Mixed Marriages: Intermarriage and Group Identity in the Second Temple Period*. Edited by Christian Frevel. LHBOTS 547. New York: T&T Clark, 2011.

Frevel, Christian, and Benedikt J. Conczorowski. "Deepening the Water: First Steps to a Diachronic Approach on Intermarriage in the Hebrew Bible." Pages 15–45 in *Mixed Marriages: Intermarriage and Group Identity in the Second Temple Period*. Edited by Christian Frevel. LHBOTS 547. New York: T&T Clark, 2011.

Fried, Lisbeth S. "The Concept of 'Impure Birth' in 5th Century Athens and Judea." Pages 121–42 in *In the Wake of Tikva Frymer-Kensky*. Edited by Steven Holloway, JoAnn Scurlock, and Richard Beal. Piscataway, NJ: Gorgias, 2009.

———. "The House of God Who Dwells in Jerusalem." Review of *Temple Restoration in Early Achaemenid Judah*, by Peter Bedford, and *Priester und Leviten im achämenidischen Juda*, by Joachim Schaper. *JAOS* 126 (2006): 89–102.

———. *The Priest and the Great King: Temple-Palace Relations in the Persian Empire*. Winona Lake, IN: Eisenbrauns, 2004.

Geertz, Clifford. *The Interpretation of Cultures*. New York: Basic Books, 1973.
Getz, Gene A. *Nehemiah: Becoming a Disciplined Leader.* Nashville: Broadman & Holman, 1995.
Grabbe, Lester L. "Ezra." Pages 313–19 in *Eerdman's Commentary on the Bible*. Edited by James D. G. Dunn and John W. Rogerson. Grand Rapids: Eerdmans, 2003.
———. *Ezra-Nehemiah*. New York: Routledge, 1998.
———. *The Persian and Greek Periods*. Vol. 1 of *Judaism from Cyrus to Hadrian*. 2 vols. Minneapolis: Fortress, 1992.
Gross, Carl. "Is There Any Interest in Nehemiah 5?" *SJOT* 11 (1997): 270–78.
Guillaume, Philippe. "Nehemiah 5: No Economic Crisis." *JHebS* 10 (2010): art. 8, pp. 2–21. doi:10.5508/jhs2010.v10.a8.
Gunn, David M., and Danna Nolan Fewell. *Narrative in the Hebrew Bible*. New York: Oxford University Press, 1993.
Halpern, Baruch. "A Historiographic Commentary on Ezra 1–6." Pages 81–142 in *The Hebrew Bible and Its Interpreters*. Edited by William H. Propp, Baruch Halpern, and David Noel Freedman. Winona Lake, IN: Eisenbrauns, 1990.
Hanson, Paul D. *Isaiah 40–66*. IBC. Louisville: John Knox, 1995.
———. "War and Peace in the Hebrew Bible." *Int* 38 (1984): 341–62.
Herzfeld, Michael. "Honour and Shame: Problems in the Comparative Analysis of Moral Systems." *Man* 15 (1980): 339–51.
Hoglund, Kenneth G. "The Achaemenid Context." Pages 54–72 in *Second Temple Studies*. Edited by Philip R. Davies. JSOTSup 117. Sheffield: JSOT Press, 1991.
———. *Achaemenid Imperial Administration in Syria-Palestine and the Missions of Ezra and Nehemiah*. SBLDS 125. Atlanta: Scholars Press, 1992.
Hopkins, David C. "Life on the Land: The Subsistence Struggles of Early Israel." *BA* 50 (1987): 178–91.
Horsley, Richard. *Scribes, Visionaries, and the Politics of Second Temple Judea*. Louisville: Westminster John Knox, 2007.
Hunt, Alice. *Missing Priests: The Zadokites in Tradition and History*. LHBOTS 452. New York: T&T Clark, 2006.
Hurowitz, Victor. *I Have Built You an Exalted House: Temple Building in the Bible in the Light of Mesopotamina and Northwest Semitic Writings*. JSOTSup 115. Sheffield: JSOT Press, 1992.

Janzen, David. "Scholars, Witches, Ideologues, and What the Text Said: Ezra 9–10 and Its Interpretation." Pages 49–69 in *Approaching Yehud: New Approaches to the Study of the Persian Period*. Edited by Jon L. Berquist. SemeiaSt 50. Atlanta: Society of Biblical Literature, 2007.

———. *The Social Meanings of Sacrifice in the Hebrew Bible: A Study of Four Writings*. BZAW 344. Berlin: de Gruyter, 2004.

———. *Witch-Hunts, Purity and Social Boundaries: The Expulsion of the Foreign Women in Ezra 9–10*. JSOTSup 350. London: Sheffield Academic, 2002.

Japhet, Sara. "Periodization between History and Ideology II: Chronology and Ideology in Ezra-Nehemiah." Pages 491–508 in *Judah and the Judeans in the Persian Period*. Edited by Oded Lipschits and Manfred Oeming. Winona Lake, IN: Eisenbrauns, 2006.

———. "Sheshbazzar and Zerubbabel against the Background of the Historical and Religious Tendencies of Ezra-Nehemiah: Part 1." Pages 53–84 in *From the Rivers of Babylon to the Highlands of Judah: Collected Studies on the Restoration Period*. Winona Lake, IN: Eisenbrauns, 2006.

Jenkins, Richard. *Social Identity*. New York: Routledge, 2008.

Jigoulov, Vadiim. "Administrataion of Achaemenid Phoenicia: A Case for Managed Autonomy." Pages 138–51 in *Exile and Restoration Revisited: Essays on the Babylonian and Persian Periods in Memory of Peter R. Ackroyd*. Edited by Gary N. Knoppers and Lester L. Grabbe, with Deirdre Fulton. LSTS 73. London: T&T Clark, 2009.

Johnson, Randal. Introduction to *The Field of Cultural Production*, by Pierre Bourdieu. Edited by Randal Johnson. New York: Columbia University Press, 1993.

Jones, Gwilym H. "The Concept of Holy War." Pages 299–321 in *The World of Ancient Israel: Sociological, Anthropological, and Political Perspectives*. Edited by R. E. Clements. Cambridge: Cambridge University Press, 1989.

———. "'Holy War' or 'Yahweh War'?" *VT* 25 (1975): 642–58.

Josephus, Flavius. *The New Complete Works of Josephus*. Edited by Paul L. Maier. Translated by William Whiston. Grand Rapids: Kregel, 1999.

Kellermann, Ulrich. *Nehemia: Quellen, Überlieferung und Geschichte*. BZAW 102. Berlin: Töpelmann, 1967.

Kessler, John. "The Diaspora in Zechariah 1–8 and Ezra-Nehemiah." Pages 119–45 in *Community Identity in Judean Historiography*. Edited by

Gary N. Knoppers and Kenneth A. Ristau. Winona Lake, IN: Eisenbrauns, 2009.

———. "Persia's Loyal Yahwists: Power Identity and Ethnicity in Achaemenid Yehud." Pages 91–121 in *Judah and the Judeans in the Persian Period*. Edited by Oded Lipschits and Manfred Oeming. Winona Lake, IN: Eisenbrauns, 2006.

Kloner, Amos, and Ian Stern. "Idumea in the Late Persian Period (Fourth Century B.C.E)." Pages 139–44 in *Judah and the Judeans in the Fourth Century B.C.E.* Edited by Oded Lipschits, Gary N. Knoppers, and Rainer Albertz. Winona Lake, IN: Eisenbrauns, 2007.

Klopfenstein, Martin. *Scham und Schande nach dem Alten Testament: Eine begriffsgeschichtliche Untersuchung zu den hebräischen Wurzeln bôš, klm und ḥpr*. ATANT 62. Zurich: TVZ, 1972.

Knauf, Ernst Axel. "Bethel: The Israelite Impact on Judean Language and Literature." Pages 291–349 in *Judah and the Judeans in the Persian Period*. Edited by Oded Lipschits and Manfred Oeming. Winona Lake, IN: Eisenbrauns, 2006.

Knoppers, Gary N. "'The City YHWH Has Chosen': The Chronicler's Promotion of Jerusalem in Light of Recent Archaeology." Pages 307–26 in *Jerusalem in Bible and Archaeology: The First Temple Period*. Edited by Andrew G. Vaughn and Ann E. Killebrew. SymS 18. Atlanta: Society of Biblical Literature, 2003.

———. "Ethnicity, Genealogy, Geography, and Change: The Judean Communities of Babylon and Jerusalem in the Story of Ezra." Pages 147–71 in *Community Identity in Judean Historiography*. Edited by Gary N. Knoppers and Kenneth A. Ristau. Winona Lake, IN: Eisenbrauns, 2009.

———. "Exile, Return, and Diaspora: Expatriates and Repatriates in Late Biblical Literature." Pages 29–61 in *Texts, Contexts and Readings in Postexilic Literature: Explorations into Historiography and Identity Negotiation in Hebrew Bible and Related Texts*. Edited by Louis Jonker. FAT 2/53. Tübingen: Mohr Siebeck, 2011.

———. "Nehemiah and Sanballat: The Enemy Without or Within?" Pages 305–31 in *Judah and the Judeans in the Fourth Century B.C.E.* Edited by Gary N. Knoppers, Rainer Albertz, and Oded Lipschits. Winona Lake, IN: Eisenbrauns, 2007.

———. "Revisiting the Composition of Ezra-Nehemiah: In Conversation with Jacob Wright's *Rebuilding Identity: The Nehemiah Memoir and*

Its Earliest Readers." JHebS 7 (2007): art. 12, pp. 1–36. doi:10.5508/jhs.2007.v7.a12.

———. "Revisiting the Samarian Question in the Persian Period." Pages 265–89 in *Judah and the Judeans in the Persian Period*. Edited by Oded Lipschits and Manfred Oeming. Winona Lake, IN: Eisenbrauns, 2006.

Knowles, Melody D. *Centrality Practiced: Jerusalem in the Religious Practice of Yehud and the Diaspora during the Persian Period*. ABS 16. Atlanta: Society of Biblical Literature, 2006.

———. "Pilgrimage Imagery in the Returns in Ezra." *JBL* 123 (2004): 57–74.

Koehler, Ludwig, Walter Baumgartner, and Johann Jakob Stamm. *The Hebrew and Aramaic Lexicon of the Old Testament*. Translated and edited under the supervision of M. E. J. Richardson. 5 vols. Leiden: Brill, 1994–2000.

Kottsieper, Ingo. "'And They Did Not Care to Speak Yehudit': On Linguistic Change in Judah during the Late Persian Era." Pages 95–124 in *Judah and the Judeans in the Fourth Century B.C.E.* Edited by Oded Lipschits, Gary N. Knoppers, and Rainer Albertz. Winona Lake, IN: Eisenbrauns, 2007.

Kraeling, Emil G. "New Light on the Elephantine Colony." *BA* 15 (1952): 50–67.

Kratz, Reinhard G. "The Second Temple of Jeb and of Jerusalem." Pages 247–64 in *Judah and the Judeans in the Persian Period*. Edited by Oded Lipschits and Manfred Oeming. Winona Lake, IN: Eisenbrauns, 2006.

Laird, Donna J. "Political Strategy in the Narrative of Ezra-Nehemiah." Pages 276–85 in *The Oxford Handbook to Biblical Narrative*. Edited by Danna Nolan Fewell. Oxford: Oxford University Press, 2015.

———. "The Temple Building Account in Ezra 1–6: Refracting the Social World." *Conversations with the Biblical World: Proceedings of the Eastern Great Lakes Biblical Society and Midwest Region Society of Biblical Literature* 31 (2011): 95–114.

Lemaire, Andrew. "Administration in Fourth-Century B.C.E. Judah in Light of Epigraphy and Numismatics." Pages 53–74 in *Judah and the Judeans in the Fourth Century B.C.E.* Edited by Oded Lipschhits, Gary N. Knoppers, and Rainer Albertz. Winona Lake, IN: Eisenbrauns, 2007.

Leuchter, Mark. "Ezra's Mission and the Levites of Casiphia." Pages 173–95 in *Community Identity in Judean Historiography: Biblical and Comparative Perspectives*. Edited by Gary N. Knoppers and Kenneth A. Ristau. Winona Lake, IN: Eisenbrauns, 2009.

———. "The Levites in Exile: A Response to L. S. Tiemeyer." *VT* 60 (2010): 583–90.

———. "Zadokites, Deuteronomists, and the Exilic Debate over Scribal Authority." *JHebS* 7 (2007): art. 10, pp. 5–18. doi:10.5508/jhs.2007.v7.a10.

Levin, Yigal, ed. *A Time of Change: Judah and Its Neighbours in the Persian and Early Hellenistic Periods.* LSTS 65. New York: T&T Clark, 2007.

Lipiński, Edward. "Marriage and Divorce in the Judaism of the Persian Period." *Transeu* 4 (1991): 63–71.

Lipschits, Oded. "Achaemenid Imperial Policy, Settlement Processes in Palestine, and the Status of Jerusalem in the Middle of the Fifth Century B.C.E." Pages 19–52 in *Judah and the Judeans in the Persian Period.* Edited by Oded Lipschits and Manfred Oeming. Winona Lake, IN: Eisenbrauns, 2006.

———. *The Fall and Rise of Jerusalem: Judah under Babylonian Rule.* Winona Lake, IN: Eisenbrauns, 2005.

———. "The History of the Benjamin Region under Babylonian Rule." *TA* 26 (1999): 155–90.

Lipschits, Oded, and Manfred Oeming, eds. *Judah and the Judeans in the Persian Period.* Winona Lake, IN: Eisenbrauns, 2006.

Lipschits, Oded, and Oren Tal. "The Settlement Archaeology of the Province of Judah: A Case Study." Pages 33–52 in *Judah and the Judeans in the Fourth Century B.C.E.* Edited by Oded Lipschits, Gary N. Knoppers, and Rainer Albertz. Winona Lake, IN: Eisenbrauns, 2007.

Lipschits, Oded, and David S. Vanderhooft. *The Yehud Stamp Impressions: A Corpus of Inscribed Impressions from the Persian and Hellenistic Periods in Judah.* Winona Lake, IN: Eisenbrauns, 2011.

———. "Yehud Stamp Impressions in the Fourth Century B.C.E.: A Time of Administrative Consolidation?" Pages 75–94 in *Judah and the Judeans in the Fourth Century B.C.E.* Edited by Oded Lipschits, Gary N. Knoppers, and Rainer Albertz. Winona Lake, IN: Eisenbrauns, 2007.

Lowenthal, David. *The Past Is a Foreign Country.* Cambridge: Cambridge University Press, 1985.

Maduro, Otto. "'Habitus' and Action as Strategy: Religious Habitus." Lecture, Drew University, Madison, NJ, 4 March 2008.

———. *Religion and Social Conflicts.* Translated by Robert R. Barr. Eugene, OR: Wipf & Stock, 1982.

Magen, Yitzhak. "The Dating of the First Phase of the Samaritan Temple on Mount Gerizim in Light of the Archaeological Evidence." Pages

157–211 in *Judah and the Judeans in the Fourth Century B.C.E.* Edited by Oded Lipschits, Gary N. Knoppers, and Rainer Albertz. Winona Lake, IN: Eisenbrauns, 2007.

Mallau, Hans H. "The Redaction of Ezra 4–6: A Plea for a Theology of Scribes." *PRSt* 15.4 (1988): 67–80.

Margalith, Othniel. "The Political Background of Zerubbabel's Mission and the Samaritan Schism." *VT* 41 (1991): 312–23.

Matzal, Stefan. "Short Notes on the Structure of Ezra 4–6." *VT* 50 (2000): 566–68.

May, Larry. "Metaphysical Guilt and Moral Taint." Pages 239–54 in *Collective Responsibility: Five Decades of Debate on Theoretical and Applied Ethics*. Edited by Larry May and Stacey Hoffman. Lanham, MD: Rowman & Littlefield, 1991.

McGeough, Kevin. "Esther the Hero: Going beyond 'Wisdom' in Heroic Narratives." *CBQ* 70 (2008): 44–65.

McKinnon, Andrew M., Marta Trzebiatowska, and Christopher C. Brittain. "Bourdieu, Capital, and Conflict in a Religious Field: The Case of the 'Homosexuality' Conflict in the Anglican Communion." *Journal of Contemporary Religion* 26 (2011): 355–70.

Mildenberg, Leo. "Yehud: A Preliminary Study of the Provincial Coinage of Judaea." Pages 183–96 in *Greek Numismatics and Archaeology: Essays in Honor of Margaret Thompson*. Edited by Otto Mørkholm and Nancy M. Waggoner. Wetteren: Cultura, 1979.

Milgrom, Jacob. *Leviticus: A Book of Ritual and Ethics*. CC. Minneapolis: Fortress, 2004.

Morrow, William. "The Affirmation of Divine Righteousness in Early Penitential Prayers: A Sign of Judaism's Entry into the Axial Age." Pages 101–17 in *The Origins of Penitential Prayer in Second Temple Judaism*. Vol. 1 of *Seeking the Favor of God*. Edited by Mark J. Boda, Daniel K. Falk, and Rodney A. Werline. EJL 21. Atlanta: Society of Biblical Literature, 2006.

Myers, Jacob M. *Ezra, Nehemiah*. AB 14. Garden City, NY: Doubleday, 1965.

Na'aman, Nadav. *Ancient Israel and Its Neighbors: Interaction and Counteraction*. Vol. 1 of *Collected Essays*. Winona Lake, IN: Eisenbrauns, 2005.

Nash, Manning. *The Cauldron of Ethnicity in the Modern World*. Chicago: University of Chicago Press, 1989.

Newman, Judith H. "Nehemiah 9 and the Scripturalization of Prayer in the Second Temple Period." Pages 112–24 in *The Function of Scripture* in *Early Jewish and Christian Tradition*. Edited by Craig A. Evans and James A. Sanders. JSNTSup 154. Sheffield: Sheffield Academic, 1998.

———. *Praying by the Book: The Scripturalization of Prayer in Second Temple Judaism*. EJL 14. Atlanta: Scholars Press, 1999.

Niditch, Susan. *Oral World and Written Words: Ancient Israelite Literature*. Louisville: Westminster John Knox, 1996.

———. *A Prelude to Biblical Folklore: Underdogs and Tricksters*. Urbana, IL: University of Illlinois Press, 2000.

———. *War in the Hebrew Bible: A Study in the Ethics of Violence*. New York: Oxford University Press, 1993.

Oded, Bustenay. "Where Is the 'Myth of the Empty Land' to Be Found? History versus Myth." Pages 55–74 in *Judah and the Judeans in the Neo-Babylonian Period*. Edited by Oded Lipschits and Joseph Blenkinsopp. Winona Lake, IN: Eisenbrauns, 2003.

Oeming, Manfred. "'See, We Are Serving Today' (Nehemiah 9:36): Nehemiah 9 as a Theological Interpretation of the Persian Period." Pages 571–88 in *Judah and the Judeans in the Persian Period*. Edited by Oded Lipschits and Manfred Oeming. Winona Lake, IN: Eisenbrauns, 2006.

Olave, María Angélica Thumala. "The Aristocracy of the Will: A Critique of Pierre Bourdieu with Illustrations from Chile." *Social Compass* 59 (2012): 52–68.

Olyan, Saul. "Purity Ideology in Ezra-Nehemiah as a Tool to Reconstitute the Community." *JSJ* 35 (2004): 1–16.

Oswald, Wolfgang. "Foreign Marriages and Citizenship in Persian Period Judah." *JHebS* 12 (2012): art. 6, pp. 1–17. doi:10.5508/jhs.2012.v12.a6.

Pakkala, Juha. "The Exile and the Exiles in the Ezra Tradition." Pages 91–101 in *The Concept of Exile in Ancient Israel and Its Historical Contexts*. Edited by Ehud Ben Zvi and Christoph Levin. BZAW 404. Berlin: de Grutyer, 2010.

———. *Ezra the Scribe: The Development of Ezra 7–10 and Nehemiah 8*. BZAW 347. Berlin: de Gruyter, 2004.

———. "Intermarriage and Group Identity in the Ezra Tradition (Ezra 7–10 and Nehemiah 8)." Pages 78–88 in *Mixed Marriages: Intermarriage and Group Identity in the Second Temple Period*. Edited by Christian Frevel. LHBOTS 547. New York: T&T Clark, 2011.

Parsons, Talcott. Introduction to *The Sociology of Religion*, by Max Weber. Translated by Ephraim Fischoff. 4th ed. Repr., Boston: Beacon, 1991.

Peristiany, J. G., ed. *Honour and Shame: The Values of Mediterranean Society*. London: Weidenfeld & Nicolson, 1965.

Pitt-Rivers, Julian. *The Fate of Shechem, or the Politics of Sex: Essays in the Anthropology of the Mediterranean*. Cambridge: Cambridge University Press, 1977.

Plevnik, Joseph. "Honor/Shame." Pages 106–15 in *Handbook of Biblical Social Values*. Edited by John J. Pilch and Bruce J. Malina. Peabody, MA: Hendrickson, 1993.

Polaski, Donald C. "What Mean These Stones? Inscriptions, Textuality and Power in Persia and Yehud." Pages 37–48 in *Approaching Yehud: New Approaches to the Study of the Persian Period*. Edited by Jon L. Berquist. SemeiaSt 50. Atlanta: Society of Biblical Literature, 2007.

Rad, Gerhard von. *Das Geschichtsbild des chronistischen Werkes*. BWANT 4/1. Stuttgart: Kohlhammer, 1930.

———. *Holy War in Ancient Israel*. Edited and translated by Marva J. Dawn. Grand Rapids: Eerdmans, 1991.

Rendsburg, Gary. "The Northern Origin of Nehemiah 9." *Bib* 72 (1991): 348–66.

Rendtorff, Rolf. "Nehemiah 9: An Important Witness of Theological Reflection." Pages 111–17 in *Tehillah le-Moshe: Biblical and Judaic Studies in Honor of Moshe Greenberg*. Edited by Mordechai Cogan, Barry L. Eichler, and Jeffrey H. Tigay. Winona Lake, IN: Eisenbrauns, 1997.

Rey, Terry. *Bourdieu on Religion: Imposing Faith and Legitimacy*. London: Equinox, 2007.

———. "Marketing the Goods of Salvation: Bourdieu on Religion." *Religion* 34 (2004): 331–43.

Rofé, Alexander. "Isaiah 66:1–4: Judean Sects in the Persian Period as Viewed by Trito-Isaiah." Pages 205–17 in *Biblical and Related Studies Presented to Samuel Iwry*. Edited by Ann Kort. Winona Lake, IN: Eisenbrauns, 1985.

Rom-Shiloni, Dalit. *Exclusive Inclusivity: Identity Conflicts between the Exiles and the People Who Remained (6th–5th Centuries BCE)*. LHBOTS 543. New York: Bloomsbury, 2013.

———. "Socio-ideological Setting or Settings for Penitential Prayers?" Pages 51–68 in *The Origins of Penitential Prayer in Second Temple Judaism*. Vol. 1 of *Seeking the Favor of God*. Edited by Mark J. Boda, Daniel K. Falk, and Rodney A. Werline. EJL 21. Atlanta: Society of Biblical Literature, 2006.

Rothenbusch, Ralf. "The Question of Mixed Marriages between the Poles of Diaspora and Homeland: Observations in Ezra-Nehemiah." Pages

60–77 in *Mixed Marriages: Intermarriage and Group Identity in the Second Temple Period*. Edited by Christian Frevel. LHBOTS 547. New York: T&T Clark, 2011.

Rowley, H. H. *Men of God*. New York: Nelson, 1963.

Sachau, Eduard. *Aramäische Papyrus und Ostraka aus einer jüdischen Militär-Kolonie zu Elephantine*. Leipzig: Hinrichs, 1911.

Schaper, Joachim. "Hebrew and Its Study in the Persian Period." Pages 15–26 in *Hebrew Study from Ezra to Ben-Yehuda*. Edited by William Horbury. Edinburgh: T&T Clark, 1999.

Schneider, Jane. "Of Vigilance and Virgins: Honor, Shame and Access to Resources in Mediterranean Societies." *Ethnology* 10 (1971): 1–24.

Schultz, Carl. "The Political Tensions Reflected in Ezra-Nehemiah." Pages 221–44 in *Scripture in Context: Essays on the Comparative Method*. Edited by Carl D. Evans, William W. Hallo, and John B. White. PTMS 34. Pittsburgh: Pickwick, 1980.

Schwiderski, Dirk. *Handbuch des nordwestsemitischen Briefformulars: Ein Beitrag zur Echtheitsfrage der aramäischen Briefe des Esrabuches*. BZAW 295. Berlin: de Gruyter, 2013.

Scott, James C. *Domination and the Arts of Resistance: Hidden Transcripts*. New Haven: Yale University Press, 1990.

Seitz, Christopher R. *Theology in Conflict: Reactions to the Exile in the Book of Jeremiah*. BZAW 176. Berlin: de Gruyter, 1989.

Ska, Jean Louis. "'Persian Imperial Authorization': Some Question Marks." Pages 161–82 in *Persia and Torah: The Theory of Imperial Authorization of the Pentateuch*. Edited by James W. Watts. SymS 17. Atlanta: Society of Biblical Literature, 2001.

Smith, Anthony D. "The Politics of Culture: Ethnicity and Nationalism." Pages 706–34 in *Companion Encyclopedia of Anthropology*. Edited by Tim Ingold. London: Routledge, 1994.

Smith, Daniel L. *The Religion of the Landless: The Social Context of the Babylonian Exile*. Bloomington, IN: Meyer Stone, 1989.

Smith, Morton. *Palestinian Parties and Politics That Shaped the Old Testament*. New York: Columbia University Press, 1971.

Smith-Christopher, Daniel L. "The Politics of Ezra: Sociological Indicators of Postexilic Judaean Society." Pages 73–97 in *Second Temple Studies*. Edited by Philip R. Davies. JSOTSup 117. Sheffield: JSOT Press, 1991.

Snell, Daniel C. "Why Is There Aramaic in the Bible?" *JSOT* 18 (1980): 32–51.

Southwood, Katherine E. "An Ethnic Affair? Ezra's Intermarriage Crisis against a Context of 'Self-Ascription' and 'Ascription of Others.'" Pages 46–59 in *Mixed Marriages: Intermarriage and Group Identity in the Second Temple Period*. Edited by Christian Frevel. LHBOTS 547. New York: T&T Clark, 2011.

———. *Ethnicity and the Mixed Marriage Crisis in Ezra 9–10: An Anthropological Approach*. Oxford: Oxford University Press, 2012.

———. "The Holy Seed: The Significance of Endogamous Boundaries and Their Transgression in Ezra 9–10." Pages 189–224 in *Judah and the Judeans in the Achaemenid Period: Negotiating Identity in an International Context*. Edited by Oded Lipschits, Gary N. Knoppers, and Manfred Oeming. Winona Lake, IN: Eisenbrauns, 2011.

Sparks, Kenton L. *Ethnicity and Identity in Ancient Israel: Prolegomena to the Study of Ethnic Sentiments and Their Expression in the Hebrew Bible*. Winona Lake, IN: Eisenbrauns, 1998.

Steiner, Richard C. "Bishlam's Archival Search Report in Nehemiah's Archive: Multiple Introductions and Reverse Chronological Order as Clues to the Origin of the Aramaic Letters in Ezra 4–6." *JBL* 125 (2006): 641–85.

Steinmann, Andrew E. "Letters of Kings about Votive Offerings, the God of Israel and the Aramaic Document in Ezra 4:8–6:18." *JHebS* 8 (2008): art. 23, pp. 2–14. doi:10.5508/jhs.2008.v8.a23.

Stern, Ephraim. *The Assyrian, Babylonian, and Persian Periods, 732–332 BCE*. Vol. 2 of *Archaeology of the Land of the Bible*. New York: Doubleday, 2001.

———. "The Persian Empire and the Political and Social History of Palestine in the Persian Period." Pages 70–87 in *Introduction; The Persian Period*. Vol. 1 of *The Cambridge History of Judaism*. Edited by W. D. Davies and Louis Finkelstein. Cambridge: Cambridge University Press, 1984.

Stern, Ian. "The Population of Persian-Period Idumea according to the Ostraca: A Study of Ethnic Boundaries and Ethnogenesis." Pages 205–38 in *A Time of Change: Judah and Its Neighbours in the Persian and Early Hellenistic Periods*. Edited by Yigal Levin. LSTS 65. New York: T&T Clark, 2007.

Stewart, Frank Henderson. *Honor*. Chicago: University of Chicago Press, 1994.

Stiebert, Johanna. *The Construction of Shame in the Hebrew Bible: The Prophetic Contribution*. JSOTSup 346. Sheffield: Sheffield Academic, 2002.

Stulman, Louis. "Encroachment in Deuteronomy: An Analysis of the Social World of the D Code." *JBL* 109 (1990): 613–32.

Swartz, David. "Bridging the Study of Culture and Religion: Pierre Bourdieu's Political Economy of Symbolic Power." *Sociology of Religion* 57 (1996): 71–85.

Talstra, Eep. "The Discourse of Praying: Reading Nehemiah 1." Pages 219–36 in *Psalms and Prayers: Papers Read at the Joint Meeting of the Society of Old Testament Study and Oudtestamentische Werkgezelschap in Nederland en Belgie*. Edited by Bob Becking and Eric Peels. OTS 55. Leiden: Brill, 2007.

Terr, Lenore. *Too Scared to Cry: How Trauma Affects Children ... and Ultimately Us All*. New York: Basic Books, 1990.

Thompson, John B. "Editor's Introduction." Pages 1–31 in *Language and Symbolic Power*, by Pierre Bourdieu. Edited by John B. Thompson. Translated by Gino Raymond and Matthew Adamson. Cambridge: Harvard University Press, 1991.

Throntveit, Mark A. *Ezra-Nehemiah*. IBC. Louisville: John Knox, 1992.

Torrey, Charles C. *Ezra Studies*. 1910. Repr., Eugene, OR: Wipf & Stock, 2006.

Trotter, James M. "Was the Second Temple a Primarily Persian Project?" *SJOT* 15 (2001): 276–94.

Urban, Hugh. "Response: Spiritual Capital, Academic Capital and the Politics of Scholarship: A Response to Bradford Verter." *MTSR* 17 (2005): 166–75.

———. "Sacred Capital: Pierre Bourdieu and the Study of Religion." *MTSR* 15 (2003): 354–89.

Uspenski, Boris. *The Poetics of Composition: The Structure of the Artistic Text and Typology of Compositionl Form*. Translated by Valentina Zavarin and Susan Wittig. Berkeley: University of California Press, 1973.

Van Leeuwen, Raymond C. "Cosmos, Temple, House: Building and Wisdom in Mesopotamia and Israel." Pages 67–90 in *Wisdom Literature in Mesopotamia and Israel*. Edited by Richard J. Clifford. SymS 36. Atlanta: Society of Biblical Literature, 2007.

Van Seters, John. "The Role of the Scribe in the Making of the Hebrew Bible." *JANER* 8 (2008): 99–129.

Verter, Bradford. "Spiritual Capital: Theorizing Religion with Bourdieu against Bourdieu." *Sociological Theory* 21 (2003): 150–74.

Veeser, H. Aram, ed. *The New Historicism*. New York: Routledge, 1989.

Walters, Stanley D. "Saul of Gibeon." *JSOT* 52 (1991): 61–76.
Weber, Max. *Ancient Judaism*. Edited and translated by Hans H. Gerth and Don Martindale. New York: Free Press, 1952.
———. *Economy and Society: An Outline of Interpretive Sociology*. Edited by Guenther Roth and Claus Wittich. Translated by Ephraim Fischoff. 2 vols. Berkeley: University of California Press, 1978.
———. *The Sociology of Religion*. Translated by Ephraim Fischoff. 4th ed. Repr., Boston: Beacon, 1991.
Weinberg, Joel. *The Citizen-Temple Community*. Translated by Daniel L. Smith-Christopher. JSOTSup 151. Sheffield: JSOT Press, 1992.
Welch, Adam C. "The Source of Nehemiah IX." *ZAW* 47 (1929): 130–37.
Werline, Rodney A. "Defining Penitential Prayer." Pages xiii–xvii in *The Origins of Penitential Prayer in Second Temple Judaism*. Vol. 1 of *Seeking the Favor of God*. Edited by Mark J. Boda, Daniel K. Falk, and Rodney A. Werline. EJL 21. Atlanta: Society of Biblical Literature, 2006.
———. *Penitential Prayer in Second Temple Judaism: The Development of a Religious Insitution*. EJL 13. Atlanta: Scholars Press, 1998.
Wiersbe, Warren. *Be Determined (Nehemiah): Standing Firm in the Face of Opposition*. Colorado Springs: Cook, 2009.
Williams, Bernard. *Shame and Necessity*. Berkeley: University of California Press, 1993.
Williamson, H. G. M. "The Aramaic Documents in Ezra Revisited." *JTS* 59 (2008): 41–62.
———. "The Belief System of the Book of Nehemiah." Pages 276–87 in *The Crisis of Israelite Religion: Transformation of Religious Tradition in Exilic and Post-Exilic Times*. Edited by Bob Becking and Marjo C. A. Korpel. OTS 42. Boston: Brill, 1999.
———. "The Composition of Ezra i–vi." *JTS* 34 (1983): 1–30.
———. "The Concept of Israel in Transition." Pages 141–61 in *The World of Ancient Israel: Sociological, Anthropological and Political Perspectives*. Edited by R. E. Clements. Cambridge: Cambridge University Press, 1989.
———. *Ezra, Nehemiah*. WBC 16. Waco, TX: Word, 1985.
Wright, Jacob L. "A New Model for the Composition of Ezra-Nehemiah." Pages 333–48 in *Judah and the Judeans in the Fourth Century B.C.E.* Edited by Oded Lipschits, Gary N. Knoppers, and Rainer Albertz. Winona Lake, IN: Eisenbrauns, 2007.
———. *Rebuilding Identity: The Nehemiah Memoir and Its Earliest Readers*. BZAW 348. Berlin: de Gruyter, 2004.

———. "Writing the Restoration: Compositional Agenda and the Role of Ezra in Nehemiah 8." *JHebS* 7 (2007): art. 10, pp. 19–29. doi:10.5508/jhs.2007.v7.a10.

Wright, John W. "Remapping Yehud: The Borders of Yehud and the Genealogies of Chronicles." Pages 67–89 in *Judah and the Judeans in the Persian Period*. Edited by Oded Lipschits and Manfred Oeming. Winona Lake, IN: Eisenbrauns, 2006.

Zlotnick-Sivan, H. "The Silent Women of Yehud: Notes on Ezra 9–10." *JJS* 51 (2000): 3–18.

Zorn, Jeffrey R. "Tell en-Naṣbeh and the Material Culture of the Sixth Century." Pages 413–47 in *Judah and the Judeans in the Neo-Babylonian Period*. Edited by Oded Lipschits and Joseph Blenkinsopp. Winona Lake, IN: Eisenbrauns, 2003.

Ancient Sources Index

Hebrew Bible/Old Testament

Genesis
19:8	335
24:3	195, 312
24:7	195
28:11–17	97
38:24	335
43:34	124

Exodus
3:7	274
3:8	307
3:22	79
7:3	274
12	172
12:1–2	294
12:35–36	77
12:36	79
13:3	294
13:14	294
14:13	209
18:11	274
22:20	213
22:24	229
22:25	239
23:16	112, 119
23:32–33	308
34:11–16	308
34:15–16	336
34:16	308
34:22	112
40:34–35	71

Leviticus
8	71
10:10	300, 304
11:47	304
16:21	309
17–27	132
18:24–25	304
18:24–30	308
19:19	305
19:33–34	132
20:24–26	300, 304
23	121
23:33–43	120–21
23:34–36	119
23:34–38	121
23:34–43	112
23:36	132
23:36–38	121
23:37–38	121–22
23:39	119
23:39–43	119
23:43	121
25	12
25:36	238–39
25:43	238
25:47–49	241
26:39–40	249
26:40–42	271
27:21	213
27:28–29	213

Numbers
1:44	84
1:50–51	295
3:17	295

-387-

Numbers (cont.)		13:16	215
3:20	295	13:17	214
3:33–36	295	14:23	263
8	71	16:2	263
8:16–19	99	16:6	263
8:21	300	16:11	263
9:1–3	294	16:13	119, 132
9:1–5	74	16:13–15	119
10:17	295	16:13–17	112
26:57–58	295	16:14	132
28:26	119	16:16	132
29	119, 121, 293	17	332
29:12–38	112	17:1–4	304
29:13–38	119	20:1	313
		22:21–24	335
Deuteronomy		23	307
3:24	263	23:3	307
4	264	23:7–8	307
4:6	262	23:19	229, 239
4:9	262	24:1–4	335
4:23	262	26:2	263
4:27	261	26:13	264
4:27–30	264	26:17	262
4:27–31	329	27:4–7	114
5:31	262	27:6–7	114
6:1	262	28:2	309
6:12	264	28:12	239
7:1	307–8	28:15	309
7:1–5	305, 336	28:21	308
7:1–6	307	28:44	239
7:2–6	214, 308	28:58	264
7:3–4	214, 305	28:63	308–9
7:6	214, 305	29:9	266
7:9	262–63	29:25	264
7:11	262	30:1–5	262
7:19	263	30:16	308–9
7:21	262	31	119, 121
8:11	264	31:9	121
8:14	264	31:9–13	112
8:19	264	31:10–12	120
10:17	262	31:10–13	120
11:2	263	31:12	132
12:11	263	31:16–18	304
13:12–18	213	31:23	313
13:13	213	34:5	262

34:12	263	9:1	307
		9:1–2	134
Joshua		9:23	96
1:7–8	313	10:10	209
1:9	313	10:28	212
1:16–18	313	10:30	212
1:18	313	10:37	212
2:1	210	10:39	212
2:5–7	211	10:40	212
2:9–11	209	11:11	214
2:9–13	155	12:8	307
2:14	210	14:1	92
2:15	210	14–21	92
2:24	209	22:16–31	262, 264
5	212	22:20	250
5:1	209		
5:9	213	Judges	
5:14	212	2:12–18	275
6:1	210–11	4:15	209
6:2	209	7:10–15	210
6:3–4	211	7:13–14	155
6:8–9	211	10:17–18	225
6:8–19	212	11	225
6:20	210	20:18	97
6:21	212	20:26	97
6:23	214		
6:24	210, 212, 214	1 Samuel	
6:26	215	1:4	124
7:1	215, 250, 262, 264	2:22	314
7:9	215	3	314
7:11	215, 326	3:13	314
7:12	215	3:18	314
7:12–15	215	7:16	97
7:13	215	10:3	97
7:15	214–15	14	134
7:19	326	14:34–35	134
7:25	214	22	97
8	134	28:6–7	137
8:1	209		
8:8	214	2 Samuel	
8:17	212	2	96
8:18	209	7	67
8:19	214	7:10	67
8:22	212–13	21	96
9	96	21:6	96

2 Samuel (cont.)		1 Chronicles	
24	134	2:7	262, 264
24:25	134	2:10	84
		3:16–17	93
1 Kings		3:18	84
2:26	96	3:24	101
3:4–5	96	4:38	84
5:3	67	5	290
5:3–5	66	5:6	84
5:4	67	5:27–41	289
5:8–11	68–69	6:3–8	289
5:13	66	6:12–14	289
8	114, 262–64	6:60	97
8:1	84	7:40	84
8:20–21	71	9:2	100
8:23	262–63	9:12	98
8:28	263	9:16	97
8:29	262, 263	9:33	99
8:30	263	9:35	96
8:31	239	10:13	262
8:33–39	247	10:13–14	137
8:42	263	15:2	99
8:44	263	15:16	99
8:46–54	247	15:17–22	99
8:47–50	263	15:22–23	99
8:48	263	16:31	117
8:52	262–63	16:34	117
8:52–53	265	16:39	96
8:53	262	19:5	251
8:56	262, 265	21	134
8:57	265	21:28–22:1	134
8:58	262	22:1–5	68
8:62	262	22:2	68
11:34	84	22:11	313
12:29	97	23:6	68
19	277	24	98
		24:8	97
2 Kings		24:18	101
17:37	274	28:8	329
19:15	282	28:9	137
19:19	282	28:10	313
22:11–23:3	269	28:20	313
24:13	65	29:21	293
24:14	90		
24:16	90		

2 Chronicles

5:13	117
6	262, 264
6:6	263
6:14	262
6:19	263
6:20	263
6:21	263
6:32	263
6:34	263
6:40	262
7:3	117
7:6	117
7:12	263
7:16	263
7:17	262
8:13	132
12:14	137, 330
17:3–4	137
19:3	330
19:10	274
20	117, 177
20:1	117
20:11	117
20:21	117
20:22	117
28:19	262, 264
30	172
30:18b–19	330
30:19	330
30:27	172
34:12–13	99
35	172
35:14	172
35:18	120
36:21	18
36:21–22	81
36:22	81
36:23	195

Ezra 80, 82–83, 90, 111–12, 183, 292
1–3	180
1–4	59, 322
1–6	1, 6–7, 44, 59, 61, 64, 67, 73, 76, 78, 80–81, 86, 99, 104, 137, 176–77, 181, 190, 192, 226, 232, 267, 292, 294, 316, 319–20, 329, 346–51, 354–55, 359
1–7	195
1:1	65, 69, 78, 81–82, 151, 160, 175
1:1–2	65
1:1–3	83
1:2	292
1:2–4	61, 82
1:3	139, 292
1:4	7, 77, 226
1:4–11	65
1:4–5	66
1:4–6	82
1:5	66, 78, 89, 322, 355
1:6	65, 69, 77, 83
1:6–7	293
1:6–11	74
1:7	65–66
1:7–8	82–83, 93
1:8	83–84
1:9–10	82
1:9–11	61, 296
1:11	84, 320
1:68	69
2	7, 21, 65, 66, 80, 83, 89–91, 93, 96, 100, 109, 112, 129, 133, 198, 294, 298, 316, 318
2:1	92–93, 104, 154, 320
2:1–67	61
2:2	78, 84, 90, 93, 316
2:2–19	94
2:2–35	94
2:3–19	90
2:4–19	95–96
2:6	92, 95
2:10–14	294
2:14	92, 95
2:16	94
2:20	96
2:20–35	90, 92, 94, 96
2:22	97
2:23	96
2:24	97
2:25	96

Ezra (cont.)

2:28	97
2:29	97
2:35	97
2:36–39	98
2:36–58	90
2:39	97
2:40	98–99
2:43–54	99
2:55–57	99
2:59	94, 98, 100, 104, 149, 319
2:59–60	100
2:59–62	92
2:59–63	90
2:59–4:5	138
2:60	101
2:61–62	100–101
2:61–63	101–102
2:62	89, 330
2:63	102
2:64	90, 102
2:64–65	90
2:65–67	90, 102
2:68	78
2:68–69	74, 83, 90, 102
2:69	108
2:70	90, 92, 95, 97, 117
3	68, 89, 104, 111–14, 118–19, 121–26, 128–34, 138–39, 142–44, 157, 327, 348, 351
3:1	111–12, 115, 117–18, 154
3:1–7	99, 111
3:1–4:5	112
3:2	93, 114–15, 155, 329
3:2–6	118
3:2–8	316
3:3	67, 117–18, 133–34, 138, 150, 354
3:3–7	115
3:4	114, 122, 132
3:4–6	116
3:5	118
3:5–7	67, 69
3:6	67, 118
3:7	65, 67–68, 74, 82, 129, 133
3:8	93, 111–12, 115, 133, 142
3:8–9	122
3:8–12	99
3:8–13	111, 115
3:9	99
3:10	67, 114, 122
3:11	67, 117, 129, 247, 328
3:12	67, 247, 322
3:12–13	116
4	6, 46, 59, 64, 66, 99, 147–49, 152, 156–61, 164, 168, 179, 348
4–6	130, 147, 155–56, 161, 330, 352
4:1	59, 86, 117, 157, 354–55
4:1–2	68, 150
4:1–3	333
4:1–5	111, 133–34, 150–51
4:1–7	150
4:1–24	150
4:1–6:22	151
4:2	135–37, 156, 330
4:2–3	133, 157, 322
4:2–5	149
4:2–13	64
4:3	68–69, 82, 138, 150–51, 159, 161, 177, 316, 319
4:4	118, 138, 150–51, 157
4:4–5	151
4:4–16	66
4:5	82, 111, 149, 157
4:5–6	140
4:6	142, 149
4:6–16	150–51
4:6–23	149, 152
4:7	149
4:7–8	156
4:7–9	156
4:7–23	156
4:8	112, 149, 186
4:8–9	93
4:8–6:15	69
4:8–6:18	61, 67, 184
4:9–10	156
4:10	156
4:11	162
4:11–16	163
4:12	138, 157

ANCIENT SOURCES INDEX

4:12–13	158	5:12–17	168
4:12–16	148	5:13	150–51, 160, 187
4:13	157	5:13–14	168
4:14	157, 162	5:13–16	82, 159
4:14–15	149	5:14–15	74
4:15	149–51, 157–58, 162, 179	5:14–16	83–84
4:16	157–58, 162	5:14–17	175
4:17	182	5:15	178
4:17–22	150–51	5:16	113
4:19	149, 157–58, 183	5:17	150–51
4:20	158	5:17–6:1	149
4:21	149, 151, 157	5:20	159
4:22	160	6	59, 82, 133, 136–37, 147, 167, 170, 172, 177, 182, 327
4:23	138		
4:23–24	150–51	6:1	187
4:24	149–50, 154	6:1–2	182
5	59, 73, 83, 99, 152, 155, 159–61, 167, 170, 182	6:1–12	150–51
		6:3	69, 118, 187
5–6	10, 148, 156, 158–60, 162, 166, 174, 188	6:3–4	69
		6:3–5	82, 160
5:1	64, 87, 138, 151, 154, 170, 175, 178	6:3–6	69
		6:5	74, 175
5:1–2	85, 154, 160, 168, 170	6:6	142
5:1–5	150–51	6:6–7	188
5:1–13	175	6:6–12	180
5:1–6:22	150	6:7	174, 178
5:2	93, 150, 154, 158, 178, 316	6:7–8	138
5:3	152, 160, 182, 187, 200	6:8	173, 187
5:3–4	151	6:8–9	74
5:3–10	64	6:8–12	151
5:4	155, 158, 168	6:9	118, 160, 175, 293
5:5	78, 138, 150–51, 154, 158, 168, 175, 178	6:10	73, 174–75
		6:11	160, 182
5:5–7	182	6:11–12	70, 183
5:6	186	6:12	160, 175, 178
5:6–17	150–51	6:13–15	150–51
5:7–17	163, 180	6:14	160, 168, 170, 174, 178–79, 187
5:7–6:12	182	6:14–15	148, 150
5:8	175, 178	6:16	70, 72, 170
5:9	168, 187	6:16–17	138
5:10	155, 158	6:16–18	70, 293
5:11	158–59, 174–75, 178, 182	6:16–20	99, 170, 320
5:11–12	158	6:17	71, 119
5:11–16	66, 158	6:17–22	71
5:12	159, 175, 179, 188	6:18	71, 85, 149, 155, 170, 183

Ezra (cont.)
6:18–20	171
6:19	70
6:19–22	70, 73, 150–51, 171
6:20–22	328
6:21	1, 71–72, 134, 136–37, 171, 173, 177, 187, 270, 304, 315, 319, 330, 333
6:22	6, 64, 70–72, 74, 149
7	7, 122, 137, 288, 292
7–8	59, 287–88, 294, 298, 324, 352
7–10	59, 247, 285–88, 319, 321–22, 327–30, 341, 346, 351–52, 354, 359
7:1	93, 286, 288
7:1–5	123, 289, 324
7:1–10	287
7:2	289
7:2–5	316
7:6	123, 288, 291–92, 294, 324, 326, 329
7:6–10	291
7:6–26	155
7:7	294, 319
7:8	286, 288
7:9	294
7:9–10	291
7:10	137, 291, 326, 329–30
7:10–11	329
7:11	123, 324, 329
7:11–26	287
7:12	123, 324, 329–30
7:12–26	184, 287, 292, 324
7:13	292, 319
7:14	293, 326, 330
7:15–16	325
7:15–23	292
7:17	293
7:18	325
7:20	325
7:20–21	325
7:21	123, 324
7:22	296
7:23–24	293
7:25	293, 322, 330
7:25–26	293, 326
7:26	230, 293, 299, 326, 330
7:27	247
7:27–28	287, 292, 294
7:28	294, 319, 322
8	198, 287, 294, 356
8–10	294
8:1	294
8:1–14	287, 294
8:2	290, 294
8:3	294
8:7	296
8:10–14	294
8:15	295, 320
8:15–19	98
8:15–32	287
8:16	295
8:16–17	322
8:17	100, 299
8:17–20	99
8:18	294–95
8:18–19	295
8:20	99, 295
8:21	296, 343
8:21–23	296, 326, 330
8:21–24	247
8:22	294, 296–97
8:23	296
8:24	295, 297, 300, 304, 315
8:24–34	296
8:25	319, 325
8:28	300
8:29	296
8:31	294, 296
8:31–32	286, 297
8:33	102, 230, 296
8:33–35	286
8:33–36	287
8:35	119, 293, 320
8:35–36	303
8:36	320
9	134, 247–48, 251, 256, 261, 270, 287, 299, 303–4, 312, 317, 321, 347
9–10	2, 13–14, 55, 59, 262, 270, 289, 293–94, 303, 308, 319, 324, 329,

	332, 334, 336, 338, 340, 342–43, 349, 355	10:6–9	320, 323
		10:7	320
9:1	95, 117, 303–4, 307–8, 315, 319, 322	10:7–8	322, 343
		10:7–9	286
9:1–5	287, 303–4, 312	10:7–12	340
9:2	264, 285, 303–4, 308, 311–12	10:8	214, 304, 311, 313, 315, 320, 334
9:3–4	326	10:9	270, 312, 315, 355
9:3–5	297	10:10	308, 312, 314, 316, 319, 324, 326
9:3–6	326		
9:4	288, 308, 312, 322, 326–27, 329	10:10–11	324, 355
9:6	250–51, 258, 305–6, 308, 316	10:11	304, 310, 313, 315, 326
9:6–7	251, 260	10:12	312, 314, 316, 322
9:6–15	247, 286–88	10:12–13	321
9:6–16	309, 326	10:13	315–16
9:7	257–58, 304–6, 308, 316	10:14	322, 334
9:8	82, 343	10:15	295, 315–16, 323
9:8–9	305–6	10:16	100, 137, 287, 294, 304, 314–15, 320, 322, 324, 330
9:9	248, 306		
9:10	257, 297, 305, 307, 321, 329	10:16–44	318
9:10–11	308	10:17	286, 312
9:10–12	305–6	10:18	312, 323
9:11	177, 304	10:18–44	312
9:11–12	306, 308	10:19	316, 334
9:12	305, 330	10:20–43	287–88
9:13	258, 303, 306–7, 309, 316	10:20–44	323
9:13–14	256, 305–6	10:21	97
9:14	249, 304–5, 307, 321, 343	10:23–24	316
9:15	82, 248, 305–7, 316	10:25	296, 316
10	98, 134, 137, 198, 287, 289, 295, 303, 306, 312, 314, 318, 352	10:26	316
		10:31	97
10:1	248, 312, 314, 320–22, 324, 326	10:44	288, 316–17
10:1–5	312, 319		
10:1–14	320	Nehemiah	
10:1–17	312	1	205, 248, 261, 264, 272, 304
10:1–19	288	1–2	195
10:2	264, 303, 308, 312, 314, 317, 319, 324	1–4	197
		1–6	197
10:2–3	322	1:1–7:5	197, 202
10:3	248, 313, 317, 322, 327	1:2	205, 212, 355
10:4	313, 322, 324	1:2–3	221, 226
10:5	288, 313–14, 319, 320, 323–24, 355	1:3	210–13, 222, 251, 267
		1:4	210–11, 260
10:5–6	320	1:5	261–64, 275, 313
10:6	308, 312, 314, 320, 324, 326	1:5–6	265
10:6–8	288, 320	1:5–11	202, 247, 260, 262, 307, 347

Nehemiah (cont.)

1:6	248, 250, 261–63, 266	4:3	333
1:6–7	258, 260–61, 263–66	4:4	211–13, 251
1:7	249, 262, 265	4:4–5	222
1:8	249, 261–62, 264–65, 303	4:6	211
1:8–9	262	4:7	101, 203–4, 211
1:9	249, 261–63	4:7–8	225
1:9–10	264–65	4:8	208
1:10	257, 263	4:9	208, 222
1:11	222, 262–67, 292	4:10	208
2	149, 205–6	4:10–12	348
2:1	199	4:11	211
2:1–3	205	4:13	94, 208
2:3	211	4:14	208, 212, 262
2:4	222, 330	4:15	204, 208, 222
2:5	221	4:18	209
2:5–8	205	4:20	209
2:8	205, 209–10, 292	4:23	230
2:9	212, 230	5	12, 120, 163, 197–98, 202. 220, 229, 232–34, 239, 245, 317, 321, 356
2:9–10	205	5:1	234
2:10	203–5, 222, 224–25, 261, 330, 333, 335	5:1–4	234
		5:1–13	233
2:10–19	101	5:2	234–35
2:12	210	5:2–5	32
2:13	211	5:3	234
2:16	356	5:4	231, 234–35, 239
2:17	211, 213, 222, 251, 267	5:5	233–35
2:17–20	209	5:6	203, 205, 238
2:18	209–10, 222	5:6–11	238
2:19	204, 225, 333	5:7	239, 321
2:20	209–10, 212	5:7–11	239
3	197–98, 202, 210	5:8	238, 241
3:1	313	5:9	213, 238, 251, 267
3:3	97	5:10	239–40
3:4	102	5:10–11	238
3:17	93, 296	5:12	238, 330
3:20	203	5:13	238, 261
3:21	102	5:14	199, 202
3:23–24	95	5:14–19	198, 202, 233, 242
3:36	267	5:15	231, 251
4	197, 209, 321	5:16	242–43
4:1	204, 211	5:17–18	243
4:1–2	225	5:18	243, 251, 330
4:1–15	208	5:19	202, 205, 233
4:2	211, 230	6	197, 220, 225, 356

6:1	204, 211, 233	8:14	132, 319
6:1–19	101	8:16	122, 123
6:7	227	8:16–17	120
6:10–13	261	8:16–18	120
6:13	251	8:17	319–20, 328
6:14	202, 205	8:18	120, 122
6:15	202, 211	9	149, 237, 248, 256, 261, 269–72, 274, 279, 295, 304, 307, 321, 347–48
6:16	204, 209		
6:17	356		
6:17–19	198, 220, 333	9:1–3	269
7	21, 90–91, 93, 96, 112, 197–98, 348	9:1–5	270–71
7:1	202, 211	9:1–12:26	198
7:2	24	9:2	250–51, 271, 280, 315, 333, 354
7:3	211	9:2–3	248
7:5–12:26	202	9:3	271
7:6–73	198	9:5	271, 295
7:7	93	9:6	271, 273, 282, 324
7:50	101	9:6–7	274
7:64	216, 330	9:6–8	272–73
7:66	20	9:6–15	274
7:67	32	9:6–31	271
7:70–72	102, 109	9:6–37	247, 271, 278
7:73	114	9:7–9	257
8	118–22, 124, 127–33, 198, 269–70, 272, 286–89, 297, 320, 326, 328–29, 346, 356, 359	9:8	273–74, 276, 313
		9:9	274
		9:9–21	272
8–9	198	9:10	274
8–10	59, 197, 261, 269	9:12–15	274
8–12	324	9:13	274
8:1	112, 118, 122, 269	9:13–14	273
8:1–2	324	9:14	274, 281
8:1–12	122, 270	9:15	273
8:1–12:26	198	9:16–17	274
8:2	122, 285, 320	9:16–21	274
8:3	121	9:17	274
8:4	122, 324	9:18	273
8:5	324	9:18–19	274
8:6	324	9:22–31	272, 275
8:7	122	9:23	273
8:8	152	9:26	249, 275
8:9	102, 122, 247, 324, 327	9:26–29	258, 275
8:11	122	9:26–30	275
8:12	123, 328	9:27	275
8:13	121–22, 125, 269, 324	9:28	249, 275
8:13–14	121	9:29	249, 275

Nehemiah (cont.)

9:30	275	12:3	102
9:31	272	12:10	313
9:32	275–77, 307, 313	12:10–11	290, 313
9:32–33	248	12:15	97
9:32–37	250, 260, 271, 275	12:22	33, 290
9:33	257, 273, 276	12:24	295
9:33–34	279	12:26	199, 324
9:34	275	12:27	330
9:35	276	12:27–30	202
9:36	273	12:27–43	202
9:36–37	283	12:28–29	97
9:37	257, 282, 321	12:30	197, 211
9:38	248, 276, 280	12:31	245
9:39	269	12:31–43	211
10	93, 197–98, 202, 270–71, 279, 281, 295	12:35–47	327
		12:36	285, 324
		12:36–43	247
10:1	93, 102	12:38	245
10:2	93	12:43	328
10:5	97	12:44	124, 324
10:11–12	295	12:45	324
10:14–16	294	12:46	124
10:16	93	12:47	324
10:25	93	13	51, 55, 197–98, 202, 216, 245, 270, 317, 336, 353, 356
10:26	93		
10:27	93, 97	13:1	95, 320
10:28	100, 269, 283, 315	13:1–3	333
10:28–30	333	13:2	261
10:29	278	13:3	215–16, 315, 354
10:30	283	13:4	314
10:30–39	269	13:4–5	205, 314
10:31	239, 280–81, 283	13:4–8	101
10:32–33	119	13:4–9	177, 198
10:32–39	281–82	13:4–14	198, 205
10:35–36	283	13:4–31	202
11:1–2	218	13:5–9	31, 148
11:21	100	13:6	198
11:21–36	198	13:6–7	202, 216
11:25–36	21	13:7	206, 215
11:31	355	13:7–9	12, 217
11:32	97	13:8–9	314
11:36	355	13:9	215
12–13	197	13:10	98, 124
12:1	93	13:13–22	216
12:1–26	198	13:14	202, 205

13:15–22	198	6:11–13	305, 314
13:17	356	6:13	304
13:18	217, 261	41:8–9	273
13:22	202, 205, 216	45:13	81
13:23	95, 312	54:4	251
13:23–24	332	56:3	143
13:23–28	316	56:3–8	143
13:23–29	285, 335	65:8–16	266
13:23–31	198	65:9	305
13:24	153	65:23	305
13:25–26	216	66:2	266, 327
13:26	216, 220, 261, 312	66:2–5	327
12:26–27	354	66:5	327–28
13:27	262, 264, 308, 312	66:22	305
13:28	12, 216, 220, 225, 313–14		
13:29	202, 205, 216, 313	Jeremiah	
13:30	216	2:26	254
13:30–31	216, 245	6:15	306
13:31	202, 205	6:19	306
		11:21–23	136
Esther		20	98
9:19	124	20:1	98
9:22	124	22:22	251
		22:24–30	85
Psalms		24:5–6	86
7	203	24:6	82
9	203	25:11–14	81
41:14	271	29:5–7	299
54	203	29:10	81
56	203	31:4–5	82
59	203	31:19	251
104:32	312	31:28	82
106	247, 272–73	31:31–34	299
106:1	272	32:7–9	136
106:7	272	35:4	314
106:15	272	36:10	314
106:17	272	38:19	136
106:18	272	39:14	136
106:23	272	40	19, 85
106:48	271	40:6	136
118	117	40:9–10	19
136	117	41:5	17
		41–42	19
Isaiah		50:18–19	81
3:5	251	52:28–30	90

Ezekiel	
11:15	33
11:17	33
18:17	239
20	274, 278
22:12	239
26:16	84
27:21	84
30:13	84
33:24	273
46:10–28	84

Daniel	195
6:28	6
9:1	6
9:4	248
9:4–19	247
9:7	264
9:20	248
10:11	312

Amos	
1–2	249–50
2:4–16	208
4:4	97
5:1–27	208
7:10	97

Jonah	
4:1	205

Haggai	
1:1	93
1:2–4	152
1:4	86, 113
1:5–11	176
1:9	176
1:9–11	65
2:19	72
2:21	72
2:23	72, 85

Zechariah	
1:16	113
4:9	113

5:1	65
6:10	101
14:16	132
14:18	132
14:19	
132	

Apocryphal/Deuterocanonical Books

Tobit	195
Judith	195

1 Maccabees	
8:17	102

1 Esdras	
5:46	95
5:50	135
9:14	315
9:36	317

3 Maccabees	195

Ancient Jewish Writers

Josephus, *Antiquities*	290
11.324	31
11.326	33
11.68	89
19.281	180

Modern Authors Index

Abdel-Nour, Farid 256–58
Ackroyd, Peter 24, 84, 197
Albertz, Rainer 85–86, 233
Alexander, Jeffrey C. 259–60, 281, 283
Allen, Graham. 208
Allen, Leslie C. 116
Alt, Albrecht 23
Amit, Yairah 234
Angel, Hayyim 91, 316
Arnold, B. T. 154–56
Arnold, William R. 16
Avrahami, Yael 250
Barstad, Hans 18
Barth, Fredrik 54, 140–41, 194
Barthes, Roland 208
Bautch, Richard J. 309
Bechtel, Lyn M. 251, 268
Becking, Bob 32, 80–81
Bedford, Peter R. 10, 17, 31, 68, 72–73
Beetham, David 147, 161, 165–66, 189, 358–59
Bell, Catherine M. 127–29, 143, 268, 281
Berlinerblau, Jacques 62, 169, 250
Berman, Joshua 154–56, 158–60
Berquist, Jon L 33–34, 176, 182, 203
Betlyon, John Wilson 16
Beuken, Wim 327
Bickerman, Elias J. 16, 81
Blenkinsopp, Joseph 25, 31, 81, 83, 90–91, 93, 97, 98, 100, 108, 112, 114, 117, 134–35, 148, 152, 180, 198–99, 201–205, 208, 211, 233, 261–64, 269–71, 273, 290, 293–95, 307, 316–17, 324, 328–29
Boda, Mark J. 7, 198–99, 248–50, 260, 265, 272, 274–76, 282
Boer, Roland 332–33
Boice, James M. 362
Bourdieu, Pierre 2–4, 14, 35–58, 61–62, 74–76, 80, 101, 104, 106–8, 111, 123–27, 131, 138–43, 158, 163–65, 167–73, 177, 184–87, 190–194, 206, 217–221, 223–24, 227. 229–230, 236–238, 240–45, 252–53, 268, 280–83, 299–301, 309–11, 319, 325, 328–29, 333, 337–43, 351–52, 356–58, 359–61, 363
Briant, Pierre 17, 28–30, 147, 180, 200, 221, 230–32, 242
Brittain, Christopher C. 58
Brown, Raymond 362
Camp, Claudia V. 340–41
Carter, Charles E. 16, 19–23, 230
Cataldo, Jeremiah 31
Celikates, Robin 310
Chance, John K. 251–53
Childs, Brevard S. 133
Chirichigno, Gregory 235
Christian, Mark A. 331–32, 341
Chrostowski, Waldemar
Clines, D. J. A. 90–91, 94–95, 97–98, 100, 112, 260, 262, 270,285
Cohen, Margaret 197
Collins, John J. 207, 218
Conczorowski, Benedikt J. 332, 334–35
Connerton, Paul 127–28, 130–31
Coogan, Michael D. 16
Cook, Stephen L. 298
Dandamayev, Muhammad A. 17, 26, 199

Davies, Gordon F.   9, 156–57, 183, 263, 265–66, 305, 311–12
Davies, Philip   12–13, 117–18, 177
Dianteill, Erwan   57, 107
Dillon, Michele   56
Domeris, W. R.   253
Douglas, Mary   315, 317
Duggan, Michael W.   269, 271–73, 283
Dyck, Jonathan E.   92–95, 97–98, 100–101, 104, 106–8, 144, 192
Edelman, Diana   6, 20–21, 24, 28, 59–60, 64, 69, 72, 100–101, 113, 148, 175, 180–81
Eidheim, Harald   194–95
Eshel, Hannan   200
Eskenazi, Tamara C.   8–9, 24, 66, 83, 91, 94, 115–16, 122, 125, 179, 181, 205–6, 244, 266, 269, 276, 280, 308, 329–30
Fantalkin, Alexander   35, 147, 307, 323
Fewell, Danna Nolan   78, 80, 125, 132, 172, 178, 234, 317, 328
Finkelstein, Israel   20, 24
Fleming, Daniel E.   207
Frei, Peter   10, 26–27, 293
Frevel, Christian   332
Fried, Lisbeth S.   10, 17, 27, 60. 64, 67, 175, 337
Geertz, Clifford   345
Getz, Gene A.   361
Grabbe, Lester L.   17, 25, 83, 91, 93, 102, 135–36, 149, 180, 203, 270, 317, 324
Gross, Carl   239
Guillaume, Philippe   233, 239–40, 244
Gunn, David M.   234
Halpern, Baruch   149, 152, 181, 187
Hanson, Paul D.   217–18, 327
Herzfeld, Michael   250, 253
Hoglund, Kenneth G.   9–11, 15–17, 20, 23–24, 27–29, 33, 147, 200–201, 285, 311
Hopkins, David C.   231, 233
Horsley, Richard   181
Hunt, Alice   289–91
Hurowitz, Victor   62–65, 67, 70–71, 73
Janzen, David   13, 72, 215, 217
Japhet, Sara   77, 83–84, 190
Jenkins, Richard   162–64
Jigoulov, Vadiim   28
Johnson, Randal   37, 42, 44–45, 47, 193
Jones, Gwilym H.   207–9
Judd, Eleanore P.   308
Kellermann, Ulrich   208
Kessler, John   34–35, 297
Kloner, Amos   25
Klopfenstein, Martin   250–51
Knauf, Ernst Axel   153
Knoppers Gary N.   8, 22–24, 148, 225–26, 289–93, 339, 341, 348
Knowles, Melody D.   79–80, 147–48
Kottsieper, Ingo   153–54
Kraeling, Emmil G.   16
Kratz, Reinhard G.   16
Laird, Donna J.   61, 209
Lemaire, André   32–33
Leuchter Mark   289–91, 295, 298–300
Lipiński, Edward   333–34
Lipschits, Oded   15–16, 18–26, 29–30, 115, 136, 200, 221
Lohfink, Norbert   213
Lowenthal, David   129–30
Lukonin, Vladimir G.   17, 26
Maduro, Otto   49, 51, 57, 309, 323
Magen, Yitzhak   31–32, 148, 200
Mallau, Hans H.   150–51, 183
Margalith, Othniel   113
Matzal, Stefan   150
May, Larry   257
McGeough, Kevin   204,
McKinnon, Andrew M.   58
Mildenberg, Leo   16
Milgrom, Jacob   132
Morrow, William   248
Myers, Jacob M.   91, 113, 115
Naʾaman, Nadav   17
Nash, Manning   54, 103–4, 138, 318, 320
Newman, Judith H.   273, 277–78
Niditch, Susan   181, 203–4, 208, 213–14, 218, 318–19, 329, 357
Oded, Bustenay   18

Oeming, Manfred 276
Olave, María Angélica Thumala 56, 58
Olyan, Saul 177
Oswald, Wolfgang 336–37
Pakkala, Juha 7–8, 287–90, 292–94, 303, 320, 323, 329–30, 335, 341
Parsons, Talcott 40
Peristiany, J. G. 252
Pitt-Rivers, Julian 252–53
Plevnik, Jooseph 252–53
Polaski, Donald C. 182, 184
Rad, Gerhard von 138, 208–10, 213
Rendsburg, Gary 277
Rendtorff, Rolf 273
Rey, Terry 56–58, 186
Rofé, Alexander 327
Rom-Shiloni, Dalit 89, 136, 178, 247–49, 278–79, 339
Rothenbusch, Ralf 289
Rowley, H. H. 225
Sachau, Eduard 16
Schaper, Joachim 60, 153
Schneider Jane 253
Schultz, Carl 225
Schwiderski, Dirk 180
Scott, James C. 186–87
Seitz, Christopher R. 135–36
Ska, Jean Louis 10
Smith, Anthony D. 144, 191–92, 282
Smith, Daniel L. 12. See also Smith-Christopher, Daniel L.
Smith, Morton 11–12, 17, 33–34
Smith-Christopher, Daniel L. 35, 148. See also Smith, Daniel L.
Snell, Daniel C. 154
Southwood, Katherine E. 14, 305, 309–10, 332, 335, 338–39, 360
Sparks, Kenton L. 103–4
Steiner, Richard C. 180, 182
Steinmann, Andrew E. 180, 182
Stern, Ephraim 16–19, 22, 25, 84, 148, 225
Stern, Ian 25, 105, 143
Stewart, Frank Henderson 252
Stiebert, Johanna 252–53
Stulman, Louis 214, 218–19
Swartz, David 42
Tal, Oren 30, 35, 147, 307, 323
Talstra, Eep 261–65
Terr, Lenore 255–59, 306
Thompson, John B. 50
Throntveit, Mark A. 91–92, 114, 116
Torrey, Charles C. 5–6, 8, 180
Trotter, James M. 176
Trzebiatowska, Marta 58
Urban, Hugh 56–58
Uspenski, Boris 154
Vanderhooft, David 22–23, 29, 200
Van Leeuwen, Raymond C. 61–62
Van Seters, John 184
Verter, Bradford 328
Veeser, H. Aram 37
Wacquant, Loïc J. D. 38, 194, 361
Walters, Stanley D. 96
Weber, Max 35, 37, 39–41, 46, 169–72, 174, 177, 179, 249, 253–54, 259, 282, 307, 357
Weinberg, Joel 9, 17, 23, 31, 94
Welch, Adam C. 277
Werline Rodney A. 247, 249, 260, 266–67
Wiersbe, Warren 361
Williams, Bernard 248, 254–55, 257–58, 268, 306
Williamson, H. G. M. 7, 59, 77, 112–16, 120, 136, 149–50, 152, 154, 180, 182, 198–99, 202, 208, 211, 233–35, 238–39, 240, 242, 261–63, 267, 269–72, 274–77, 285–86, 289–90, 292, 295–97, 307, 312–13, 315–17, 322, 324–25
Wright, Jacob L. 7–8, 59, 120, 122–23, 131, 137, 149, 197–98, 201, 204, 211, 226, 287–88, 303
Wright, John W. 25
Zlotnick-Sivan, H. 317–18, 337
Zorn, Jeffrey R. 25

www.ingramcontent.com/pod-product-compliance
Lightning Source LLC
Chambersburg PA
CBHW020121020526
44111CB00048B/136